SAP PRESS e-books

Print or e-book, Kindle or iPad, workplace or airplane: Choose where and how to read your SAP PRESS books! You can now get all our titles as e-books, too:

▸ By download and online access
▸ For all popular devices
▸ And, of course, DRM-free

Convinced? Then go to **www.sap-press.com** and get your e-book today.

SuccessFactors™ with SAP® ERP HCM

PRESS

SAP PRESS is a joint initiative of SAP and Galileo Press. The know-how offered by SAP specialists combined with the expertise of the Galileo Press publishing house offers the reader expert books in the field. SAP PRESS features first-hand information and expert advice, and provides useful skills for professional decision-making.

SAP PRESS offers a variety of books on technical and business-related topics for the SAP user. For further information, please visit our website: *www.sap-press.com*.

Amy Grubb, Luke Marson

SuccessFactors™ with SAP® ERP HCM

Business Processes and Use

Galileo Press

Bonn • Boston

Galileo Press is named after the Italian physicist, mathematician, and philosopher Galileo Galilei (1564 — 1642). He is known as one of the founders of modern science and an advocate of our contemporary, heliocentric worldview. His words *Eppur si muove* (And yet it moves) have become legendary. The Galileo Press logo depicts Jupiter orbited by the four Galilean moons, which were discovered by Galileo in 1610.

Editor Sarah Frazier
Acquisitions Editor Emily Nicholls
Copyeditor Miranda Martin
Cover Design Graham Geary
Photo Credit Shutterstock.com/190772951/© ChaiyonS021
Layout Design Vera Brauner
Production Graham Geary
Typesetting III-satz, Husby (Germany)
Printed and bound in the United States of America, on paper from sustainable sources

ISBN 978-1-4932-1173-9

© 2015 by Galileo Press Inc., Boston (MA)
2nd edition 2015

Library of Congress Cataloging-in-Publication Data
Grubb, Amy.
SuccessFactors with SAP ERP HCM : business processes and use / Amy Grubb and Luke Marson. -- 2nd edition.
pages cm
Includes index.
ISBN 978-1-4932-1173-9 (print : alk. paper) -- ISBN 1-4932-1173-0 (print : alk. paper) -- ISBN 978-1-4932-1174-6 (ebook)
ISBN 978-1-4932-1175-3 (print and ebook : alk. paper) 1. SAP ERP. 2. Personnel management--Data processing.
3. Personnel management--Computer programs. 4. Manpower planning--Computer programs. 5. SuccessFactors (Firm)
I. Marson, Luke. II. Title.
HF5549.5.D37G78 2014
658.300285'53--dc23
2014037916

Contents at a Glance

Dear Reader,

Go ahead and take another peek at the cover of this book. Don't worry, I'll wait.

Much like the rowing team seen on this cover, organizations thrive through strategic alignment and individual accountability. In many ways, SuccessFactors functions similarly to a rowing coxswain—steering and leading a company by measuring and aligning the individual talents and goals of employees towards one overarching objective. Beyond the sporting metaphors, this book presents how to best use SuccessFactors as a tool for bettering HR workflow and business processes—making your life that much easier.

Now, just as the world of SuccessFactors has expanded, so has this second edition, with the latest in features and functionalities. Brought together once again by the leadership of author Luke Marson (our literary coxswain), his team includes co-author Amy Grubb, and contributor Atif Siddiqui. Together, they present a detailed look at how to best integrate your HCM strategy—whether you have an existing on-premise business solution or are looking to integrate into the cloud. From talent management to payroll, get your head in the game, and take strides towards your company's success.

We want to hear from you! What did you think about the second edition of *Success-Factors with SAP ERP HCM: Business Processes and Use*? Your comments and suggestions are the most useful tools to help us make our books the best they can be. We encourage you to visit our website at *www.sap-press.com* and share your feedback.

Thank you for purchasing a book from SAP PRESS!

Sarah Frazier
Editor, SAP PRESS

Galileo Press
Boston, MA

sarah.frazier@galileo-press.com
www.sap-press.com

Contents

4 Platform and Extensibility 141

13 Workforce Analytics 503

14 Workforce Planning 539

Foreword

We live in one of the most important and interesting days in the history of enterprise software. Our industry is going through a major transformation, and, without a doubt, cloud software is at the forefront of these changes. The cloud enables software to be created, delivered, updated, and consumed quickly and inexpensively.

But cloud is not the only interesting trend—myriad factors have converged to create this shift. Millennials are replacing Baby Boomers in the workforce. Consumer software, such as Facebook, Twitter, and Google, has changed our lives by creating new expectations around user experience, immediacy, and content accessibility, all wrapped up in the ability to connect with similar users while doing everything on the go. Companies such as Apple have introduced us to beautiful, sleek, and easy-to-use devices. SAP HANA has introduced the world to in-memory platform at scale. And the list goes on.

Here at SuccessFactors, we are incredibly lucky to be at the intersection of these trends. We get to build software that is relevant to today's workforce and that is social, mobile, and engaging employees to deliver business results every day. We are grateful to learn and benefit from thousands of customers with tens of millions of employees, who teach us every day. They share their best practices with us, allow us to incorporate these practices into our software, and share this knowledge with others. We get to observe trends in the consumer software market, learn from them, and then deliver enticing experiences to enterprises. We consider ourselves fortunate to be at the right place, at the right time, moving at the right speed in the right direction, to deliver our innovative solutions to customers. I am convinced that when we look back on this period in our professional lives many years from now, we will appreciate it even more.

The second edition of *SuccessFactors for SAP ERP HCM: Business Processes and Use* is a comprehensive book to broadly describe the capabilities we have been building for more than a decade. The book highlights different parts of the suite and how they fit together. It goes into detail about key areas of the product—core HR, payroll, talent management, learning, recruiting, compensation, social, and mobile—from both functional and experiential perspectives. Finally, it covers important elements that are required to fully understand the solution, including management, configuration, security, and maintenance of the system. Authors Luke and Amy, along with contributor Atif, did an unbelievable job in the first edition in learning the software, looking under the covers, and describing it to the readers in an accessible yet detailed way. We made their lives somewhat more challenging adding substantial amount of new functionality in the past years, but they were clearly up to the task and have done a phenomenal job staying in sync with the product in this second edition.

I think you will find this well-written and comprehensive book to be useful, and I hope you will use the software to transform your business and help your employees achieve their dreams.

Dmitri Krakovsky
Senior Vice President, Global Product Management
SuccessFactors

Acknowledgments

We would like to dedicate this book to all those who have supported us in this long and exciting journey. We have sacrificed a great deal of time and effort to produce this book, and we greatly appreciate the support our loved ones have provided during the long nights and even longer weekends.

We also appreciate the support that SAP, SuccessFactors, and members of the community have given to ensure that we are able to provide a book of the highest caliber. The SAP ERP HCM industry is currently in a time of transition, and it is disconcerting to read and hear inaccuracies and myths regarded as cutting-edge information. For this reason, we are grateful to all those who have helped ensure that this title provides our readers with confidence in its authenticity, accuracy, and relevance.

We are especially thankful to Dmitri Krakovsky, Senior Vice President of Global Product Management at SAP for taking the time, energy, and passion to write an excellent foreword to this book.

In addition to expressing appreciation for each other's hard work and dedication, each author would like to thank specific individuals that have provided support and/or input that has positively affected the final result of this book.

Amy would like to thank Don Grubb, Jill Venable, Brian Stiles, Jane Sedlecky, Scott Vinkemulder, Dan Frederick, Robert Cramer, Brandon Toombs, Kara Pastorek, Mary Poppen, Jeff Pytel, Paige Cherny, Donna Cohen, Ed Steiger, Melissa Scruggs, Matt Jones, Jerry McBrayer, Nicole Mercurio, and Leigh Kelleher.

Luke would like to thank Kira Swain, Andrea Meyer, Deb Lyons, Shawn Price, Mike Ettling, Dmitri Krakovsky, Thomas Otter, Joachim Förderer, Eva Woo, Phil Morley, Prashanth Padmanabhan, Steve Schnoll, Murali Mazhavanchery, Yannick Peterschmitt, Paru Sankar, Frans Smolders, Kouros Behzad, Henner Schliebs, Volker Stiehl, Bianka Woelke, Mike Rossi, Heiko Zintgraf, Petra Ligthart, Chiara Bersano, Carrie Lande, Udo Paltzer, Philip Haine, Dagmar Becker, Wolfgang Dittrich, Adrienne Whitten, Heiko Lenk, Oliver Conze, David Ludlow, Yariv Zur, Paul Hopkins, Mary Poppen, Brian Clendenin, Brandon Toombs, Donna Cohen,

Tim Simmons, Joe Lee, Jyoti Sharma, Regan Klein, Jörg Schreiber, Heike Kolar, Naomi Bloom, Philip Piek, Meg Conley, Katy Spencer, Jon Kent, Kelly Grace Weaver, Matthew Partridge, Atif Siddiqui, Robert Thomson, Paul Marson, Carol Styler, Jarret Pazahanick, Chris Paine, Dick Hirsch, Jon Reed, Mark Finnern, Jennifer Heavysege, and Brandy Henricks. A special mention is made in the memory of Judson Wickham.

Atif would like to thank Anup Yanamandra and Paul Hopkins.

Last, but not least, we would collectively like to give a big thank you to Sarah Frazier, Emily Nicholls, Graham Geary, Aja Walkes, and the rest of the team at SAP PRESS who put up with missed deadlines, extension requests, spelling mistakes, and grammar faux pas and ensured that we were able to deliver this title to the high standards set by those individuals that want a world-class title.

A leader in talent management and social collaboration software in the cloud, SuccessFactors provides a full range of human capital management solutions that are suitable for any organization.

1 Introduction

It has been more than two and a half years since SAP completed the acquisition of SuccessFactors. During this time, both the enterprise software industry and SAP have witnessed a transformation as cloud computing moves to the forefront of enterprise technology adoption. SAP has created a dual strategy for HCM customers; on-premise continues to be supported and enhanced, while SuccessFactors leads the way. SAP has augmented its strategy with a series of integrations for both the talent management applications and its continually growing core HRIS, Employee Central.

Our experience since the release of the first edition of this book has shown that there is huge interest in SuccessFactors, whether this is just to take advantage of the market-leading performance management capabilities or to replace an outdated core HRIS with Employee Central. In this updated and expanded edition, we will look at the new, cutting-edge features released since the last edition of this book. In addition, we have expanded the content to add more practical information for readers who already have one or more SuccessFactors applications implemented.

1.1 Terminology and Concepts

Before we look at the topic of SuccessFactors, it's worth understanding what the terminology and concepts behind cloud computing really mean. Enterprise software, particularly from SAP, is rooted in client-server technology and based on older but highly customizable architectures. Despite being flexible, these systems often have user interfaces (UIs) that, by twenty-first century standards, are antiquated and complex. This technology—installed at a customer's or outsourcing provider's premises—is commonly referred to as *on-premise*.

By contrast, modern applications, such as those on computers, in the cloud, or via mobile apps, have slick graphics and easy-to-use functionality. As a result, many users find a mismatch between the applications they use in the workplace and the applications they consume on the Internet and on their personal mobile devices. The rise of smartphones and tablets means that attractive and simple applications are available for a cost-effective price—quite often free—and can easily be used for leisure and professional use. And, because the Internet allows software to be consumed as a service, organizations and individuals can access data and applications anywhere at any time.

Providing employees with a means of working anywhere lets them perform tasks that were once restricted to the workplace. For example, many employees are likely to check their email outside of work or submit their timesheets while they are commuting home. This essentially means that time spent in the workplace is more productive because employees are performing smaller, bite-size activities at times when they would otherwise be out of the office and unproductive—during "dead" time. Because of these shifts in application consumption, workers are becoming more productive outside of the workplace, whether this is during travel or leisure time. It is not unheard of for busy individuals to keep on top of their workload while on vacation!

Of course, whether this is positive or negative for employees depends on the view of the individual, but businesses benefit because increased efficiency and productivity ensure survival in a competitive marketplace.

1.1.1 Cloud Computing

Cloud computing—or simply the *cloud*—has been around for a number of years and, for many, it is a common term. Many readers are already using the cloud in their everyday lives, maybe accessing Facebook or their email. But when it comes to enterprise software, cloud computing is a fairly new concept, and many individuals may not yet be using cloud-based software professionally.

So what is cloud computing? To put it simply, cloud computing is when software or servers are hosted remotely and accessed via a network, such as the Internet. Cloud software exists "in the cloud."

Modern-day hardware and the speed of common Internet connections have made it possible to offer cloud-based services that are truly as effective as those operated on an organization's premises. And, because there is now significant uptake in cloud services, costs are becoming easily affordable by individual consumers and companies. With no need to host, install, maintain, or upgrade software, cloud computing is hassle-free for individuals or organizations who simply want software that is easy to consume. In particular, the *Software as a Service (SaaS)* concept allows organizations to consume enterprise resource planning (ERP) software through the cloud.

1.1.2 Software as a Service

Software-as-a-Service (SaaS) is a concept in cloud computing whereby enterprise software is offered—as the name suggests—as a service. It is consumed via a web browser and is often licensed on a subscription basis. In relation to cloud, if the cloud is the platform to provide services, then SaaS is the application that provides those services.

SaaS applications are usually more visually attractive and easier to use than typical enterprise software applications. Many SaaS vendors, particularly in the Human Capital Management (HCM) area, use highly innovative features in their applications to provide a user experience superior to that found with traditional, on-premise enterprise software.

In addition to SaaS and on-premise delivery methods, *mobile* is also widely used and is often an integral part of most SaaS vendors' offerings. Another integral component of SaaS offerings is the regular delivery of updates to applications, which can be as often as every quarter. These updates often contain new features and bug fixes with a focus on introducing enhancements to the core application in every release. This strategy creates a focus on product development and innovation so that customers can get new features quickly, rather than waiting on the common 12-, 18-, or 24-month cycles that are typical for on-premise enterprise software releases.

SaaS offers customers additional benefits. For example, customers do not need to pay for hardware, maintenance and support, or solution upgrades because the vendor handles all of these.

A key architectural difference from on-premise is the use of *multi-tenancy*, in which each customer uses the same instance of the software but has their own unique configuration of the software. This type of architecture facilitates improved upgradability and system maintenance because every customer uses the exact same version of the software. It also enables new capabilities, like benchmark analytics, to be produced: anonymous aggregates of the analytical data in all tenants are available to customers. This is a feature of SuccessFactors Workforce Analytics and will be covered in Chapter 14. This type of scenario is simply not possible with on-premise.

Of course, SaaS also has its downsides. It requires that customers trust their vendor to adequately maintain the system and protect their sensitive employee data. Multi-tenant systems give only limited control to the customer, who must work within the vendor's guidelines. While SaaS systems are stronger on configuration that on-premise systems are, they are comparatively weak on customization. Although this can be a disadvantage for many customers, the inability to do heavy customizing means that systems are easy to upgrade and extend while remaining stable and high performing. The growth of extensibility capabilities—of which SuccessFactors is a leader—means that customers can add custom functionality to a system without customizing it. In essence, it is customizing without customizing.

There are some misconceptions about SaaS, and, although some of these are valid, they often vary between different vendors rather than being common across vendors. For example, security (both the protection of data stored in the cloud and in day-to-day operations) is a key concern for customers, and each vendor has different standards and systems for protecting data. For some organizations, there is a clear risk that they cannot prevent data from being accessed by the wrong employees.

All in all, SaaS demonstrates how a cloud-based delivery model can provide a wealth of benefits for customers, not just from a practical perspective, but also from the innovation that these young enterprise software companies are investing in. The growth in SaaS clearly shows that this new age of application delivery is the future of enterprise software.

1.2   About SuccessFactors

SuccessFactors was founded in 2001 as an SaaS performance management software vendor. It quickly evolved its strategy to focus on providing "Business Execution" software and, thus, expanding its offering to cover talent management and analytics. Headquartered in San Francisco, California, SuccessFactors also has offices in more than 35 locations around the world and more than 3,500 customers in 168 territories using 35 different languages. Among these customers are some highly recognizable companies and brands, including 20th Century Fox, Adobe, American Airlines, AstraZeneca, Bayer Corporation, Capital One, Comcast, Department of Homeland Security, Drug Enforcement Administration, McAfee, NASA, PepsiCo, Siemens, Starbucks, Timken, and VMware.

SAP announced its intention to acquire SuccessFactors on December 3, 2011, and the acquisition was formally completed in February 2012. SuccessFactors became "SuccessFactors, an SAP company" shortly thereafter. The acquisition was significant for SAP in a number of ways: it provided SAP with access to genuine cloud expertise and enabled it to offer a full cloud-based HCM suite. It also gave both SAP and SuccessFactors significant exposure within and outside the SAP ERP HCM ecosystem.

SuccessFactors' applications are a suite of applications called the SuccessFactors HCM suite. They cover the spectrum of HCM processes, including core HR, talent management, workforce planning, analytics, and social collaboration. SuccessFactors has a particular strength in talent management and social collaboration, while its vendor-agnostic analytics solution has 30 years of experience behind it and provides well over a thousand predefined analytics. Its range of talent management solutions covers all of the key process areas: performance management, recruitment, compensation management, learning, succession, and development. Its core HR solution has grown extensively since the appointment of Thomas Otter as Vice-President, Product Management—Employee Central.

In both Gartner's 2013 and 2014 Magic Quadrant for Talent Management suites, SuccessFactors came out head and shoulders above all other vendors and was ranked as the leader in the Forrest Wave for Talent Management, Q1 2013. In IDC's 2012 Integrated Talent Management MarketScape report, IDC ranked SuccessFactors as a leader in six key areas: Talent Management, Recruiting, Learning, Performance, Compensation, and Social Technology.

1.3   SuccessFactors HCM Suite

The SuccessFactors HCM suite covers core HR, talent management, analytics, and social collaboration. Content, integration, and extensibility underpin the suite.

SuccessFactors has more than 12,000 pieces of standard content, covering skills, competencies, and goals. The suite contains the following applications, which we will cover in this book:

- Platform
- Employee Central
- Performance & Goals
- Compensation
- Recruiting Execution
- Onboarding
- Learning
- Succession & Development
- Workforce Planning
- Workforce Analytics
- SuccessFactors Mobile
- SAP Jam

Figure 1.1 is the graphic used by SAP and SuccessFactors to visualize the HCM suite.

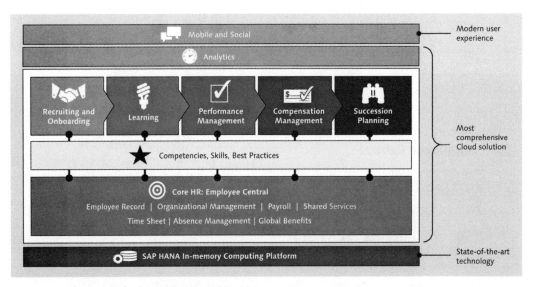

Figure 1.1 The SuccessFactors HCM suite

Let's walk through the 11 key components of the SuccessFactors HCM suite.

1.3.1 Platform

The SuccessFactors Platform is the technical foundation for the entire SuccessFactors HCM suite. It provides core functionality, such as the Public Profile, Talent Profile, Org Chart (shown in Figure 1.2), Badges, email notifications, Metadata Framework (MDF), Presentations, and more. It is required when the first SuccessFactors application(s) is configured and provides all prerequisite technical elements required to run any suite applications.

Figure 1.2 The Org Chart

More information on the SuccessFactors Platform can be found in Chapter 4.

1.3.2 Employee Central

SuccessFactors Employee Central is the core HRIS of the SuccessFactors HCM suite. It provides enterprise-level HCM functionality in an intuitive UI for HR professionals, executives, managers, and employees. It allows users to view, maintain, audit, and report on employee and organizational data across different countries, cost centers, legal entities, and employee types. Event-based transactions, workflows, and HR processes are available to fully manage everyday HR operations and activities.

Employee Central also offers payroll functionality optionally with SAP's hosted payroll solution, Employee Central Payroll (see Figure 1.3).

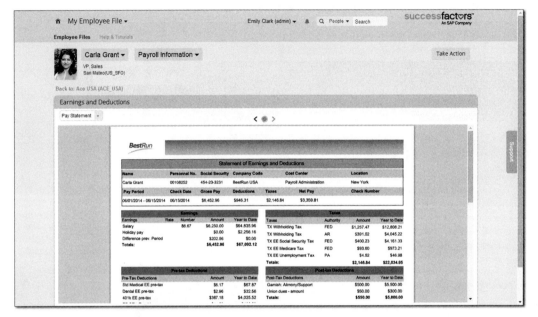

Figure 1.3 Employee Central Payroll

More information on SuccessFactors Employee Central and Employee Central Payroll can be found in Chapter 6.

1.3.3 Performance & Goals

SuccessFactors Performance & Goals is the performance management and goal-setting solution. One of the strongest modules of the SuccessFactors HCM suite, it is feature-rich, supports organizations to deliver more meaningful employee reviews, and aligns employee goals with business goals by using Management by Objectives (MBO) principles.

To help users assign appropriate goals to employees and cascade those goals back to the managers and departments that assigned them, the application comes with a SMART wizard and library of more than 500 goals. While completing performance review forms, it is easy for managers to add ratings and comments using the writing assistant, coaching advisor, and legal scan to ensure meaningful, legally robust, and compliant remarks.

Other functions available to managers during the assessment process include team overview, team evaluation (as shown in Figure 1.4), calibration, 360 Multi-Rater assessments, competency gap assessments, and dashboards.

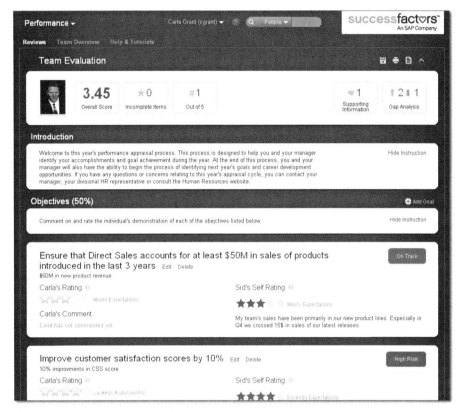

Figure 1.4 Team Evaluation in Performance & Goals

More information on SuccessFactors Performance & Goals can be found in Chapter 7.

1.3.4 Compensation

SuccessFactors Compensation, shown in Figure 1.5, covers the compensation management processes and provides a range of functionality expected in an enterprise-level compensation management solution. For managers, there is a wealth of functionality in compensation planning, including the following:

- ▶ Access-controlled compensation plans
- ▶ Budgeting
- ▶ Calibration
- ▶ Variable pay options
- ▶ Pay-for-performance

SuccessFactors Compensation also features hierarchy-based approvals, departmental budget roll-ups, and total rewards statements. Dashboards and analytics measure the impact of compensation measurements and adjustments on budgets in real time.

Figure 1.5 Compensation and Bonus Plan in SuccessFactors Compensation

SuccessFactors Variable Pay is a module offered within the SuccessFactors Compensation solution that facilitates the administration of complex bonus programs impacted by business and employee performance measures.

More information on SuccessFactors Compensation and Variable Pay can be found in Chapter 8.

1.3.5   Recruiting Execution

SuccessFactors Recruiting Execution supports attracting, engaging, and selecting hires more efficiently. The application comprises two core modules: Recruiting Management (RCM) and Recruiting Marketing (RMK). RCM is a mobile and collaborative recruiting management platform, whereas RMK is a social recruiting marketing platform. Together, they aim to make every job opening into a marketing campaign in itself.

By using techniques such as search engine optimization (SEO), customizable job landing pages, and social network integration, SuccessFactors Recruiting Execution can offer a truly attractive, 21st-century recruiting platform to engage applicants. Career site optimization, SocialMatcher, and the use of QR codes help further support the social aspects of recruiting,

Analytics dashboards help recruiters and managers identify the number of visitors, source of visitors, and areas where the recruiting process needs to be adjusted. Integration between candidate sourcing and Employee Central enable accurate evaluation of candidates versus position requirements. Figure 1.6 shows a JOB REQUISITION in SuccessFactors Recruiting.

Figure 1.6 Job Requisition in SuccessFactors Recruiting Execution

More information on SuccessFactors Recruiting Execution can be found in Chapter 9.

1.3.6 Onboarding

SuccessFactors Onboarding is the newest solution in the SuccessFactors HCM suite and provides onboarding functionality for new hires. As shown in Figure 1.7, it allows new hires to gain access to the online portal, where they can access and complete required documentation, get an overview of their new team, view their Learning Plan, see and interact in SAP Jam groups, and ask questions of their new colleagues.

In addition, it gives managers and HR professionals an easy way to ensure that new hires get access to the right information, the right documents, and the right people so they can hit the ground running at their new company.

Figure 1.7 Home Page of SuccessFactors Onboarding

More information on Onboarding can be found in Chapter 10.

1.3.7 Learning

SuccessFactors Learning is a learning management system (LMS) that features heavy use of social and mobile features to enhance the learning experience.

With SuccessFactors Learning, courses can be delegated by supervisors, and employees can search the course catalog. The To-Do List, Easy Links, and Status pods allow employees to track their learning activities and visit their most frequently performed tasks. Managers can track due and overdue courses (as shown in Figure 1.8) and identify skills gaps for their employees.

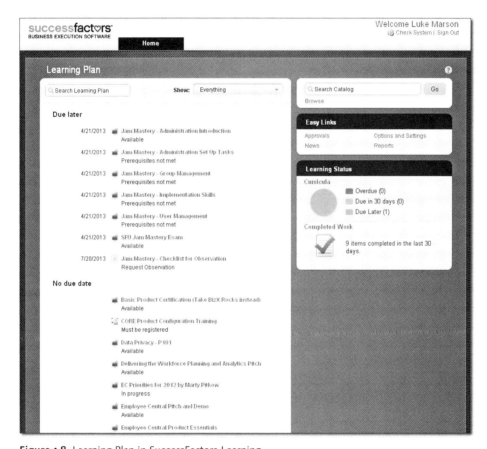

Figure 1.8 Learning Plan in SuccessFactors Learning

Learning administrators have a wealth of options for creating and managing different types of courses and course content, in addition to managing overall learning activities across the organization. Analytics dashboards and reports also let them track the benefits of learning activities to the organization in relation to overall goals. E-learning content can be created, managed, and delivered using iContent, which is a CaaS platform.

More information on SuccessFactors Learning can be found in Chapter 11.

1.3.8 Succession & Development

SuccessFactors Succession & Development is a succession planning and career development solution for helping to objectively identify high-potential individuals, assign successors to key positions, and create development plans for successors.

The Succession Org Chart—built on top of the standard Org Chart functionality— allows an overall view of health of positions, employee risks, and successor readiness. As shown in Figure 1.9, you can highlight key positions, identify the risk and impact of loss of position holders, assess successors' readiness, and make nominations.

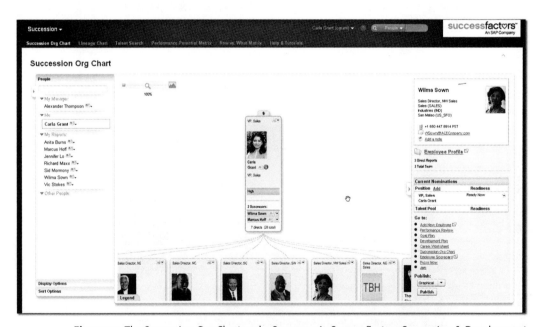

Figure 1.9 The Succession Org Chart and a Successor in SuccessFactors Succession & Development

The competency-based Talent Search, side-by-side comparison, and Performance-Potential Matrix (nine-box grid) enable talent specialists to find the best employees and successors across the organization. You can use calibration to ensure that performance and potential ratings are adequate for a selection of employees.

You can create development plans to track career development activities for employees and successors. Career Worksheets enable employees to track favored positions and identify the competencies needed to progress toward those roles. Identified competencies can be assigned as Development Goals.

More information on Succession & Development can be found in Chapter 12.

1.3.9 Workforce Planning

SuccessFactors Workforce Planning, shown in Figure 1.10, enables organizations to match workforce supply to workforce demand in the long-term future. It helps organizations predict long-term workforce needs and forecast the costs and skills associated with meeting those needs.

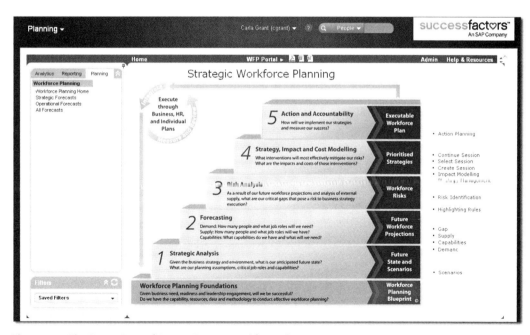

Figure 1.10 The Home Page of SuccessFactors Workforce Planning

Strategic workforce plans can be created that forecast demand, supply, and gaps in workforce requirements. You can generate "what-if" scenarios using various data and models made to simulate the cost impact of different scenarios. Predictive capabilities allow SuccessFactors Workforce Planning to forecast how the future supply will look if present trends continue, and different variables can be set to produce forecasts and gap analyses of employees and competencies. More information on SuccessFactors Workforce Planning can be found in Chapter 14.

1.3.10 Workforce Analytics

SuccessFactors Workforce Analytics is a comprehensive, vendor-agnostic analytics and reporting solution that comes with more than a thousand predefined analytics and key performance indicators (KPIs). Because it can connect to various systems simultaneously, Workforce Analytics provides a complete and unified view of how various talent-based activities, such as recruiting and learning, impact metrics such as retention, engagement, and performance. Analytics such as headcounts, retention, mobility, diversity, and profit-per-employee can be measured and correlated with business KPIs focused on revenue, profitability, and costs. Figures can also be examined further and deeper with drill-down and slicing capabilities.

The solution also features built-in industry benchmarks so that users can compare various analytics and metrics from their own businesses with like-for-like organizations of similar size, industry, and geographical locations. By using the Questions functionality, organizations can spot trends and then use the interpretation guides to understand data, identify issues, and find resolutions. Ad hoc reports can be built based on on-the-spot requirements, and automated, personalized reports can be set up for a set frequency with predefined format and content for each target user, such as managers or executives. Figure 1.11 provides an example of the OBJECTIVE DASHBOARD within SuccessFactors Workforce Analytics.

More information on Workforce Analytics can be found in Chapter 13.

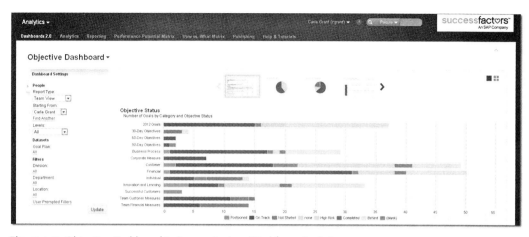

Figure 1.11 Objective Dashboard in SuccessFactors Workforce Analytics

1.3.11 SuccessFactors Mobile

SuccessFactors Mobile is the mobile solution to view notifications, arrange and review meetings, perform SAP Jam activities, view and manage open To-Do activities, and display the Org Chart while on the go. SuccessFactors Mobile is available on Apple, Android, and BlackBerry devices. Figure 1.12 shows SuccessFactors Mobile on one such smartphone.

Figure 1.12 The Home Page of SuccessFactors Mobile

More information on SuccessFactors Mobile can be found in Chapter 15.

1.3.12   SAP Jam

SAP Jam—formerly SuccessFactors Jam—is a social collaboration platform that is designed to enhance communication, sharing, content creation, and collaborative working throughout an organization. It is cross-function and designed to be used by employees from different branches across the organization, not just HR. It is modeled after popular social networking sites, such as Twitter, YouTube, and Facebook. Figure 1.13 shows the SAP Jam feed.

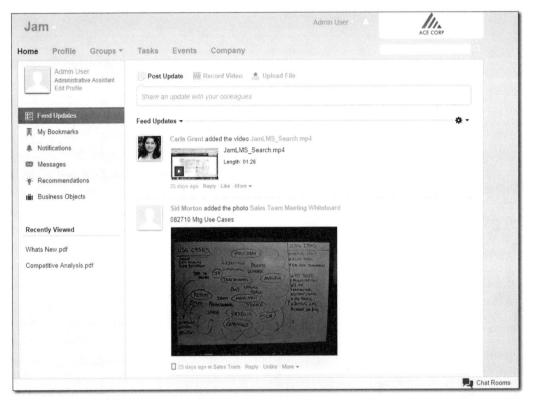

Figure 1.13 The Feed in SAP Jam

As a social collaboration platform, it allows users to post documents, articles, and videos, as well as create wikis and groups, with either open membership across the organization or automated membership for particular target groups or employees. This type of platform can be used to accelerate onboarding, allow informal learning, and encourage knowledge sharing. It also encourages managers and HR professionals to view the work and activities that employees are performing, evaluate relationships that they have established, and see who is proactive in helping colleagues achieve their goals and the organization's goals. More information on SAP Jam can be found in Chapter 16.

1.4   SAP Strategy and Roadmap

Both SAP and SuccessFactors announced their unified product direction in February 2012, shortly after the acquisition had closed.

1.4.1   Product Strategy and Roadmap

In SAP and SuccessFactors' unified product direction, the SuccessFactors HCM suite talent management applications (Performance & Goals, Compensation, Recruiting Execution, Learning, and Succession & Development) are the go-forward solutions for talent management.

> **Go-Forward**
>
> SAP defines "go-forward" as the solutions that new customers for a process will be offered. On-premise solutions will still be available and, when appropriate, these are the solutions that will be offered to new customers instead of the cloud solutions. Some customers—for example, those in the defense sector or those with right-to-left language requirements—will be offered on-premise solutions because they are the best fit for the customer. SAP intends to offer both options for customers, but for talent management, it makes more sense for SAP to offer the SuccessFactors HCM suite because of the continuous and regular innovations that SuccessFactors is working on.

For core HR, workforce analytics, and mobility, both the SAP and SuccessFactors solutions will be the go-forward offerings for new customers. The solutions available in the SAP ERP HCM portfolio are outlined in Table 1.1, with asterisks for the go-forward solutions.

	On-premise Solution	Cloud Solution
HR Core	SAP ERP HCM*	SuccessFactors Employee Central*
Performance and Goals	SAP ERP HCM	SuccessFactors Performance & Goals*
Compensation	SAP ERP HCM	SuccessFactors Compensation*
Succession and Development	SAP ERP HCM	SuccessFactors Succession & Development*
Recruiting	SAP E-Recruiting	SuccessFactors Recruiting Execution*
Learning	SAP Learning Solution	SuccessFactors Learning*
Social Talent Management		SAP Jam*
Workforce Planning		SuccessFactors Workforce Planning*
Workforce Analytics	SAP BusinessObjects for HCM Analytics*	SuccessFactors Workforce Analytics*
Mobile HCM	SAP Mobile apps based on Sybase Unwired Platform*	SuccessFactors Mobile*

Table 1.1 Solution Portfolio for SAP ERP HCM

If you are reading this book, there is a strong likelihood that you are considering or have implemented one or more SuccessFactors HCM suite solutions. However, if you have any on-premise investments that you want to retain, be reassured that SAP intends to continue to sell, enhance, and support the on-premise portfolio until at least 2025. This was the date to which SAP extended support for the SAP ERP ECC 6.0 suite in 2014. Few enhancements will be made to the on-premise Talent Management portfolio, and no further innovations are planned. For core HR and analytics, SAP will continue to make dual investments in innovation in both on-premise and cloud solutions. There will be a period of accelerated investment in SuccessFactors Employee Central, but SAP is also investing in core HR with initiatives such as HR Renewal and SAP Business Suite powered by SAP HANA. SAP Organizational Visualization by Nakisa (SOVN) will remain SAP's on-premise solution suite of choice for organizational visualization and planning. Of course, this information is accurate at the time of writing and may change at any time as SAP sees fit.

SAP has three models for offering some or all of the SuccessFactors HCM suite to customers: the *Talent Hybrid* model, *Full Cloud HCM* model, and *Side-by-Side* model.

1.4.2 Talent Hybrid Model

When a customer uses SAP ERP HCM on-premise for core HR processes, such as personnel administration and payroll, and SuccessFactors HCM suite for talent management, they are using the Talent Hybrid model. SAP Jam, Workforce Planning, and Workforce Analytics are also considered part of the Talent Hybrid model, although, from an integration perspective, SAP Jam is treated separately from the rest of the solutions in the Talent Hybrid model due to its cross-functional nature. We'll discuss integration in more detail in Chapter 3.

1.4.3 Full Cloud HCM Model

The Full Cloud HCM model refers to using the entire SuccessFactors HCM suite and can include Employee Central Payroll. Customers new to SAP can choose either the Full Cloud HCM model or the Talent Hybrid model with SAP ERP HCM as the system of record.

1.4.4 Side-by-Side Model

The Side-by-Side model was launched in August 2014 and allows customers to run SAP ERP HCM and Employee Central side by side as dual systems of record. Each system is the master system for a defined group of employees (referred to as "mastered" employees), and data is synchronized between SAP ERP HCM and Employee Central. Standard integration is provided by SAP, and UI mashups mean that WebDynpro applications from SAP ERP HCM can be run within Employee Central for those employees mastered in SAP ERP HCM.

1.4.5 SAP's Cloud Strategy

SAP has a diversified cloud strategy that covers human resources, marketing, sales, service, procurement, and more. It is underpinned by the SAP HANA cloud platform for application development and integration and Fiori for user experience. SuccessFactors HCM suite is the solution for the human resources category. Figure 1.14 shows SAP's overall cloud strategy.

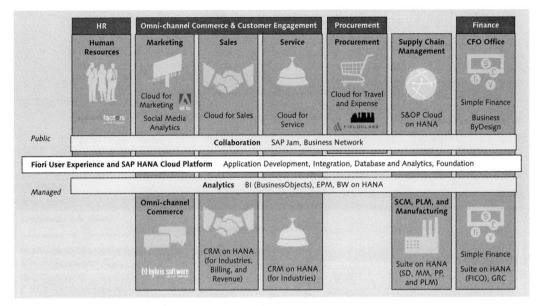

Figure 1.14 SAP's Cloud Strategy

1.5 Licensing

Like most SaaS applications, SuccessFactors is licensed on a subscription basis. Each SuccessFactors HCM suite solution is licensed for a single fee on a per-user per-year basis, with no additional maintenance costs. In contrast, SAP ERP HCM is licensed for a one-off fee on a per-user basis in perpetuity, plus maintenance at a rate of around 20%. Additional applications, such as Employee Interaction Center or SAP Talent Visualization by Nakisa, are charged additionally on the same basis plus maintenance.

The SaaS licensing module reduces the large capital expenditure for licenses, meaning that customers are charged only for what they use. This is often considered an Operational Expense (OpEx). In the on-premise model, a customer buys a fixed number of licenses at a fixed cost and, if fewer users use the system, the price does not change. This is usually a Capital Expenditure (CapEx). In the subscription model, a customer can cancel the contract at the end of the term, which tends to be a year, without incurring any additional costs. In an on-premise scenario, the customer will likely lose that license investment.

1.6   Summary

SAP purchased SaaS HCM vendor SuccessFactors to provide a full HCM suite in the cloud and improve its talent management offering while simultaneously protecting its position as the world's primary ERP HCM vendor. The acquisition brought genuine cloud DNA and market-leading SaaS HCM functionality into SAP and enabled it to get a foothold in a market where it had previously struggled to establish a presence.

SuccessFactors can be designed and configured to support customers' processes, and tested and deployed in weeks rather than months. Orienting yourself to the difference between configuration and development is the key to understanding the implementation of SuccessFactors HCM.

2   Implementing SuccessFactors HCM

The SuccessFactors HCM suite is a highly configurable, cloud-based system that can be implemented successfully in a compressed timeline and in a remote manner. SuccessFactors has worked for years to develop and hone its project methodology to support customers in implementing best-in-class talent management solutions for millions of users in the cloud. By choosing to implement the SuccessFactors HCM suite, you are embarking on a new adventure that will present you with a different way of approaching a systems implementation than you may be accustomed to.

As a cloud technology, SuccessFactors HCM suite can be implemented from wherever an Internet connection and web browser are available. By leveraging built-in best practices and focusing on system configuration and business process changes, rather than developing functionality to close system requirement gaps, you can implement your SuccessFactors HCM suite in a much shorter timeframe than an on-premise solution.

This chapter will discuss important topics for you to consider when embarking upon a SuccessFactors HCM suite implementation (see Section 2.1), provide an overview of a typical project structure (see Section 2.2), take a look at the methodology used to implement SuccessFactors (see Section 2.3), and offer insight into how SuccessFactors projects are delivered (see Section 2.4).

2.1   Implementation Considerations

There are many things to consider when planning to undertake any system implementation, and these considerations are no different if you plan to implement a cloud solution or an on-premise solution. Take this opportunity to review the applicable business processes, taking care to revisit why you do things the way you do and evaluate how they can be improved. Understand whether the processes exist because they are best practices, because they supported the legacy system, or because that is simply the way business has always been done. This is your chance to adequately prepare the organization for the change that is coming. When you implement SuccessFactors HCM suite, this change may have the biggest impact on the business process owners in HR, rather than on the employee end users.

2.1.1 Setting the Strategic Objectives of the Project

The success of any project, especially a system implementation, depends upon aligning the project with the strategic objectives of the company. By developing a strong business case for making the move from on-premise to the cloud, you set your success criteria from the beginning.

If you are engaged with an implementation partner in these early stages of the project, they can assist you with business case development and should be able to provide resources to perform live demonstrations of system functionality to your key stakeholders. Demonstrations often help facilitate buy-in and foster enthusiasm for the change you are about to make. Whether in the business case or in the first weeks of the project, take time to identify the business objectives of the project. This is critical for ensuring that all project team members, key stakeholders, and partners are on the same page from the beginning. Once business objectives are identified, agree to the success criteria that will be used to evaluate the overall success of the project. These should be closely aligned to the business objectives. The most successful system implementations are those for which project objectives and success criteria are set at the start and used for measurement throughout the project.

2.1.2 Planning for the Implementation

Are you looking to implement the full SuccessFactors HCM suite? Not sure where to start? Although there is no set order to implement the modules within SuccessFactors HCM suite, you should keep some considerations in mind when planning how to approach the implementation. Several modules are very complementary and are usually implemented together as a kind of bundle. Others are more suited to being implemented on their own. Next, we'll walk through some examples of how you might bundle the implementation phases of your full-suite project from a process viewpoint. Keep in mind that implementing the SuccessFactors HCM suite platform module is necessary for any modules that you implement and is always included in the first project phase. The platform module includes a minimum level of configuration for business rule settings within the instance, Employee Profile, Single Sign-On (SSO), and Role-Based Permissions (RBP).

Performance Review Process

The performance review process most often includes reviewing performance for the previous review period and setting objectives for the coming performance period. In this way, the Performance Management (PM) and Goal Management (GM) modules of SuccessFactors HCM Suite are intricately integrated and almost always implemented together. Goal plans can be pulled into performance review forms so that employees can be rated on their performance toward the goals from the previous year. Also, it's possible to link the coming year's goal plan in the performance review form so that goal setting can be accomplished at the same time the performance review is completed. Additional integration with the Development module includes adding a Development Plan section to the performance review template so that Development goals can be created when they are most often identified: during the performance review.

Complementary to PM and GM, the 360 Multi-Rater module is often implemented in conjunction with PM and GM. Results from the 360 Multi-Rater review can be accessed from within the performance review, giving any manager completing an employee review easy access to third-party reviewers.

Performance and Salary Planning Process

Additional complementary modules are PM and GM with Compensation and Variable Pay. Because the merit and bonus planning cycle follows the performance or focal review process, the Compensation and Variable Pay modules are often implemented at the same time as PM and GM. Performance forms can be integrated into the compensation form so that managers can view an employee's performance review rating on the salary planning sheet, as well as access the details by clicking the hyperlink and opening the performance review in a new window.

Succession Planning Process

The Scorecard is accessed from the Employee Profile of SuccessFactors HCM suite, and many companies opt to implement these two modules together. If the Employee Profile was implemented at an earlier project phase, the Succession Planning implementation is a good time to review the configuration of the Employee Profile and make any changes or updates. Succession Planning is also a good candidate for implementation in conjunction with PM and GM.

Another module often implemented in conjunction with Succession is the Development module. Many companies use the Succession process to identify development areas or goals for successors nominated to certain positions, so it makes sense for them to implement Development with Succession to support their process.

Development and Learning Process

The Development module is very similar to the GM module and includes defining a development plan whereby employees and managers can create and maintain development goals. Development goals can be linked with learning activities that are pulled from the learning catalogs assigned to employees in the Learning Management System (LMS). Consequently, customers often choose to implement Development and LMS together.

Recruiting Process

SuccessFactors HCM suite offers two recruiting modules: Recruiting Marketing (RMK) and Recruiting Management (RCM). These two modules are now offered as Recruiting Execution (RX). While the RMK module is always implemented with or after the RCM module, customers often choose to implement RCM on its own.

Both RCM and RMK modules contain a tremendous amount of functionality, so implementing one or both of these in an environment of high-volume sourcing or detailed processes is quite an undertaking. Because these business process owners are often different from those who own the performance and merit processes, implementation of the RX module can also be undertaken in parallel with any other modules, but will have a longer project life due to the complexity of the product and all of the configuration decisions involved.

2.1.3   Business Processes

Before you embark on an implementation, we advise you to spend some time reviewing the business processes involved. Although business process review should be included during the implementation, understanding the weaknesses or limitations of your existing processes facilitates a more robust kickoff meeting and expedites the system configuration decisions post-kickoff. Because SuccessFactors HCM suite can be configured but not developed, it's possible that not all system requirements are met by existing system functionality and configuration possibilities. This is typical of a cloud-based solution, so be prepared to use a combination of system configuration and business process change to address outstanding system requirements. A good understanding of the as-is processes and any legal or corporate requirements becomes key in these situations.

2.1.4   Competencies and Job Roles

Revising or adopting a competency model can be one of the most time-consuming activities you undertake when implementing any performance management solution; in fact, it's fair to say that you can't begin this preparation soon enough. If you haven't adopted a competency model for the organization, SuccessFactors HCM suite offers more than 80 best-practice behavioral competencies that can be used in the performance and development processes. If your company already has a behavioral competency model, SuccessFactors lets you create and maintain custom competencies, as well.

Another critical activity is determining how to manage job roles within the organization and how these are represented within SuccessFactors HCM suite. This should include a thorough review of how your jobs and positions are defined and organized in SAP ERP HCM, so this activity may also require some modification on the SAP ERP HCM side before bringing these over to SuccessFactors HCM suite. Although your implementation consultant can assist you through these reviews and decisions, this is something that should be undertaken during the initial planning phases of the project to ensure adequate time before go-live.

2.1.5   Employee Data

SuccessFactors HCM suite leverages a set of employee data that is brought over from SAP ERP HCM. Numerous standard fields such as name, manager, address, job title, and others are supported; up to 15 custom columns may also be defined to house additional data necessary to support the talent management processes completed in SuccessFactors HCM suite. This is covered in detail in Chapter 3. As with competencies and job roles, the sooner you begin reviewing the employee data requirements, location, and cleanliness of the data, the less impact there is on the overall project schedule.

2.2 Project Structure

Although the project structure of a SuccessFactors implementation varies depending on the number of modules undertaken at one time, you can expect to see some baselines. Implementation can be as varied as the Partners in the ecosphere; however, you should ensure that your consultants have product expertise in the implemented module(s), coupled with process and best practice expertise.

The project team can comprise the following types of resources:

- Implementation consultant(s)
- Project manager
- Project sponsor
- Technical resource
- Functional/business resource
- Stakeholder group representatives
- Training/communication resource

Let's look at each of these resources.

2.2.1 Implementation Consultant

The implementation consultant is your product expert. They should have the requisite training and product experience in the modules they are implementing so that they can configure the system and guide the customer through process discussions, offering best practices where applicable. Training on the SuccessFactors HCM suite is now offered by SAP Education, and a new certification program is being introduced, similar to the certification for other SAP modules.

You may have several consultants implementing on your team, but it's also normal for one consultant to implement multiple modules. For example, you could have one consulting resource implementing GM, PM, 360 Multi-Rater, and Employee Profile.

Implementation consultant responsibilities include the following:

▸ Conducting the kickoff meeting

▸ Conducting regular (usually weekly) project meetings by module

▸ Addressing customer questions on functionality, best practices, and system functionality

▸ Guiding the customer in completing the configuration workbook

▸ Configuring the system to customer requirements, as defined in the configuration workbook

▸ Testing the configuration to ensure completeness and functionality

▸ Leading the customer through testing each iteration configuration

▸ Conducting administrator training for customer administrators

▸ Maintaining project plan, issues log, and risks for their respective module(s)

2.2.2 Project Manager

As on any project, the project manager's role is to manage the work plan, project issues and risks, and keep resources aligned and on track. You may have both a consulting project manager and a client project manager working together to manage the entire project. If there isn't a consulting project manager, the implementation consultant may serve in a project management capacity, keeping the work plan updated and assisting the project manager in understanding the BizXpert phases and deliverables.

If you are implementing the entire SuccessFactors HCM suite, you likely have a project manager dedicated by your implementation partner who will remain consistent across all modules. This resource will work closely with the client project manager throughout the life of the project and through all project waves until all modules have gone live and are in support.

2.2.3 Project Sponsor

Project sponsors champion the project within the client organization and assist with issue resolution, when appropriate. They serve as key stakeholders in the change management and communication plan and are often a delivery channel for key messages. They also ultimately sign off on the business processes and system configuration. Often, the project sponsor is the one who signs off on the configuration workbooks and other project milestone sign-off gates.

2.2.4 Technical Resource

One or more technical resources are involved with various aspects of implementation, mainly related to data and integration. Traditionally, the technical resources are engaged to provide an extract of employee data to feed SuccessFactors HCM suite and set up the automated feed after the project has gone live. They are also involved with setting up SSO and any data migration that might be undertaken. For customers moving from on-premise solutions to SuccessFactors HCM suite, the technical resources are involved with setting up the various data connectors and integration packages. As SAP works to build total integration between SAP ERP HCM and SuccessFactors HCM suite, the role of a technical resource in an on-premise to cloud implementation will continue to grow.

2.2.5 Functional/Business Resource

The functional and business resources are possibly the most critical of the project because they define the end-state business processes and corresponding system configuration. Numerous resources are usually involved per module implemented. We recommend that you keep project-dedicated resources to a minimum while keeping a larger pool of functional/business resources involved for input, validation, and testing. Your core team of functional resources will prove critical to providing business process knowledge and context when you are working with the implementation consultant in fleshing out system capabilities to arrive at a satisfactory configuration that meets system and business process requirements.

Functional/business resources should be engaged early in the project planning so that they can begin working on the previously mentioned competency and job role work, review the applicable business processes, and assist with communication and training strategies.

2.2.6 Stakeholder Group Representatives

Stakeholder group representatives play a key role in project communication and training strategies and execution. Like project sponsors, they deliver key project messages and drive user adoption after the project is live. Key stakeholders should be involved in various times throughout the project to help validate the to-be business processes, participate in testing, and provide input to training plans. These are your change champions within the organization.

2.2.7 Training/Communication Resource

The key to any successful systems implementation is consistent and frequent communication to stakeholders and appropriate, just-in-time training for all end-user groups. Even though SuccessFactors HCM suite is an extremely intuitive solution with "toy-like" qualities, the training plan should not be overlooked. Often, you roll out SuccessFactors in conjunction with significant process updates; ensuring that your employees and managers are informed and prepared for the change is just as important for a SuccessFactors implementation as it is for an SAP ERP HCM implementation. Involve the training and communication resources early in the project and keep them engaged through to post-go-live.

Now, let's shift our focus to how SuccessFactors' modules are implemented by discussing project methodology.

2.3   Project Methodology

Prior to March 2013, SuccessFactors had various project methodologies to implement modules within the suite. Core modules utilized the Empower methodology; SuccessFactors Learning utilized Enable; and Employee Central, Workforce Planning and Analytics, and Recruiting Marketing were each implemented with a slightly different methodology. In March 2013, SAP introduced a new project implementation methodology that unifies implementation across the entire SuccessFactors HCM suite: *BizXpert*.

The BizXpert methodology draws from the strengths of the existing project methodologies and includes best practices from industry standards (such as PMP, PRINCE2, and Agile) while leveraging best practices from the SAP cloud experience. Readers familiar with SAP implementations will recognize many components in BizXpert.

As shown in Figure 2.1, the BizXpert methodology includes four phases: Prepare, Realize, Verify, and Launch.

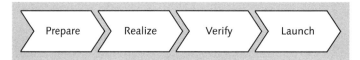

Figure 2.1 BizXpert Project Methodology Phases

We'll take a high-level look at each phase next.

2.3.1 Phase 1: Prepare

The Prepare phase lays the groundwork for a successful implementation. Tasks are focused on kicking off the project and developing the implementation project plan, as well as ensuring that the customer is prepared for the implementation process and the key differences in a cloud-based implementation. Key tasks in the Prepare phase include the following:

- Project team orientation
- Kickoff meeting
- Requirements-gathering workshops
- Project plan development

Project team orientation includes orienting the team to the project framework, guidelines, and schedule. It may also include some project team tool training on the particular module(s) being implemented.

The kickoff meeting focuses on the following:

- Project scope
- Methodology
- Key project business drivers
- Initial timeline/project plan
- Customer resources, such as Customer Community
- Project team roles and responsibilities

Table 2.1 lists the estimated duration of kickoff meetings by module, not including detailed process mapping.

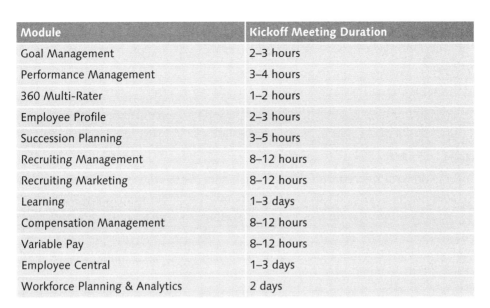

Module	Kickoff Meeting Duration
Goal Management	2–3 hours
Performance Management	3–4 hours
360 Multi-Rater	1–2 hours
Employee Profile	2–3 hours
Succession Planning	3–5 hours
Recruiting Management	8–12 hours
Recruiting Marketing	8–12 hours
Learning	1–3 days
Compensation Management	8–12 hours
Variable Pay	8–12 hours
Employee Central	1–3 days
Workforce Planning & Analytics	2 days

Table 2.1 Kickoff Meetings by Module

Requirements-gathering workshops are the focus of the Prepare phase. This is when the consulting team identifies the customer's system requirements and details the business processes impacted by the implementation. The entire project team, consultants, and business stakeholders work together to identify the system configuration required to meet the customer's needs.

Requirements gathering is typically conducted as part of the kickoff meeting, and the length of the sessions are determined by the modules being implemented. For modules such as PM and GM, these sessions can likely be covered in a day. But for modules such as Learning, Compensation, and Employee Central, it may take several days or more to talk through the configuration options and document decisions. While many decisions can be made during the configuration workshops, the workbooks should be completed over a span of days or a few weeks. The end result is the completion of a detailed configuration workbook, which consultants then use to complete the system configuration. Typically, the longer it takes to document the first iteration, the more complete it is, and the fewer changes are made in later iterations.

Data migration and technical workshops (if applicable) are centered on ancillary implementation work, such as migrating legacy data and implementing custom connectors or other third-party integrations. These are conducted on an as-needed basis; the length of the workshops is determined by the services required and the complexity of the scope of work.

Project plan development is also completed during this phase, outlining key tasks, deliverables, and milestones necessary for project success. As with any implementation, project planning is an ongoing task throughout the project.

2.3.2 Phase 2: Realize

During the Realize phase, the focus is on system configuration and data migration (if applicable). The system design and requirements identified during the Prepare phase are built in the customer's test instance. The implementation consultants are responsible for configuring all modules, with the exception of Learning and SAP Jam. For these modules, the customer is heavily involved in configuration, guided by the implementation consultant. Configuration for these modules is heavy in administrative tasks and can be done directly via the administrative interface in the instance.

Configuration Cycles

The configuration is completed in the test instance, with the exception of SAP Jam, which is completed directly in the production instance. Customers are typically given one SAP Jam instance, which is integrated with their SuccessFactors HCM suite production instance. The following is a simplified process for most modules:

1. Consultant completes configuration per the requirements identified during the Prepare phase.
2. Configuration is made available to the customer for testing.
3. Customer tests the configuration to the business processes impacted and provides feedback to the consultant on necessary changes.

Depending on the modules being implemented, you could have up to three cycles of configuration updates and testing. This depends upon the complexity of the requirements and the business processes impacted. Each cycle of configuration consists of smaller requirements-gathering sessions. These are typically conducted virtually and can occur over a series of meetings. Configuration workbooks are updated and given back to the consultant to update system configuration. The customer then retests the updated configuration, and the cycle repeats itself until complete. Traditionally, there are three iterations of configuration and testing.

In the case of the Learning module, the customer provides feedback on the configuration, and the consultants work closely with the customer administrator to refine the system configuration. With Learning, the majority of the configuration is master data that is controlled directly in the instance. When the customer administrator is involved from the beginning, training and knowledge transfer occurs throughout the project, resulting in a fully capable customer administrator by go-live.

Data Migration or Other Technical Services

If the customer is migrating data from a legacy system or has included other technical services or custom connectors in the project scope, data migration or other technical activities run parallel to the configuration cycles during the Realize phase. Much of the data migration activities focus on getting the customer up to speed on how data is brought into the SuccessFactors HCM suite. Many self-service tools, videos, documents, and sample files are available to the customer team in the Customer Welcome Kit.

If the customer is migrating data into Learning, a small sample file is created so that the customer can test the upload via OneAdmin or via the Secure File Transfer Protocol (SFTP). Data cleansing and validation are critical during this testing phase. After the sample file loads cleanly, the larger data file can be prepared. It is advisable to load the full file into the customer's test instance toward the end of the Realize phase and before the Verify phase.

2.3.3 Phase 3: Verify

Once configuration is signed off, the Realize phase concludes, and the project transitions to the Verify phase. The tasks conducted during Verify are all focused on testing and organizational readiness for the impending go-live. The customer executes the testing plan developed during the Prepare phase to prove that the system is configured as designed and is "fit for purpose." Because the test plan and script development are a key customer deliverable, samples are available in the Customer Welcome Kit, and the implementation consultant can provide input based on project experience, as well.

Testing

The types of testing included in the test plan are familiar as the same testing that occurs in most systems implementations. The customer can determine which testing activities to conduct, but the following are typically included:

▶ **Unit testing**
Confirms that each item identified in the configuration workbook has been configured and is working as expected. Unit testing is the responsibility of the implementation consultant.

▶ **Application testing**
Confirms that the system configuration meets the customer's functional requirements. It's critical to confirm that the system is ready for end-to-end testing. The customer project team is responsible for application testing.

▶ **Integration testing**
Required if other systems will be integrated with SuccessFactors. If integration testing occurs, it is the responsibility of the customer project team, usually focused on IT personnel and key stakeholders representing the systems integrating with SuccessFactors. Because integration deals with existing customer systems, the customer bears responsibility to develop detailed testing scripts. At the conclusion of integration testing, there is often a customer sign-off before moving forward.

▶ **User acceptance testing (UAT)**
Confirms that the system is configured to meet the end-to-end business requirements and is the responsibility of the customer UAT team. The most successful user testing includes testers from outside the core project team and has representation from the key business areas impacted by the system.

Preparing the Organization

While testing is underway, the communication and training plans begin execution. Any successful systems implementation hinges on clear communication and preparation of end users. These tasks are typically owned by the customer, so it's advisable to engage any customer teams that provide change management and training services. Because SuccessFactors HCM suite modules touch on employee performance, compensation, and career development, it's critical that any change in process or system is deployed with the utmost care and planning. Although SuccessFactors HCM suite is an intuitive system that can be picked up with minimal training, it is often accompanied by radical process change. These changes, and the business reasons driving them, should be "over-communicated" to employees and management alike.

2.3.4   Phase 4: Launch

The Launch phase is all about preparing for go-live, launching the system, and transitioning to Customer Success for ongoing support. After all testing activities are completed, identified issues are addressed and retested, and final sign-off of testing is achieved, the implementation consultant begins cutting over configuration from the test instance to the customer's production instance.

The *cutover checklist* is a critical deliverable of this phase that is used to monitor progress of all cutover activities, responsibilities, and statuses. The implementation consultant prepares the cutover checklist, and tasks are determined by the modules implemented. Cutting over can take from one day to many days, depending on the complexity of the modules, configuration, and business processes impacted. For example, an RMK cutover of moderate complexity with no data migration takes approximately four days, while a PM and GM cutover can be completed in one day. Cutover also includes enabling the production SFTP and final user connector for employee data, as well as enabling SSO, if applicable.

At the completion of cutover, including data migration as applicable, the customer begins production validation. After that is complete, the transition to the SuccessFactors' support organization Customer Success begins. The final deliverable of the project is the production readiness sign-off document, which is submitted to Customer Success when submitting the case to have customer accounts created. This process not only provides the customer access to the SuccessFactors support portal, but also notifies SuccessFactors that the customer has successfully transitioned into the production instance and is now live.

2.4   Project Delivery

Recall that a big difference between implementations of SuccessFactors HCM suite and on-premise SAP ERP HCM is that the emphasis is on configuration rather than development. As an SaaS solution, SuccessFactors offers a series of configuration options that can be deployed as needed to support a customer's business processes. If the system cannot be configured to a specific requirement, the applicable business process needs to be changed accordingly. Customers can then submit enhancement requests through the customer community to request functionality that they would like to see added to the roadmap and worked into the solution.

Because the project focuses on configuration rather than development, the customer project team can get its hands on the system almost immediately. To support the kickoff meeting, the implementation consultant often performs some best-practice, baseline configuration in the customer's test instance so that the customer project team can log in and "play" in a sandbox environment while discussing and making configuration decisions. This is an excellent way to confirm Iteration 1 configuration decisions before submitting them to the implementation consultant. In this way, the system configuration is being continually tested throughout the entire Realize phase.

A new concept to most on-premise SAP ERP HCM customers is *virtual project delivery*. As a cloud-based solution, SuccessFactors can be configured anywhere an Internet connection and web browser are available. After an onsite kickoff meeting, most of the implementation has traditionally been done in a virtual manner, with implementation consultants working from their home offices and supporting the customer project team over regular web conferences.

The main objective of the BizXpert implementation methodology is to empower customers to own their solutions, so activities are designed to give them the tools to do just that. Implementation consultants work with the project team on a mutually agreed upon, regular basis (not less than weekly) to review system configuration questions and decisions. The features in the OneAdmin section of SuccessFactors HCM suite are covered in detail as they apply to the implemented modules.

While project delivery varies depending on the implementation partner and complexity of the customer's business processes and scope, the days of teams of consultants camping out in client offices for months on end are no longer necessary. SuccessFactors had more than 10 years of successful implementations using this model with some of the largest companies in the world prior to being acquired by SAP.

2.5 Summary

Implementing your SuccessFactors HCM suite solution should be an opportunity to review existing business processes and add efficiency while providing enhanced system functionality.

By selecting SuccessFactors, you have taken the first step toward a best-practice core HCM or talent management landscape in your organization. The BizXpert methodology provides the structure, milestones, and deliverables necessary to ensure a successful project. Staffing your project team appropriately and providing them with the tools to deliver a fully configured system is critical to ensuring that your resulting system meets the needs of the organization and stakeholders. You can ensure successful go-live by teaming up with an experienced implementation partner who has deep business process knowledge and can provide best practices, along with deep knowledge of the SuccessFactors modules you are implementing. Lastly, preparing your organization for the new system and processes that will drive their performance and career planning is crucial to ensuring user adoption. The importance of this element cannot be overstated.

In the next chapter, we'll look at the integration between SuccessFactors HCM and SAP ERP HCM.

SuccessFactors HCM suite has been integrated with SAP ERP HCM hundreds of times with varying approaches and technologies. Since acquiring SuccessFactors, SAP has worked on providing packaged integration content for a variety of different integration scenarios.

3   Integration with SAP ERP HCM

Before using any solutions of the SuccessFactors HCM suite with other systems, you need to integrate those systems. The SuccessFactors HCM suite has been integrated with SAP ERP HCM by more than 700 SuccessFactors customers, so there is sufficient evidence of successful integration, even if, at the time of this writing, a number of these customers have built their integrations autonomously. SAP has since extended integration to cover more of SAP ERP than just SAP ERP HCM, as well as provided integration for other SAP systems and third-party applications.

SAP recognizes that many customers retain SAP ERP for multiple business processes and that some customers wish to retain SAP ERP HCM for core HR. Therefore, SAP has been building standard integration content for customers for its different delivery models. Many of these leverage SAP and non-SAP technology. SAP is focusing its efforts on providing data integration, process integration, and user experience integration that support a variety of different HR, payroll, and talent management processes.

Because SAP ERP HCM and the SuccessFactors HCM suite both store data, it's necessary to create integration so that data can flow between the systems and reside in one central system of record. The process of integration requires technology and mapping of the relevant fields in one system with those in the other and rules for data transformation and validation. Different process steps and triggers can also be part of an integration process, although this will depend on the extent to which integration is required. However integration is designed, a certain level of complexity is required—and SAP intends to reduce this complexity with standard content.

In this chapter, we'll evaluate the different technologies available to customers who want to integrate SuccessFactors solutions with SAP ERP HCM (see Section 3.2), plus the standard integration content available from SAP (see Section 3.3, Section 3.4, and Section 3.5) and the different Application Programming Interfaces (APIs) found in the SuccessFactors system (see Section 3.6). We'll also look at some of the additional documentation available from SAP (see Section 3.7).

Additional Resources

You can read more about integration between SuccessFactors and SAP ERP in the SAP PRESS book *Integrating SuccessFactors with SAP* by Venki Krishnamoorthy, Donna Leong-Cohen, Prashanth Padmanabhan, and Chinni Reddygari (2015).

3.1 Integration Strategy

SAP has a deep, detailed, and evolving integration strategy. Although we will look at the key points of this strategy, we will not cover all elements of it. SAP has designed and adopted a cloud integration framework to do the following:

▸ Identify and prescribe cloud deployment models for all products

▸ Support each cloud deployment model with packaged integrations

▸ Deliver fixed-price professional services packages and best practices for implementation

▸ Publish APIs to enable custom integrations

▸ Provide integration middleware technology in the cloud and on-premise

As part of this strategy, SAP has developed, productized, and released various packaged content to integrate the SuccessFactors HCM suite with SAP ERP HCM (for core HR, talent management, and analytics), SAP ERP (for other processes, such as payroll), Employee Central Payroll, and third-party solutions (such as time and attendance, and benefits). Integrations exist for all of the deployment models previously introduced.

3.1.1 Integration Pillars

The integration strategy looks to address three types of integration challenges through three strategic pillars:

▸ Data integration

▸ Process integration

▸ User experience integration

Data integration creates a basic data foundation within the SuccessFactors HCM suite so that core HR and talent management processes can be performed. This type of integration has been delivered for all deployment models. Two examples are the employee master data integration for Employee Central and Workforce Analytics extractors.

Process integration is event-driven, bi-directional data integration designed for specific HR processes that span both SuccessFactors and SAP ERP HCM. These include the pay-for-performance (compensation management), attract-to-hire (recruiting), and define-to-hire (recruiting) processes. With this type of integration, data can be transferred to SuccessFactors, and data produced in the Success-Factors HCM suite is transferred to SAP, where it can be used in SAP-dependent parts of processes or stored in the system of record. SAP delivers this type of integration on an ongoing basis.

User experience integration is centered on creating a unified, single point of access for end users, irrespective of whether the processes being performed are within the SAP Enterprise Portal or the SuccessFactors HCM suite. This includes Single Sign-On (SSO) and integration of SuccessFactors processes into Employee Self-Services (ESS) and Manager Self-Services (MSS) menus. The intention is that end users can move between Web Dynpro applications and SuccessFactors solutions within the SAP Enterprise Portal or SAP NetWeaver Business Client (NWBC) without even noticing that they have changed applications. SAP delivered the SSO cookbook resource to configure SSO between SAP Enterprise Portal and Success-Factors HCM suite.

3.1.2 Integrations for Deployment Scenarios

SAP intends to deliver a number of integration scenarios that align with the three pillars of its integration strategy. These vary for each deployment model.

Talent Hybrid

For the Talent Hybrid deployment model, SAP's aim is to provide packaged integrations to cover each of the integration pillars: data, process, and user experience.

They enable changes to data in the SuccessFactors HCM suite to be written back to the SAP ERP HCM system at the point the data is needed for further processing. For example, the compensation process integration delivered by SAP is designed to write data to SAP only when it needs to become part of the Payroll process.

SAP provides a number of packaged integrations for the Talent Hybrid model. These packages provide a set of programs, tools, and methodologies to help leverage SAP/SuccessFactors processes seamlessly and with both minimal risk and low TCO. These integrations are robust; however, as they are packaged, they may require additional effort to extend the standard integration if custom fields or logic is required beyond the predefined standard.

It's important to note that all data transfers between SAP ERP HCM and the SuccessFactors HCM suite are always initiated from the SAP ERP HCM side or from the middleware. No data is "pushed" from the SuccessFactors HCM suite; rather, it is always "pulled" from SAP ERP HCM or the middleware.

A number of the Talent Hybrid scenarios have already been delivered or are in ramp-up, and SAP intends to continue delivering these scenarios to cover common talent management scenarios for the Talent Hybrid model. This is covered in more detail in Section 3.3.

Full Cloud HCM

Integration for the Full Cloud HCM deployment model has three focuses: integration with SAP ERP, data replication to Employee Central Payroll, and integration to third-party solutions. All integrations are from Employee Central, and the Talent Hybrid integrations are not needed in this scenario. The integrations are largely related to being able to support other processes, like payroll or time and attendance.

Side-by-Side

Side-by-Side integration covers bi-directional integration to ensure that Employee Central and SAP ERP HCM are synchronized. This leverages the Full Cloud HCM integrations, as well as some Side-by-Side specific integrations, to transfer data between SAP ERP HCM and Employee Central.

Full Cloud HCM, Talent Hybrid, and Side-by-Side specific integrations may be needed in the Side-by-Side deployment model, depending on the business scenario.

3.2   Integration Technology

Several technologies are available to integrate the SuccessFactors HCM suite with other systems that offer different features, ease of setup, cost, and flexibility. Previous integrations have used a variety of platforms; many of these are still available for customers, even if they aren't supported by SAP's packaged integrations.

Some of the technologies available for integrating SuccessFactors HCM suite with other systems include the following:

- Flat-file transfer
- SAP Process Integration (PI)
- SAP HANA Cloud Integration (HCI)
- Dell Boomi AtomSphere® (Boomi)
- Social Media ABAP Integration Library (SAIL)
- SAP Data Services
- SuccesFactors APIs, custom-built APIs, or other middleware

Although the majority of existing integrations use flat-file or custom-built APIs, SAP wants to enable customers to use packaged content that leverages either SAP PI or SAP HANA Cloud Integration for Talent Hybrid and Dell Boomi AtomSphere or SAP HANA Cloud Integration for Full Cloud HCM and Side-by-Side. Table 3.1 summarizes the technologies available for standard packaged content from SAP.

Technology	Talent Hybrid	Full Cloud HCM/Side-by-Side
Flat-file transfer	X (partial)	
SAP PI	X	
SAP HANA Cloud Integration (HCI)	X	X
Boomi		X
SAIL		
SAP Data Services		
Custom-built APIs or other middleware	X	X

Table 3.1 Technology Options for Each Deployment Model

Figure 3.1 shows an example of the architecture of middleware technology in an SAP ERP HCM and SuccessFactors scenario.

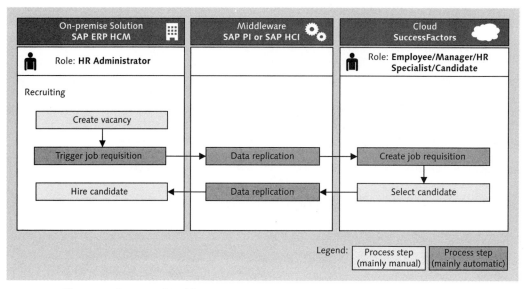

Figure 3.1 Diagram of Middleware Integration

We'll now run through these technology options in a bit more detail.

3.2.1 Flat-File Integration

Flat-file integration has been around for a number of years and is still a quick and reliable way to transfer data between two systems, albeit with a lack of standards and security compared to other mechanisms. Flat-file transfer usually involves extracting a file of data—often a comma-separated values (CSV) or text (TXT) file—from a system and then uploading it to another system. A *File Transfer Protocol* (FTP) or *Secure File Transfer Protocol* (SFTP) server is often used to transfer the file between the systems. Although this method is fairly simple to create and maintain, it does have some disadvantages that might be undesirable to some customers, such as a lack of security or encryption, standards or validation for data, and transformation and mapping capabilities. However, some tools are available that can validate or transform data in flat files. CSV files used to send data to SuccessFactors support *Pretty Good Privacy* (PGP) software to encrypt the file. SuccessFactors supports only SFTP.

In SAP ERP HCM, a report provided in the integration add-on can be used to export a flat file of data to be uploaded to SuccessFactors. No other transactions are available within SAP that allow the export of data within a format accepted by the SuccessFactors HCM suite (*see* Section 3.6). Within the SuccessFactors HCM suite, a flat file of data can be imported from the SuccessFactors SFTP using one of the many options in OneAdmin or, on a regular basis, using a job set up by your implementation partner in the MANAGE SCHEDULED JOBS page within Provisioning. Flat-file transfer can also be used to perform ad hoc or one-time data imports for Metadata Objects, employee data, Employee Central foundation data, translations, and more. These will be covered throughout the specific product chapters.

The Integration Add-On for SAP ERP HCM and SuccessFactors (covered later in this chapter) can leverage flat-file technology to transfer basic organizational and employee data between SAP ERP HCM and the SuccessFactors HCM suite for use in talent management processes.

3.2.2 SAP Process Integration

SAP PI is SAP's reliable/high-performance service-oriented architecture (SOA) middleware product for integrating and transferring message-based data between SAP systems and between other internal or external systems. Approximately 35% of SAP ERP HCM customers currently use SAP PI to integrate SAP systems.

> **Note**
>
> SAP PI was called SAP Exchange Infrastructure (SAP XI) until version 7.0.

SAP PI allows multiple different systems to connect to each other and exchange messages via the central SAP PI Integration Engine component. Various adapters allow connectivity to a variety of systems and handle messages to ensure they are processed correctly by the Integration Engine. Business logic and transformations can be applied to messages to ensure compatibility of data between systems. Figure 3.2 depicts a typical message flow within the SAP PI system.

Although SAP provides a large number of adapters, customers and integration partners can also build their own adapters to fill gaps within the SAP-delivered adapters or to connect to a brand new system, such as the SuccessFactors HCM suite. The SuccessFactors Adapter—launched in early 2014—simplifies the process to build custom interfaces between SuccessFactors and SAP ERP HCM.

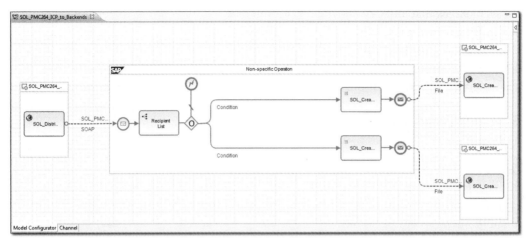

Figure 3.2 Message Flow in SAP PI

The license for SAP PI is included in the SAP licenses that every SAP customer should have. This means there are no licensing implications for using SAP PI as an integration middleware.

Additional Resources

You can read more about SAP PI in the SAP PRESS book *SAP NetWeaver Process Integration* (2nd edition, SAP PRESS, 2010) by Mandy Krimmel and Joachim Orb.

3.2.3 SAP HANA Cloud Integration

As a cloud-based alternative to SAP PI, SAP HANA Cloud Integration provides the same level of middleware integration among multiple systems as is found in SAP PI. SAP HANA Cloud Integration is an *Integration-as-a-Service* (IaaS) platform with an easy-to-use and intuitive UI.

SAP HANA Cloud Integration is specifically designed to integrate SAP's range of cloud solutions (such as SAP Cloud for Travel and Expense and, of course, the SuccessFactors HCM suite) with other cloud applications and on-premise systems. However, the platform does support integration of numerous external systems.

For customers who are not using SAP PI, SAP HANA Cloud Integration is a reasonable alternative. Like the SuccessFactors HCM suite, it benefits from many of the advantages that an SaaS does, such as leveraging a subscription model, offering multi-tenancy, and being hosted and supported remotely. It also offers the same functionality expected from any enterprise-level middleware integration platform. Modeling of integration content is done in web-based UI, as shown in Figure 3.3.

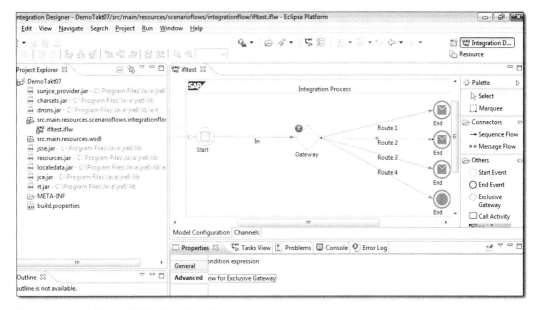

Figure 3.3 Modeling in SAP HANA Cloud Integration

The integration packages that SAP supplies for the Talent Hybrid model leverage SAP HANA Cloud Integration alongside SAP PI. Integration content built-in SAP HANA Cloud Integration is backward-compatible with SAP PI, meaning that content created by other customers or partners on SAP HANA Cloud Integration can be provided to customers using SAP PI. However, it's worth noting that content created in SAP PI can't be used in SAP HANA Cloud Integration.

SAP HANA Cloud Integration also contains standard integration content and templates for integrating SuccessFactors Employee Central with SAP ERP HCM, SuccessFactors Employee Central Payroll, and third-party systems.

Like for SAP PI, a SuccessFactors Adapter was released for SAP HANA Cloud Integration in early 2014.

3.2.4 Dell Boomi AtomSphere

Dell Boomi AtomSphere is a *Platform-as-a-Service* (PaaS) integration platform designed to integrate on-premise and cloud-based systems without the need for additional coding, software, or technology. Dell Boomi AtomSphere is offered to Success-Factors Employee Central customers as part of their subscriptions, at no extra cost. This technology is used primarily to integrate SuccessFactors Employee Central with other systems, but the platform can be used to support integration of other solutions in the SuccessFactors HCM suite.

As a PaaS solution, Dell Boomi AtomSphere benefits from many of the same advantages as SaaS solutions, such as subscription pricing, regular releases, scalability, and lower TCO. In addition, it offers an easy-to-use graphical interface with wizard-based designers that provide the ability to design workflows using drag and drop, create data transformations and model complex business logic, perform integrity checks and validate data, introduce decision handling, create event-based messages, cleanse data, and build unique connectors.

Dell Boomi AtomSphere also features generic templates, prebuilt connectors, and integration scenarios and leverages newly designed components for all customers.

When you use Dell Boomi AtomSphere to connect to SAP ERP, it is possible to use SAP PI as a pass-through so that Dell Boomi AtomSphere and SAP ERP are not connected directly.

3.2.5 SAP Data Services

SAP Data Services is a solution that offers data integration, data quality, data profiling, and text data processing. It is used primarily with analytics-based scenarios that require transferring data from SAP ERP to SAP Business Warehouse (SAP BW), SAP HANA, SAP Rapid Marts, SAP Sybase IQ server, and non-SAP data stores.

SAP Data Services is an *extract, transform, load* (ETL) solution, so its primary purpose is to extract data, transform the data, and load the data to and from any application for use in data integration or data warehouse projects. It provides a development workbench, metadata repository, data connectivity layer, runtime environment, and management console.

SAP Data Services can be used to integrate the SuccessFactors HCM suite with SAP BW. More details can be found in Section 3.7.3.

3.2.6   Single Sign-On

For user experience integration, SSO technology enables multiple technologies to be integrated from a security and logon perspective so that the user can seamlessly switch between applications. Although the switch from one technology to another might not be seamless visually, from an access perspective, the user is not aware that they have been authenticated against another system using the credentials from their first point of access.

Many systems use a variety of industry-standard security mechanisms to provide SSO and protect against unauthorized access. The use of HTTPS as a secure protocol is widespread and provides additional security to data that is transmitted over internal or external networks. Technology such as OAuth, Security Assertion Markup Language 2.0 (SAML2) assertion, and Secure Sockets Layer (SSL) are used both between internal systems and with web-based applications.

SAP's Social Media ABAP Integration Library (SAIL) leverages these protocols when integrating SAP ERP HCM with SAP Jam.

3.2.7   Other Integration Technology

Even with all of these technologies, there is still room for a number of other platforms. Customers may already be using another middleware platform, such as Mule ESB or IBM Cast Iron, and they may want to continue leveraging the platform or to build custom APIs. The SAP platform is open and technology agnostic, so customers can use various integration technologies to integrate SAP ERP HCM with SuccessFactors solutions. This provides a great deal of flexibility and allows customers to retain existing technology and infrastructure that is being used for other solutions.

The SuccessFactors API (SFAPI) and OData API provide a high level of integration capabilities with SuccessFactors. Both APIs enable any web services–based middleware to query, read, and modify data in SuccessFactors. SuccessFactors are constantly enhancing their OData API to add new features and data access capabilities. See Section 3.6 for more details.

3.3 Talent Hybrid Integration Packages

In May 2012, SAP began delivering on its integration strategy with the first packaged integration for the Talent Hybrid model, SAP & SuccessFactors Integration Add-On 1.0. This is delivered as an ABAP add-on for SAP ERP. This initial shipment was followed by a number of support packages and subsequent add-on releases to extend the functionality delivered in the first release and provide additional stability and bug fixes. Subsequent packaged integrations have been released and are planned for release. The latest release of the integration add-on covers a number of Talent Hybrid packages, which can be seen in Figure 3.4 below. The dotted lines represent planned integrations.

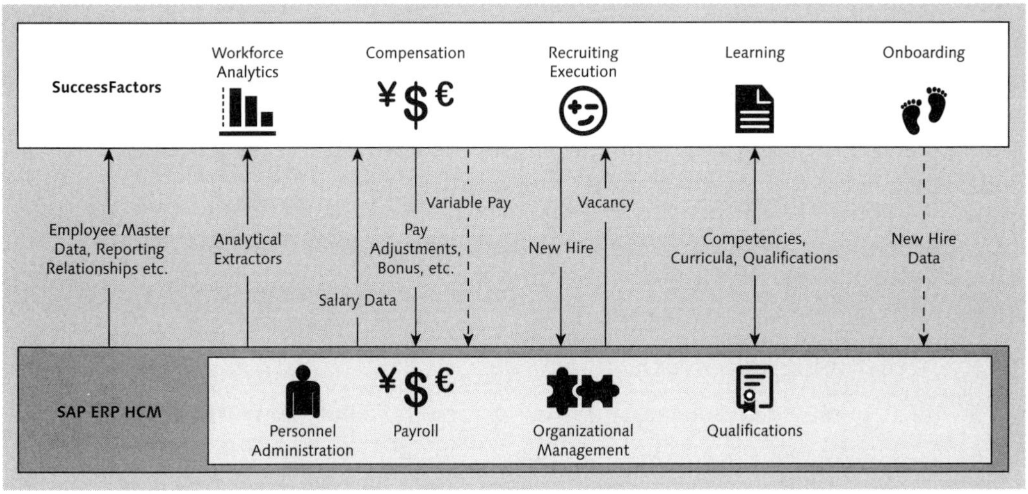

Figure 3.4 The Talent Hybrid Integrations and Immediate Roadmap

SuccessFactors has delivered a number of Employee Central integrations and standard generic templates with every release, which we will cover in Section 3.5.

The current version of the integration add-on (SFIHCM03) covers the following data and process integrations at the time of writing:

- **Basic employee and organizational data**
  - Employee data from SAP ERP HCM to SuccessFactors
- **Evaluation data**
  - Data from SAP ERP HCM to SuccessFactors Workforce Analytics

▶ **Recruiting process**

- ▷ Vacant position data from SAP ERP HCM to SuccessFactors Recruiting Execution

- ▷ New hire data from SuccessFactors Recruiting Execution to SAP ERP HCM

▶ **Compensation process**

- ▷ Salary data from SAP ERP HCM to SuccessFactors Compensation

- ▷ Compensation planning data from SuccessFactors Compensation to SAP ERP HCM

▶ **Qualifications process**

- ▷ One-time upload of Qualification Catalog and employee qualification history to SuccessFactors

- ▷ Changes in employee qualifications and competencies to SAP ERP HCM

The first two scenarios are available for both flat-file and middleware integration methods. The remaining integrations are available only via middleware platforms. These are SAP Process Integration (PI) or SAP HANA Cloud Integration (HCI).

Important Note

The Employee Data integration should always be triggered before all other integration scenarios. The only exception is evaluation data, where this is no dependency.

The integration add-on can be downloaded from SAP Service Marketplace and is available in eight languages: English, German, Spanish, French, Portuguese, Russian, Chinese, and Japanese. The latest versions of the Administrator guides—including all technical prerequisites for the add-on—can be found on SAP Service Marketplace via the path RELEASE & UPGRADE INFO • INSTALLATION & UPGRADE GUIDES • SAP BUSINESS SUITE APPLICATIONS • SAP ERP ADD-ONS • INTEGRATION ADD-ON FOR SAP ERP HCM AND SUCCESSFACTORS BIZX. SAP Notes can be found on SAP Service Marketplace under components PA-SFI-TM and PA-SFI-TM-MW.

Because the integration add-on is delivered as an ABAP add-on, customers who are not familiar with this process should consult SAP Note 1708986 (Installation of SFIHCM01 600). For the middleware integration using SAP PI, version 7.0 of SAP PI and Enterprise Services Repository (ESR) content are required. HTTPS communication between each system and SAP PI is mandatory.

> **Important Note**
>
> The latest version of the integration add-on should always be used, irrespective of which data and/or process integrations are used. It contains all previous packaged integration content, plus bug fixes and new content introduced via support packages and SAP notes.

Further information on Talent Hybrid integrations can be found in SAP Online Help at *http://help.sap.com/erp_sfi_addon30*.

Basic Settings for Integration

There are a number of basic settings that can be configured for the add-on. These are all found in the IMG via the menu path PERSONNEL MANAGEMENT • INTEGRATION ADD-ON FOR SAP ERP HCM AND SUCCESSFACTORS BIZX • BASIC SETTINGS.

Customer-specific logic for authorizations and super users can be defined in the IMG via the menu path PERSONNEL MANAGEMENT • INTEGRATION ADD-ON FOR SAP ERP HCM AND SUCCESSFACTORS BIZX • BASIC SETTINGS • BADI: AUTHORIZATION CHECK FOR SFSF INTEGRATION. This can also be done with BAdI HRSFI_B_AUTHORITY_CHECK (Authorization Check for SFSF Integration), which is called whenever the list of imported data is viewed in SAP ERP HCM and displays the data records that the user has authorization to view.

Additionally, settings for defining how the personnel numbers and SuccessFactors user IDs are determined (e.g., if there are duplicates) are performed in the IMG via the menu path PERSONNEL MANAGEMENT • INTEGRATION ADD-ON FOR SAP ERP HCM AND SUCCESSFACTORS BIZX • BASIC SETTINGS • BADI: DETERMINATION OF SAP ERP PERSONNEL NUMBERS AND SFSF USER IDS. These are also configurable via BAdI implementation HRSFI_RCT_PERNR_USERID of BAdI HRSFI_B_PERNR_USERID (Determination of SAP ERP Personnel Numbers and SFSF User IDs).

When you use middleware, settings for credentials and package size need to be configured in the IMG via the menu path PERSONNEL MANAGEMENT • INTEGRATION ADD-ON FOR SAP ERP HCM AND SUCCESSFACTORS BIZX • BASIC SETTINGS • SETTINGS FOR MIDDLEWARE.

3.3.1 Employee Data

Employee Data integration was introduced in the first integration package released by SAP: Integration Add-On 1.0 for SAP ERP HCM and SuccessFactors

(SFIHCM01). The integration provides basic employee data to populate the basic user import in SuccessFactors.

This integration add-on provides one-way transfer of data from SAP ERP HCM to the SuccessFactors HCM suite to populate the User Data File (UDF) for use in talent management processes. We cover the UDF in Chapter 4, Section 4.5. The add-on can use either flat-file or middleware technology to transfer data. A series of ABAP programs, Web Dynpro applications, authorization roles, and BAdIs are included to extract data on a periodic basis to export to SuccessFactors HCM suite and monitor the process.

The add-on supports 49 standard UDF fields and can be extended to add more fields as required. Within these 49 fields are 34 predefined fields and 15 custom fields that can be freely defined. Nine of the fields are mandatory in SuccessFactors and so must be extracted from SAP. The fields are listed in Table 3.2.

Field	Use	Required
STATUS	Employment status from PA0000-STAT2	X
USER ID	Central person ID or person ID from PA0709	X
USER NAME	Employee's user ID or central person	X
FIRST NAME	First name from PA0002	X
LAST NAME	Last name from PA0002	X
MIDDLE NAME	Middle name from PA0002	
GENDER	Gender from PA0002	
EMAIL	Email address	X
MANAGER	Manager using relationship B012 or A002	X
HUMAN RESOURCE	HR administrator from PA0001	X
DEPARTMENT	Organizational unit or cost center from PA0001	
JOB CODE	Job from PA0001	
DIVISION	Company code from PA0001	
LOCATION	Personnel area from PA0001	
TIME ZONE	Time zone of user	X
HIRE DATE	Initial hire date from feature entry	
EMPLOYEE ID	Personnel number	

Table 3.2 Predefined Fields Used in the Extraction and Synchronization Reports

Field	Use	Required
TITLE	Position or job from PA0001	
BUSINESS PHONE	Business phone number from PA0032 or PA0105 SUBTY 0020	
FAX	Fax number from PA0105 SUBTY CELL	
ADDRESS 1	Description of personnel area from PA0001	
ADDRESS 2	Street of personnel area from PA0001	
CITY	City of personnel area from PA0001	
STATE	Region of personnel area from PA0001	
ZIP	ZIP code of personnel area from PA0001	
COUNTRY	Country key or country grouping of personnel subarea from PA0001	
REVIEW FREQUENCY	Performance appraisal frequency	
LAST REVIEW DATE	Date of last performance appraisal	
MATRIX MANAGER	Dotted-line manager using relationship A002	
DEFAULT LOCALE	Default locale of employee	
CUSTOM MANAGER	Custom manager	
SECOND MANAGER	Second manager	
PROXY	Proxy user	
LOGIN METHOD	Type of login (SSO or PWD)	

Table 3.2 Predefined Fields Used in the Extraction and Synchronization Reports (Cont.)

For each of the fields, a default field mapping selection exists. Customers can also define their own logic. The custom fields can be customized in the Implementation Guide (IMG) via the menu path PERSONNEL MANAGEMENT • INTEGRATION ADD-ON FOR SAP ERP HCM AND SUCCESSFACTORS BIZX • INTEGRATION SCENARIO FOR EMPLOYEE DATA • EXTEND EXTRACTION OF EMPLOYEE DATA. This logic can also be created directly in the BAdI implementation HRSFI_B_EMPL_DATA_REPLICATION (Replication of Employee's Data).

The format to be used for the FIRST NAME and LAST NAME fields can be customized in the IMG via the menu path PERSONNEL MANAGEMENT • INTEGRATION ADD-ON FOR SAP ERP HCM AND SUCCESSFACTORS BIZX • INTEGRATION SCENARIO FOR EMPLOYEE DATA • DEFINE NAME FORMAT FOR FIELDS FIRSTNAME AND LASTNAME.

Figure 3.5 shows the selection screen for the integration report.

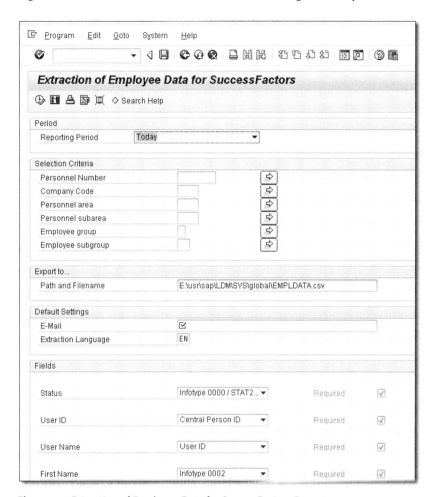

Figure 3.5 Extraction of Employee Data for SuccessFactors Report

Additional parameters of the SFAPI can be set up in the IMG via the menu path
PERSONNEL MANAGEMENT • INTEGRATION ADD-ON FOR SAP ERP HCM AND SUCCESS-
FACTORS BIZX • INTEGRATION SCENARIO FOR EMPLOYEE DATA • BUSINESS ADD-INS
(BADIS). This can also be done with BAdI HRSFI_B_SFSF_API_PARAMETER (Parame-
ters for Checks of Employee Data Transfer).

> **Important Note**
>
> Although the integration add-on provides a report to extract the employee data (RH_SFI_TRIGGER_EMPL_DATA_REPL) and a report for synchronization of data (RH_SFI_SYNCHRONIZE_EMPL_DATA), we recommend that you use the synchronization report at all times.

Concurrent Employment

The add-on considers concurrent employment, but because SuccessFactors currently handles concurrent employment differently than SAP ERP HCM, additional configuration is required before the extraction reports can be run. SuccessFactors is introducing concurrent employment, but at the time of writing, this has not been rolled out across the suite.

Each employee with multiple assignments (e.g., multiple personnel numbers [PERNRs]) must have their main assignments defined in infotype 0712 using subtype SFSF. This ensures that the main assignment and all related assignments are transferred to the SuccessFactors HCM suite. If no main assignment is maintained, the extraction report selects one of the assignments for data extraction, or if BAdI HRSFI_B_LEADING_CONTRACT (Determine the Leading Assignment for a Central Person) is defined, the logic of the active implementation is used.

Employee Data Extraction

Data transfer from SAP ERP HCM to the SuccessFactors HCM suite is triggered using report RH_SFI_SYNCHRONIZE_EMPL_DATA. This report was introduced in Service Package 2.0 for integration add-on 1.0. If this report is not available, report RH_SFI_SYNCHRONIZE_EMPL_DATA can be used. Please note that this report does not support middleware integration. To transfer employees to SuccessFactors prior to their being hired (for example, to provide access to SuccessFactors Onboarding or SAP Jam), use report RH_SFI_PREHIRE_EMPL_DATA.

For flat-file transfer, the location of the CSV file and the regular scheduling of the report as a job should be configured in the IMG via the menu path PERSONNEL MANAGEMENT • INTEGRATION ADD-ON FOR SAP ERP HCM AND SUCCESSFACTORS BIZX • INTEGRATION SCENARIO FOR EMPLOYEE DATA • DEFINE FILE PATH AND NAME FOR STORING THE GENERATED FILES. Both reports can also be scheduled as a job via Transaction SM36. A job must be set up in the SuccessFactors HCM suite by an implementation partner to import the flat file. This is set up under MANAGED SCHEDULED JOBS in the Provisioning module. Figure 3.6 shows the CREATE NEW JOB page.

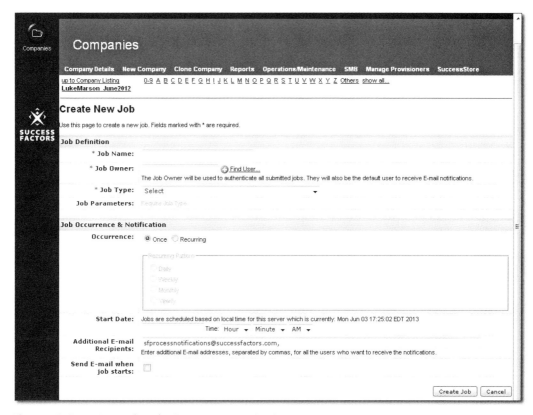

Figure 3.6 Create New Job in the SuccessFactors HCM Suite Provisioning

The flat file can also be imported on an ad hoc basis using the IMPORT EMPLOYEE DATA page under MANAGER USERS in OneAdmin.

If you are using middleware, the middleware integration platform needs to be configured in the IMG via the menu path PERSONNEL MANAGEMENT • INTEGRATION ADD-ON FOR SAP ERP HCM AND SUCCESSFACTORS BIZX • BASIC SETTINGS • SETTINGS FOR MIDDLEWARE.

A variant is required to run the extraction report, and this is created in the IMG via the menu path PERSONNEL MANAGEMENT • INTEGRATION ADD-ON FOR SAP ERP HCM AND SUCCESSFACTORS BIZX • INTEGRATION SCENARIO FOR EMPLOYEE DATA • SPE-

CIFY ALLOWED VARIANTS FOR DELTA EXTRACTION. If multiple variants are used, they should always be run with the same frequency and in the same sequence.

Various fields are available within the report as selection criteria, including PERSONNEL NUMBER, EMPLOYMENT STATUS, COMPANY CODE, PERSONNEL AREA, PERSONNEL SUBAREA, EMPLOYEE GROUP, and EMPLOYEE SUBGROUP. The type of transfer (middleware or file transfer), default email address, extraction language, and fields to transfer are configured as part of a variant but can also be changed after a variant has been selected. A default email address must be configured because this is a mandatory field in the SuccessFactors HCM suite. The FORCED SYNCHRONIZATION option forces a full data load. After the report is executed, either a flat file is generated, or, if middleware integration is selected, the data is transferred directly to the SuccessFactors HCM suite. The log is also displayed to show any success, warning, or error messages. Figure 3.7 shows an example of the log.

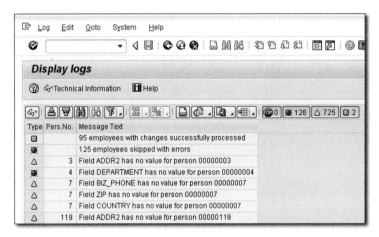

Figure 3.7 Display Log Screen in the Employee Data Synchronization Report

When the report is executed, Table HRSFI_D_EXTR_LOG is updated with all synchronized employees. If an error occurs, the employee is stored in Table HRSFI_D_ERR_LOG, and Table HRSFI_D_EXTR_LOG is not updated for the employee. When the report is subsequently executed, a check is done against Table HRSFI_D_EXTR_LOG to see if any employees have changed, and, if so, they are extracted from SAP ERP HCM. The report also checks for employees marked as inactive in Table HRSFI_D_INACT_EE.

Report RH_SFI_SYNCHRONIZE_EMPL_DATA can be scheduled to regularly transfer data from SAP ERP HCM to SuccessFactors.

Monitoring the Extraction Process

SAP supplies the Web Dynpro application HRSFI_MONITORING_EMPL (Success Factors—Transfer Monitoring) to monitor the transfer of employee data from SAP ERP HCM to SuccessFactors that is triggered by report RH_SFI_SYNCHRONIZE_ EMPL_DATA. The application can be seen in Figure 3.8, where the EMPLOYEE DATA TRANSFER area shows several backend messages.

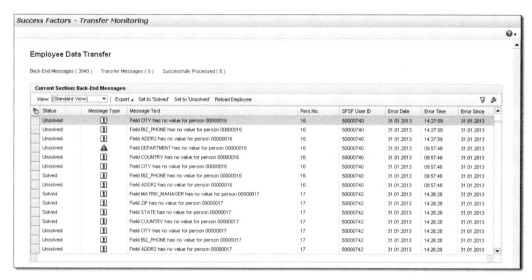

Figure 3.8 Employee Data Transfer in the Transfer Monitoring Application

The EMPLOYEE DATA TRANSFER list displays the messages that have been triggered during the data transfer process. The messages are displayed with a status, message type (error, warning, or success), employee number and SuccessFactors user ID, extraction variant, and date and time. For the compensation transfer, the SuccessFactors Compensation template ID and field set name are also displayed. Any fields can be hidden from display using the SETTINGS DIALOG option.

Messages can be viewed by type, as follows:

▶ **Backend messages**
Messages that were triggered in SAP ERP HCM

▶ **Transfer messages**
Messages that were triggered during transfer of data

▶ **Successfully processed**
List of employees with successful data transfer

Some actions can be taken to track and re-extract data for issues. The status can be switched to Solved and back to Unsolved using the Set to 'Solved' and Set to 'Unsolved' buttons. After issues with the employee data extract have been manually corrected in the backend and marked as Solved, they can be re-extracted on an ad hoc basis. This is done by selecting a record and using the Reload Employee button; it uses the same variant as in the original processing.

Data Administration and Cleanup

Several reports are available to administer data used in the transfers.

After employees leave the company and the period of data retention has passed, report RPUDELPP can be used to delete the personnel IDs of those individuals in the synchronization logs. The BAdI implementation HRPAYXX_DELETE_PERNR (Personnel Number Deletion Reports) is used to define the logic for selecting the employee(s) to be deleted. There is a dual control principle for the authorization object P_DEL_PERN that is used by the report. Both the role used for requesting the deletion and the role used for performing the delete must have this authorization object assigned.

The extraction of employee data can be stopped for one or more employees by using Report RH_SFI_WITHDRAW_VARIANT. This report can be used to halt the extraction for employees using the same selection criteria available in the employee data synchronization report or the compensation extraction report.

3.3.2 Evaluation Data

The integration add-on contains 30 extractors to transfer evaluation data from various infotypes to SuccessFactors Workforce Analytics. It outputs a number of text (TXT) files for the SuccessFactors SFTP to retrieve. These reports can be used as standard but configured to use customer-specific logic or fields in Transaction SE38. In total, 35 reports can be run to export a text file to be uploaded into SuccessFactors Workforce Analytics.

The reports should be run as a batch job periodically to create the TXT files. Each report can be run individually and contains basic selection criteria to run the report for a group of employees or a group of objects.

A list of the reports and infotypes can be found in Table 3.3 below.

Report	Infotype
RH_SFI_HRP1000	1000 (Objects)
RH_SFI_HRP1001	1001 (Relationships)
RH_SFI_PA0000	0000 (Actions)
RH_SFI_PA0001	0001 (Organizational Assignments)
RH_SFI_PA0002	0002 (Personnel Data)
RH_SFI_PA0007	0007 (Planned Working Time)
RH_SFI_PA0008	0008 (Basic Pay)
RH_SFI_PA0016	0016 (Contract Elements)
RH_SFI_PA0025	0025 (Appraisals)
RH_SFI_PA0041	0041 (Date Specifications)
RH_SFI_PA0077	0077 (Personnel Actions)
RH_SFI_PA0302	0302 (Additional Actions)
RH_SFI_T001	T001 (Company Codes)
RH_SFI_T001P	T001P (Personnel Subareas)
RH_SFI_T500P	T500P (Personnel Areas)
RH_SFI_T501T	T501T (Employee Group Names)
RH_SFI_T503T	T503T (Employee Subgroup Names)
RH_SFI_T505S	T505S (Ethnic Origin Texts)
RH_SFI_T510A	T510A (Pay Scales Types)
RH_SFI_T510G	T510G (Pay Scale Areas)
RH_SFI_T512T	T512T (Wage Type Texts)
RH_SFI_T513F	T513F (Appraisal Criteria Texts)
RH_SFI_T527O	T527O (Organizational Key Validation)
RH_SFI_T529T	T529T (Personnel Events Text)
RH_SFI_T529U	T529U (Status Values)
RH_SFI_T530T	T530T (Event Reasons Text)
RH_SFI_T542T	T542T (Employment Contracts)
RH_SFI_T545T	T545T (Corporation Texts)
RH_SFI_T548T	T548T (Date Types)
RH_SFI_T549T	T549T (Date Types)

Table 3.3 Extraction Reports for Evaluation Data

Report	Infotype
RH_SFI_T554T	T554T (Absence and Attendance Texts)
RH_SFI_T5U13	T5U13 (Jobs)
RH_SFI_T5UEE	T5UEE (EEO Occupational Categories)
RH_SFI_THOC	THOC (Public Holiday Calendar)
RH_SFI_THOL	THOL (Public Holidays)

Table 3.3 Extraction Reports for Evaluation Data (Cont.)

Authorization role SAP_HR_SFI_ANALYTICS is required for the analytics extraction.

3.3.3 Compensation Data

Integration of compensation data—both salary data from SAP ERP HCM and compensation planning results from SuccessFactors HCM—ensures that SuccessFactors Compensation can be used for salary planning with SAP ERP HCM data and have the resulting salary changes written back to SAP ERP HCM and staged prior to releasing into Payroll. Figure 3.9 shows the process flow of the integration.

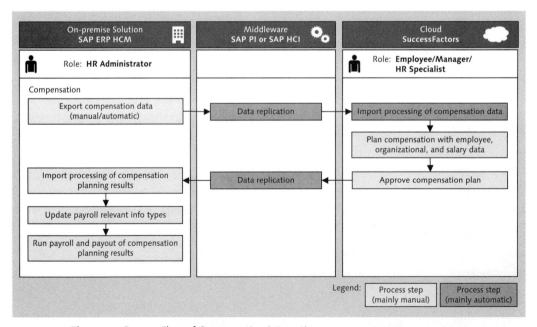

Figure 3.9 Process Flow of Compensation Integration

> **Important Note**
>
> No configuration is required in the SAP ERP HCM Enterprise Compensation Management module for this integration.

Setting Up the Compensation Integration

Before data can be transferred to SuccessFactors, the field sets for the data export and import need to be configured in the IMG via the menu path PERSONNEL MANAGEMENT • INTEGRATION ADD-ON FOR SAP ERP HCM AND SUCCESSFACTORS BIZX • INTEGRATION SCENARIO FOR COMPENSATION DATA • DATA TRANSFER FROM SAP ERP TO SUCCESSFACTORS BIZX • DEFINE FIELDS FOR EXTRACTING COMPENSATION DATA. These are also configurable via BAdI HRSFI_B_COMP_FIELD_EXTRACTOR (Extraction of Compensation Data).

Some fields can also be set to have their values entered at the time of activation, rather than being predefined. These values can then be changed during the activation part of the process. BAdI HRSFI_B_COMP_DATA_ACTIVATION (Activation of Compensation Data Imported from SFSF) is used to determine how compensation data is imported into and activated in SAP ERP HCM. The BAdI HRSFI_B_COMP_ACTIVATION_CUST (Customizing Information Needed for Compensation Activation) can be used to determine additional data from SAP ERP HCM that is required to activate the imported compensation data but that cannot be imported from SuccessFactors Compensation.

Before the integration is run, the Compensation form should already be created in SuccessFactors Compensation and assigned to a Compensation Group ID. This Compensation Group ID is required as part of the synchronization report in SAP. An ad hoc report must be created in SuccessFactors Compensation for the SuccessFactors API to extract the data for import into SAP ERP HCM; this ad hoc report must contain the columns required for extraction, plus the form template ID and the user ID. The column for the user ID must have the property CONSTRAINABLE. Only fields from complete forms must be extracted.

Transferring Salary Data to SuccessFactors Compensation

Report RH_SFI_SYNCH_COMP_DATA is provided for transferring salary data to SuccessFactors. Thirty-nine fields are available as standard, including the following:

- ▶ SALARY
- ▶ PAYMENT INTERVAL
- ▶ CURRENCY
- ▶ CAPACITY UTILIZATION LEVEL
- ▶ PAY GRADE
- ▶ JOB LEVEL
- ▶ START DATE
- ▶ BONUS ELIGIBILITY
- ▶ COMPENSATION ELIGIBILITY
- ▶ LUMP SUM ELIGIBILITY
- ▶ CONTROLLER

Figure 3.10 shows the selection screen for the report to transfer compensation data to the SuccessFactors HCM suite from SAP ERP HCM.

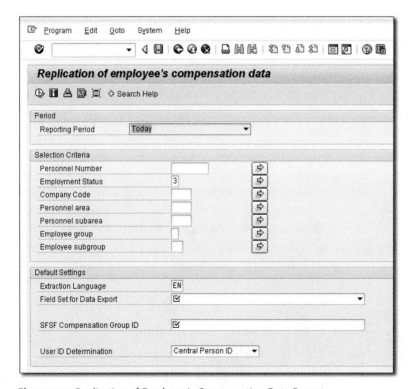

Figure 3.10 Replication of Employee's Compensation Data Report

The selection screen for report RH_SFI_SYNCH_COMP_DATA requires the reporting period to be selected, alongside the extraction language, set of fields to be used, Compensation Group ID from SuccessFactors Compensation, and field to determine the employees' user IDs. The field to determine the user IDs of employees should be the same as that defined for the employee data extraction. Additionally, the same selection criteria fields that are available in the employee data synchronization report are also available in this report. After the report is executed, the data is transferred directly to the SuccessFactors HCM suite, and the log is also displayed to show any success, warning, or error messages.

Transferring Compensation Planning Results to SAP ERP HCM

After the compensation planning process is performed in SuccessFactors Compensation using the salary data transferred with the method described in the previous section, the resultant compensation planning data can be imported into SAP ERP HCM. Report RH_SFI_IMPORT_COMP_DATA is provided for this purpose. In addition, once the data is imported into the system, it must be separately activated at the point it is required in the payroll run. This is done with Report RH_SFI_ACTIVATE_COMP_DATA.

The selection screen for Report RH_SFI_IMPORT_COMP_DATA is very similar to the selection screen for Report RH_SFI_SYNCH_COMP_DATA and requires similar fields to be provided, such as the reporting period, the set of fields to be used, the name of the ad hoc report in SuccessFactors, and the field to determine the employees' user IDs. After the report is executed, the data is imported into the staging tables in SAP ERP HCM, and the log is displayed to show any success, warning, or error messages.

The next and final stage of the compensation integration process is activating the data in SAP ERP HCM so that it is available within the Payroll infotypes. This is done with Report RH_SFI_ACTIVATE_COMP_DATA. The report selection screen requires the reporting period to be selected, alongside the set of fields to be used and the SuccessFactors Compensation Template ID. Additionally, the same selection criteria fields that are available in the compensation data synchronization report are available in this report.

You can run the report in test mode by selecting the TEST ONLY checkbox. During the configuration of the field set to be used, if some fields were selected to be entered during the activation stage, then these can be changed using the ENTER FIELDS button. After the report is executed, the data is imported from the staging tables into the basic pay and associated infotypes in SAP ERP HCM. The log is also displayed to show any success, warning, or error messages.

The compensation data integration process is now complete.

Monitoring the Data Transfer

The Web Dynpro application HRSFI_MONITORING_COMP is provided to monitor the compensation data extraction from SuccessFactors. The application HRSFI_MONITORING_EMPL is used to monitor the transfer of salary data from SAP ERP HCM to SuccessFactors, as seen in Figure 3.11.

Compensation Data Transfer

Back-End Messages (7638)   Transfer Messages (2741)   Successfully Processed (3)   Transfer Log

Current Section: Back-End Messages

View: [Standard View] ▼ | Export ▲ | Set to 'Solved' | Set to 'Unsolved'   Filter Settings

Status	Message Type	Message Text	Pers.No.	SFSF User ID	Error Date	Error Time	Error Since	Field Set for Data Export
Unsolved	⚠	Salary at 100% capacity cannot be calculated: Cap. util. level is 0%	7012	00000304	05.02.2013	08:07:31	05.02.2013	ZBW_TEST
Unsolved	⚠	Field CUR_SALARY has no value for person 00000623	22100	00000623	05.02.2013	08:07:31	05.02.2013	ZBW_TEST
Unsolved	⚠	Field CUR_SALARY has no value for person 00000624	22101	00000624	05.02.2013	08:07:31	05.02.2013	ZBW_TEST
Unsolved	⚠	Field CUR_SALARY has no value for person 00000627	1402	00000627	05.02.2013	08:07:31	05.02.2013	ZBW_TEST
Unsolved	⚠	Field CUR_SALARY has no value for person 00000862	900050	00000862	05.02.2013	08:07:31	05.02.2013	ZBW_TEST
Unsolved	⚠	Field CUR_SALARY has no value for person 00000863	900051	00000863	05.02.2013	08:07:31	05.02.2013	ZBW_TEST
Unsolved	⚠	Field CUR_SALARY has no value for person 00000864	900052	00000864	05.02.2013	08:07:31	05.02.2013	ZBW_TEST
Unsolved	⚠	Field CUR_SALARY has no value for person 00000865	900053	00000865	05.02.2013	08:07:31	05.02.2013	ZBW_TEST
Unsolved	⚠	Field CUR_SALARY has no value for person 00000866	900054	00000866	05.02.2013	08:07:31	05.02.2013	ZBW_TEST
Unsolved	⚠	Field CUR_SALARY has no value for person 00000868	900056	00000868	05.02.2013	08:07:31	05.02.2013	ZBW_TEST
Unsolved	⚠	Field CUR_SALARY has no value for person 00000934	900122	00000934	05.02.2013	08:07:31	05.02.2013	ZBW_TEST
Unsolved	⚠	Field CUR_SALARY has no value for person 00001036	901001	00001036	05.02.2013	08:07:31	05.02.2013	ZBW_TEST
Unsolved	⚠	Field CUR_SALARY has no value for person 00001037	901002	00001037	05.02.2013	08:07:31	05.02.2013	ZBW_TEST
Unsolved	⚠	Field CUR_SALARY has no value for person 00001038	901003	00001038	05.02.2013	08:07:31	05.02.2013	ZBW_TEST
Unsolved	⚠	Field CUR_SALARY has no value for person 00001039	901004	00001039	05.02.2013	08:07:31	05.02.2013	ZBW_TEST

Figure 3.11 Compensation Data Transfer in the Transfer Monitoring Application

The HRSFI_MONITORING_COMP (Compensation Monitor—Import and Activation) application is similar to the employee data transfer monitoring application. The application is split up into two lists:

▶ The COMPENSATION DATA TRANSFER list displays an overview for each of the processes (TRANSFER, MAPPING, TEST, and ACTIVATED) in the importing and activation of data from SuccessFactors Compensation to SAP ERP HCM. It uses a traffic light system of icons to show whether there were errors, warnings, or success messages for employees in each of the four processes. These can be seen in Figure 3.12. The list displays the personnel number, person ID, SuccessFactors user ID, the SuccessFactors Compensation Template ID, set of fields used, SuccessFactors ad hoc report, and a column for each of the four processes.

- The ALL EMPLOYEES list displays messages that have been triggered during the data transfer process for each employee. It displays the status, message type, message text, personnel number, SuccessFactors user ID, SuccessFactors Compensation Template ID, field set, SuccessFactors ad hoc report, and date and time. The status of each message can be switched to SOLVED and back to UNSOLVED using the SET TO 'SOLVED' and SET TO 'UNSOLVED' buttons, as with the other monitoring application.

As with the employee monitoring application, any fields in either list can be hidden from display using the SETTINGS DIALOG option.

Messages in both lists can be viewed by type:

- **Transfer messages**
  Messages that were triggered during transfer of data to SAP ERP HCM

- **Mapping messages**
  Messages that were triggered during transformation of data

- **Messages on test activation**
  Messages that were triggered during the test run of the activation

- **Messages on activation**
  Messages that were triggered during the activation

The main screen of the application is shown in Figure 3.12, which shows the status of each step of the compensation integration process.

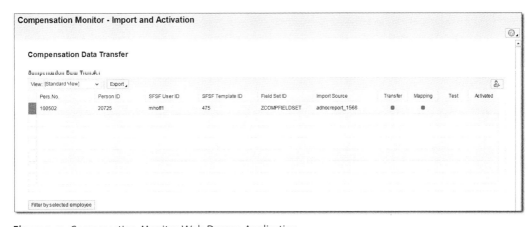

Figure 3.12 Compensation Monitor Web Dynpro Application

Data Administration and Cleanup

Data in the internal log tables used for the transfer of compensation data can be deleted using Report RH_SFI_CLEANUP_COMP_REPL (for data synchronization with the SuccessFactors HCM suite) and Report RH_SFI_CLEANUP_COMP_IMP (for importing data into SAP ERP HCM).

3.3.4 Recruiting Data

For the recruiting process, SAP provides integrations for the attract-to-hire and define-to-hire processes. These enable requisition requests to be created in SuccessFactors Recruiting Execution using organizational and position vacancy data from SAP ERP HCM and allow hiring or transfer actions to be started in SAP ERP HCM with data from SuccessFactors Recruiting Execution after a candidate has accepted an offer. These integrations were released in Integration Add-On 2.0 for SAP ERP HCM and SuccessFactors BizX (SFIHCM02) and in the second service package. Figure 3.13 shows the process flow of the integration.

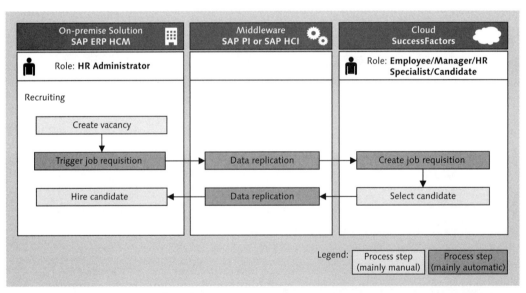

Figure 3.13 Process Flow of Recruiting Integration

Unlike the previous integrations, this integration features various integration points between SAP ERP HCM and SuccessFactors Recruiting Execution. In the compensation integration, compensation data was transferred to SuccessFactors before the compensation planning process was performed in SuccessFactors Compensation, and then the resultant data was transferred back to SAP ERP HCM after it was completed. With these integrations, data is transferred from one system to another at different stages of the recruiting process. This will be detailed shortly. The process for the recruiting integrations is as follows:

1. A vacancy record is created for a position.

2. A report in SAP ERP HCM is run to send vacant position information to SuccessFactors Recruiting Execution to create Job Requisitions.

3. Job Requisitions are created in SuccessFactors RECRUITING EXECUTION WITH THE VALUE OF THE STATE FIELD SET TO PRE-APPROVED. Infotype 1107 in SAP is updated with the Requisition ID, along with fields such as REQUISITION TEMPLATE ID and NAME, etc.

4. The recruiting process is performed in SuccessFactors Recruiting Execution.

5. A report in SAP ERP HCM is run to extract all JobApplication objects with status SENTTOSAP into a staging table in SAP ERP HCM.

6. For each JobApplication object that is sent to SAP ERP HCM, the status field in SuccessFactors Recruiting Execution is updated to TRANSFEREDTOSAP if the transfer was successful or TRANSFEREDTOSAPERROR if the transfer was unsuccessful.

7. SuccessFactors Recruiting Execution fields are mapped to SAP ERP HCM fields.

8. Transaction HRSFI_RCT_HIRE is run to check the data from the data import and launch a personnel action to hire, rehire, or transfer a candidate.

9. The status of the JobApplication object in SuccessFactors is set to HIREDATSAP, and the date is saved in the EXPORTED ON field.

10. The new employee's data is transferred to the SuccessFactors HCM suite using the employee data integration.

In addition, a new infotype (1107) is introduced to enable handling of vacant positions for Job Requisitions.

The flow of data between SAP ERP HCM and the SuccessFactors HCM suite for the new hire process is illustrated in Figure 3.14.

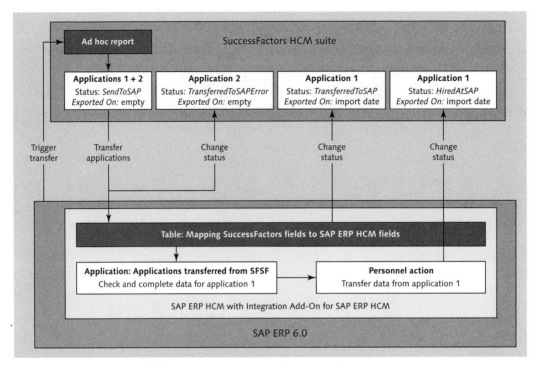

Figure 3.14 End-to-End Process Flow of the Recruiting Integrations

Setting Up the Recruiting Integrations

Various settings must be made in the IMG in SAP ERP HCM and SuccessFactors Recruiting Execution for you to use the integrations.

The first setting to be made is defining the integrations to be used. This is done by setting one or both of the parameters CANDIDATE_UPDATE_ACTIVE and JOB_REQUISITION_INTEGR_ACTIVE to X in the IMG via the menu path PERSONNEL MANAGEMENT • INTEGRATION ADD-ON FOR SAP ERP HCM AND SUCCESSFACTORS BIZX • INTEGRATION SCENARIO FOR RECRUITING DATA • ACTIVATE ADDITIONAL FUNCTIONS.

The BAdI used to determine which Job Requisition ID should be used for each group of Positions (should more than one be used) must be defined, if applicable. This is configured in the IMG via the menu path PERSONNEL MANAGEMENT • INTEGRATION ADD-ON FOR SAP ERP HCM AND SUCCESSFACTORS BIZX • INTEGRATION SCENARIO FOR RECRUITING DATA • TRANSFER OF JOB REQUISITION DATA FROM SAP ERP TO SUCCESSFACTORS BIZX • BADI: DETERMINATION OF JOB REQUISITION TEMPLATE FROM

SFSF. This can also be configured via BAdI `HRSFI_B_TEMPLATE_DETERMINATION` (Determination of Job Requisition Template from SFSF).

For positions with an existing, active record in infotype 1007, records are created in new infotype 1107 automatically (we'll cover this in the next section). However, these records are not transferred to SuccessFactors Recruiting Execution by default. To modify this behavior, you can make settings in the IMG via the menu path PERSONNEL MANAGEMENT • INTEGRATION ADD-ON FOR SAP ERP HCM AND SUC-CESSFACTORS BIZX • INTEGRATION SCENARIO FOR RECRUITING DATA • TRANSFER OF JOB REQUISITION DATA FROM SAP ERP TO SUCCESSFACTORS BIZX • SPECIFY HANDLING OF EXISTING VACANCIES DURING DATA TRANSFER. Report RH_SFI_MIGRATE_VACAN-CIES is used to migrate existing vacancies to SuccessFactors Recruiting and create requisitions.

Once these steps are complete, most of the Requisition integration is setup. Some further steps are required during the configuration of the New Hire integration, when fields from both integrations need to be assigned to field sets.

The New Hire integration steps begin with defining the settings for how the country grouping and personnel actions are determined. These are configured in the IMG via the menu path PERSONNEL MANAGEMENT • INTEGRATION ADD-ON FOR SAP ERP HCM AND SUCCESSFACTORS BIZX • INTEGRATION SCENARIO FOR RECRUITING DATA • TRANSFER OF DATA FROM SUCCESSFACTORS BIZX TO SAP ERP • BADI: DETERMI-NATION OF FURTHER DATA FOR RECRUITING SCENARIO FROM SFSF. These are also con-figurable via BAdI `HRSFI_B_RECRUIT_MAPPING` (Determination of Further Data for Recruiting Scenario from SFSF), although no standard implementation exists within the system.

There are three Customizing activities available to configure the application HRSFI_RCT_HIRE in the IMG via the menu path PERSONNEL MANAGEMENT • INTE-GRATION ADD-ON FOR SAP ERP HCM AND SUCCESSFACTORS BIZX • INTEGRATION SCENARIO FOR RECRUITING DATA • TRANSFER OF DATA FROM SUCCESSFACTORS BIZX TO SAP ERP • FURTHER PROCESSING OF IMPORTED DATA. With these, you can do the following:

▸ Define more columns for the TRANSFERRED JOB APPLICATIONS list

▸ Specify the headers and field labels

▸ Change the PDF overview for job requisition

Within SuccessFactors Recruiting Execution, you need to make several settings. It is a prerequisite that the JobApplication object has the field SAPERROR available and that the HIRE status category can be filtered. Four statuses must be made available in the CANDIDATESTATUS selection list that is used by the APPLICATION STATUS (RCM_APP_STATUS_STATUS_NAME) field:

▸ SFSF_APPL_STATUS_HIRED: HIREDATSAP

▸ SFSF_APPL_STATUS_SEND_SAP: SENDTOSAP

▸ SFSF_APPL_STATUS_TRANSFERRED: TRANSFERREDTOSAP

▸ SFSF_APPL_STATUS_TRANSF_ERR: TRANSFERREDTOSAPERROR

The statuses can be changed in SuccessFactors Recruiting Execution and, if so, must also be changed in the IMG via the menu path PERSONNEL MANAGEMENT • INTEGRATION ADD-ON FOR SAP ERP HCM AND SUCCESSFACTORS BIZX • INTEGRATION SCENARIO FOR RECRUITING DATA • TRANSFER OF DATA FROM SUCCESSFACTORS BIZX TO SAP ERP • CHANGE APPLICATION STATUS VALUES USED IN SUCCESSFACTORS BIZX.

An ad hoc report needs to be created to transfer all JobApplication objects to SAP with the status SEND TO SAP, including the fields to be transferred. The fields listed in Table 3.4 must be included in the ad hoc report. The XML templates for the SuccessFactors Recruiting Execution objects must contain all of the required fields.

Object	Field
JobApplication	RCM_APPLICATION_CAN_JOB_MAP_ID
JobApplication	RCM_APP_STATUS_STATUS_NAME
JobApplication	APP_TEMPLATE_APP_TEMPLATE_ID
LastOfferDetail	OFFER_DETAIL_LATEST_JOB_REQ_JOB_START_ DATE

Table 3.4 Fields Required for the Ad Hoc Report

We recommend that you also add the fields listed in Table 3.5.

Object	Field
JobApplication	RCM_APPLICATION_FIRSTNAME
JobApplication	RCM_APPLICATION_LASTNAME
JobApplication	RCM_APPLICATION_GENDER

Table 3.5 Fields Recommended for the Ad Hoc Report

Object	Field
JobApplication	RCM_APPLICATION_DOB
JobRequisition	RCM_JOB_REQ_EXT_TEXT1

Table 3.5 Fields Recommended for the Ad Hoc Report (Cont.)

After the Customizing in SAP ERP HCM has been performed, the ad hoc report must be created in SuccessFactors Recruiting Execution. The ad hoc reports, fields, and metadata for this template and the Job Requisition template need to be imported into SAP ERP HCM to configure the remainder of the integration. This is done via Report RH_SFI_SYNCH_METADATA or in the IMG via the menu path Personnel Management • Integration Add-On for SAP ERP HCM and SuccessFactors BizX • Basic Settings • Importing Metadata from SuccessFactors BizX. When any of these objects change in SuccessFactors, the report must be run to re-import the objects. When you run the report, there is only one option that can be run for recruiting data: SFSF Ad-hoc Reports. This report can also be used to import compensation metadata from SuccessFactors Compensation.

After the report is run, the imported ad hoc report needs to be mapped to field sets for both the Job Requisition and New Hire fields. This is performed in the IMG via the menu path Personnel Management • Integration Add-On for SAP ERP HCM and SuccessFactors BizX • Integration Scenario for Recruiting Data • Assign SuccessFactors BizX Objects to Field Sets. It can also be performed in Transaction S_NWC_37000012.

Following this, fields from the field sets need to be mapped to SAP ERP HCM fields. Here, each SuccessFactors Recruiting Execution field can have its mapping mode defined (Mapped via Table, Mapped via BAdI, or Not Individually Mapped, e.g., display-only), whether the field is country-group dependent, and whether the field should be a required field. This is performed in the IMG via the menu path Personnel Management • Integration Add-On for SAP ERP HCM and SuccessFactors BizX • Integration Scenario for Recruiting Data • Map SuccessFactors BizX Fields and SAP ERP Fields to Each Other. These are also configurable via BAdI `HRSFI_B_FIELD_MAPPING` (Mapping of SFSF Fields to SAP ERP Infotype Fields). It is important to note that not every field needs to be mapped via a BAdI.

> **Important Note**
>
> The Customizing performed in ASSIGN SUCCESSFACTORS BIZX OBJECTS TO FIELD SETS and MAP SUCCESSFACTORS BIZX FIELDS AND SAP ERP FIELDS TO EACH OTHER are not transportable and must be completed in each of the target SAP ERP HCM systems.

Once all fields are mapped to field sets, a check should be run to ensure that all of the fields that are to be transferred to and from SuccessFactors Recruiting Execution exist and are set to REQUIRED. This is performed in the IMG via the menu path PERSONNEL MANAGEMENT • INTEGRATION ADD-ON FOR SAP ERP HCM AND SUCCESS-FACTORS BIZX • INTEGRATION SCENARIO FOR RECRUITING DATA • CHECK FIELD SETS FOR REQUIRED FIELDS AND CORRECT. This can be done directly with report RH_SFI_RECRUIT_REQ_FIELDS.

Multiple fields can be mapped to one or more fields in the IMG via the menu path PERSONNEL MANAGEMENT • INTEGRATION ADD-ON FOR SAP ERP HCM AND SUCCESSF-ACTORS BIZX • INTEGRATION SCENARIO FOR RECRUITING DATA • TRANSFER OF DATA FROM SAP ERP TO SUCCESSFACTORS BIZX • BADI: MAPPING OF SFSF FIELDS TO ERP IT FIELDS: CHANGE OF MAPPING RESULT for Job Requisition integration and via the menu path PERSONNEL MANAGEMENT • INTEGRATION ADD-ON FOR SAP ERP HCM AND SUCCESSFACTORS BIZX • INTEGRATION SCENARIO FOR RECRUITING DATA • TRANSFER OF DATA FROM SUCCESSFACTORS BIZX TO SAP ERP • BADI: MAPPING OF SFSF FIELDS TO ERP IT FIELDS: CHANGE OF MAPPING RESULT for New Hire integration. These are also configurable via BAdI HRSFI_B_CHANGE_MAPPING_RESULT (Mapping of SFSF Fields to ERP Infotype Fields: Change of Mapping Result).

Transferring Vacant Position Data to SuccessFactors Recruiting

After the configuration is completed in SAP ERP HCM and SuccessFactors Recruiting Execution, the integration process can begin.

Before the integration is actually run, Infotype 1107 must be maintained for one or more vacant positions that need to be recruited for in SuccessFactors Recruiting Execution. This is done automatically when a position is set to vacant in Infotype 1007. Job Requisition data for a position can be viewed in one of the following transactions:

- Create Organization and Staffing (Transaction PPOCE)
- Change Organization and Staffing (Transaction PPOME)
- Display Organization and Staffing (Transaction PPOSE)

Within these transactions, the user can select a position and navigate to the SFSF JOB REQUISITION tab to view the vacancy and requisition trigger information. If Infotype 1007 is not used, a user can create and manage vacancy and requisition trigger information here. Infotype 1107 has two subtypes that can be set in this tab: Open Job Requisition (subtype 0001) and Closed Job Requisition (subtype 0002). These affect whether a Job Requisition is created and/or remains active in SuccessFactors Recruiting Execution. This tab also displays information about the open Job Requisitions and any other Job Requisitions for the position. Only one open Job Requisition can exist at any one time. Figure 3.15 shows the SFSF JOB REQUISITION tab in Transaction PPOME.

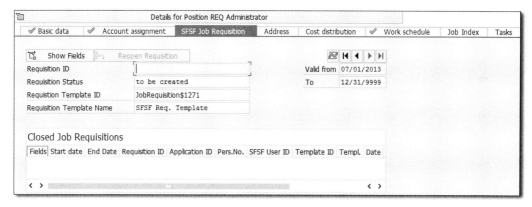

Figure 3.15 The SFSF Job Requisition Tab in Transaction PPOME

To create Job Requisitions in SuccessFactors Recruiting Execution for vacant positions, Report RH_SFI_TRIGGER_JOB_REQUISITION is used. This sends information about vacation positions to SuccessFactors Recruiting Execution and triggers the Job Requisition process.

Transferring Candidate Data to SAP ERP HCM

There are two steps to the data integration process: data import and further processing.

After a job offer has been accepted by a candidate in SuccessFactors Recruiting Execution, the status of the requisition can be changed to SENTTOSAP so that the JobApplication and other data can be imported into SAP ERP HCM. Report RH_SFI_IMPORT_RECRUITING_DATA is used to import the data. In the report selection screen, select the ad hoc report to be run in SuccessFactors Recruiting Execution. This also selects the field set defined for the ad hoc report during Customizing. After the report is executed, the data is transferred from the SuccessFactors HCM suite into the staging table, and the log is also displayed to show any success, warning, or error messages. Figure 3.16 shows the selection screen for the report to import recruiting data to SAP ERP HCM.

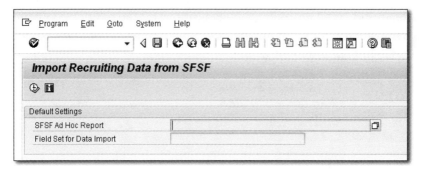

Figure 3.16 Selection Screen of Import Recruiting Data from SFSF Report

Report RH_SFI_IMPORT_RECRUITING_DATA can be scheduled to regularly transfer data from SuccessFactors to SAP ERP HCM.

The second step is the further processing of the imported Recruiting Execution data. This is performed in Transaction HRSFI_RCT_HIRE. The transaction displays a list of all job application data that has been transferred to the SAP ERP HCM staging area. The first three columns of the list display icons: the check status (green if a personnel action can be started, or red if one cannot), notes (either the CREATE NOTE or CHANGE NOTE icons), and an icon if any messages were generated during the transfer. Selecting the MESSAGE icon shows the messages that were generated.

The subsequent 9 columns display the applicant's first name and last name, start date, personnel number, action type, application ID from SuccessFactors Recruiting Execution, country grouping, status, and company code. Selecting any record provides information in the bottom panel of messages, notes, or details for the selected employee. The DETAILS tab displays data about the applicant, application, data from SuccessFactors, and last processor of the data/record.

Figure 3.17 shows the main screen for Transaction HRSFI_RCT_HIRE.

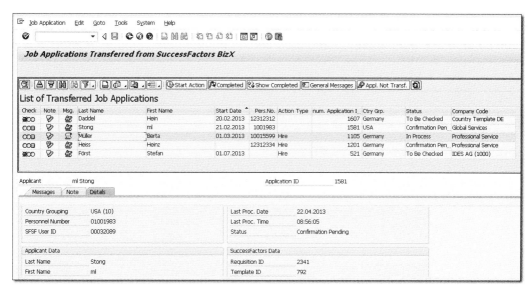

Figure 3.17 Transaction HRSFI_RCT_HIRE

Above the list are several options. In addition to the standard options for an SAP List Viewer (ALV) list, such as sorting and exporting, there are several application-specific actions:

- ▶ DATA OVERVIEW (PDF)
  Display a PDF of the job application information

- ▶ START ACTION
  Trigger a personnel action for the job application

- ▶ COMPLETED
  Manually mark the job application as COMPLETED

- ▶ SHOW COMPLETED
  Display records that are marked as COMPLETED

- ▶ GENERAL MESSAGES
  Display records that have general messages (e.g., middleware connection issues)

- ▶ APPL. NOT TRANSF.
  Display job applications that were not transferred correctly to SAP ERP HCM

The PDF produced when you click the DATA OVERVIEW (PDF) button displays basic information about the application, the fields and data transferred from Success-Factors Recruiting Execution to SAP ERP HCM, the SAP ERP HCM fields that data has been transferred to, and what data has been transferred to the SAP ERP HCM fields. Figure 3.18 shows an example of the first page of the PDF document.

Job Application Data

Name	Mark RECR4		Transfer Date	01/29/2013
Start Date	02/01/2013		Transfer Time	13:51:19
Requisition	1602		Status	New
Country Grp.	Germany (01)		Last Changed	GUNDELFINGER
Action	Hire (01)		Ad Hoc Rep. ID	AdhocReport_3482
Application	682		Ad Hoc Report	Hire Data SFI Final 2

SFSF Field	Content
Template ID	792
HiringManager_USERS_SYS_ID	RECR3
OFFER_DETAIL_LATEST_JOB_REQ_JO	2013-02-01
RCM_APPLICATION_ADDRESS	Colima Avenue NW
RCM_APPLICATION_CANDIDATE_ID	1041
	682
RCM_APPLICATION_CITY	San Diego
RCM_APPLICATION_COUNTRY_CODE	US
RCM_APPLICATION_DOB	
RCM_APPLICATION_EMAIL_ADDRESS	reiner_do@yahoo.de
RCM_APPLICATION_EXPORTED_ON	
RCM_APPLICATION_FIRSTNAME	Mark
RCM_APPLICATION_FORMER_EMPLOYE	N
RCM_APPLICATION_GENDER	
RCM_APPLICATION_HOME_PHONE	858-123456
RCM_APPLICATION_LASTNAME	RECR4
RCM_APPLICATION_MIDDLE_NAME	
RCM_APPLICATION_STATE	California
RCM_APPLICATION_ZIP	85413
RCM_APP_STATUS_STATUS_NAME	SendToSAP

Figure 3.18 PDF of Job Application Data in HRSFI_RCT_HIRE

The STATUS column indicates whether the record requires action, can be processed, or is being processed. When a record is set to TO BE CHECKED, the record requires action before it can be set to START ACTION and processed further.

To set the status to START ACTION, the record must be completed. Selecting the red light in the CHECK column opens the CHECK AND CHANGE DATA window. Here, any potential duplicates are displayed, and the COUNTRY GROUPING and PERSONNEL ACTION fields are displayed in the PROCESS DATA section. SAP ERP HCM uses the first name, last name, and date of birth to check whether any employees already exist in the system. If a potential duplicate is found, then the correct record must be selected. If either value is missing in the PROCESS DATA section, the correct value must be selected from the available dropdown values.

In the PERSONNEL ACTION dropdown, the type of action that should be started is selected. The COUNTRY GROUPING field must be selected because this selects the country-specific infotypes used during the selected PERSONNEL ACTION. Figure 3.19 displays the CHECK AND CHANGE DATA window.

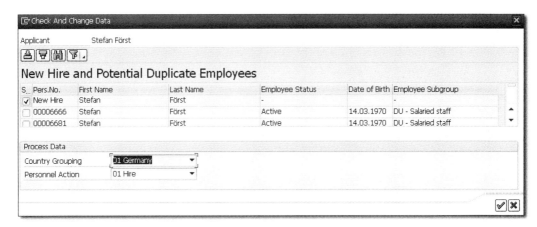

Figure 3.19 Check and Change Data Window in HRSFI_RCT_HIRE

After the record is corrected and the window closed, the record is set to START ACTION in the STATUS column.

You can start a personnel action by selecting a record with the status START ACTION and selecting the START ACTION button. Transaction PA40 (Personnel Actions) opens for the appropriate action and pre-fills the relevant data that has been sent over from SuccessFactors Recruiting Execution. By default, this is the start date, position ID, personnel area, employee group, and employee subgroup in the CREATE ACTIONS screen (Infotype 0001); first name and last name in the PERSONNEL DATA screen (Infotype 0002); and address details in the CREATE ADDRESSES screen (Infotype 0006).

After the action is completed, the candidate is now hired into the SAP ERP HCM system, and Personnel Actions (Transaction PA40) is closed. The list of job applications in HRSFI_RCT_HIRE is once again displayed, and the record that has been processed in Personnel Actions is no longer displayed in the list. Use the SHOW COMPLETED button, to display the record, along with all other completed job applications. In SuccessFactors Recruiting Execution, the STATUS column of the job application changes to HIREDATSAP.

You can manually close a job application by selecting the record and clicking the COMPLETED button. This may be used if a personnel action needs to be manually performed (for example, if insufficient data is sent from SuccessFactors Recruiting Execution or if a personnel action has been performed already).

It's possible to retransfer one, multiple, or all job applications from SuccessFactors Recruiting Execution in the TOOLS menu using either the REMAP DATA FOR JOB APPLICATION or the REMAP DATA FOR ALL JOB APPLICATIONS menu options. It's also possible to retransfer the status update for a job application marked as COMPLETED to SuccessFactors Recruiting Execution if the original message was not sent (e.g., if the middleware was unavailable). This is done in the TOOLS menu using menu option RESEND FAILED CONFIRMATIONS TO SFSF.

A job application that is no longer required for processing can be removed from the list. This doesn't remove the job application in SuccessFactors Recruiting Execution, however. To perform the deletion, the user must have super user authorization. This also means that the user sees *all* job applications in the list. The deletion can be performed in the JOB APPLICATION menu using the DELETE menu option.

3.3.5 Qualification Data

For the learning process, SAP provides integrations to manage qualification and competency assignments in SuccessFactors. This allows organizations to manage competency assignments via SuccessFactors HCM suite and/or SuccessFactors Learning and retain a full and updated Qualification Profile in SAP ERP HCM. These integrations were released in Integration Add-On 3.0 for SAP ERP HCM and SuccessFactors BizX (SFIHCM03). This integration differs from previous integrations in that it is triggered by the middleware rather than by a report in SAP ERP HCM.

The integration enables a one-time transfer of the Qualifications Catalog and Employee Qualification History from SAP ERP HCM to SuccessFactors. Success-Factors is then considered the system of record for employee qualification data, and SAP ERP HCM is considered read only for this data. Periodic transfer of changes to qualification data and employee qualifications is then sent back to SAP ERP HCM from SuccessFactors. The process flow for the competency-based qualification integration can be seen in Figure 3.20.

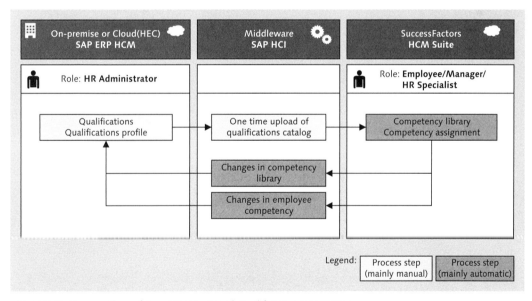

Figure 3.20 Process Flow of Competency-Based Qualification Integration

Likewise, the process flow for the curricula-based qualification integration can be seen in Figure 3.21.

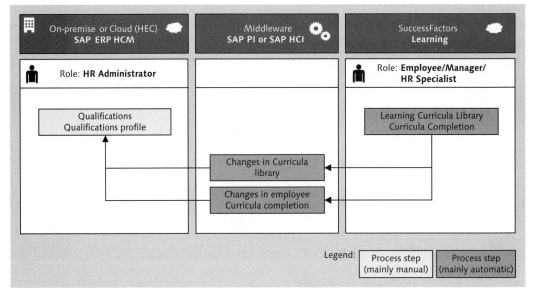

Figure 3.21 Process Flow of Curricula-Based Qualification Integration

The integration can handle either the use of Competencies or Curricula as methods of storing employee competencies in SuccessFactors. Depending on which one is used, SuccessFactors updates qualification data in SAP ERP HCM with either of the following:

▶ Changes to the competency catalog and employee competencies in SuccessFactors HCM suite

▶ Changes to the curricula catalog and employee curricula in SuccessFactors Learning

> **Important Note**
>
> The integration supports only the legacy competencies in SuccessFactors; it does not support MDF-based competencies. In addition, the integration supports only parts of competencies that interact directly with the employee. It does not cover skills, behaviors, teasers, or tuners.

The integration supports qualifications stored in SAP ERP HCM in either Personnel Administration (PA) or Organizational Management (OM)/Personnel Development (PD), and the integration automatically determines this by reading the

PLOGI QUAL integration switch in SAP. No configuration is required in Success-Factors or in the integration add-on. If the PLOGI QUAL integration switch is changed from one value to the other during operation of the integration, then the integration should be re-implemented.

Integration Notes

There are some important notes to remember when considering or using the integration:

▶ At the time of writing, both SAP HANA Cloud Integration and SAP Gateway 2.0 SP07 are required for the integration.

▶ Qualification data is transferred from SuccessFactors to SAP ERP HCM using integration processes in SAP HANA Cloud Integration.

▶ Competencies or curricula that are deleted in SuccessFactors must be manually deleted or delimited in SAP ERP HCM.

▶ When mapped to SAP ERP HCM qualification proficiencies, competency ratings may be rounded up or down.

▶ If items attached to the curricula catalog in SuccessFactors are changed, the replicated status of the curriculum for related employees is invalid, and a full, forced synchronization must be triggered by an administrator.

▶ The integration does not affect the qualification hierarchy; it only transfers the individual competencies and proficiencies, and not relationships between competencies.

▶ Transfer of competencies or skills to SuccessFactors Learning is not supported by the integration.

We'll now look at setting up the integration.

Setting up Competency-Based Qualification Integration

The qualification catalog in SAP ERP HCM can be exported using Report RH_SFI_EXPORT_QUALI. This report can also be run via Transaction HRSFI_QUAL_DATA_EXPT. The exported file can then be imported into SuccessFactors via Provisioning or OneAdmin. Figure 3.22 shows the selection screen of Report RH_SFI_EXPORT_QUALI.

The one-time upload of Employee Qualifications Profiles is done using the integration process *com.sap.SFIHCM03.hcm2bizx.EmployeeQualificationRating* in the packaged integration content in SAP HANA Cloud Integration.

If PD qualifications are used, a default QUALIFICATION GROUP must be configured in the SAP HANA Cloud Integration middleware for Curricula that do not have a parent Curricula Type. This is because the Curricula Type is optional in SuccessFactors Learning, but the equivalent QUALIFICATION GROUP object in SAP is mandatory.

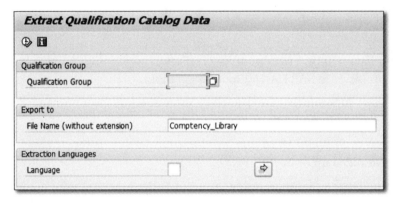

Figure 3.22 Selection Screen of Report RH_SFI_EXPORT_QUALI

In addition to the configuration of SAP HANA Cloud Integration, the ODATA APIs for Qualifications Data must be enabled in SAP Gateway. Details can be found in the IMG via the menu path PERSONNEL MANAGEMENT • INTEGRATION ADD-ON FOR SAP ERP HCM AND SUCCESSFACTORS BIZX • INTEGRATION SCENARIO FOR QUALIFICATION DATA • BASIC SETTINGS • GATEWAY CONFIGURATION.

Determination of Personnel Numbers in SAP ERP from the User ID in SuccessFactors HCM suite must be configured in the IMG via the menu path PERSONNEL MANAGEMENT • INTEGRATION ADD-ON FOR SAP ERP HCM AND SUCCESSFACTORS BIZX • INTEGRATION SCENARIO FOR QUALIFICATION DATA • BASIC SETTINGS • BADI: DETERMINE SAP ERP PERSONNEL NUMBERS AND SUCCESSFACTORS USER IDS.

If any existing Qualification objects in SAP ERP need to be mapped to Competency objects in SuccessFactors HCM suite, this is configured in the IMG via the menu path PERSONNEL MANAGEMENT • INTEGRATION ADD-ON FOR SAP ERP HCM AND SUCCESSFACTORS BIZX • INTEGRATION SCENARIO FOR QUALIFICATION DATA • TRANSFER

OF QUALIFICATIONS CATALOG FROM SAP ERP TO SUCCESSFACTORS HCM SUITE • MAINTAIN RELATIONSHIP BETWEEN QUALIFICATION ID AND SUCCESSFACTORS ID.

Finally, the mapping of Competency ratings in SuccessFactors HCM suite to a rating scale of Qualifications in SAP ERP can be made in the IMG via the menu path PERSONNEL MANAGEMENT • INTEGRATION ADD-ON FOR SAP ERP HCM AND SUCCESSFACTORS BIZX • INTEGRATION SCENARIO FOR QUALIFICATION DATA • TRANSFER OF QUALIFICATIONS RATING FROM SUCCESSFACTORS HCM SUITE TO SAP ERP • BADI: CONFIGURE VALUE MAPPING FOR QUALIFICATION RATING.

Setting Up Curricula-Based Qualification Integration

The one-time upload of the qualification catalog to SuccessFactors Learning is not supported in the integration.

If PD qualifications are used, a default Qualification Group must be configured in the SAP HANA Cloud Integration middleware for Curricula that do not have a parent Curricula Type. This is because the Curricula Type is optional in SuccessFactors Learning, but the equivalent Qualification Group object in SAP is mandatory.

In addition to the configuration of SAP HANA Cloud Integration, the ODATA APIs for Qualifications Data must be enabled in SAP Gateway. Details can be found in the IMG via the menu path PERSONNEL MANAGEMENT • INTEGRATION ADD-ON FOR SAP ERP HCM AND SUCCESSFACTORS BIZX • INTEGRATION SCENARIO FOR QUALIFICATION DATA • BASIC SETTINGS • GATEWAY CONFIGURATION.

Determination of Personnel Numbers in SAP ERP from the User ID in SuccessFactors Learning must be configured in the IMG via the menu path PERSONNEL MANAGEMENT • INTEGRATION ADD-ON FOR SAP ERP HCM AND SUCCESSFACTORS BIZX • INTEGRATION SCENARIO FOR QUALIFICATION DATA • BASIC SETTINGS • BADI: DETERMINE SAP ERP PERSONNEL NUMBERS AND SUCCESSFACTORS USER IDS.

If any existing Qualification objects in SAP ERP need to be mapped to Curricula objects in SuccessFactors Learning, this is configured in the IMG via the menu path PERSONNEL MANAGEMENT • INTEGRATION ADD-ON FOR SAP ERP HCM AND SUCCESSFACTORS BIZX • INTEGRATION SCENARIO FOR QUALIFICATION DATA • TRANSFER OF QUALIFICATIONS CATALOG FROM SAP ERP TO SUCCESSFACTORS HCM SUITE • MAINTAIN RELATIONSHIP BETWEEN QUALIFICATION ID AND SUCCESSFACTORS ID.

Finally, the mapping of COMPLETED and INCOMPLETED statuses of Curricula in SuccessFactors Learning to a rating scale in SAP ERP must be made in the IMG via the menu path PERSONNEL MANAGEMENT • INTEGRATION ADD-ON FOR SAP ERP HCM AND SUCCESSFACTORS BIZX • INTEGRATION SCENARIO FOR QUALIFICATION DATA • TRANSFER OF QUALIFICATIONS RATING FROM SUCCESSFACTORS HCM SUITE TO SAP ERP • BADI: CONFIGURE VALUE MAPPING FOR QUALIFICATION RATING.

Transferring Competency-Based Qualification Data to SAP ERP HCM

When you use the competency object in SuccessFactors HCM suite, you use the integration process *com.sap.SFIHCM03.bizx2hcm.UserCompetencyRating*. This transfers competency rating data for employees from the competency rating object in SuccessFactors to SAP ERP HCM.

When a new Competency Library is created in SuccessFactors HCM suite, a new Qualification Group is created in SAP. When a new child Competency is created in SuccessFactors HCM suite, a new child Qualification of the Qualification Group is created in SAP.

Transferring Curricula-Based Qualification Data to SAP ERP HCM

When you use the Curricula object in SuccessFactors Learning, you use two integration processes: *com.sap.SFIHCM03.bizx2hcm.CurriculumCatalogue* and *com.sap.SFIHCM03.bizx2hcm.UserCurriculumStatus*. These transfer the changes to the competency catalog (either the competency object or curricula object) from SuccessFactors to SAP ERP HCM and changes to the curriculum status object for employees from SuccessFactors to SAP ERP HCM.

Only Curricula with the status COMPLETED are considered in the integration. The expiry date of a Curriculum with multiple child item objects is taken from the object with the earliest expiry date. If no expiry date exists, the default end date of 31.12.9999 is used. The start date is always the date of the integration.

When a new Curricula Type is created in SuccessFactors Learning, a new Qualification Group is created in SAP. When a new child Curriculum is created in SuccessFactors Learning, a new child Qualification of the Qualification Group is created in SAP.

3.4   Other Talent Integration Content

SAP has released other types of talent integration content for SAP ERP HCM, from integration for third-party applications to "cookbooks."

3.4.1   Integrations for Third-Party Applications

There are several other standard integrations provided for SuccessFactors' talent solutions that enable integration with third-party systems. These are currently available for SuccessFactors Recruiting Execution and SuccessFactors Learning.

For SuccessFactors Recruiting Execution, there are two integrations available to enable candidate assessments to be performed with PeopleAnswers and SHL. These leverage Dell Boomi AtomSphere and enable assignment of assessments to job requisitions, prompt applicants to fill out assessments, and view assessment statuses and results in the assessment portlet within SuccessFactors Recruiting Execution.

For SuccessFactors Learning, there are three integrations available:

- Virtual Meeting Rooms (VLS), such as WebEx and Adobe Connect
- PayPal Payflow Pro
- Cross Domain Online Content Servers using SuccessFactors Learning Cross Domain Solution (CDS)

Further details can be found on the website *http://help.sap.com/cloud4hr*.

3.4.2   Cookbooks and How-To Guides

SAP has released various "cookbooks" and how-to guides to help customers and partners to enable system-related integration, such as user experience or connecting multiple SAP ERP systems to SuccessFactors. These cookbooks are essentially how-to documents on enabling this connectivity. These types of documents are released when human intervention is required more than a standard software solution. SAP has released the following cookbooks and how-to guides to date:

- *Integration of SuccessFactors Business Execution into SAP Enterprise Portal via Single Sign-On*
- *Integration of Multiple SAP ERP Human Capital Management Systems with SuccessFactors Business Execution*
- *Integrating Compensation Management Using Multiple Compensation Group IDs*
- *Enhancing the Extraction of Employee Data with Customer-Specific Fields*
- *PI Configuration Example*

The *Integration of SuccessFactors Business Execution into SAP Enterprise Portal via Single Sign-On* cookbook provides information on the prerequisites for setting up

SSO integration between the SAP Enterprise Portal and the SuccessFactors HCM suite solutions, as well as the steps to do the following:

- Configure SAML2.0 in the SAP Enterprise Portal
- Collect required information from SuccessFactors
- Configure SSO in SuccessFactors
- Create links within the SAP Enterprise Portal

The *Integration of Multiple SAP ERP Human Capital Management Systems with SuccessFactors Business Execution* cookbook discusses various scenarios and the impact of those scenarios when you are integrating multiple instances of SAP ERP HCM with one instance of SuccessFactors. It covers SAP ERP HCM as both the source system and the target system.

The *Integrating Compensation Management Using Multiple Compensation Group IDs* how-to guide provides the steps required to enable integration between SuccessFactors Compensation and SAP ERP HCM when multiple Compensation Group IDs are used in SuccessFactors Compensation.

The *Enhancing the Extraction of Employee Data with Customer-Specific Fields* how-to guide provides the steps required to extend the employee data integration extraction reports for customer-specific fields in SuccessFactors. It doesn't cover the steps to add fields in SuccessFactors—only the steps for SAP PI and SAP ERP HCM.

A *PI Configuration Example* how-to guide provides a practical example of configuring SAP PI for using with the Talent Hybrid model.

All of the cookbooks and how-to guides can be downloaded from *http://help.sap.com/erp_sfi_addon30#section3*.

3.5   Employee Central Integrations

For SuccessFactors Employee Central, a host of integrations are available, all based on Dell Boomi AtomSphere and SAP HANA Cloud Integration. These integrations allow Employee Central to transfer data to and/or from other systems, such as SAP ERP or a third-party payroll or time and attendance provider. Figure 3.23 shows the current and planned integrations for Employee Central.

Let's look at some of these integrations in a bit more detail.

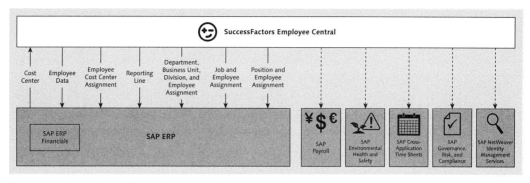

Figure 3.23 Current and Planned Employee Central Integrations

3.5.1 SAP ERP

Several integrations exist for transferring data between Employee Central and SAP ERP. This is largely because many SAP ERP customers want to run their core HR processes in Employee Central instead of SAP ERP HCM but still retain other processes in SAP ERP. The most common integration scenario is to run SAP ERP Payroll. The employee master data integration is also used for Employee Central Payroll.

SAP Notes can be found on SAP Service Marketplace under the following components:

- PA-SFI-EC for Employee Central integration
- LOD-EC-INT-EE for ERP to Employee Central integration
- LOD-EC-INT-ORG for Employee Central to ERP Organizational Integration
- LOD-EC-GCP-ANA for Employee Central Reporting and Analytics
- LOD-EC-GCP-PY for Employee Central Payroll & Integration
- LOD-EC-GCP-PY-GLO for Employee Central Payroll & Integration — Globalization

> **Important Note**
>
> By default, many of the fields in Employee Central have a greater field length than SAP ERP and the Dell Boomi AtomSphere middleware support. It is important to consider this during the Employee Central design because many of the fields in Employee Central must have their field lengths reduced in order to integrate with SAP ERP.

Employee Master Data

HR master data—the data stored in Personnel Administration (PA) infotypes—is replicated from Employee Central to SAP ERP using a standard integration. This is often referred to as the mini-master. It enables a core set of employee data to be replicated to SAP ERP to support a number of processes. It is also used for integration with Employee Central Payroll. The integration includes the following data:

- Biographical information
- Personal information
- Address information
- Email address
- Job information
- Compensation information (recurring and non-recurring)
- Cost distribution
- Direct deposit
- National ID information

This integration is served by component PA_SE_IN 100 in SAP ERP and integration package iFlow EC to EC Payroll Employee Replication v1.0 Multi-Installation in Dell Boomi AtomSphere. For PA_SE_IN 100, Service Package 3 is required, but Service Package 6 or 7 is recommended.

The integration works by Dell Boomi AtomSphere calling SuccessFactors APIs (see 3.6) and retrieving data. This data is then converted as necessary and sent to SAP ERP, where it is processed by inbound web service interface EmployeeMasterDataReplicationRequest_In and written to SAP ERP HCM infotypes. Records are created, edited, or delimited as required based on the data sent and the infotype framework in SAP ERP.

The add-on is configured in the IMG via menu path PERSONNEL MANAGEMENT • PERSONNEL ADMINISTRATION • INTERFACES AND INTEGRATION • INTEGRATION OF SAP ERP HR MASTER DATA AND SUCCESSFACTORS EMPLOYEE CENTRAL.

The following fields are part of the standard integration:

- Biographical Information
  - Person ID external
  - Birth Name (PA0002-NAME2)

- ▷ Date of Birth (PA0002-GBDAT) *
- ▷ Country of Birth (PA0002-GBLND)
- ▷ Place of Birth (PA0002-GBORT)
- ▷ Region of Birth (PA0002-GBDEP)
- ▶ Personal Information
  - ▷ First Name (PA0002-VORNA) *
  - ▷ Middle Name (PA0002-MIDNM)
  - ▷ Last Name (PA0002-NACHN) *
  - ▷ Additional Family Name (PA0002-NACH2)
  - ▷ Suffix (PA0002-NAMZU)
  - ▷ Salutation (PA0002-ANRED) *
  - ▷ Marital status (PA0002-FAMST) *
  - ▷ Native preferred language (PA0002-SPRSL) *
  - ▷ Gender (PA0002-GESCH) *
  - ▷ Nationality (PA0002-NATIO) *
- ▶ Address Information
  - ▷ Address type (PA0006-ANSSA) *
  - ▷ Start Date (PA0006-BEGDA) *
  - ▷ End Date (PA0006-ENDDA) *
  - ▷ Address1-8 (PA0006; *country-dependent*)
  - ▷ City (PA0006-ORT01)
  - ▷ State/Province/County (PA0006-STATE)
  - ▷ ZIP Code (PA0006-PSTLZ)
  - ▷ Country (PA0006-LAND1) *
- ▶ Email Address Information
  - ▷ Email address (PA0105-USRID_LONG) *
  - ▷ Email address type (PA0105) *
  - ▷ Primary Indicator (PA0105)
- ▶ Job Information
  - ▷ Event (PA0000-MASSN) *

- ► Event Reason (PA0000-MASSG)
- ► Job Code (PA0001-ANSVH) *
- ► Location (PA0001-BTRTL and PA0001-WERKS) *
- ► Company (PA0001-BUKRS) *
- ► Cost Center (PA0001-KOSTL)
- ► Employee Class (PA0001-PERSG) *
- ► Employment Type (PA0001-PERSK) *
- ► Is Full-Time Employee (PA0007-TEILK)
- ► Working Days per Week (PA0007-WKWDY) *
- ► Pay Scale Area (PA0008-TRFGB) *
- ► Pay Scale Type (PA0008-TRFAR) *
- ► Work Schedule Rule (PA0007)
- ▶ Compensation Information
  - ► Pay Group (PA0001-ABKRS) *
- ▶ Pay Component Recurring
  - ► Pay Component (PA0008-LGA01 to PA0008-LGA40 or PA0014-LGART) *
  - ► Currency Code (PA0008-WAERS) *
  - ► Amount (PA0008-BET01 to PA0008-BET40 or PA0014-BETRG) *
  - ► Frequency (PA0014-ZEINZ and PA0014-ZANZL) *
- ▶ Pay Component Non-Recurring
  - ► Pay Component (PA0015-LGART) *
  - ► Pay Date (PA0015-UWDAT) *
  - ► Currency Code (PA0015-WAERS) *
  - ► Amount (PA0015- BETRG) *
  - ► Alternative Cost Center (PA0015-KOSTL)
- ▶ Cost Distribution
  - ► Start Date (PA0027-BEGDA)
  - ► End Date (PA0027-ENDDA)
  - ► Cost Center (PA0027-KST01 to PA0027-KST12)
  - ► Percentage (PA0027-KPR01 to PA0027-KPR12)

- ▶ Direct Deposit
  - ▹ Payment Method (PA0009-ZLSCH) *
  - ▹ Account Type (PA0009-BKONT)
  - ▹ Account Number (PA0009-BANKN)
  - ▹ Account Name (PA0009-EMFTX)
  - ▹ Routing Number (PA0009-BANKL)
  - ▹ IBAN (PA0009-IBAN)
  - ▹ Bank Control Key (PA0009-BKONT)
  - ▹ Bank Country (PA0009-BANKS) *
  - ▹ Deposit Type (PA0009-BNKSA)
  - ▹ Processing Type (PA0009-BNKSA) *
  - ▹ Payment Type Code (PA0009-ZLSCH)
  - ▹ Currency (PA0009-WAERS)
  - ▹ Amount (PA0009-BETRG or PA0009-ANZHL)
- ▶ National ID Card
  - ▹ Country (PA0002) *
  - ▹ National ID (PA0002-PERID) *

* indicates a required field. Please note that some fields not marked with * are required for certain countries.

In addition to these fields, dates are replicated to Infotype 0041 for date events such as global assignments and payroll periods.

Many fields, such as marital status or gender, have different mappings in Employee Central, and special consideration should be taken during implementation to ensure correct values and mappings. Additionally, mapping tables exist for some mapping values, such as address type.

Two BAdIs are provided to modify the logic and behavior of replicated fields. The first is to determine the Employee Central field to use for Personnel Number, and the second is to exclude infotype records from deletion for specific subtypes. Both of these are configured in the IMG.

Additionally, various mapping tables are provided to map values between Employee Central and SAP ERP. These include the following:

- ▶ Employee Central object codes to SAP ERP global data types (GDT)
- ▶ Employee Central object codes to SAP ERP code value lists
- ▶ Employee Central codes to SAP ERP code value lists for country-dependent fields
- ▶ Employee Central date types to SAP ERP date types
- ▶ Employee Central company object codes to SAP ERP company keys
- ▶ Employee Central cost center object codes to SAP ERP cost center keys
- ▶ Employee Central location codes to SAP ERP place of work keys
- ▶ Employee Central pay component and country combinations to SAP ERP Infotype 0008 or Infotype 0014

Other IMG settings are available that allow currencies to be assigned to wage types (so that currencies with more than two decimal places can be used without rounding to two decimal places), restrict which infotypes are replicated for certain countries, and filter which infotypes are replicated for which countries.

The integration supports replicating custom-specific fields in Personal Information and Job Information portlets to Infotypes 0001, 0002, 0007, and 0008 in SAP ERP. The integration supports replication to any fields in Infotypes 0001 and 0002, Work Schedule Rule (PA0007-SCHKZ) in Infotype 0007, and the Pay Scale Group (PA0008-TRFGR) and Pay Scale Level (PA0008-TRFST) fields in Infotype 0008. The fields are automatically replicated by the middleware, but must be mapped to SAP ERP fields in the IMG

For more information on the details of the integration, field mappings, and BAdIs, refer to the *Employee Master Data Replication* handbook.

Employee Organizational Data

For employees' organizational data, several types of information can be replicated from Employee Central to SAP ERP:

- ▶ Reporting relationships
- ▶ Employee's business unit, division, department, and job assignment
- ▶ Employee cost center assignment

This integration is served by component PA_SE_IN 100 in SAP ERP and integration package iFlow Solution: EC—ERP Organizational Management v1.0 in Dell

Boomi AtomSphere (different processes of the integration package are used for different integration scenarios). For PA_SE_IN 100, Service Package 3 is required, but Service Package 6 or 7 is recommended.

The integration works by Dell Boomi AtomSphere calling SuccessFactors APIs (see Section 3.6) and retrieving data. This data is then converted as necessary and sent to SAP ERP, where it is processed by inbound web service interface EmployeeOrganisationalAssignmentReplicationRequest_In and written to SAP ERP HCM infotypes. Records are created, edited, or delimited as required based on the data sent and the infotype framework in SAP ERP.

For replication of business unit, division, and department objects, as well as their assignment to employees, the ID of the object in Employee Central is mapped to an organizational unit ID in table SFIOM_KMAP_OSI (Organizational Structure Item Key Mapping) in SAP ERP. This can also be done manually. Alternatively, BAdI EX_SFIOM_KEY_MAP_ENH_ORG_STRUC (Enhancements for key mapping of organizational structure items) in Enhancement Spot ES_SFIOM_PROCESSING can be used to define the logic to be used for determining mapping of these objects. Upon first replication, if no new organizational units need to be created, the mapping table should be maintained with all mappings.

The employee cost center assignment in Employee Central is stored against the employee's position in SAP ERP.

Cost Center Objects

SAP provides a standard integration to replicate cost centers from SAP ERP FICO to Employee Central. This integration is served by component ODTFINCC 600 in SAP ERP and integration package iFlow Solution: SAP ERP to EC Cost Center Replication 1308 in Dell Boomi AtomSphere.

In SAP ERP, the data can be transferred by either IDOC or flat-file (CSV). Report ODTF_REPL_CC is provided to replicate the cost centers from SAP ERP to Employee Central.

The logic used to define cost center IDs can be modified using a BAdI that is part of enhancement spot ODTF_CC_REPLICAT_IDOCS_MODIFY. Depending on whether IDOC or flat-file integration is used, the BAdI varies. For IDOC integration, the BAdI ODTF_CC_REPLICAT_IDOCS_MODIFY • MODIFY_COST_CENTER_EXTRACTOR is used, and for flat-file integration, the BAdI ODTF_CO_REPL_IDOC_COST_C_CSV • MODIFY_COST_CENTER_EXTACT_CSV is used.

Side-by-Side

The Side-by-Side deployment model enables data transfer from SAP ERP HCM to SuccessFactors Employee Central so that the data for all employees is stored in Employee Central. Employees whose system of record is SAP ERP HCM are considered "mastered" in that system. The standard integrations for Employee Central to SAP ERP are used to replicate data of employees to SAP ERP HCM who are mastered within that system. The integration is provided in component PA_SE_IN 100 SP07 in SAP ERP and integration package Packaged Integration: SAP ERP to EC Employee Replication v1.0 in Dell Boomi AtomSphere.

The Side-by-Side add-on is configured in the IMG via menu path PERSONNEL MANAGEMENT • PERSONNEL ADMINISTRATION • INTERFACES AND INTEGRATION • INTEGRATION OF SAP ERP HCM TO SUCCESSFACTORS EMPLOYEE CENTRAL SIDE BY SIDE.

Side-by-Side integration currently supports the following Employee Central data:

▶ Basic User Import
▶ Biographical Information
▶ Employment Information
▶ Job Information
▶ Email Information
▶ Phone Information
▶ Global Assignments

Side-By-Side supports the following actions:

▶ Hire
▶ Rehire
▶ Transfer
▶ International Transfer
▶ Global Assignment
▶ Termination

Template Groups are used to assign the field mappings between SAP ERP HCM and Employee Central. Two sample Template Groups are provided in SAP ERP HCM; a customer can create their own Template Groups as required. The following five fields are considered standard fields and cannot be mapped in the Template Groups (see Table 3.6).

SAP ERP HCM	Employee Central
Personnel ID (PERNR)	user_id
Central Person ID (ID of employee's CP object)	person_id_external
Hire Date (from Infotype 0041)	start_date
First Hire Date (from Infotype 0041)	originalStartDate
Manager (from table ECPAO_EE_MGNR)	manager_id

Table 3.6 Standard Fields in Side-By-Side Integration

Employee-manager relationships are stored in Table ECPAO_EE_MGNR. Report ECPAO_MNGR_EXTRACTION is provided to generate employee-manager relationships using relationship 012 and stores them in this table. Employee-manager relationships for employees are stored in Employee Central. You must maintain them in SAP ERP HCM by creating a user profile in Transaction SU01 and assigning it to a manager position in Transaction PPOSE or Transaction PPOME.

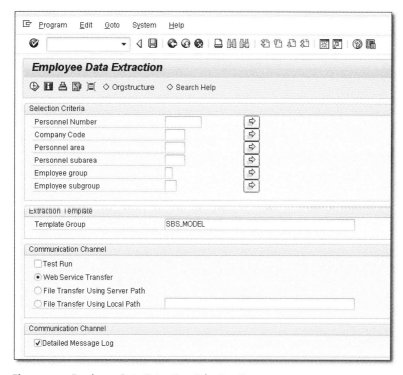

Figure 3.24 Employee Data Extraction Selection Screen

Report ECPAO_EMPL_EXTRACTION (Employee Data Extraction) is used to extract data from SAP ERP HCM to send to Employee Central. Figure 3.24 shows the select screen for Report ECPAO_EMPL_EXTRACTION.

Delta synchronizations are possible. Report RBDMIDOC creates change pointers whenever employee master data is changed. The change pointers are read by Report ECPAO_EMPL_EXTRACTION, and the delta changes are then synchronized to Employee Central.

The mapping of SAP ERP HCM and Employee Central fields is performed in view cluster VC_ECPAO_MAP. There are three methods available to map fields:

- **Infotype Mapping**
  Map each Employee Central field to an SAP ERP HCM infotype and field.

- **Preconfigured Mapping**
  Use SAP's predefined mappings from table ECPAO_PREMAPPING, ECPAO_PREMAP_TT).

- **BAdI Mapping**
  Use BAdI EX_ECPAO_EMP_DATA_EXTRACT_OUT (Mapping of EC and SAP ERP Data for Employee Replication) to determine mappings between Employee Central fields and SAP ERP HCM infotype fields.

Optional BAdIs exist to overwrite the employee data extracted from SAP ERP HCM (EX_ECPAO_ERP_EMP_DATA_MODIFY) and define groups of employees to replicate to Employee Central (EX_ECPAO_EMP_VALIDITY_TAB). Additionally, BAdI EX_ECPAO_EMP_USYID_PRN_UNM_MAP (Mapping of User ID, Person ID, and User Name) can be implemented to map User ID, Person ID, and User Name of employees.

In addition to the data integration, a UI integration exists so that Employee Central can be used as the central hub for managers and employees. It enables a Web Dynpro application to be run inside Employee Central to perform actions on employees who are mastered in SAP ERP HCM.

Notes

The inbound service in SAP for integration between Employee Central and SAP ERP using Dell Boomi has certain character limitations that may not match with Employee Central. In addition, the standard character length of some Employee Central fields exceeds the character limitation of the inbound service in SAP as well as some of the object code fields and transparent table fields.

Not all SAP objects exist in Employee Central, and vice-versa. For example, Personnel Area doesn't exist in Employee Central and, likewise, the org structure in Employee Central has objects that have no corresponding object in SAP. These must be considered when designing Employee Central and the integration. Additionally, value mappings could be needed to map Business Unit, Division, and Department objects from Employee Central with Organizational Units in SAP, as well as mapping of company code and cost center keys among other mappings. Further effort might be needed to program BAdIs to ensure that the relevant mapping and value transformation logic exists.

For more details, the handbooks provided by SAP and referenced in this section should be reviewed in deta.

3.5.2 Employee Central Payroll

Employee Central Payroll is based on SAP ERP Payroll, and, therefore, integration between Employee Central and Employee Central Payroll reuses the employee mini-master integration covered in Section 3.5.1.

Integration also exists between Employee Central Payroll and BSI TaxFactory SaaS™ for calculation of US employees' withholding taxes and, if required, BSI eFormsFactory™ for employees to maintain tax details. For more details, refer to the *Integrating BSI SaaS Solutions with Employee Central Payroll* handbook.

3.5.3 Payroll BPO

Integration is provided between Employee Central and two Payroll BPO providers, ADP GlobalView and NorthgateArinso euHReka. Because both systems are built on SAP ERP Payroll, the integration and mash-ups are similar to those offered in the standard integration for SAP ERP. Single Sign-On (SSO) also exists between Employee Central and these systems. Like with SAP ERP Payroll and Employee Central Payroll, Employee Central can display a pay slip directly from these systems.

SAP also provides a standard payroll integration template that can be used to integrate Employee Central with other payroll systems and payroll BPO providers. This is covered in Section 3.5.7.

3.5.4 Time and Attendance

SAP provides integrations between Employee Central and both WorkForce Software EmpCenter and Kronos Workforce Central for time and attendance processes. Both are out-of-the-box integration packages and require no manual mapping for the United States; for other countries, additional configuration may be necessary. Both integrations also feature SSO, native UI integration, and data export to Employee Central Payroll, if required.

SAP also provides a standard time and attendance integration template that can be used to integrate Employee Central with other time and attendance systems. This is covered in Section 3.5.7.

WorkForce Software EmpCenter

For WorkForce Software EmpCenter integration, data is exported from the following Employee Central portlets:

- Personal Information
- Phone Information
- Email Information
- Address Information
- Job Information
- Job Relationships
- Compensation Information
- Recurring Pay Components

SSO can be configured with the WorkForce Software EmpCenter application so that a UI mash-up can be accessed by employees directly in an Employee Central portlet.

For more details on the integration and UI mash-up, refer to the *SuccessFactors Employee Central and WorkForce Software* integration handbook.

Kronos Workforce Central

For Kronos Workforce Central integration, data is exported from the following Employee Central portlets:

- ▶ Personal Information
- ▶ Phone Information
- ▶ Email Information
- ▶ Job Information
- ▶ Employment Information
- ▶ Recurring Pay Components

For more details, refer to the *SuccessFactors Employee Central and Kronos Workforce Central* integration handbook.

SSO can also be configured with Kronos Workforce Ready to enable a UI mash-up within Employee Central. This enables employees to maintain time and attendance data directly in Kronos Workforce Ready within an Employee Central portlet. More details can be found in the *Implementing Single Sign-On with Kronos Workforce Ready* implementation handbook.

3.5.5 Benefits

Benefits integration is provided for Aon Hewitt Core Benefits Administration, Benefitfocus, and Thomsons Darwin. Both are out-of-the-box integration packages and require no manual mapping. Both integrations also feature data export to Employee Central Payroll, if required.

SAP also provides a standard benefits integration template that can be used to integrate Employee Central with other benefits administration systems. This is covered in Section 3.5.7.

Aon Hewitt Core Benefits Administration

For Aon Hewitt Core Benefits Administration integration, data is exported from the following Employee Central portlets:

- ▶ Person Information
- ▶ Personal Information

- Phone Information
- Email Information
- Address Information
- Job Information
- Employment Information
- Compensation Information
- Recurring Pay Components
- National ID Card

For more details on the integration, refer to the *Integrating SuccessFactors Employee Central with Aon Hewitt Core Benefits Administration* integration handbook.

Benefitfocus

For Benefitfocus integration, data is exported from the following Employee Central portlets:

- Person Information
- Personal Information
- Phone Information
- Email Information
- Address Information
- Employment Information
- Compensation Information
- Recurring Pay Components
- National ID Card
- Emergency Contacts Information

SSO can be configured with the Benefitfocus application so that a UI mash-up can be accessed by employees directly in an Employee Central portlet.

For more details on the integration and UI mash-up, refer to the *SuccessFactors Employee Central and Benefitfocus* integration handbook.

Thomsons Darwin

For Thomsons Darwin integration, data is exported from the following Employee Central portlets:

- Person Information
- Personal Information
- Phone Information
- Email Information
- Address Information
- Employment Information
- Job Information
- Compensation Information
- Recurring Pay Components
- National ID Card

SSO can be configured with the Thomsons Darwin application so that a link directly to the application can be accessed by employees directly in the Employee Central navigation menu.

For more details on the integration and UI mash-up, refer to the *Employee Central and Thomsons Darwin* integration guide.

3.5.6 SAP HANA Cloud Platform

SAP HANA Cloud Platform enables extensions to be built for Employee Central. It features OData integration to enable transfer of Employee Central and Metadata Framework data between Employee Central and the extension.

3.5.7 Standard Integration Templates

SAP provides three standard integration templates that can be used for integrating to the following systems:

- Payroll
- Time and Attendance
- Benefits

Each template uses the Employee Central Compound API and Dell Boomi Atom-Sphere to send a CSV file to the target system. Refer to Section 3.6.3 for details on the Employee Central Compound API.

Payroll

The standard payroll integration template is configured to export the following data from Employee Central:

- Person Information
- Personal Information
- Address Information
- Phone Information
- Email Information
- Employment Information
- Job Information
- Compensation Information
- Recurring Pay Components
- Non-Recurring Pay Components
- Recurring Deductions
- Non-Recurring Deductions
- Alternative Cost Distribution
- Dependents
- Direct Deposit

For more details, refer to the *Standard Payroll Integration Template for SuccessFactors Employee Central* integration handbook.

Time

The standard time integration template is configured to export the following data from Employee Central:

- Person Information
- Personal Information

- Address Information
- Phone Information
- Email Information
- Employment Information
- Compensation Information
- Recurring Pay Components
- National ID Card
- Manager
- Pay Group foundation object

For more details, refer to the *Standard Time Integration Template for SuccessFactors Employee Central* integration handbook.

Benefits

The standard benefits integration template is configured to export the following data from Employee Central:

- Person Information
- Personal Information
- Address Information
- Phone Information
- Email Information
- Employment Information
- Job Information
- Compensation Information
- Recurring Pay Components
- Non-Recurring Pay Components
- Dependents
- National ID Card
- Manager
- Pay Group foundation object

For more details, refer to the *Standard Benefits Integration Template for SuccessFactors Employee Central* integration handbook.

3.5.8 Planned Integrations

Integrations are planned from Employee Central to the following:

- SAP Environmental Health & Safety (EHS)
- SAP Cross-Application Timesheet (CATS)
- SAP Governance, Risk, and Compliance (GRC)
- SAP Identity Service (IDS)

Details for these are not yet confirmed.

3.6 Application Programming Interfaces (APIs)

SuccessFactors provides three APIs for querying data in and out of the SuccessFactors system using web services. Each API has different flexibility, depending on the intended use. Further details, including details handbooks, can be found on the website *http://help.sap.com/cloud4hr*.

We'll now take a brief look at each of these APIs.

3.6.1 SuccessFactors Data API (SFAPI)

The SuccessFactors Data API (SFAPI) is provided by SAP to allow querying of data from and updating data in SuccessFactors via SOAP web services. It was the first API provided by SuccessFactors. It provides four operations to query data in SuccessFactors—create, read, update, and delete—as well as exposing the data entities to the API as *SFObjects* to enable the entities and their fields to be listed and available to the API.

API Operations

The SFAPI supports multiple operations that can be triggered through SOAP web services, including web services–based middleware application. The SFAPI supports the following operations:

- Create an SFAPI session

- End an SFAPI session

- Check whether the current SFAPI session is valid

- List and describe all of the entities available to the SFAPI

- Insert a new record for an entity

- Update or delete an existing record for an entity

- Query the SFAPI using SuccessFactors Query Language (SFQL)

- Submit, check, list, or cancel asynchronous jobs

Integration Tools

Three tools exist to support and monitor API operations, all of which are available in OneAdmin under COMPANY SETTINGS. These are as follows:

- API AUDIT LOG: Captures payload details for the last 10,000 API calls

- API METERING DETAILS: Provides analytics on API usage over the last 30 days

- API DATA DICTIONARY: Lists all data entities available to the SFAPI

Further Information

For more details, refer to the *HCM Suite SFAPI handbook*.

3.6.2   OData API

The OData API is built on the Open Data Protocol (OData) v2.0, a standardized protocol for creating and consuming data. It is a new API designed to add more standardization and flexibility for developers than the SFAPI. Although OData is a standardized protocol, SuccessFactors still has the ability to disable some operations. This is the case for deleting a user entity, for example.

This API is used in Employee Central employee organizational data integration to replicate Foundation Objects into SAP ERP and Employee Central Payroll.

Supported Entities

At the time of writing, the OData API supports only the following applications/ features:

- ▶ Platform
  - ▶ User Entity
  - ▶ Photo
  - ▶ To Do
  - ▶ Employee Profile
  - ▶ Role-Based Permissions
- ▶ Employee Central
  - ▶ Foundation Objects
  - ▶ Personal Information
  - ▶ Employment Information
  - ▶ Picklists
  - ▶ Workflows
  - ▶ Fiscal Year Variants
  - ▶ Country
  - ▶ Currency
- ▶ Compensation
  - ▶ Advances
  - ▶ Benefits
  - ▶ Deductions
  - ▶ Income Tax Declarations
- ▶ Succession Planning
  - ▶ Talent Pools

API Operations

The OData API supports multiple operations that can be triggered through an HTTP call, including web services-based middleware application. The OData API supports the following operations:

- ▶ Create, query, or update data
- ▶ Select, order, filter, skip, top, format, or expand queries
- ▶ Create, update, or delete links between entities

Integration Tools

Two tools exist to support and monitor API operations, all of which are available in OneAdmin under COMPANY SETTINGS. These are as follows:

▸ API AUDIT LOG: Captures payload details for the last 10,000 API calls

▸ MANAGE API OPTION PROFILE: Manages account settings for a User Entity

Further Information

For more details, refer to the *HCM Suite OData API handbook* and *HCM Suite OData API Reference* handbook.

3.6.3 Employee Central Compound API

The Employee Central Compound API is a SOAP web services–based API provided to extract employee data from Employee Central. The focus of the API is to replicate data from Employee Central to SAP ERP, payroll, and benefits systems and, as such, fields designed for these types of replication scenarios are supported by the API. Because not all fields are supported, we recommend that you check that the API supports the required fields prior to implementing an integration that leverages the API.

This API is used in Employee Central employee master data integration to replicate employee data and assignments into SAP ERP and Employee Central Payroll.

Supported Entities

At the time of writing, the Employee Central Compound API supports the following data entities:

▸ Person Information

▸ Person Relationships

▸ Personal Information

▸ Address Information

▸ Phone Information

▸ Email Information

▸ Dependents

- ▶ National ID Card
- ▶ Job Information
- ▶ Job Relationships
- ▶ Employment Information
- ▶ Compensation Information
- ▶ Recurring Pay Components
- ▶ Non-Recurring Pay Components
- ▶ Direct Deposit
- ▶ Payment Information
- ▶ Alternative Cost Distribution
- ▶ Recurring Deductions
- ▶ Non-Recurring Deductions
- ▶ Global Assignments

API Operations

The API uses an SQL SELECT statement to extract data and support the WHERE clause. It does not support the Order By clause, nor does it support updating or deleting data because the API is designed only to extract data. The FROM clause is always FROM CompoundEmployee. Below is an example statement to extract Person Information and Job Information for employees whose company is SAP and whose data was modified after 01/01/2000:

```
SELECT person, job_information
FROM CompoundEmployee
WHERE company='SAP'
AND last_modified_on > to_datetime ('2000-01-01','YYYY-MM-DD')
```

Integration Tools

Two tools exist to support and monitor API operations, all of which are available in OneAdmin under COMPANY SETTINGS. These are as follows:

- ▶ API AUDIT LOG: Captures payload details for the last 10,000 API calls
- ▶ API METERING DETAILS: Provides analytics on API usage over the last 30 days

Further Information

For more details, refer to the *Employee Central—Compound Employee API* handbook.

3.6.4   Other APIs

There are a few other APIs that exist, including:

▶ Onboarding API

▶ Workforce Analytics OData API

▶ SAP Jam OData API

For more details on the Onboarding API, refer to the *SuccessFactors Onboarding API Reference* handbook.

3.7   Other Integration Content

In addition to the standard integrations that have been and will be released, SAP has also released various other types of content for integrating SuccessFactors HCM suite with SAP ERP (or vice versa) and other systems not covered by the aforementioned integrations or deployment models.

3.7.1   SuccessFactors Adapter

Two SuccessFactors Adapters have been released, one each for SAP PI and SAP HANA Cloud Integration. We'll take a brief look at these now.

SAP PI

SAP NetWeaver Process Integration, connectivity add-on 1.0 was introduced to enable SAP Process Integration to be used to integrate between SuccessFactors and SAP ERP. The add-on runs on the SAP Process Integration Adapter Framework, based on the Java Connector Architecture (JCA). We recommend that you use Service Package 1.

The add-on supports using the SFAPI and, as of Service Package 1, the OData API. The Operations Modeler can be used to model integrations based on these APIs to create integrations simply and intuitively for integrations specialists.

Further details can be found at *http://help.sap.com/nw-connectivity-addon101*.

SAP HANA Cloud Integration

Similarly to the *SAP NetWeaver Process Integration, connectivity add-on 1.0*, an adapter for SAP HANA Cloud Integration is available. The *SFSF Adapter* supports integration between SuccessFactors HCM suite and SAP ERP via SFAPI, OData API, and the Employee Central Compound API. The Operations Modeler allows simple and easy modeling of integrations, as is the case with SAP PI.

Further details can be found in the *Developer's Guide—Managing Integration Content* that is found at *http://help.sap.com/cloudintegration*.

3.7.2 Social Media ABAP Integration Library

To integrate SAP Jam with SAP modules—including SAP ERP HCM—the Social Media ABAP Integration Library (SAIL) was delivered by SAP in late 2012. SAIL is part of SAP and is available as of SAP_BASIS versions 7.02 SP11, 7.30 SP07, and 7.31 SP03. To use SAIL, the business function `BC_SRV_STW_01` must be activated.

SAIL allows for SAP Jam objects, such as groups and feeds, to be available in multiple applications, such as SAP ERP HCM, SAP CRM, or custom applications. Integration is focused on two parts:

▸ Establishing an HTTP connection between SAP and SAP Jam

▸ Setting up authentication between SAP and SAP Jam

Unlike other integration activities between SAP and the SuccessFactors HCM suite solutions, SAP Jam doesn't require any mapping of fields. Rather, because the application is focused on social media activities, collaboration, and sharing non-SAP data, there is no requirement for SAP data to be stored outside of the SAP system.

SAIL is configured in the IMG via the menu path APPLICATION SERVER • BASIS -SERVICES • COLLABORATION. In the first release of SAIL, the SAP StreamWork subnode is used, but as of SAP_BASIS 7.31 SP06, the SAP Jam subnode is used.

Authentication is via OAuth, Security Assertion Markup Language 2.0 (SAML2) assertion, and Secure Sockets Layer (SSL) for HTTPS communication.

Full details of configuring integration of SAP Jam using SAIL can be found in the SAP guide *SAP Jam ABAP Integration—Configuration Guide*, which is available as a document on the SAP Community Network in the Social Software space at *http://scn.sap.com/community/socialsoftware*. There are two versions of the configuration guide: one version for SAP_BASIS version 7.31 SP06, and one version for SAP_BASIS versions 7.31 SP05, 7.30 SP08, and 7.02 SP12.

3.7.3 SAP Data Services Adapter

A standard SuccessFactors adapter is provided in SAP Data Services 4.1 SP1 to integrate talent data from the SuccessFactors HCM suite into SAP BW or SAP HANA. Potentially, data can also be transferred bi-directionally into the SuccessFactors HCM suite.

The adapter connects to the SuccessFactors API and extracts database tables that can be processed and sent to SAP BW or SAP HANA. The data can also be subject to transformations and quality checks during processing. It is worth noting that the standard talent management InfoCubes in SAP BW don't map entirely with data from the SuccessFactors HCM suite, so new InfoCubes may need to be created.

For more information, see the *SAP Business-Objects Data Services 4.1 Support Package 1 (14.1.1.0) Integrator's Guide*, available on SAP Help at *http://help.sap.com/boall*.

3.8 Summary

SAP is making progress on its journey to build and deliver robust packaged integration content. It has already laid out a detailed foundation of how to reach its goal, which is to ensure that customers have relevant, specific, and maintainable integration content. SAP has set its strategy and chosen to leverage SAP and Dell Boomi AtomSphere technology to provide bi-directional middleware integration between the SuccessFactors HCM suite, SAP ERP, and other systems.

Shortly after completing the acquisition of SuccessFactors, SAP delivered the first of its packages of packaged integration content and followed these up with cookbooks to facilitate additional integration scenarios, such as SSO for the SAP Enterprise Portal. SAP has continued to deliver additional integration content to cover talent management process integration for compensation and recruitment processes and for qualifications management. SAP has also built a set of integrations for Employee Central to enable it to integrate with SAP ERP and other systems so that organizations can run end-to-end HR processes in the cloud and on-premise.

Having read this chapter, you should now be familiar with SAP's strategy, the integration technology and content that SAP offers, and how to configure and use this content for core HR and talent processes. Next, we'll look at the platform and extensibility, as well as cover some of the technical aspects and considerations of the SuccessFactors HCM suite.

The basis of the SuccessFactors HCM suite is the platform. It provides the basic data and functionality framework required by each of the applications in the suite. The underlying platform now serves integration and extensibility needs that make the suite flexible for many customer needs.

4 Platform and Extensibility

As the basis of the suite, the platform provides the fundamental cross-suite functionality required by all applications in the SuccessFactors HCM suite. This could be compared to the SAP NetWeaver platform that SAP ERP runs on. The platform's functionality is highly configurable and, with the Metadata Framework and extensions offered on the SAP HANA Cloud Platform, it is now possible to create custom objects, screens, business rules, logic, and even applications.

The platform provides a host of the foundational functionality required by the system:

▶ System configuration and administration

▶ User management

▶ Authentication and password policy

▶ Permissions framework

▶ User interface

▶ Home page

▶ Email notifications

▶ Theme and logo

▶ Picklists

▶ Data imports

▶ Application Programming Interfaces (APIs)

In addition, it also provides some applications that are either cross-suite or not specific to any SuccessFactors application. These include the following:

- Employee Profile
- Org Chart
- Presentations
- Skills and Competencies
- Job Families and Roles
- Job Profile Builder
- Upgrade Center
- Metadata Framework

All features and applications that form part of the platform are inclusive in the platform licenses; no additional licensing is necessary to use features such as Org Chart or Presentations.

The first time that any SuccessFactors application is implemented, the platform must be implemented. This requires configuring the Employee Profile, importing user data to create user accounts, setting up Role-Based Permissions, and defining password policies. There are many optional configurations that can be made, such as email notifications and the tiles used on the home page.

In this chapter, we'll walk through an overview of the key pieces of provided platform functionality before taking a look at extensibility options with the Metadata Framework (MDF) and SAP HANA Cloud Platform (see Section 4.16 and Section 4.17). To begin, we'll take a look at the technical architecture of SuccessFactors, the technical aspects of the solution, and how it differs from SAP (see Section 4.1). We'll also look at some of the security aspects of SuccessFactors (see Section 4.2). Although APIs are part of the platform, these are covered in Chapter 3.

Now, let's take a look at the basics of how the SuccessFactors system works.

4.1   Technical Architecture

Although the technical architecture and system design of SuccessFactors are very different from those of SAP ERP HCM, SuccessFactors is able to maintain highly scalable and effective procedures not only to store and run data, but also to maintain secure data while keeping applications fast and stable. The SuccessFactors architecture allows for very fast, stable, and customizable solutions that remain performant from the hosted location.

The approach for examining the technical architecture of SuccessFactors varies greatly from on-premise SAP ERP HCM solutions in several ways. The days of creating custom tables from scratch and implementing completely custom functionality in house using specialized skillsets are no more. And, because SuccessFactors is a cloud solution, everything from security to moving configuration from one system to another system is different.

But, that's not to say that SuccessFactors is not flexible. SuccessFactors delivers significant functionality by default and uses the Metadata Framework and the Rules Engine to customize your own objects and screen elements. The flexibility of the architecture allows for endless customization. Extensibility with SAP HANA Cloud Platform enables entirely customizable applications to be built and integrated into SuccessFactors.

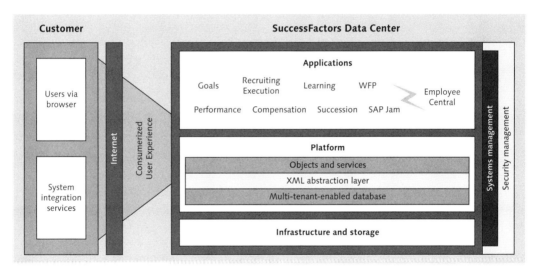

Figure 4.1 SuccessFactors Structure Stack

In Figure 4.1, you can see that the overall architecture of the SuccessFactors application landscape runs similarly to many other web-enabled applications. There are the core application and database in the SuccessFactors Data Center, and then there is the client-side web browser that consumes the application from the Data Center. Architecturally, SuccessFactors is split into three layers; two are within the Data Center, and one connects the Data Center to the client:

▸ Within the Data Center, the *database layer* contains the underlying application metadata configuration and the customer data.

▸ The *application layer*, also within the Data Center, contains the actual application and overall logic of the SuccessFactors HCM suite.

▸ The *communication layer* lies between the application layer and the client web browser.

As with all cloud applications, security is generally a main concern. We'll cover security in depth later in this section. First, we'll briefly look at each of the layers.

4.1.1 Database Layer

SuccessFactors houses all of the customer's data in an Oracle database, but it plans to switch this to an SAP HANA database from 2014 onwards.

Because the SuccessFactors HCM suite is a multi-tenant Software-as-a-Service (SaaS) suite, customers share infrastructure, web servers, database instances, and the application itself. However, each customer has their own partition in the database, along with the customer-specific database schema. They also have their own configuration of the software ("tenant"). This allows for high flexibility and the export of any customer data from the database at any time with no effect on any other customer. Because the database partition is separated from other customer data and linked specifically to the customer's tenant, data cannot be accessed from any place except the customer's instance of SuccessFactors. This also means that configuration in one customer tenant does not affect any other customer tenant running on the same instance of the software.

Of course, sharing database space with another customer's sensitive HR data raises some obvious security concerns to those not familiar with the technical architecture of the database landscape. We'll address how SuccessFactors rigorously tests each level of the stack to ensure data security later in this section.

4.1.2 Application Layer

One of the most important aspects of a SaaS solution is that it is multi-tenant. Because of the multi-tenant architecture, all of the users share the same core code base of the application, but they each have their own tenant of configuration. This differs from on-premise solutions, wherein each instance of the system requires different hardware, versions, and operating systems. Having all users on the same code base has many advantages:

▶ **Scheduled releases**
The SuccessFactors development team is constantly updating the software to improve performance and increase functionality. Users get regular, scheduled updates automatically (every quarter), instead of paying to upgrade their own on-premise software. Many of the new features that are delivered must be pro-actively activated by the customer to be used (opt-in), so there are no "nasty surprises" for customers.

▶ **Latest version across all customers**
With the scheduled releases, all customers are up-to-date on the latest version all the time. This means that there are no more costly upgrades, creating different versions for different customers. It also means all customers get all bug fixes.

▶ **No hardware, operating systems, or database licenses**
A single subscription licensing fee is paid to use SuccessFactors and includes all necessary costs for hardware, database, and support.

▶ **Optimal hardware and software combination**
SuccessFactors resides on hardware that is optimized for its own software.

▶ **Consistent performance and stability**
All customers use the same software and hardware, so the fast, stable, and secure experience is shared by all customers.

▶ **More manageable and efficient support and maintenance**
SuccessFactors can easily support and maintain its software because it is stan-dardized.

▶ **Data mining and aggregation for analytical benchmarking**
Analytics can easily be pulled with maximum efficiency due to the standardiza-tion of software and hardware.

Now, let's take a closer look at the application architecture itself. Figure 4.2 shows a more in-depth overview of the SuccessFactors components within the applica-tion engine.

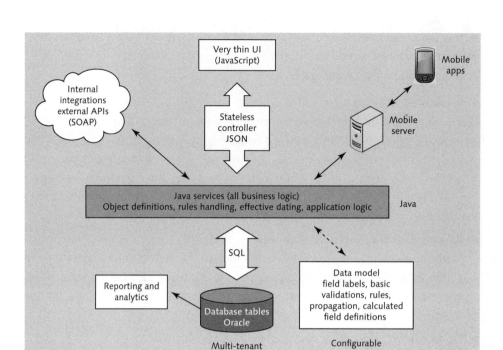

Figure 4.2 Technologies Used with SuccessFactors

The applications are written in the Java programming language using Java Platform Enterprise Edition (J2EE) specifications, so they conform to a standard set of programming logic.

The Java application uses JavaScript Object Notation (JSON) to send the data to the client or end user. With JSON, the web page that the user sees is dynamically created and rendered using JavaScript. This makes it a very lightweight application on the client side and allows for a dynamic display of data. This also lets the application perform many of the user-friendly animations that appear and gives great flexibility within the design of the user interface (UI). We'll cover the UI itself later in this chapter.

Because the JSON interchange allows for an efficient and powerful exchange of data from the Java application to the end user, SuccessFactors applications are *stateless*. Stateless application design means that there are no static HTML pages being called from the server. Each page is dynamically created and sent securely to the end user. This allows for complete flexibility and lightweight application design.

Also within this layer are the APIs and connectors to other web services (e.g., Recruiting Management can connect to Job Boards), mobile application services, and all the logic that drives the entire application.

4.1.3 Communication Layer

The communication layer transports the data for the application to the web browser for rendering and communications data calls to and from the Data Center. This is important from an architectural perspective because this layer is sending sensitive application and personal HR information across the Internet. As a result, SuccessFactors has implemented well-known standards for data transfer, including Secure Shell (SSH), VeriSign-certified Secure Sockets Layer (SSL)/Transport Layer Security (TLS), and Secure File Transfer Protocol (SFTP).

Now that you understand the various layers of the application, let's take a look at how SuccessFactors secures data within the application.

4.2 Security

SuccessFactors takes security and protecting its customers' sensitive data very seriously. Because its systems store sensitive HR data from multiple customers, every aspect of technology used is thoroughly tested and includes many security standards to ensure proper security. Data is secured in two ways: through authentication and through security applied to each of the layers described previously in this section.

4.2.1 Authentication Security

SuccessFactors has many different levels of security on all layers. It supports the SSL and TLS encryption languages that are leveraged by standard web providers. In addition are the following authentication methods:

▶ **Internal authentication**
Using an internal repository of user profiles, this authentication occurs on the SuccessFactors side when customers choose not to integrate their own identity management system.

▶ **Federated authentication (SSO)**
SSO implementation requires users to first be authenticated through their own authorization systems (LDAP) using tokens (MD5, SHA-1, HMAC encryption, DES, 3DES) or Security Assertion Markup Languages (SAML 1.1, 2.0). The user is then redirected to the SuccessFactors instance using HTTPS.

▶ **SSO without federation**
This method uses a public encryption key that is sent to the customer's authentication server from SuccessFactors. By using this key, users can connect to SuccessFactors by using a pre-established authentication method.

▶ **Separate security applications**
Because authorization is usually deeply integrated in source code in standard solutions, SuccessFactors uses a separate authorization and authentication application from that of the data and functions. This allows for future growth of security throughout the application, as needed. This security application logs every action of the user and validates each request to prevent cross-site scripting (XSS) attacks.

▶ **Password protection**
Strong passwords with regular password changes are required by SuccessFactors. Administrators can also set custom rules for passwords that users must abide by.

4.2.2 Layer Security

The SuccessFactors environment is made up of multiple layers of security. The security layers and accompanying encryption and technology are shown in Figure 4.3.

The data center itself also conforms to many security standards:

▶ EU 95/46 EC

▶ PCI-DSS

▶ ISO 27002

▶ BS7799

▶ ASIO-4

▶ FIPS Moderate

▶ BS10012

▶ SSAE-16/SOC2

Because of these safeguards, customers' information is encrypted and protected, so even if the data is stolen, it is inaccessible and unusable.

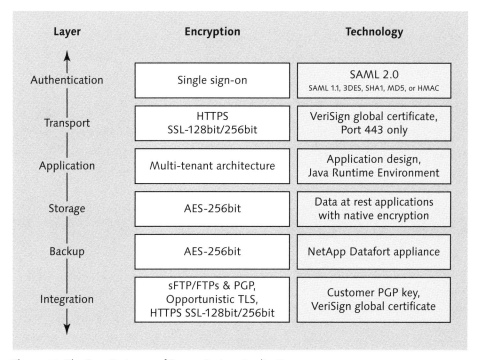

Figure 4.3 The Security Layers of SuccessFactors Applications

4.2.3 Role-Based Permissions Security

The Role-Based Permission (RBP) framework in SuccessFactors provides a flexible, robust, and granular approach to securing data and functionality to the right groups of users for specified target groups of employees. It allows authorizations and security to be managed at all levels, including the function, transaction, field, and data levels. Field-level permissions can also be set so that data can be hidden, viewable, or viewable and editable for specific roles. We will discuss the RBP further in Section 4.4.

Now that you understand how the data and layers are secured, let's explore some of the key components of the SuccessFactors platform.

4.3   OneAdmin

Administrators within SuccessFactors have many powerful tools at their fingertips, including those that enable administration of features such as employee and organizational data, forms used in various SuccessFactors HCM suite solutions, Picklists, and notification emails. In this section, we'll explore the *OneAdmin* tool (previously known as Admin Tools) and see how it supports easy configuration of the SuccessFactors instance.

When you log in to your SuccessFactors instance as a user with the appropriate permission to administer parts of one or more application (typically an administrator user), you have the ability to access OneAdmin. This can be accessed through one of two ways: either click the navigation menu in the top-left of the application (where the current module name is displayed), or click your user name and then select the ADMIN TOOLS OPTION from the menu. If configured, OneAdmin can also be accessed from a tile on the home page.

Once you are in OneAdmin, many useful administration tools are available to enable an administrator to set up various features, functions, objects, and data imports. These all depend on the different permissions assigned to the user's role. Figure 4.4 shows the OneAdmin home page.

> **Note**
>
> You can also switch to the old Admin Tools, which is a text-based list of the options available in OneAdmin, by clicking BACK TO OLD ADMIN TOOLS in OneAdmin.

The icons on the screen in Figure 4.5 display some of the standard functions that are available for those particular applications (e.g., PERFORMANCE MANAGEMENT, COMPENSATION, and RECRUITING). When you choose an icon, a dynamic menu appears on the screen to show the functions and activities available for that application. Figure 4.6 shows an example of the SuccessFactors Recruiting Execution application dynamic menu.

Here, you can see many useful functions of the Recruiting Management application of the SuccessFactors Recruiting Execution solution. The administrator can easily navigate to these key functions all within the same page. Notice that many functions are available, which can be overwhelming for new users who are not familiar with the system.

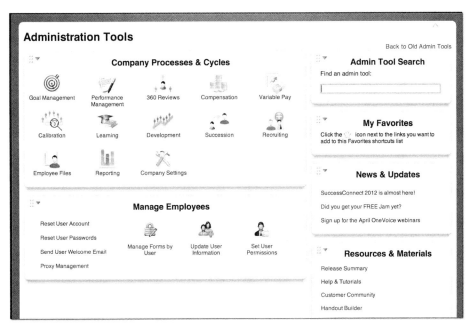

Figure 4.4 OneAdmin Home Page

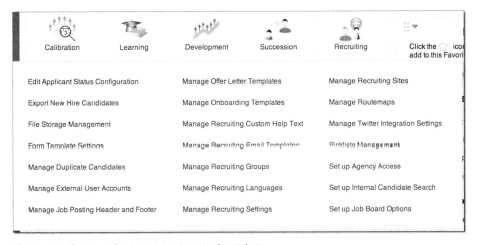

Figure 4.5 Choosing the Recruiting Icon in OneAdmin

Thankfully, SuccessFactors comes with a live search function right on the OneAdmin home page (see Figure 4.6). This useful function displays the search results as you type, making navigation within the OneAdmin home page very easy.

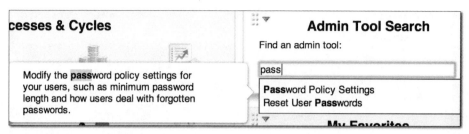

Figure 4.6 Live Search Function in OneAdmin

We will cover some of the practical administration activities in Chapter 5.

4.4 Role-Based Permissions

The Role-Based Permission (RBP) framework in SuccessFactors is similar in use to the authorization concept in SAP ERP, although its application to users differs. Unlike in SAP, the RBP framework is focused on assigning roles to groups of users that are identified based on various available criteria. Because a user can be assigned multiple roles, it makes administration of RBPs simpler. We will cover this in more detail in the next subsection.

> **Important Note**
>
> The RBP framework cannot be used alongside Administrative Domains (the legacy SuccessFactors permissions framework). If Administrative Domains is used and the RBP framework is needed, all Administrative Domains permissions must be migrated to the RBP framework.

At present, the RBP framework supports organizations with up to 300,000 employees.

4.4.1 Configuration and Audits

The RBP framework is configured in the SET USER PERMISSIONS menu in the MANAGE EMPLOYEES section of OneAdmin. In addition, permissions can be checked for users in this menu. The following menu options are available:

▶ MANAGE PERMISSION GROUPS: Create, edit, copy, delete, view summary of, and view change history of Permission Groups

▸ MANAGE PERMISSION ROLES: Create, edit, copy, delete, view summary of, and view change history of Permission Roles

▸ SECURITY PERMISSION REPORTS: View the Proxy Management report

▸ VIEW USER PERMISSION: View permissions assigned to a user

We will cover some of these options as we look deeper into the RBP framework.

4.4.2 How the RBP Framework Works

The core authorization concepts of the RBP framework are built primarily upon three elements:

▸ *Permission Roles:* Group of permissions

▸ *Granted Users*: Users who are assigned a Permission Role

▸ *Target Population*: Employee population on which the permissions in the Permission Role are applied

Practically, these work together as such: Granted Users are assigned a Permission Role that is effective on the Target Population. This is summarized visually in Figure 4.7.

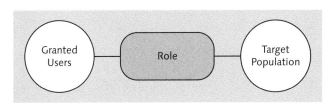

Figure 4.7 Core Authorization Concept in the RBP Framework

We'll look at each of these three components of the RBP framework in the remainder of this section. However, we'll first take a look at *Permission Groups* because they are a key component of the RBP framework that supports these aforementioned concepts.

4.4.3 Permission Groups

Permission Groups are simply groups of either Granted Users or Target Employees. In some instances—depending on the design—the same group can be used for both.

Permission Group Membership

Many different criteria are available to identify the members of each Permission Group. By default, these are the fields from the User Data File, although Employee Central fields can be added to this list. The default list contains fields such as COUNTRY, DEPARTMENT, DIVISION, HIRE DATE, JOB CODE, JOB TITLE, LOCATION, and USERNAME.

Within a Permission Group, one or more *People Pools* can be created. One or more criteria can be used within each People Pool, and so combinations can be used to narrow down groups of employees. For example, a Permission Group criterion could be created with a PEOPLE POOL to select employees with a JOB CODE of MANAGER and a LOCATION of CHICAGO, and another PEOPLE POOL to select employees with a LOCATION of BOSTON. Figure 4.8 shows a PERMISSION GROUP and how this example would look.

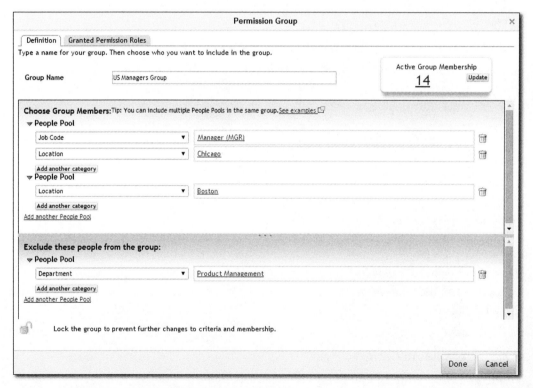

Figure 4.8 An Example of a Permission Group

In addition to identifying members to include in a Permission Group, the same criteria can be used to exclude members from a Permission Group. In Figure 4.8, the PRODUCT MANAGEMENT department has been excluded.

Creating Permission Groups

Permission Groups are created in OneAdmin in SET USER PERMISSIONS • MANAGE PERMISSION GROUPS. In the MANAGE PERMISSION GROUPS screen, click the CREATE NEW button to create a new Permission Group. The PERMISSION GROUP window opens, and it looks similar to Figure 4.8. The PERMISSION GROUP window is split into two tabs: DEFINITION and GRANTED PERMISSION ROLES.

The DEFINITION tab is where the Permission Group name and People Pools for included and excluded members can be defined, as mentioned previously. The ACTIVE GROUP MEMBERSHIP box displays the number of members in the Permission Group, which can be seen in the upper-right corner in Figure 4.8. Clicking the number shows a list of the members in the Permission Group. The UPDATE button can be used to update this figure in real time.

The GRANTED PERMISSION ROLES tab displays which Permission Roles this Permission Group has been assigned to.

4.4.4 Granted Users

As mentioned earlier, Granted Users are users who are assigned a Permission Role for the Target Population of employees. Granted Users are assigned directly to a Permission Role with one of the following options:

▶ PERMISSION GROUP: Granted Users are selected from a Permission Group.

▶ MANAGERS: Granted Users are all employees who have direct reports.

▶ HR MANAGERS: Granted Users are all employees assigned as one or more employee's HR Manager.

▶ MATRIX MANAGERS: Granted Users are all employees assigned as one or more employee's Matrix Manager.

▶ CUSTOM MANAGERS: Granted Users are all employees assigned as one or more employee's Custom Manager.

▶ SECOND MANAGERS: Granted Users are all employees assigned as one or more employee's Second Manager.

▶ CALIBRATION FACILITATORS: Granted Users are those who facilitate Calibration sessions in the Calibration module.

▶ HOME MANAGERS: Granted Users are all employees who have direct reports who are out on global assignment elsewhere in the organization.

▶ HOME HR MANAGERS: Granted Users are all employees who are assigned as HR Manager to one or more employees out on global assignment elsewhere in the organization.

▶ HOST MANAGERS: Granted Users are all employees who have direct reports who are on Global Assignment in their team.

▶ HOST HR MANAGERS: Granted Users are all employees who are assigned as HR Manager to one or more employees who are on global assignment in their area of responsibility.

▶ EVERYONE: All employees are selected as the Granted Users.

All options—except PERMISSION GROUP and EVERYONE—can be filtered with one or more Permission Groups. Depending on the option selected, the available options for the Target Population vary. These options will be covered in the next section.

Note

The CALIBRATION FACILITATORS role displays only if the Calibration application is enabled. The four Global Assignment options display only if the Global Assignment functionality is enabled in Employee Central.

4.4.5 Target Population

The Target Population are those employees who can be accessed by the Granted Users. The options depend on which Granted User option is selected.

Permission Group or Everyone

If the option selected for the Granted Users is either PERMISSION GROUP or EVERYONE, the Target Population options are as follows:

▶ EVERYONE: All employees are the Target Population.

▶ GRANTED USER'S DEPARTMENT: All employees in the Granted User's department are the Target Population.

- GRANTED USER'S DIVISION: All employees in the Granted User's division are the Target Population.

- GRANTED USER'S LOCATION: All employees in the Granted User's location are the Target Population

- GRANTED USER: The Granted User themselves is the Target Population

Figure 4.9 shows the granting of Granted Users to a Target Population for a Permission Role using Permission Groups.

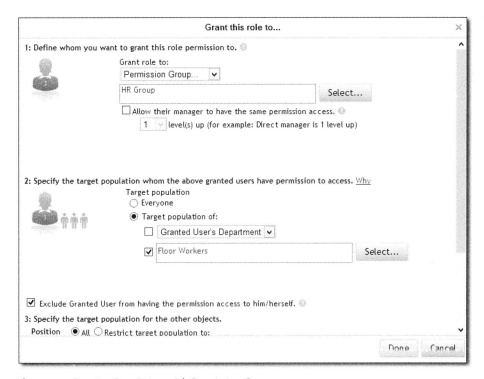

Figure 4.9 Granting Permission with Permission Groups

Managers

If the option selected for the Granted Users is any type of manager (e.g., Manager, HR Manager, Home HR Manager, etc.), the Target Population options are as follows:

- GRANTED USER'S DIRECT REPORTS: All of the Granted User's direct reports are the Target Population.

▶ GRANTED USER'S DIRECT REPORTS IN A SPECIFIC PERMISSION GROUP: All of the Granted User's direct reports in a specific Permission Group are the Target Population.

For all manager roles, with the exception of the Global Assignment manager roles, the number of levels of indirect reports can be selected. The options are one level down, two levels down, three levels down, or all levels down. The manager can also select to include themselves in this population with the option INCLUDE ACCESS TO GRANTED USER (SELF). Managers can be further filtered with one or more Permission Groups.

Figure 4.10 shows the granting of Granted Users to a Target Population for a Permission Role for managers. In this example, only managers in the Permission Group HR GROUP are granted the role for the manager's direct reports and one level of indirect reports.

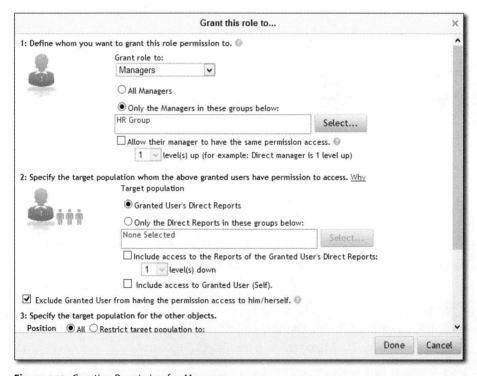

Figure 4.10 Granting Permission for Managers

Calibration Facilitator

When the Calibration Facilitator option is selected for the Granted Users, the Target Population is automatically set to GRANTED CALIBRATION SUBJECTS.

4.4.6 Permission Roles

Permission Roles are simply the collection of permissions that are assigned to Granted Users. They are created in OneAdmin in SET USER PERMISSIONS • MANAGE PERMISSION ROLES. A role has two parts to its definition: the selected permissions and the granting of the role to Granted Users for a Target Population. A Permission Role can be granted multiple times to different Granted Users and Target Populations.

Permissions

Permissions are split into two categories: *user permissions* and *administrator permissions*. User permissions cover all of the permissions that allow a user to access functionality or create, edit, and/or delete data. Administrator permissions provide administrators the ability to access administrative functions and allow integration users to query and update data via APIs. Within each of these categories are a number of sub-categories that cover application-specific or system-specific functionality and data fields, such as Career Development Planning or Succession Planners. Permissions can have three types of settings, depending on what the effect is:

▸ **Non-Effective-dated fields**: View and Edit

▸ **Employee Central Effective-dated fields**: View Current, View History, Edit/Insert, Correct, and Delete

▸ **Functionality/Settings**: On or off

> **Important Note**
>
> Module-page permissions for Performance Management, Goal Management, Compensation, and CDP are controlled at the form level.

Non-effective data is data found in Employee Central and the Employee Profile, which you can see in Figure 4.11. If you select the checkbox in the VIEW column, the field is visible as read-only to the user. If you select the checkbox in the EDIT column, the field is editable by the user. Clicking EDIT will automatically select VIEW because a field must be visible in order to be editable. If neither column is selected, the field is not visible to the user.

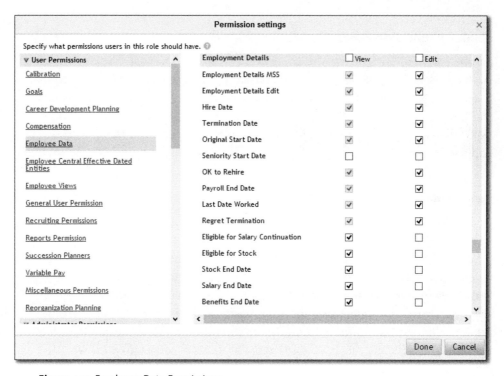

Figure 4.11 Employee Data Permissions

For Employee Central effective-dated fields, there are multiple options available, as specified above. These are as follows:

▶ VIEW CURRENT: Allows the user to see the field in the respective portlet

▶ VIEW HISTORY: Allows the user to access the History link on the respective portlet, which when selected displays all records

▶ EDIT/INSERT: Allows the user to insert a new record

▶ CORRECT: Allows the user to edit ("correct") any record

▶ DELETE: Allows the user to delete any record

Figure 4.12 shows the Employee Central effective-dated fields permissions.

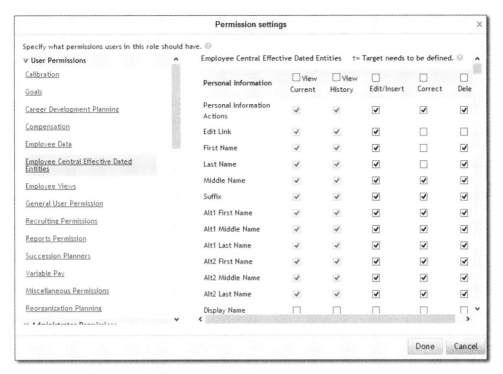

Figure 4.12 Employee Central Effective-Dated Field Permissions

More often than not, only HR or system administrators are given CORRECT or DELETE permissions.

The permissions for enabling functionality or settings are, for the most part, a simple checkbox. Some of these permissions may require a target population to be defined, which is indicated with a † next to the permission. This can be seen in Figure 4.13. In addition, some functionalities require one or multiple selections of that functionality to be made. This applies to forms (such as Compensation, Variable Pay, and Goal Management) and reports. This is also seen in Figure 4.13 for Compensation forms.

Generic Object permissions, usually under Miscellaneous permissions, work in a similar way for functionality or settings. The only real difference is that they have multiple options per object, such as VIEW or EDIT. The options depend on whether the Generic Object is effective-dated or not. In addition, individual field-level overrides are possible for each Generic Object field (see Figure 4.14).

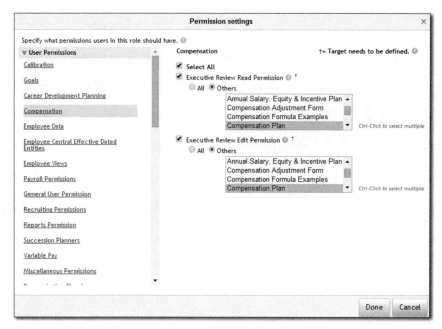

Figure 4.13 Functionality and Settings Permissions

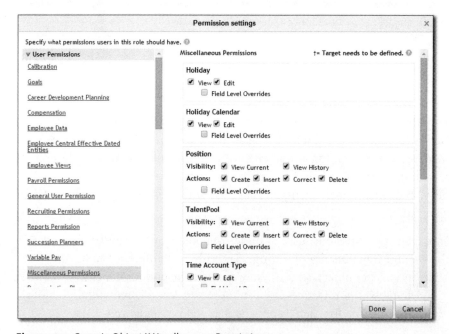

Figure 4.14 Generic Object/Miscellaneous Permissions

Assigning Permission Roles

The assignment of Permission Roles—called *granting*—is done to Granted Users for Target Populations. This is done once a Permission Role is configured and can be modified as required. Without granting, a Permission Role remains inactive in the system. Figure 4.15 shows a summary of the granting of a Permission Role, as seen at the bottom of the screen when configuring a Permission Role.

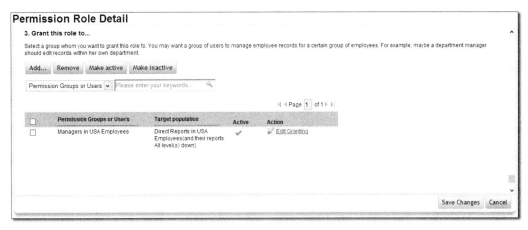

Figure 4.15 Summary of Granting of a Permission Role

A user can be granted multiple Permission Roles as part of one or more Permission Groups or managers. When this happens and a user is granted the same permission with different rights (e.g., VIEW and EDIT access for the same field) the user receives the most powerful permission.

4.4.7 Reporting and Audit

Four ad hoc reports are available in the system for reporting on RBPs:

- ▸ *RBP User to Role Report*: Displays users assigned to each Permission Role
- ▸ *RBP Permission to User Report*: Displays permissions assigned to each user
- ▸ *RBP User to Group Report*: Displays users assigned to each Permission Group
- ▸ *RBP Permission Roles Report*: Displays details about each Permission Role

The can be created and run in the Analytics module by navigating to the REPORTING module, selecting AD HOC REPORTS in the left side menu, selecting the CREATE NEW REPORT button, selecting any of the four reports from the REPORT DEFINITION

TYPE dropdown list, and then selecting the CREATE button. This dropdown list can be seen in Figure 4.16.

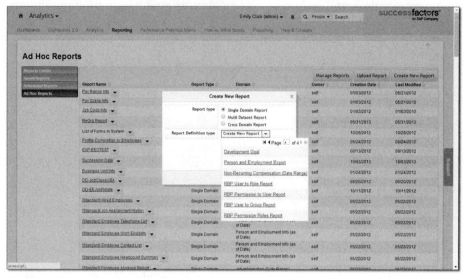

Figure 4.16 Selecting an Ad Hoc Report

In Figure 4.17, a preview of an RBP USER TO ROLE REPORT ad hoc report that was generated by a user is displayed.

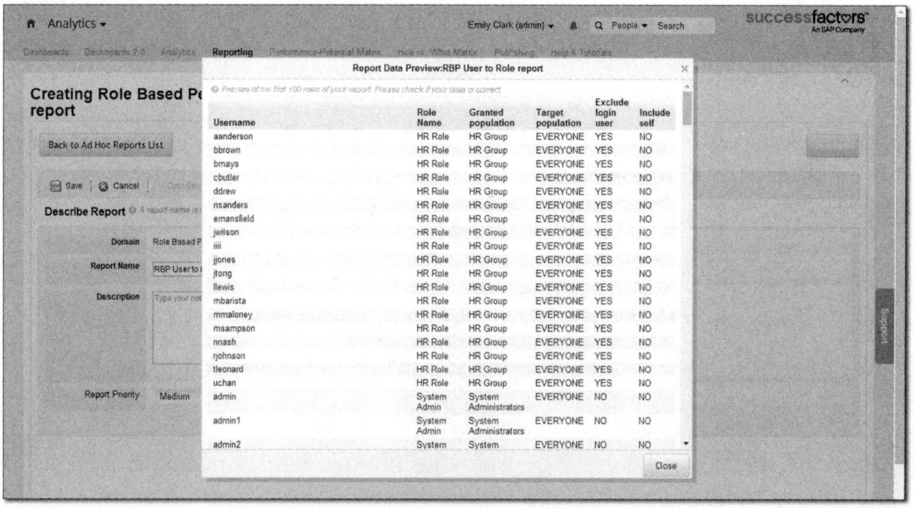

Figure 4.17 A Preview of the RBP User to Role Report

In addition to the ad hoc reports, an administrator can view the permissions assigned to any user in OneAdmin in Set User Permissions • View User Permission. This displays each of the permissions and from which Permission Roles these have been assigned. Figure 4.18 shows the report.

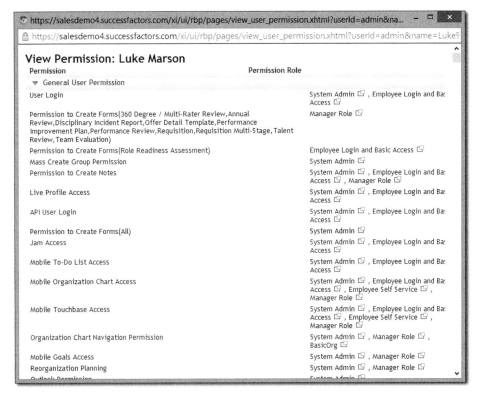

Figure 4.18 The View User Permission Window

4.4.8 Copying RBP Configuration between Instances

RBP configuration can be copied one from instance to another in Provisioning using the option Copy Permission Roles from Another Instance. This can be performed bi-directionally between test and production systems and can be useful for cutting over to production during an implementation or to keep a test system synchronized with a production system. An option to perform a dry run is available to test whether the process would work.

Within the feature, the target instance must be selected, followed by either Dry Run or Copy RBP Configuration, as shown in Figure 4.19.

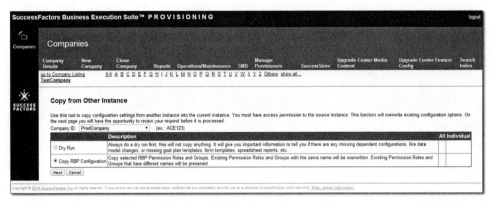

Figure 4.19 Copy RBP Configuration Selection Screen

Click NEXT, and then the main RBP copy screen is shown. Here, you can select one of three options:

▶ COPY SPECIFIED ROLES: Copies the selected Permission Roles and associated Permission Groups

▶ COPY ALL RBP ROLES: Copies all Permission Roles and associated Permission Groups

▶ COPY SPECIFIED GROUPS: Copies the selected Permission Groups

Figure 4.20 shows the selected COPY SPECIFIED ROLES option and two selected Permission Roles.

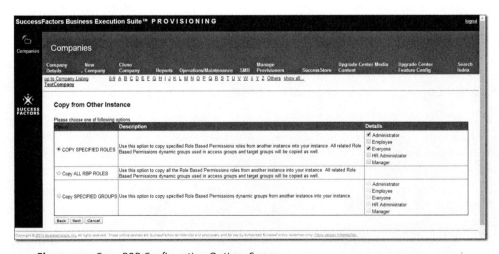

Figure 4.20 Copy RBP Configuration Options Screen

After clicking NEXT, they are presented with the summary of the RBP copy operation, as seen in Figure 4.21.

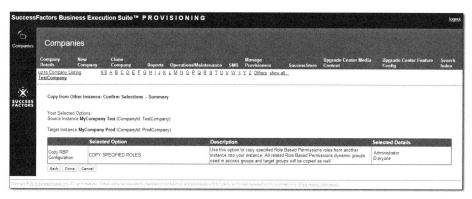

Figure 4.21 Copy RBP Configuration Summary Screen

Selecting DONE brings up a pop-up window to confirm the copy operation. After clicking OK, the summary screen is displayed. The copy operation job can then be viewed in the MONITOR SCHEDULED JOB page.

4.5 User Data File (UDF)

The *User Data File* (UDF)—also known as the *Basic User Import*—is the basic user data required by the SuccessFactors HCM suite to run talent applications. In an integration concept, the data stored in the system is called the *user entity*. The packaged integration from SAP populates the UDF with data from SAP ERP HCM.

It is made up of the 49 standard elements from the Succession Data Model: 34 fields, plus 15 customizable fields available for any use. Nine of these fields are mandatory in SuccessFactors and must be defined. The standard elements used in the UDF are defined in the view template *sysUserDirectorySetting* in the Succession Data Model. We recommend that you leave the standard fields as they are provided in the data model. The standard fields are as follows:

▸ STATUS: Employee status (active or inactive) *
▸ USERID: Unique identifier *
▸ USERNAME: Employee's user name to login *
▸ FIRSTNAME: First name *

- ▶ NICKNAME: Nickname
- ▶ MI: Middle name
- ▶ LASTNAME: Last name *
- ▶ SUFFIX: Name suffix
- ▶ TITLE: Job title
- ▶ GENDER: Gender
- ▶ EMAIL: Email address *
- ▶ MANAGER: Manager *
- ▶ HR: HR administrator *
- ▶ DEPARTMENT: Department
- ▶ JOBCODE: Job code
- ▶ DIVISION: Division
- ▶ LOCATION: Location
- ▶ TIMEZONE: Time zone of user *
- ▶ HIREDATE: Hire date
- ▶ EMPID: Employee's ID
- ▶ BIZ_PHONE: Telephone number
- ▶ FAX: Fax number
- ▶ ADDR1: Address line 1
- ▶ ADDR2: Address line 2
- ▶ CITY: City
- ▶ STATE: State/Province
- ▶ ZIP: Zip Code/Postal Code
- ▶ COUNTRY: Country
- ▶ REVIEW_FREQ: Performance appraisal frequency
- ▶ LAST_REVIEW_DATE: Date of last performance appraisal
- ▶ MATRIX_MANAGER: Dotted line (matrix) manager
- ▶ DEFAULT_LOCALE: Default locale of employee
- ▶ PROXY: Proxy user

▶ CUSTOM01: Customizable field 1

▶ ..

▶ CUSTOM15: Customizable field 15

Fields marked with * are mandatory and cannot be left blank. Although MAN-AGER and HR cannot be left blank, an entry can be made to define that the user does not have a manager or HR administrator by using values NO_MANAGER *and* NO_HR, respectively. If you are defining a manager or HR administrator, that user's USERID field value is used.

The values for the TIMEZONE field are pre-defined, and the correct values must be used. These can be obtained from a SuccessFactors implementation specialist or from SuccessFactors Professional Services.

All date formats are stored in format MM/DD/YYYY.

4.5.1 Managing the UDF

When you use Employee Central and hire a new employee in the HIRE NEW EMPLOYEE transaction, a UDF record is created automatically. When an employee is rehired, their UDF record status is changed from INACTIVE to ACTIVE. In OneAdmin, the UDF can be exported and imported under UPDATE USER INFORMATION using the EMPLOYEE EXPORT and IMPORT EMPLOYEE DATA options, respectively. Figure 4.22 shows an example of an exported UDF with some data.

	A	B	C	D	E	F	G	H	I	J	K	L
1	STATUS	USERID	USERNAME	FIRSTNAME	LASTNAME	SUFFIX	TITLE	GENDER	EMAIL	MANAGER	HR	DEPARTMENT
2	active	54645	awan	Adam	Wan		HR Administrator	M	aadmin1@ACECompany.com	65324	122326	Industries
3	active	8324	abagot	Alain	Bagot		Program Manager	M	ABagot@ACECompany.com	65324	43789	Client Service (SVCS)
4	active	123123	achin	Alan	Chin		Recruiter - HC	M	AChin@ACECompany.com	43535	34349	Talent Management (TALENT)
5	active	8253	alake	Alan	Lake		VP, Operations	M	ALake@ACECompany.com	NO_MANAGER	22455	Operations (OPS)
6	active	84543	aanderson	Alex	Anderson		Sr. Manager, Analytics	M	AAnderson@ACECompany.com	74545	5938	Talent Management (TALENT)
7	active	27857	athompson	Alexander	Thompson		President	M	AThompson@ACECompany.com	23777	6477	Alliances (ALNCE)
8	active	58677	afong	Alice	Fong		Recruiter	F	AFong@ACECompany.com	54555	24667	Talent Management (TALENT)
9	active	73782	amick	Alison	Mick		Director, IT Support	F	AMick@ACECompany.com	92133	NO_HR	IT (IT)
10	active	42421	akohne	Amanda	Kohne		Director, IT	F	AKohne@ACECompany.com	123331	NO_HR	IT (IT)

Figure 4.22 The UDF with Data

When you are not using Employee Central, adding a UDF record for an employee is performed through OneAdmin, through the MANAGE USERS option under UPDATE USER INFORMATION. This is seen in Figure 4.23. Here, the user has the option of doing a quick add for the required fields, or entering a full record. Both options are found under the ADD NEW USER button.

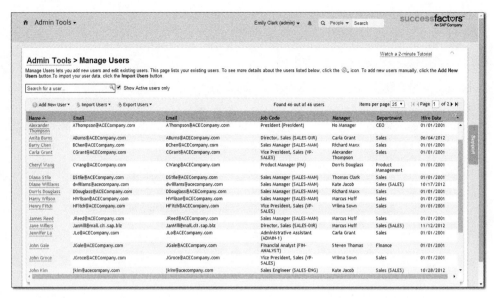

Figure 4.23 The Manage Users Screen

4.5.2 Importing and Exporting Data

Employee data is imported and exported in OneAdmin, under UPDATE USER INFORMATION. No matter whether Employee Central is used, the UDF can be exported using the option EMPLOYEE EXPORT.

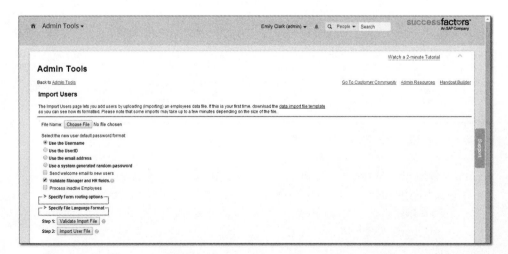

Figure 4.24 Employee Import Screen

When you use Employee Central, data is imported using the IMPORT EMPLOYEE DATA option under UPDATE USER INFORMATION. When you're not using Employee Central, data is imported using the EMPLOYEE IMPORT option under UPDATE USER INFORMATION. This has to be enabled for specific users in OneAdmin in MANAGE EMPLOYEE IMPORT under SET USER PERMISSIONS.

4.5.3 HRIS Sync

Employee Central data can be synchronized to the User Data File. Certain fields are synchronized automatically in real time when changes are made to employee data in Employee Central, including the following:

▸ First name

▸ Last name

▸ Division

▸ Department

▸ Job code

▸ Manager

▸ HR administrator

▸ Email address

Other Employee Central fields are mapped to UDF fields in the Succession Data Model. These are synchronized by a daily job that must be set up in Provisioning. Typically, Employee Central data is mapped to the customizable fields in the UDF so that they can be displayed in the Employee Profile or used in filters. Employee Central fields can also be synchronized to user-info elements.

4.6 User Interface

The SuccessFactors user interface (UI) has been designed to provide an engaging and enriching user experience (UX) for the end user. The simple design provides powerful benefits to employees and managers who have minimal training or exposure to SAP or SuccessFactors. SuccessFactors has leveraged their SMART design principles in every aspect of the UI: Social, Mobile, Analytical, Rich, and Toy-like. The modular and easy-to-use UI provides enhanced productivity through intuitive navigation and data presentation. The aesthetics of the UI provide a much richer visual UX than SAP ERP or other pre-Web 2.0 applications.

The UI is designed to conform to the needs of organizations of various sizes that operate in a wide array of industries and territories. Unlike traditional software applications that target one level of user in an organization, this solution is designed to adapt to the different needs of various types of users, from C-level executives to HR business partners, line managers, and even entry-level employees.

Now, let's take a look at some of the aspects of the UI.

4.6.1   Navigation Menu

Each of the applications that the user is permissioned to access can be reached via the navigation menu in the top-left corner of the application. Figure 4.25 shows the navigation menu in SuccessFactors. This is where each of the licensed applications in the suite can be accessed.

Figure 4.25 The Navigation Menu in SuccessFactors

Depending on the number of licensed modules and the permission design, the menu in Figure 4.26 may be much smaller for some or all audiences in your organization.

4.6.2 User Menu and Options

The *user menu* provides the user with access to options and—depending on user permissions—the Proxy feature and/or OneAdmin. The user can also log out of the system here.

The user accesses the user menu by clicking their name at the top of the screen, as seen in Figure 4.26.

Figure 4.26 User Menu

The OPTIONS page allows the user to personalize the UX. It contains features such as the following:

▶ Change password

▶ Set start page when logging into SuccessFactors

▶ Configure notifications

▶ Change language

▶ Enable accessibility

▶ Configure proxy settings

▶ Create groups

▶ Enable SuccessFactors mobile functionality

The Proxy feature allows the user to log in on behalf of another user if the appropriate permissions have been assigned. For example, a manager could proxy in as a direct report during the direct report's annual vacation to approve a stalled workflow.

4.6.3 SAP Jam Notifications

Located to the right of the user menu is the SAP Jam notifications icon. The bell icon shows the number of notifications from SAP Jam if SAP Jam is used and integrated with SuccessFactors. Selecting the icon brings up the most recent notifications and provides a link to view all SAP Jam notifications (see Figure 4.27).

Figure 4.27 The User Menu, Jam Notifications Icon, and People Search

4.6.4 People Search

The quickest way to find an employee and view that employee's quickcard and profile is with the PEOPLE search feature at the top of the screen. This is typically located between the User Menu and the company logo. We can see this in Figure 4.27. If you partially enter a name, a list of employees appears in a dropdown menu below the search box. Highlighting one of the entries shows the quickcard, which you can see in Figure 4.28.

Figure 4.28 The Quickcard for an Employee

Selecting the TAKE ACTION button in the quickcard shows the extended options available to the user for this employee. Figure 4.29 shows a wealth of actions and pages to navigate to for the user Carla Grant. These options are controlled by RBPs.

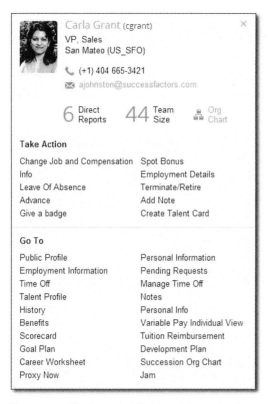

Figure 4.29 The Extended Quickcard for an Employee

4.6.5 Theme

The last, but not least, of the UI features is, of course, the theme. Configuration of the theme and logo is extremely flexible and can adhere to most corporate branding themes. Different themes can also be assigned to different user groups.

Company Logo

The company logo can be defined by an administrator in OneAdmin by selecting Upload Company Logo. It displays in the top-right of the application and on the logon screen.

Theming

You can configure the theme of the instance by selecting THEME MANAGER under COMPANY SETTINGS. Multiple themes can exist in the system, but only one default theme can be set. Depending on which setting is made in Provisioning, different themes can be assigned to specific divisions, departments, or locations. Selecting a theme brings up the EDIT THEME page, which looks similar to Figure 4.30.

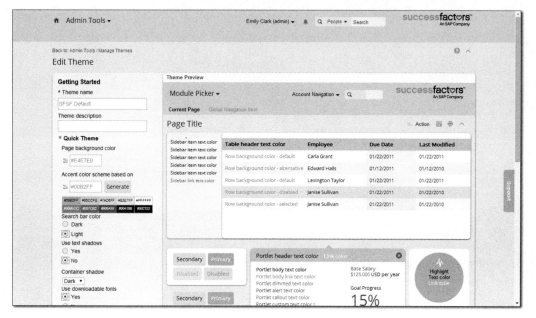

Figure 4.30 The Edit Theme Page

4.6.6 Languages

The SuccessFactors UI supports multiple languages across the suite. Each module supports a number of languages, with translations provided across the application as standard. Right-to-left (RTL) languages are also supported for some modules.

SuccessFactors are able to provide the most up-to-date list of languages available for the applications you are using or considering using.

Next, we will explore the SuccessFactors home page for employees.

4.7 Home Page

The home page is the main landing page for employees when they log on to the SuccessFactors system. It is the default landing page, although employees have the option to change their default landing page in the options that we covered in Section 4.6.2. Figure 4.31 shows a typical home page.

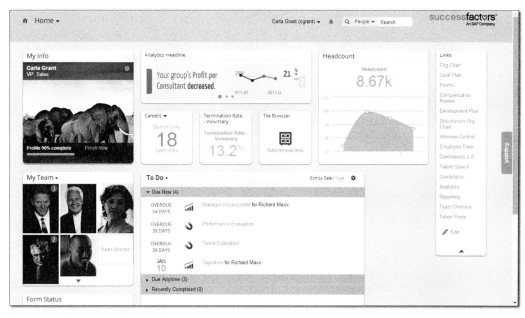

Figure 4.31 The SuccessFactors Home Page

The home page consists of a number of *tiles*. Tiles show a snapshot of information and allow the user to perform certain actions, depending on the tile. Tiles can be moved around, and the TILE BROWSER tile enables tiles to be added to or removed from the home page. Some tiles can be expanded or reduced by clicking the EXPAND button in the top-right corner of the tile. In addition to the standard-delivered tiles, custom tiles can be added. We'll cover those shortly.

Several tiles come delivered in the system:

▶ *To Do*: Lists all of the outstanding actions and activities of the user, such as workflows to be approved or performance evaluations to be assessed

- *Links*: Provides a list of links to different applications and processes, such as Org Chart and Employee Files

- *My Team*: Displays the user's direct reports and allows actions to be launched for team members

- *My Admin Favorites*: Lists all of the OneAdmin options added as favorites

- *My Info*: Displays basic info about the user and enables self-service actions to be launched by the user

- *Tile Browser*: Allows tiles to be enabled or disabled

- *Admin Alerts*: Displays alerts for administrator users, such as stalled workflows and HR data issues

In addition, each application has its own tiles that become available once that application is implemented. For example, Recruiting introduces the CAREERS and RECRUITING tiles. Figure 4.32 shows the MY TEAM tile.

Figure 4.32 The My Team Tile

4.7.1 Managing Tiles

Tiles are managed in OneAdmin in MANAGE V12 HOME PAGE under COMPANY SETTINGS, which is shown in Figure 4.33. Here, the default tiles, as well as which other tiles are available to users or not available at all, can be defined. Each tile can also be defined to be removable or non-removable by users, and the default size can be set. Certain tiles have additional settings that can be configured.

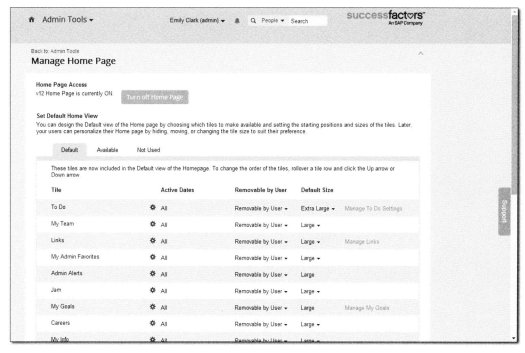

Figure 4.33 Manage Home Page Screen

4.7.2 Adding Custom Tiles

Custom tiles can be added to the system in the MANAGE HOME PAGE screen by clicking ADD CUSTOM TILE at the bottom of the list of tiles. The ADD CUSTOM TILE screen, as seen in Figure 4.34, enables a custom tile to be created for all or a specific group of employees with static or dynamic content in one or more languages. Tiles can also be set to display only over a certain date period.

The content editor allows a variety of different content types, including HTML code, Flash objects, images, and hyperlinks. Text can also be formatted in common methods, such as font face and size, color, alignment, bold, italic, underline, etc. This enables flexible types of content to be added to reflect a number of use cases and scenarios.

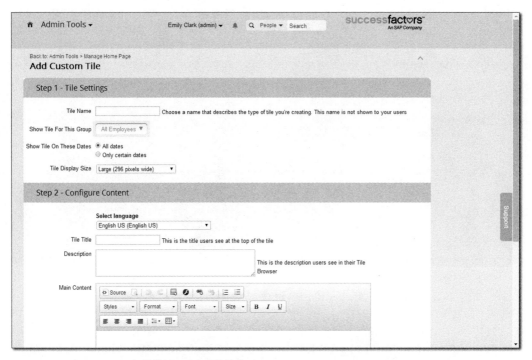

Figure 4.34 The Add Custom Tile Screen

4.8 Employee Profile

Employee Profile is the foundation for many of the talent applications in Success-Factors. With widespread user adoption, it is the housing area for employee history, accomplishments, and employment performance details. Employee Profile helps encourage employee engagement by providing employees with a place to connect with their colleagues and actively participate in their personal careers and development planning.

Employee Profile enables customers to create a continuously updated, easily searchable directory of employee skills, interests, and expertise. Employees can maintain their own data, find colleagues with relevant or similar skills and interests, and publicly recognize their peers. Managers can view workforce information to identify skill gaps in their organization and ensure that they are working with the right people and on the right things, aligning them with team and company objectives.

Employee Profile comprises numerous elements that work together to provide a complete picture of an employee's Talent Profile. These elements are used by many people in an organization to view data about an employee. Managers use the data stored on Employee Profile and Scorecard as data points into the Talent and Succession Planning process. Other employees can view the Public Profile to quickly get contact information for their colleagues. Tags help employees identify interests they want to associate themselves with find other employees with the same interests or skills.

Data in the Employee Profile is synced from three places: Employee Central if the customer is utilizing it for HR data, the Candidate Profile if SuccessFactors Recruiting is used and this integration is configured, or the source HRIS (SAP, PeopleSoft, etc.) via the UDF or web service–based integration. This includes data from fields such as Name, Job, Division, Department, and Manager.

4.8.1 Public Profile

The Public Profile was introduced as part of the SuccessFactors v12 release of Employee Profile. The Public Profile provides an attractive, usable view for employees to access data on colleagues. It provides all employees with a snapshot of anyone in the organization, along with that person's contact information, such as job title, department, phone number, and email address, as shown for Carla Grant in Figure 4.35. Colleagues can view details such as a brief description about the employee and the employee's interests, contact information, organization chart, local time, badges, and tags

An employee's Public Profile can be standard or expressive. Through the Expressive Public Profile, SuccessFactors provides employees the opportunity to visually express themselves to their colleagues by choosing a background photo. They can choose from images already provided by SuccessFactors or upload their own personal photo, depending on company guidelines. This provides a personalized feel that allows employees to stand out to their colleagues.

Figure 4.35 Expressive Public Profile

The Standard Profile, which is shown in Figure 4.36, contains the same elements as the expressive Profile but is displayed like the rest of Employee Profile. Many customers choose to maintain a uniform appearance to their Employee Profile and elect to have only the Standard Profile deployed.

Figure 4.36 Standard Profile

An editable profile allows employees the opportunity to provide a snapshot of themselves to colleagues. Features such as recording audio and video files to share personal and professional profile information make Public Profile interactive multimedia experience, as shown in Figure 4.37.

Figure 4.37 Editing Expressive Public Profile

Badges

SuccessFactors incorporates Web 2.0 functionality with badges, which are used to recognize colleagues' achievements and efforts. Badges allow employees and managers to recognize each other outside of the normal performance and compensation management processes, which are often private. Badges are meant to be awarded by others; employees cannot award badges to themselves.

Badges are selected from a static BADGES menu and displayed on the employee's PROFILE. As of February 2014, customers can now define custom badges that reflect their company values and branding. Administrative users can control the use of badges by enabling or disabling default badges and custom badges or localizing badge names in OneAdmin. Figure 4.38 provides an example of the Badge portlet displaying one of the default badges. Permissions for viewing badges have the same configuration and behavior as other data elements and are governed by the RBP model created in the instance and permissions defined in the Succession data model.

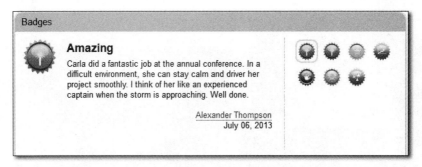

Figure 4.38 Badges Background Element

Permissions for adding or deleting badges have the same configuration and behavior as the edit permissions for any other data elements, except that you must be the creator or recipient of a badge to delete it—that is, employees cannot delete other employees' badges at will. Editing of existing badges isn't supported.

Badges are also displayed in the My Info tile on the v12 Home page (see Figure 4.39).

Figure 4.39 Badges Displayed in My Info Tile

Tags

Further expanding Web 2.0 functionality into the system, tags provide a way for users to self-identify group affiliation such as professional associations/organizations and community activity groups, both internally and externally; several examples are shown in Figure 4.40. You are able to see all employees who have selected certain tags and leverage the system to stay connected to those in the tag group. Unlike badges, users can add tags to their own profile to identify with groups or interests within the organization with which they want to be affiliated. Tags can also be assigned by other users.

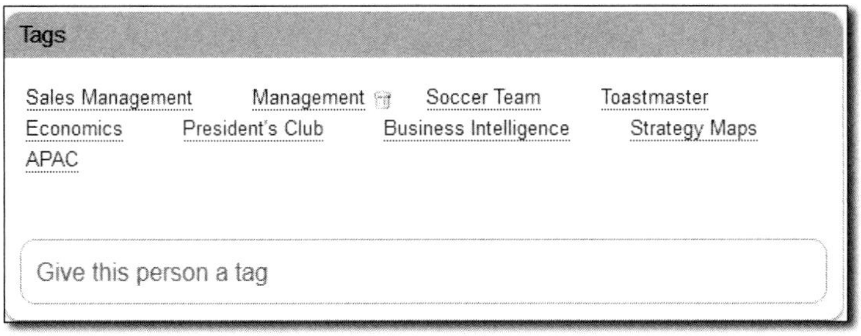

Figure 4.40 Tags

Because tags are displayed on the COMPANY INFO page when you are searching the Employee Directory (shown in Figure 4.41) and on the Public Profile, you can more easily find other employees who share the same tags, thereby increasing company cohesiveness and fostering a greater sense of community and collaboration.

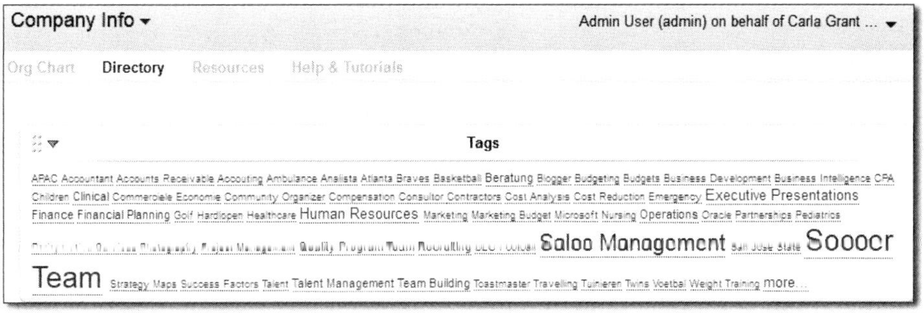

Figure 4.41 Tags in the Company Directory

4.8.2 Employee (Talent) Profile

The Employee or Talent Profile serves as an employee's online résumé by providing an area to add details about the employee's background, work history, job experience, and skills. SuccessFactors provides numerous standard background elements in the Succession data model that can be configured on the Employee

Profile to capture the information pertinent to each company. These portlets display system-generated information together with employee-generated data on the Talent Profile to provide a holistic view of an employee.

Employee Overview

The Talent Profile generally begins with an overview of the employee displayed in the OVERVIEW and EMPLOYEE INFORMATION background elements, as shown on the left in Figure 4.42. Here, information from the employee's data record in the SuccessFactors HCM suite can be displayed because it's pertinent to the talent process. These fields can be permissioned for viewing and editing based on role and in the Succession data model.

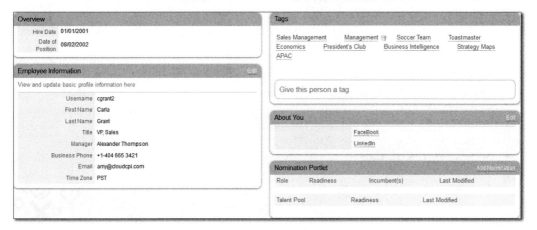

Figure 4.42 Employee Overview in the Talent Profile

Background Elements

The SuccessFactors data model comes with standard background elements that can be configured on the Profile via the OneAdmin feature in the instance. These background elements can be used as they come or modified to add or remove fields and make fields required or optional. We'll look at these background elements in the following sections.

Experience

An employee's experience is captured in numerous background elements that are designed to reflect the roles employees have held within the company, the type of functional experience they've had in those roles, any leadership experience they have had, and previous employment. This information can be captured in the following standard background elements, which are shown in Figure 4.43:

▶ DOCUMENTS

▶ WORK EXPERIENCE WITHIN COMPANY

▶ FUNCTIONAL EXPERIENCE

▶ LEADERSHIP EXPERIENCE

▶ PREVIOUS EMPLOYMENT

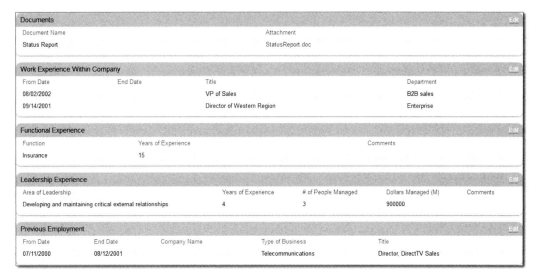

Figure 4.43 Work/Experience Background Elements

Education and Interests

An employee's educational background and specialty interests can be captured in standard background elements, as well. Along with gathering information on whether an employee is open to relocating, these background elements capture their career goals and interests to assist managers and HR in career planning for the employee.

Finally, this section also documents any special assignments, roles, or projects the employee has participated in that aren't directly tied to their role but are relevant to their experience and development. This information can be captured in the following standard background elements, which are shown in Figure 4.44:

▶ FORMAL EDUCATION

▶ CAREER GOALS/INTERESTS

▶ GEOGRAPHIC MOBILITY

▶ SPECIAL ASSIGNMENTS/PROJECTS

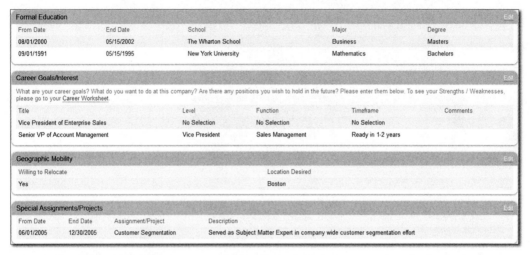

Figure 4.44 Education and Interests Background Elements

Other Employee Skills

Finally, companies are able to gather data around outside training and certifications that employees have obtained, as well as languages spoken. An employee's professional memberships, honors, and community involvement can also be documented in various background elements. This information can also be critical to the talent and development processes because it underscores the qualifications employees have for future positions and other roles within the company. This information can be documented in the following background elements, which are shown in Figure 4.45:

▶ COURSES/WORKSHOPS/SEMINARS

▶ CERTIFICATIONS/LICENSES

▶ LANGUAGE SKILLS

▶ PROFESSIONAL MEMBERSHIPS

▶ HONORS/AWARDS

▶ COMMUNITY/VOLUNTEER INVOLVEMENT

Figure 4.45 Other Employee Skills

4.8.3 Scorecard

The Scorecard is the section of the Employee Profile that is used as key data input to the Succession Planning process. The Scorecard is not visible to employees—only managers and other roles designated with permission can view the Scorecard. A series of standard portlets and background elements are intended to provide data specifically geared for evaluating employees for placement on the nine-box report and finding successors for key positions. We'll discuss Succession Planning in more detail in Chapter 12; this section is intended to cover those touch points between Succession Planning and Employee Profile.

The portlets and background elements that capture Succession-related data can reside anywhere. Many companies prefer to keep all data on one tab and combine the elements of the Employee Profile and Scorecard together, using permissions to govern who can see and do what. Other organizations prefer to keep these two separated, as they come out of the box. This is a configuration decision that is made during implementation.

Regardless of where the data resides, the important point to note here is that this type of information is typically considered highly confidential and isn't made available for viewing to a wide population. Again, this is a configuration decision that is made according to the company's process and data requirements, but the system allows a great amount of flexibility and a granular level of security through RBP and adding permissions to data and background elements in the Succession data model. Your implementation consultant will help guide you through considerations for making these critical configuration decisions.

Employee Overview

From a Scorecard perspective, several portlets can be configured to give a snapshot of the employee and provide an overview of the employee's Succession data, such as performance and potential rating and placement on the nine-box report. The OVERVIEW portlet shown in Figure 4.46 is generally visible only to the manager, upline managers, HR representatives, and the custom manager (if that role is utilized in Succession Planning).

Given the correct permissions, managers and HR personnel may be able to update an employee's placement on both the PERFORMANCE-POTENTIAL MATRIX (see Figure 4.47) and the How vs. What matrix reports directly from the OVERVIEW portlet. By selecting the UPDATE link, users can update the placement by selecting the correct box and entering effective date information. These matrices are discussed in detail in Chapter 12.

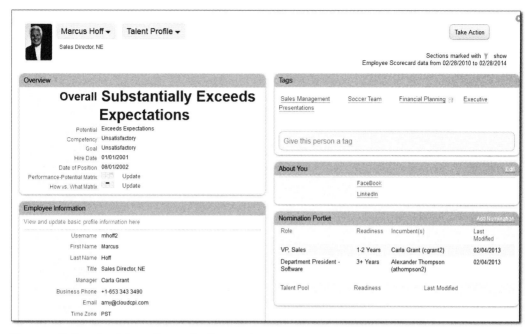

Figure 4.46 Overview Information on the Scorecard

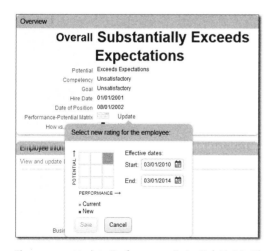

Figure 4.47 Update Performance-Potential Matrix Placement

Nomination Portlet

The standard background element Nomination Portlet displays an employee's existing Succession nominations and enables managers to add new nominations directly in the portlet, as shown in Figure 4.48. Nominations can also be made on the Succession Org Chart (as discussed in Chapter 12).

Figure 4.48 Nomination Portlet

Competency and Objective Portlets

Companies can choose to display standard background elements that display an employee's competencies, objectives, and related ratings. This information may be relevant and helpful during the talent review and Succession Planning process by providing ready access to how employees are developing and performing against their core and job-specific competencies. Easy access to the COMPETENCY and OBJECTIVE portlets prevents managers and talent planners from navigating away from the Talent Profile to the REPORTS tab or pulling up the employee's past performance reviews to get this data; these are shown in Figure 4.49.

Competency Portlet					Edit
Start Date	End Date	label		Source	Module
09/01/2011	12/31/2013	2.0-Meets Expectations		Calibration	Calibration
11/25/2013	11/25/2013	0.0-		Performance Review	Performance Manager
09/01/2013	10/31/2013	1.0-Exceeds Expectations		Calibration	Calibration
09/01/2013	10/31/2013	1.0-Exceeds Expectations		Calibration	Calibration
09/01/2013	10/31/2013	1.0-Exceeds Expectations		Calibration	Calibration
09/01/2011	10/31/2013	1.0-Does Not Meet		Calibration	Calibration
03/01/2013	03/01/2013	1-Does Not Meet		Scorecard	Scorecard
03/01/2013	03/01/2013	1-Does Not Meet		Scorecard	Scorecard

Objective Portlet					Edit
Start Date	End Date	label		Source	Module
09/01/2011	12/31/2013	1.0-Does Not Meet		Calibration	Calibration
11/25/2013	11/25/2013	0.0-		Performance Review	Performance Manager
09/01/2013	10/31/2013	1.0-Exceeds Expectations		Calibration	Calibration
09/01/2013	10/31/2013	1.0-Exceeds Expectations		Calibration	Calibration
09/01/2013	10/31/2013	1.0-Exceeds Expectations		Calibration	Calibration
09/01/2011	10/31/2013	1.0-Does Not Meet		Calibration	Calibration
03/01/2013	03/01/2013	1-Does Not Meet		Scorecard	Scorecard
03/01/2013	03/01/2013	2-Meets Expectations		Scorecard	Scorecard

Figure 4.49 Competency and Objective Portlets

Talent Information

The TALENT INFORMATION portlet, shown in Figure 4.50, captures data that can be used as flags and icons on the Succession Org Chart. Talent flags like the following are determined by each customer during implementation:

- ▶ RISK OF LOSS
- ▶ IMPACT OF LOSS
- ▶ REASON FOR LEAVING
- ▶ BENCH STRENGTH
- ▶ FUTURE LEADER
- ▶ KEY POSITION

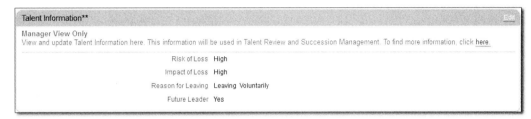

Figure 4.50 Talent Information Portlet

Performance and Potential

Two background elements are available to display historical information around performance and potential ratings (see Figure 4.51). The PERFORMANCE **MANAGER VIEW ONLY and POTENTIAL **MANAGER VIEW ONLY portlets are not available to employees. These are intended to store historical performance/potential ratings relevant to Succession Planning and are an input into the OVERALL rating in the OVERVIEW portlet on the Scorecard. These two portlets can be permissioned so that managers or custom managers can add both performance and potential scores directly in the background elements during the Succession Planning process.

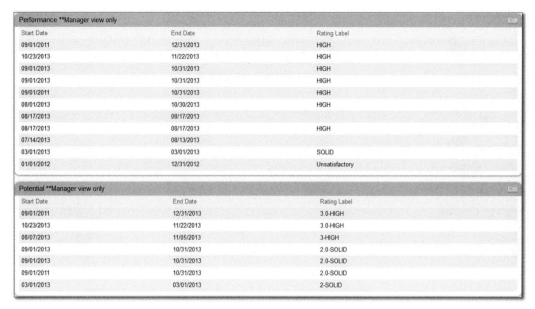

Figure 4.51 Performance and Potential **Manager View Only

4.8.4 Other Features

SuccessFactors has other features available on the Employee Profile to keep employees linked to social media and professional networking applications. The ABOUT YOU background element can link to an employee's Facebook and/or LinkedIn profiles (see Figure 4.52).

Figure 4.52 About You

Facebook

Facebook integration allows you to easily look up an employee in the *Facebook.com* application. You can click the FACEBOOK link to search for all users on *Facebook.com* with the same first and last name as the employee that you are looking for. If you sign up as a Facebook user and accept the *Facebook.com* cookie, you experience seamless integration between SuccessFactors and Facebook.

LinkedIn

LinkedIn integration allows you to easily look up an employee on the *LinkedIn.com* application. You can click on the LINKEDIN link to search for all users at *LinkedIn.com* with the same first and last name as the employee that you are looking for.

4.8.5 Configure Employee Files

The beauty of Employee Profile and all of its components is that it's highly configurable directly from the OneAdmin interface, putting the control in the hands of the customer. After the requisite data and background elements are configured in the Succession data model, the customer may add, remove, and reorder the elements on the Employee Profile and Scorecard, as well as copy and create new views, as required.

Any system administrator with the appropriate permission may choose to configure employee files directly from the OneAdmin page by clicking the CONFIGURE EMPLOYEE FILES option, shown in Figure 4.53. Any changes made to the employee files are effective immediately upon saving the dashboard, so it's critical that this administrative privilege not be widely dispersed and that care be taken to make changes that don't impact users during business hours.

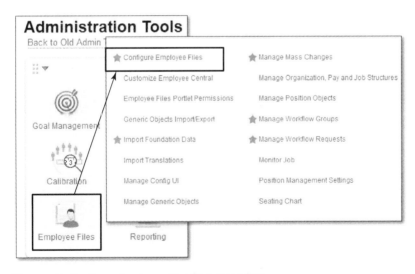

Figure 4.53 Configure Employee Files from OneAdmin

You can add, copy, or delete employee file layouts. Not all layouts may be deleted—there are some standard layouts that cannot be deleted—but they do not have to be displayed. This is controlled from the SHOW/HIDE column shown, in Figure 4.54.

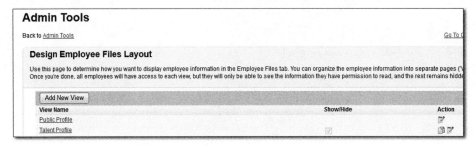

Figure 4.54 Design Employee Files Layout

Within each layout or dashboard, you can move layout elements around in a matter of mouse clicks. Use the up, down, left, and right arrows to place the elements where they should live. Use the red DELETE icon, shown in Figure 4.55, to remove the element from the layout. To edit each background element, select the edit icon under the ACTION column. Here, you can rename the portlet and make other changes, depending on the portlet you are working with.

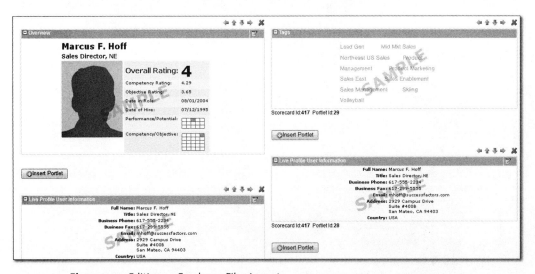

Figure 4.55 Editing an Employee Files Layout

4.9   Company Info

The *Company Info* application provides employees with the ability to access organizational information, such as the Org Chart, Directory, and general help and resources. We will cover each of these in the next few sections.

4.9.1   Org Chart

The Org Chart is a central component of the platform and a core component of succession planning. It enables users to have a visual view of the organization's reporting structure and shows a manager their direct and indirect reports. The Org Chart, which is shown in Figure 4.56, is accessed by selecting COMPANY INFO in the navigation menu. Some basic configuration can be performed in OneAdmin via ORG CHART CONFIGURATION under COMPANY SETTINGS.

Figure 4.56 The Org Chart

When accessing the Org Chart, the user always sees their own team. They can view the team of another employee by searching for that employee in the SEARCH ORG CHART box, which can be seen in the top-left of the ORG CHART screen in Figure 4.56. In the top-right of the ORG CHART screen, the user can zoom in or out of the Org Chart, access options to display direct or matrix reports, add a new employee (if they have the appropriate permissions), print the chart, and hide the top navigation panel of the screen.

By clicking the box of an employee, users can access that employee's quickcard. We covered the quickcard in Section 4.6.4. If an employee has direct reports, a small section at the bottom of the box displays the number of direct and indirect reports. Clicking this expands the Org Chart to show the direct reports of that employee. Employees who have a matrix relationship show under their matrix manager with a dotted line. In Figure 4.56, you can see a dotted line for Thomas Clark.

The Position Org Chart—shown in Figure 4.57—can be accessed by clicking POSITION ORG CHART. This shows the position reporting relationships that are stored in SuccessFactors.

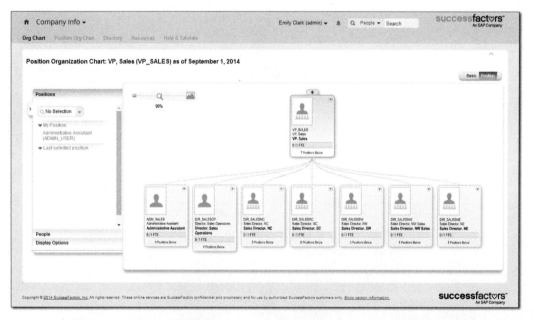

Figure 4.57 Position Org Chart

From the Position Org Chart, it is possible to perform a number of actions, including viewing the incumbent history of a position, adding other positions, or—if enabled—launching requisitions in SuccessFactors Recruiting. A print or export of the Position Org Chart can also be made.

4.9.2 Directory

The Directory is where employees can search for other employees. There are a variety of different options available to search with:

▶ TAGS: Allows employees to be searched by any tags assigned to them (see Section 4.7.1 for more information on tags)

▶ FACES: Allows users to find others by browsing through employee photos

▶ DIRECTORY SEARCH: Provides a free text search to find employees

▶ SKILL SEARCH: A search by skills to find employees

Figure 4.58 shows the DIRECTORY screen.

Figure 4.58 The Directory

4.9.3 Company Resources

Company Resources is where an organization can provide information and resources to its employees about the system and topics such as HR processes, guides, reference documents, and videos. An example of these can be seen in Figure 4.59. The COMPANY RESOURCES page also features the DIRECTORY SEARCH that is found on the DIRECTORY page. The COMPANY RESOURCES page is a configurable page and has the same editing options as when adding custom tiles, which we covered in Section 4.7.2. The Company Resources can be added in each of the languages enabled in the system.

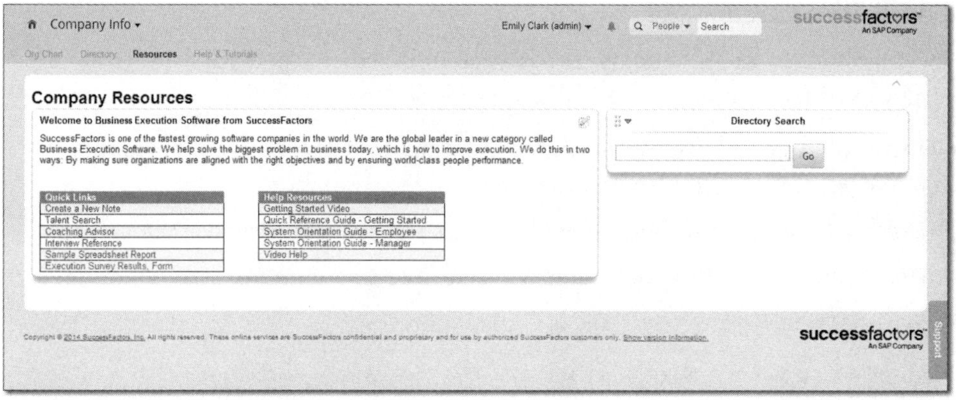

Figure 4.59 Company Resources Page

4.9.4 Help & Tutorials

The HELP & TUTORIALS page provides a selection of standard tutorials for various parts of the SuccessFactors sysatem. It also features a customizable panel to add some company-specific information. Figure 4.60 shows the HELP & TUTORIALS page. The page can be disabled if it is not required. This is done by selecting the DISABLE IT NOW button.

Figure 4.60 Help & Tutorials Page

4.10   Talent Card

The *Talent Card* is an overview of an employee's talent information from the Profile and Employee Profile, such as organizational information, badges, and work experience. It is highly configurable and is used within the Presentations application (which we'll cover in Section 4.11) and the Position Tile view in the Succession Org Chart. Only one Talent Card can exist per application. Figure 4.61 shows an example of a TALENT CARD.

Figure 4.61 A Talent Card

Talent Cards are configured in OneAdmin, in the MANAGE TALENT CARDS option under EMPLOYEE FILES. Here, a blank Talent Card is provided with an overview prefilled. The overview is standard, but each field can be disabled, and the department field can be overridden with any piece of data from the UDF.

The main body of the Talent Card can be configured to include the following information:

- Internal work experience
- Previous work experience
- Education
- Performance & Potential Matrix
- Competency & Objective Matrix
- Badges
- Custom section

Five fields can be added to each section, and the available fields depend on what has been configured for the Employee Profile already.

4.11 Presentations

Presentations is an application designed for quickly producing interactive talent review presentations that can be used in a variety of meetings. Typically, a significant amount of time is spent creating meeting presentations and compiling data and visuals for them. With Presentations, this can be done in an hour or so by uploading a Microsoft PowerPoint template to SuccessFactors and adding a variety of different types of dynamic content that is both interactive and displayed in real time. Because the dynamic content and data comes directly from the system, it is already prepared and ready to be used in a meeting.

Presentations can be used to support a number of use cases, particularly talent review meetings. However, they can also be used for compensation reviews, succession planning, and recruiting talent pool reviews.

4.11.1 Presentations Overview

You access the Presentations application by selecting PRESENTATIONS in the NAVIGATION menu. This takes you the PRESENTATIONS screen that is shown in Figure 4.62.

Here, any existing presentations are displayed, as well as any that have been shared with the user. Each of these presentations can be run, edited, or deleted as required. A new presentation can be created by clicking the + button on the right side of the screen. This opens a pop-up window for naming our new presentation, which appears on the TALENT REVIEW MEETING screen that is shown in Figure 4.63.

Figure 4.62 The Presentations Application

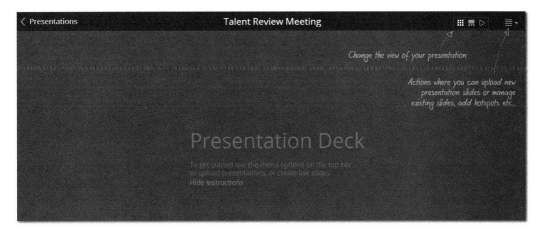

Figure 4.63 Talent Review Meeting Screen

The MENU button in the top-right corner of the screen is used to upload Microsoft PowerPoint slides, add a Live Slide of dynamic content, edit details of the presentation, or delete the presentation. Figure 4.64 shows the menu.

Figure 4.64 The Options Menu

4.11.2 Dynamic Content

Different types of dynamic content can be added to a presentation by selecting the option ADD A LIVE SLIDE, as shown in Figure 4.64. These options—which can be seen later in Figure 4.67—are:

▸ PERFORMANCE-POTENTIAL MATRIX: Adds a Performance-Potential Matrix slide for a definable team and date period

▸ HOW VS. WHAT MATRIX: Adds a How vs. What Matrix slide for a definable team and date period

▸ SUCCESSION ORG CHART: Adds a Succession Org Chart showing a manager's direct reports, matrix reports, and their successors

▸ TEAM VIEW: Adds a view of a manager's direct and matrix reports

▸ TALENT POOL: Adds a list of one or more MDF-based Talent Pools

▸ PEOPLE GRID: Adds a grid of grouped employees

▸ COMPENSATION REVIEW: Adds a Compensation executive review template

Each type of content reads data from SuccessFactors in real time and can be inserted anywhere within the PowerPoint presentation that is uploaded to the system. Now that we've taken a look at the application and dynamic content, let's create a presentation to see how this might look.

4.11.3 Creating a Presentation

To create a presentation, we first need to upload a Microsoft PowerPoint presentation. This is done by selecting UPLOAD POWERPOINT SLIDES in the top-right menu—as seen in Figure 4.64—and uploading the file in the pop-up window. Once this is done, we see our presentation in the SLIDE HOLDING AREA at the bottom of the TALENT REVIEW MEETING screen, which you can see in Figure 4.65.

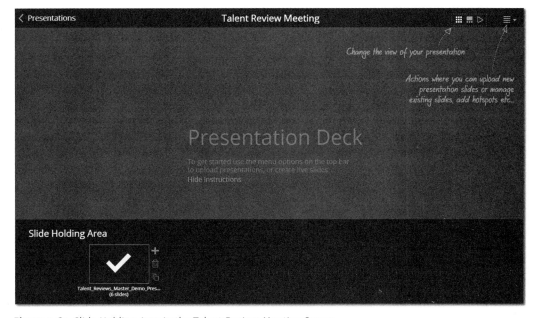

Figure 4.65 Slide Holding Area in the Talent Review Meeting Screen

Selecting the EXPAND button (the bottom of the three buttons on the right side of the presentation in the SLIDE HOLDING AREA) shows a preview of all of the slides in a film strip–style view. Figure 4.66 shows the slides preview. This becomes useful when we begin to build the presentation later.

Now, we're going to add a Live Slide to the presentation. We do this by selecting the option ADD A LIVE SLIDE. This shows us the different dynamic content options, which you can see in Figure 4.67.

We'll select PERFORMANCE-POTENTIAL MATRIX for our presentation. This gives us a further set of options for this Live Slide. We want to focus this presentation on Carla Grant's team, so we enter her name in the TEAM VIEW STARTING FROM box and enter a date range for the review. Because we want to look at the previous period, we select 1st January 2014 to 31st December 2014. You can see this in Figure 4.68.

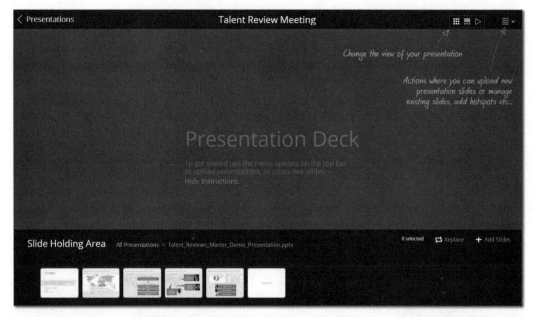

Figure 4.66 Presentation Slides Preview in Slide Holding Area

Figure 4.67 Dynamic Content Options for a Live Slide

Figure 4.68 Options for the Performance-Potential Matrix Live Slide

After we enter these details, we click the ADD LIVE SLIDE button. We now see our new Live Slide in the top of the screen, as seen in Figure 4.69.

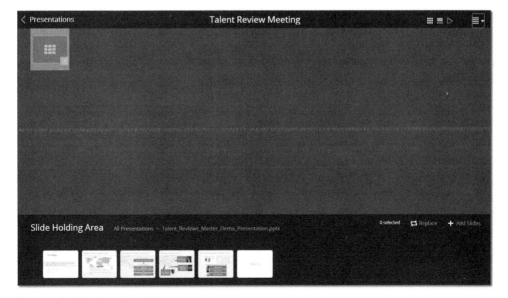

Figure 4.69 The New Live Slide

We can preview our Live Slide by clicking the LIVE SLIDE menu button (the blue button seen on the Live Slide in Figure 4.69) and selecting VIEW SLIDE. In this menu—shown in Figure 4.70—we can also access options to edit the Live Slide, remove it, add further Live Slides, or upload an additional PowerPoint presentation.

Figure 4.70 The Live Slide Menu

When we select VIEW SLIDE, a preview of the Live Slide is shown, which is similar to the screen seen in Figure 4.71.

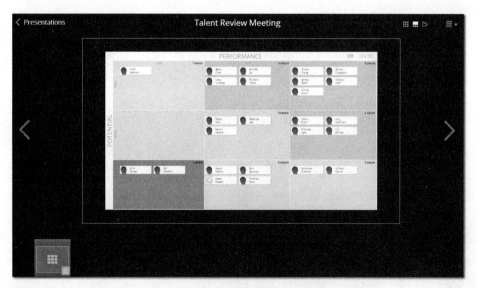

Figure 4.71 Preview of the Performance-Potential Matrix Live Slide

Once we return to the Talent Review Meeting screen, we can now compile our presentation using the PowerPoint presentation that we uploaded earlier and our new Live Slide. To do this, we simple drag each of the PowerPoint slides from the Slide Holding Area into the main area where our Live Slide is. Once this is done, the result should look similar to Figure 4.72.

Figure 4.72 The Compiled Presentation

We can now preview each of these slides by selecting the View Slide Timeline button in the top-right of the screen (the middle of the three buttons located to the left of the options menu). Our preview can be seen in Figure 4.73.

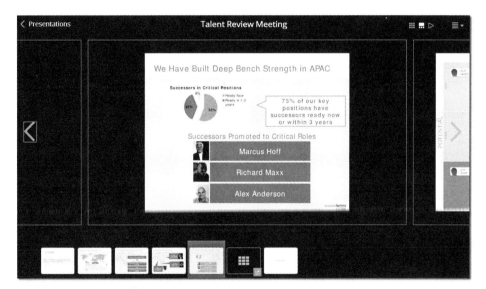

Figure 4.73 A Preview of the Presentation

A feature for static slides (i.e., those slides from an uploaded PowerPoint presentation) is the ability to add *Hotspots*. Hotspots allow part of a static slide to be linked to dynamic content, such as a Talent Card or an external link. These Hotspots can then be selected during the actual presentation.

Now, if we return to the main PRESENTATIONS screen, we can see our presentation, along with a preview of the slides that we added. We can see this in Figure 4.74.

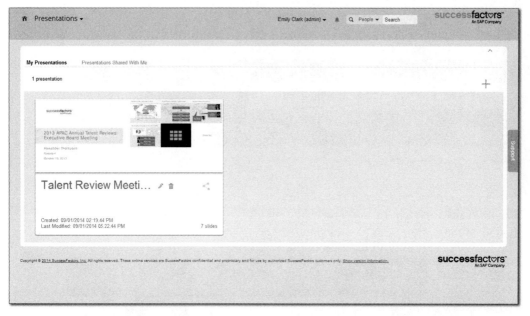

Figure 4.74 Our Presentation in the Presentations Application Screen

Created presentations can be shared with colleagues by using the SHARE button on the right side of the presentation. Once presentations are shared, the share icon is yellow, and the number of users that the presentation is shared with displays next to the SHARE icon. Now, let's take a look at conducting our presentation.

4.11.4 Running a Presentation

Presentations are conducted by selecting the presentation on the PRESENTATIONS screen that we showed in Figure 4.74 and then selecting the START PRESENTATION MODE button in the top-right of the screen (the rightmost of the three buttons located to the left of the OPTIONS menu). Now, our presentation can be begin, as we see in Figure 4.75.

During our presentation, it is possible to view the Talent Card for employees in a Live Slide by simply clicking them. Talent Cards can also be opened for side-by-side comparison. Figure 4.76 shows an example of this.

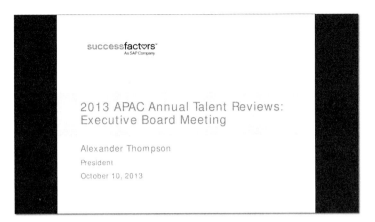

Figure 4.75 Our Presentation in Action

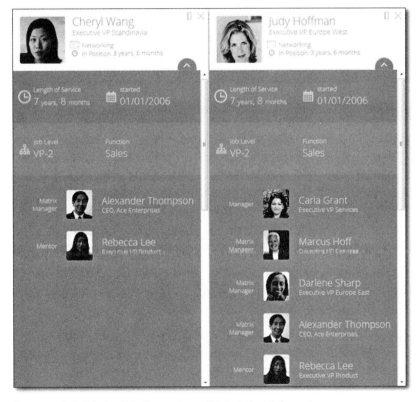

Figure 4.76 A Side-by-Side Comparison of Talent Card Information

4.12   Skills and Competencies

SuccessFactors features an extensive *Competency Library* that can be used across the talent applications. It delivers a wide range of competencies that each contain a variety of other content to Performance & Goals, Succession & Development, and Recruiting Execution. The Competency Library includes four types of content:

▸ **Competencies**
Behavioral categories that influence job performance, such as "building relationships," "managing stress," or "planning and organizing"

▸ **Skills**
Knowledge and experience required for jobs such as "C++ programming," "employment law," or "post-merger integration"

▸ **Behaviors**
Traits that describe how a competency is performed or achieved

▸ **Teasers**
Content for Writing Assistant/Coaching Advisor (WACA) that can be used to input comments onto a performance appraisal form

The standard SuccessFactors system comes with more than 80 competencies. Competency Libraries are managed in OneAdmin in MANAGE COMPETENCIES under COMPANY SETTINGS, which is seen in Figure 4.77.

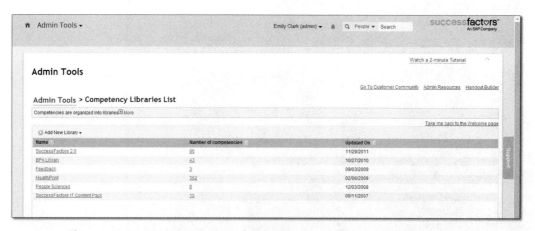

Figure 4.77 Managing Competency Libraries

Here, the Competencies in each Competency Library can be viewed, and new competencies can be added to existing Competency Libraries. Figure 4.78 shows the CREATE NEW COMPETENCY screen.

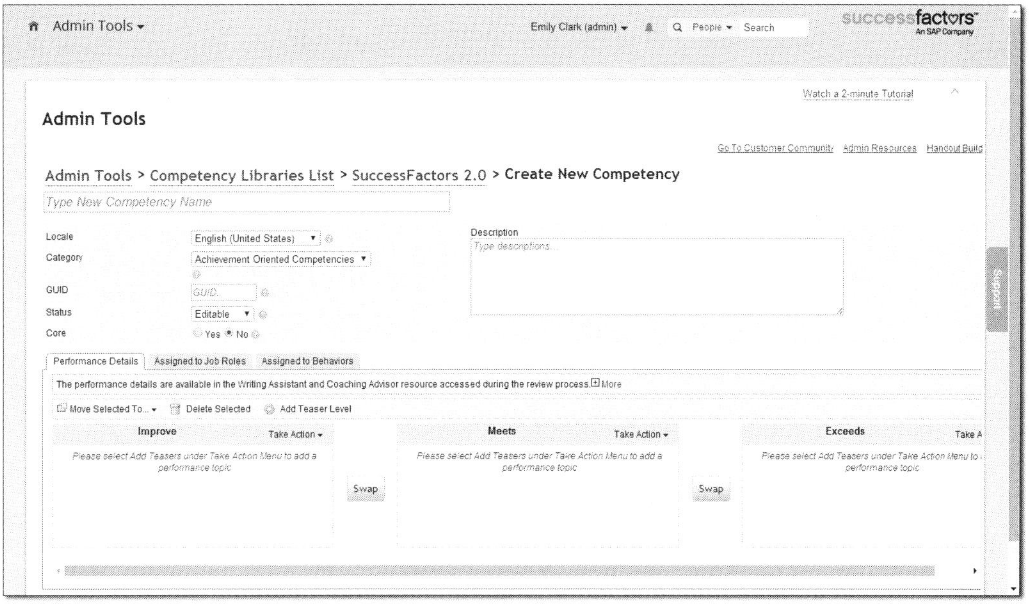

Figure 4.78 Create New Competency Screen

Competency Libraries and Competencies can also be imported into the system using the ADD NEW LIBRARY button—which can be seen in Figure 4.77—and then selecting IMPORT FROM FILE… from the list of available options.

> **Important Note**
>
> Recently, MDF-based Competencies have been released. This functionality is based on the MDF and is used with Job Profiles, which we will cover in the next section. It is not compatible with the Competency Library functionality discussed in this section.

4.13 Job Profile Builder

SuccessFactors provides a framework for managing Job Profiles for using talent applications such as Performance & Goals, Succession & Development, and Recruiting

Execution. These Job Profiles allow the assignment of Job Families and Job Roles, which in turn are linked to Job Codes and competencies, as well as providing job descriptions and other related job content. Essentially, Job Profiles help organizations have the right person in the right job at the right time.

Job Families are used to define job categories, such as Sales or Engineering, and contain a number of *Job Roles*. Each Job Role can have one or more associated Job Codes, which are used to map role-specific competencies to users for use in Performance Management, Succession, and Development.

Job Profiles are managed in the *Job Profile Builder* application. Previously, the *Job Families & Roles* functionality could be used to set up and manage this functionality on a more basic level. This functionality is still available and widely used by many customers, but has since been superseded by Job Profile Builder.

> **Important Note**
>
> When Job Profile Builder is enabled, the Competency Library functionality is automatically disabled. Using Job Profile Builder also means leveraging the MDF-based competencies across the organization.

As part of the Job Profile Builder, more than 13,000 industry-verified skills in more than 250 pre-defined Job Families are provided. Each Job Family comes with 4-7 Job Roles with Skills pre-mapped, each with five levels of proficiency. This is a significant amount of content and enables the use of Skills to be almost instantaneous once the Job Profile Builder is used.

4.13.1 Job Profile Builder Overview

Job Profile Builder enables administrators to build content repositories for the various types of content required for a Job Profile, as well as Job Profile Templates that are used to provide robust formats from which to create the Job Profiles. The following content can be created and managed in Job Profile Builder and used to build Job Profile Templates:

- ▸ Families and Roles
- ▸ Certifications
- ▸ Competencies
- ▸ Employment Conditions

- Education (Degree and Major)
- Interview Questions
- Job Responsibilities
- Physical Requirements
- Relevant Industries
- Skills

In addition, a SKILL PROFILE portlet is provided for the Employee Profile so that employees and managers can maintain an employee's skills profile. This is shown in Figure 4.79.

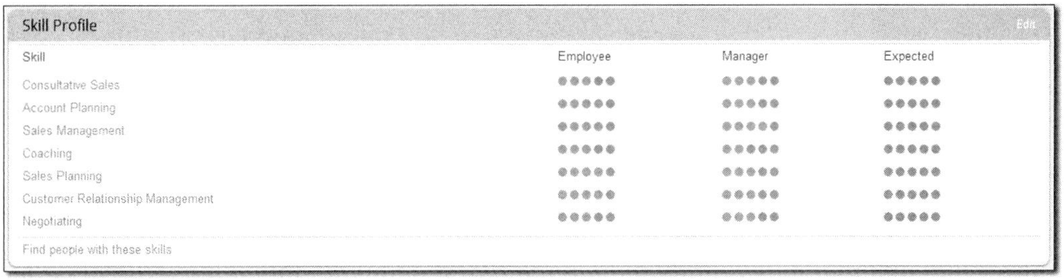

Skill Profile				Edit
Skill		Employee	Manager	Expected
Consultative Sales		●●●●●	●●●●●	●●●●●
Account Planning		●●●●●	●●●●●	●●●●●
Sales Management		●●●●●	●●●●●	●●●●●
Coaching		●●●●●	●●●●●	●●●●●
Sales Planning		●●●●●	●●●●●	●●●●●
Customer Relationship Management		●●●●●	●●●●●	●●●●●
Negotiating		●●●●●	●●●●●	●●●●●
Find people with these skills				

Figure 4.79 Skill Profile Portlet on Employee Profile

4.13.2 Managing Job Profile Content

Job Profile content can be created in SuccessFactors or imported into the system, both in OneAdmin under COMPANY SETTINGS. Job Profile content is created in MANAGE JOB PROFILE CONTENT, and data is imported or exported in MANAGE JOB PROFILE CONTENTS IMPORT/EXPORT. The date import/export uses the same engine as importing and exporting MDF data and covers all types of Job Profile content.

Figure 4.80 shows the different content options that can be created in MANAGE JOB PROFILE CONTENT.

We'll take a look at the option SET UP FAMILIES AND ROLES. This lists all of the Job Families in the system and enables new Job Families to be created using the CREATE FAMILY button or imported from the SuccessFactors SuccessStore using the ADD FAMILIES FROM SUCCESSSTORE button. You can see this in Figure 4.81.

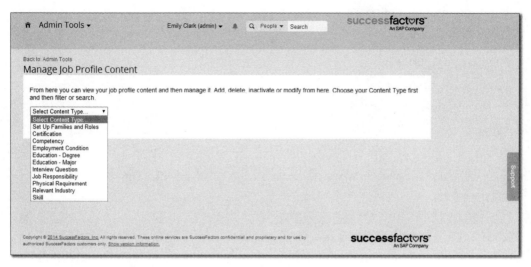

Figure 4.80 Manage Job Profile Content Screen

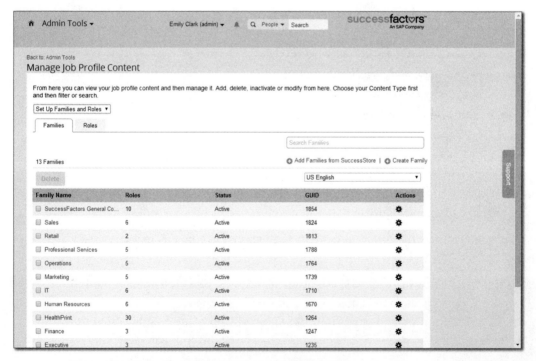

Figure 4.81 Job Families within Manage Job Profile Content

The two tabs at the top of the screen enable the user to switch between the FAMILIES (the default option) and the ROLES. Switching to the ROLES provides a list of all of the roles in the system, similar to the list of families. Roles can be created or imported from the SuccessStore in a similar fashion as the families can.

By clicking a FAMILY or ROLE, the user can see more details about each object. Selecting a FAMILY shows all of the Roles associated with it. Similarly, SKILLS and COMPETENCIES assigned directly to the Family can also be viewed by switching between the tabs.

Selecting a Role within a Family or within the ROLES tab displays details about that Role. Here, the user can view the FAMILY that the ROLE is assigned to, as well as the mapped JOB CODES, SKILLS, COMPETENCIES, and TALENT POOLS. Additional mappings can also be made here. Skills can be assigned with a proficiency level, while Competencies can be mapped with a WEIGHT and RATING, as you can see in Figure 4.82.

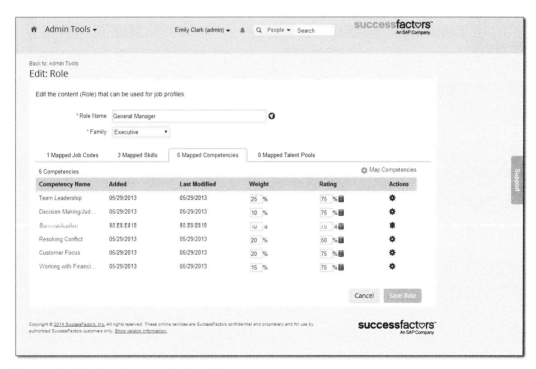

Figure 4.82 Mapping Competencies to a Role

Now that we've taken a brief look at Families and Roles, let's take a look at creating some Job Responsibility content.

On the MANAGE JOB CONTENT screen that we saw in Figure 4.80, we select JOB RESPONSIBILITY from the dropdown menu. We then see all of the JOB RESPONSIBILITY content listed, as well as options to filter the list and create new JOB RESPONSIBILITY content. Figure 4.83 shows this screen.

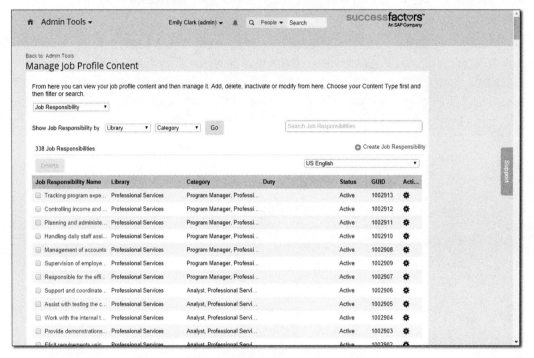

Figure 4.83 Job Responsibility Content

JOB RESPONSIBILITY content is organized into *libraries* and categorized with a *category*. A *duty* can also be assigned. If we select a JOB RESPONSIBILITY, we can see and edit the details of it, as you can see in Figure 4.84.

Figure 4.84 Editing a Job Responsibility

Now that we've looked at creating some Job Profile content, we can take a look at creating Job Profile Templates.

4.13.3 Creating Job Profiles Templates

Job Profile Templates define the structure and layout of the Job Profiles. They do not contain data on the Job Profile; rather, they have content types, specify the order of the sections, and define what sections are required and the formatting of Job Profiles, among other things. Companies may have one Job Profile Template that is used for all Job Profiles, or they may create multiple Job Profile Templates.

Job Profile Templates are created and managed in OneAdmin, in MANAGE JOB PROFILE TEMPLATES under COMPANY SETTINGS. Here, you can manage existing templates or create new ones from a default template. Figure 4.85 shows some Job Profile Templates in SuccessFactors.

We'll now go through the process of creating a Job Profile Template. Job Profile Templates are created in a two-step process by clicking CREATE TEMPLATE on the Job Profile Templates screen, which you can see in Figure 4.85. The first step is to define the name of the Job Profile Templates and the Job Families to associate with it. We call our Job Profile Template "Manager Job Profile." The second step is where the template itself is designed.

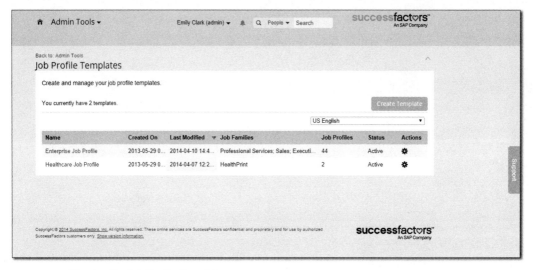

Figure 4.85 Job Profile Templates

Fourteen different types of sections can be added to the Job Profile Template using the ADD SECTION button. These fourteen types include all of the Job Profile content plus SHORT DESCRIPTION, LONG DESCRIPTION, HEADER, and FOOTER. Sections can be added and deleted easily, reordered via drag and drop, individually formatted, set as required, set to show in a Job Requisition, and, if required, set to be viewable only by administrators.

We will add some sections to the standard default template design, including CONDITIONS OF EMPLOYMENT and JOB RESPONSIBILITIES. We will also rename the SHORT DESCRIPTION section to DESCRIPTION. Our Job Profile Template with these sections can be seen in Figure 4.86.

Once we're done with designing our Job Profile Template, we click the I'M DONE button to save the Job Profile Template and make it available to use to create Job Profiles. We'll now look at the process of creating a Job Profile.

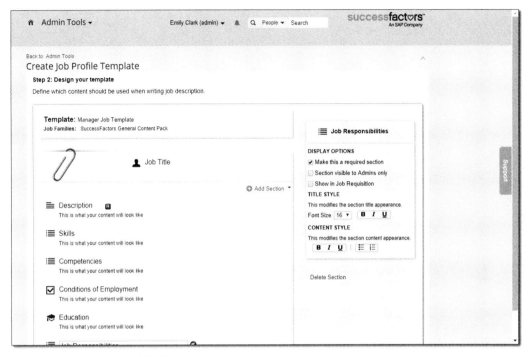

Figure 4.86 Designing a Job Profile Template

4.13.4 Creating Job Profiles

Once Job Profile Templates have been defined, you are ready to create the Job Profiles in OneAdmin, in MANAGE JOB PROFILES under COMPANY SETTINGS. The first thing you'll see are all the existing Job Profiles within the system, similar to Figure 4.87.

Job Profiles can be searched and filtered, and clicking any Job Profile displays that Job Profile. Job Profiles also subject to an approval workflow can be viewed in the IN-WORKFLOW JOB PROFILE tab. We'll now create a Job Profile by using the CREATE JOB PROFILE button.

The first step of creating a Job Profile is to select the Job FAMILY and ROLE for which you want to create a Job Profile. Once these have been selected, click the NEXT button, and then the Job Profile Template associated with the Job Family and Role is displayed. Figure 4.88 shows the JOB PROFILE for the Job Profile Template we just created.

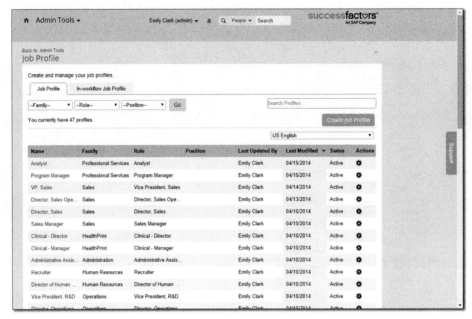

Figure 4.87 Job Profiles

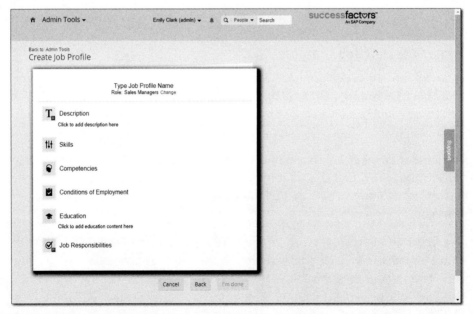

Figure 4.88 Creating a Job Profile Based on a Job Profile Template

Job Profile content can be added either as free-form text or by selecting from the content libraries. In Figure 4.89, we are adding some Competencies to the Job Profile.

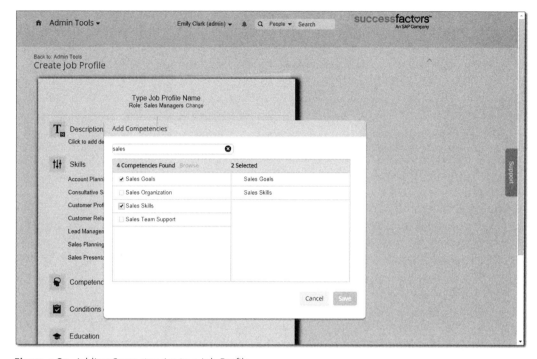

Figure 4.89 Adding Competencies to a Job Profile

Once we have added the appropriate content, our Job Profile is complete. Figure 4.90 shows our completed Job Profile.

To save our completed Job Profile, we click the I'M DONE button at the bottom of the screen. All Job Profiles are saved as drafts until they are made active, which is done by selecting the checkbox of the Job Profile in the main JOB PROFILE screen (see Figure 4.87) and clicking ACTIVATE in the actions menu. Draft Job Profiles are not visible to end users.

Job Profiles can also be created and edited via workflow, if this is enabled. Workflow enables a collaborative process of creating Job Profiles among several team members. If workflow is enabled, it is still possible to create Job Profiles in OneAdmin. However, if a Job Profile is then edited, it goes through workflow, even though it was initially created without workflow. When a Job Profile is created or edited in workflow, once approved, it immediately impacts all users in that role, regardless of whether the final approver is the manager or HR Business Partner of all the users. For this reason, it is important to think through who has access to create or edit Job Profiles.

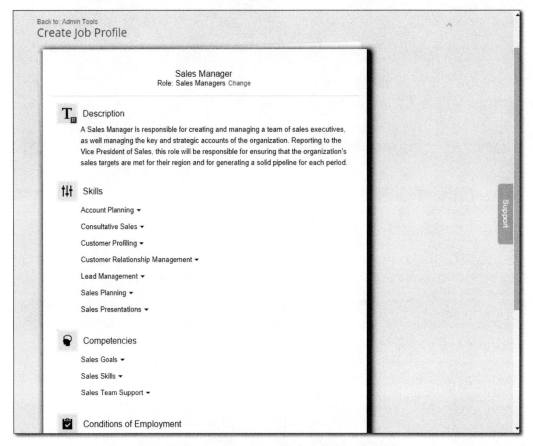

Figure 4.90 A Completed Job Profile

4.14 Picklists

Picklists are the dropdown lists of input values a user must choose from when entering data. They are used throughout SuccessFactors and are defined in a central location. Picklists are very similar to the F4 Help selection menus found in the SAP system. Picklists are managed in OneAdmin, in PICKLISTS MANAGEMENT under COMPANY SETTINGS. We will cover this in more detail in Chapter 5.

Important Note

MDF Picklists differ from standard Picklists, in that they are used only with Generic Objects and are configured in a different part of the application. We will cover MDF Picklists in Section 4.16.5.

4.15 Upgrade Center

The Upgrade Center allows customers to apply certain enhanced features and functionality to their instances without having to log a Customer Support ticket or engaging an implementation partner. Not all enhancements are available via the Upgrade Center, but many are. The Upgrade Center categorizes upgrades as follows:

▸ IMPORTANT UPGRADES

▸ RECOMMENDED UPGRADES

▸ OPTIONAL UPGRADES

Each upgrade has a detailed description of the upgraded feature, what to expect once the upgrade is applied, and other supporting information, as applicable. The Upgrade Center is accessed via a portlet in OneAdmin, located in the top-right corner. Figure 4.91 shows the UPGRADE CENTER portlet.

Figure 4.91 Upgrade Center Portlet in OneAdmin

Within the Upgrade Center, the screen is split into three columns that represent each of the categories that we mentioned. The available updates for each category are displayed in each column, and they can be filtered by application. Figure 4.92 shows the Upgrade Center with several updates available to install.

Details of any update can be viewed by selecting the LEARN MORE & UPGRADE NOW link found under the name of the update. For future-dated or upcoming changes, the link is called LEARN MORE.

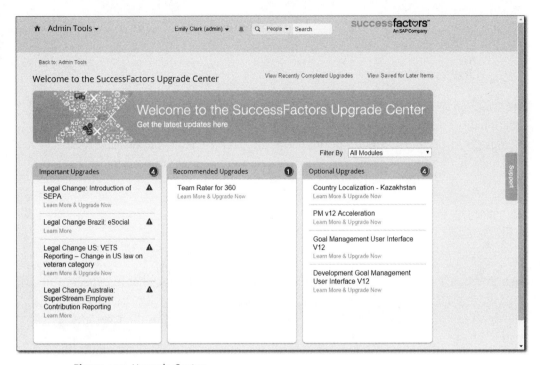

Figure 4.92 Upgrade Center

Here, a description of the update is provided, along with important notes and any RBP requirements needed to run the upgrade. Figure 4.93 shows an update in the Upgrade Center.

To apply an update, select the UPGRADE NOW button at the bottom of the screen. You are then prompted to confirm that you want the update to be made. Once it is confirmed, the update is applied to the system. This needs to be done separately in the Test and Production systems.

This concludes our look at some of the cross-application functionality that is available in SuccessFactors. Let's now take a look at the powerful extensibility framework in SuccessFactors, the Metadata Framework.

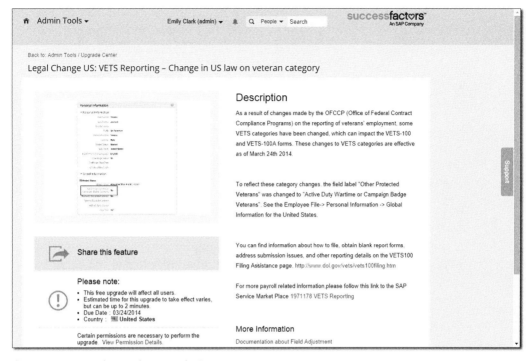

Figure 4.93 An Update in the Upgrade Center

4.16 Metadata Framework

The Metadata Framework (MDF) is a framework for creating, modifying, and maintaining objects, screens, and business rules within the SuccessFactors system. It is a powerful, flexible, and safe mechanism for customers and consultants to extend the SuccessFactors system and introduce custom objects and screens In an easy-to-use interface that is both stable and unaffected by upgrades and quarterly releases. It reduces a large proportion of the technical aspects required to create new objects in the system and puts control in the hands of business users and system administrators. The possibility to extend the SuccessFactors system is no longer reliant on technical consultants or deep knowledge of complex structures or procedures; now, customers can benefit from a flexible system that be changed at will to meet the ever-changing demands of the business.

The MDF consists of a framework that uses metadata to allow easy creation and maintenance of objects using a generic set of components that are reused by all objects. As a result, nothing related to new objects or the enhancement of existing objects is hard-coded within the SuccessFactors system, and no programming or coding is required—even for objects introduced by SuccessFactors. In fact, it is easier for SuccessFactors to introduce new objects and functionality into the system. Functionality such as Time Off, Job Profile Builder, and Position Management are built on MDF.

The specialized nature and design of the MDF means that you can create multiple objects while retaining a high level of performance within the system. For individuals from a solely SAP-based background, the concept of the MDF may seem new and unfamiliar.

The objects created in the MDF are called *Generic Objects*; they can be new objects, new screens for existing objects, new rules, or new fields—for example, a job classification or a work center. A screen and a set of rules could also be configured through the MDF—for example, to support administration of the company car plan. Generic Objects are easily configurable through the OneAdmin interface without programming or editing XML files. However, some applications within the SuccessFactors HCM suite do not yet leverage the MDF, although SuccessFactors aims to finish rolling this out across the entire SuccessFactors HCM suite in the future.

For customers or consultants who are used to creating new objects and infotypes in SAP, the MDF may seem simplistic or alien. However, simplicity offers some advantages:

▶ Reliance on technical or external assistance to add new objects or fields is no longer required.

▶ Stability and upgradability are maintained because standard objects and components are not changed.

▶ There is a consistency across objects, such as the look and feel of the UI, searching, and auditing.

▶ A minimal level of training is required to use the MDF because it has an easy-to-use GUI, and it isn't necessary to understand the technical aspects.

▶ The performance of Generic Objects is superior to the performance of standard SuccessFactors objects.

▶ The standard UIs delivered by SuccessFactors are fully compatible with the MDF and can leverage Generic Objects.

More details about the Metadata Framework can be found in the *Metadata Framework (MDF) Implementation Guide* at *http://service.sap.com/sfsf* under *Platform*.

4.16.1 Technical Aspects

Each object within the SuccessFactors is made up of a number of components, including an API, Controller, UI, Workflow implementation, Database table, set of Java Services, and reporting integration. Each of these objects has its own instances of these components. Within the MDF, only one instance of each of the components exists; this single instance of each object is used for *all* Generic Objects. Through the definition and structure of the metadata, these generic components can operate without error no matter how the objects are created and what metadata is used.

Because the components required for Generic Objects already exist, only their behavior needs to be configured. For example, the name of the fields, the field data type, and the rules used for validation must be configured. However, you don't need to take the UI, object controller, and database tables into consideration when configuring the object. This means that the overall complexity of creating new or extending existing objects in SuccessFactors is reduced significantly through this framework.

The objects created in the MDF are also automatically exposed via the OData APIs, so they can be integrated with other systems, such as SAP ERP HCM. As a result, data can be transferred to or from Generic Objects. Import templates for new objects are automatically generated.

4.16.2 Generic Object Definitions

Generic Object definitions are created in OneAdmin, in CONFIGURE OBJECT DEFINITIONS under COMPANY SETTINGS by selecting OBJECT DEFINITION in the CREATE NEW dropdown.

Generic Objects definitions have a number of fixed attributes that must be defined during creation; some are mandatory, and others are optional. In addition to these attributes, up to 200 custom fields can be configured for each Generic Object. A number of attributes are required for each Generic Object, including the object code and whether it is effective-dated. Optional attributes include label, workflow configuration, whether data should be displayed before or after a workflow has been approved, the To-Do category to use for workflow, whether the Generic Object is visible to the API, and additional fields. Labels can be maintained in multiple languages for systems that have more than one language enabled. These can be seen in Figure 4.94.

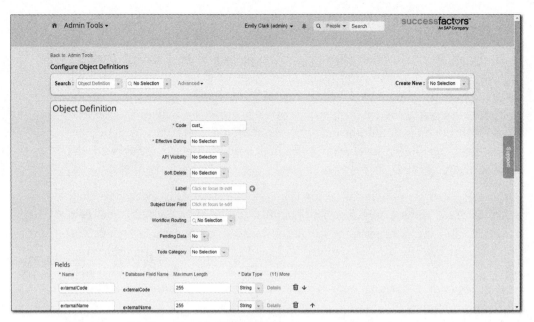

Figure 4.94 Creating a Generic Object Definition

Standard fields exist for a Generic Object, including the code and name. If the object is effective-dated, a START DATE field is added to the definition. A number of fields are automatically assigned by the system once a Generic Object is saved.

Like standard objects and Foundation Objects, Generic Objects can have associations assigned to them. Associations designate a relationship with another object and define attributes of these relationships. Associations have the following attributes:

- **Name**
  - Name of association
- **Type**
  - Composite (the associated object can exist only as a child of the object)
  - Valid When (valid with or without the existence of the associated object)
- **Multiplicity**
  - One-to-One (one object can be related to only one object)
  - One-to-Many (one object can be related to many objects)

▶ **Destination object ID**

   ▷ ID of the destination object type

▶ **Required**

   ▷ Yes (at least one child record is required)

   ▷ No

▶ **Visibility**

   ▷ Editable (users can view, add, edit, or delete child records)

   ▷ Not Visible (users cannot see the child records)

   ▷ Read Only (users can only view the child records)

▶ **Label**

   ▷ Label for the association on the UI

Each Generic Object can have searchable fields assigned, just as standard objects do. As the term suggests, these are fields of the object that can be searched upon.

Once a Generic Object has been created, data for the object is maintained in OneAdmin, in MANAGE DATA in EMPLOYEE FILES. This is demonstrated in Figure 4.95.

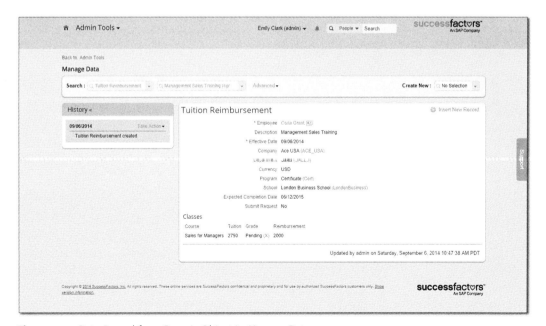

Figure 4.95 Data Record for a Generic Object in Manage Data

4.16.3 Configuration UIs

For end users, a UI can be created and added to the EMPLOYEE FILES menu so that data can be maintained as part of an employee's overall profile. An example of this—TUITION REIMBURSEMENT—is shown in Figure 4.96.

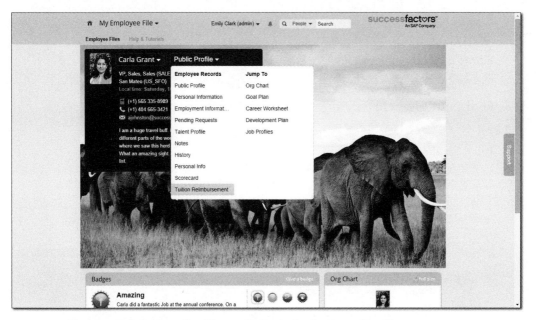

Figure 4.96 A Configuration UI as an Option in the Employee Files Menu

If you create a Configurable UI, users can maintain user-specific functionality without the need for access to OneAdmin. Figure 4.97 shows the Configurable UI for the TUITION REIMBURSEMENT Generic Object.

Configurable UIs are configured in OneAdmin in MANAGE CONFIGURATION UI in EMPLOYEE FILES. The Manage Configuration UI designer is a what-you-see-is-what-you-get (WYSIWYG), drag-and-drop UI editor that lets users style the UI for a Generic Object exactly as they require.

By default, the designer creates the UI layout with the same design as in the MANAGE DATA screen. The user can then modify this screen as required by moving fields, changing the layout of the fields, adding new fields, and adding rules. Groups of fields (called *Groups*) can also be added to separate a group of fields with its own header. Groups can be assigned titles, have borders, and be collapsible. Figure 4.98 shows a new UI being created in the designer.

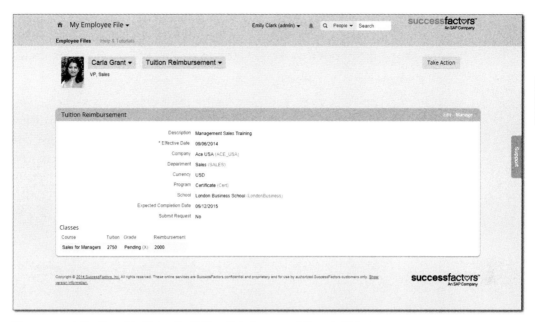

Figure 4.97 A Configurable UI for the Tuition Reimbursement Generic Object

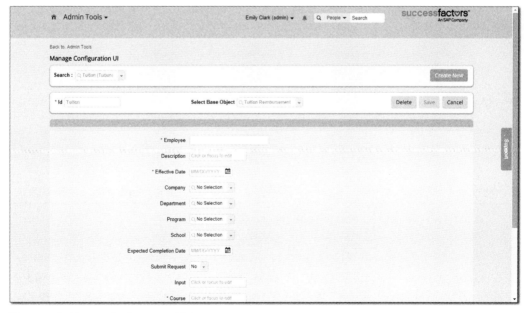

Figure 4.98 Manage Configuration UI Screen

Once a Configuration UI has been created, it is added to the EMPLOYEE FILES menu in OneAdmin in CONFIGURE EMPLOYEE FILES in EMPLOYEE FILES. The ADD NEW VIEW button—above the list of VIEWS—is used to add a View. We'll briefly run through this process.

After clicking ADD NEW VIEW, you are taken to the EMPLOYEE SCORECARD DASH-BOARD PROPERTIES screen. Click the upper-left INSERT PORTLET button. This takes you to the ADD PORTLET(S) screen. Here, navigate to the bottom of the list and select the CREATE & ADD button alongside the LIVE PROFILE MDF INFORMATION hyperlink. You now find yourself in the LIVE PROFILE MDF INFORMATION screen. In this screen, enter the title for the VIEW dashboard and select the ID of the Config-uration UI that we created earlier in the MDF SCREEN ID dropdown. Figure 4.99 shows how this should look.

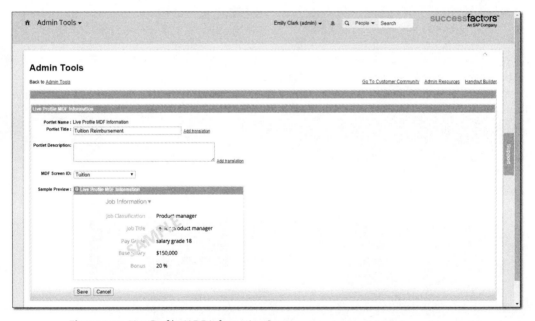

Figure 4.99 Live Profile MDF Information Screen

Click the SAVE button to return to the ADD PORTLET(S) screen. Enter the name of the View in the DASHBOARD NAME field and then click the SAVE DASHBOARD but-ton. You are taken back to the CONFIGURE EMPLOYEE FILES screen, where the new View should have the checkbox in the SHOW/HIDE column checked. Like other

Views, the up and down arrows in the SORT ORDER column can be used to position the view at the desired position within the EMPLOYEE FILES menu. Your View can now be accessed in the EMPLOYEE FILES menu, as we saw in Figure 4.96.

4.16.4 Rules Engine

The MDF features a robust and comprehensive *Rules Engine* that can be used to design complex rules so that you can apply your rules and business logic to SuccessFactors. They can be used in a variety of different use cases, such as defining default field values, changing the values of fields based on the values of other fields, pre-populating ID fields, showing or hiding fields based on other field values, performing numerical field calculations, identifying groups of employees for program eligibility, and much more. Rules are configured in OneAdmin, in CONFIGURE BUSINESS RULES under COMPANY SETTINGS.

Rules are not exclusive to Generic Objects; on the contrary, they can be used across each of the Employee Central objects and for Compensation planning eligibility. In addition, many of the Employee Central objects have a version called the Model that allows field attributes to be set (e.g., visibility). For example, Job Information Model allows any field on Job Information to have its attributes changed by a rule.

Rules are modeled with statements (using conditions such as AND and OR) and flow logic to define the business logic used; once created, they can be assigned to fields or objects. Through this functionality, you can easily modify standard system behavior or add your own business rules or logic to a host of actions or data fields throughout the SuccessFactors system.

Rules have a standard logic flow and are configured with three sections:

▶ **Rule attributes**: Attributes such rule name, ID, type, base object type, effective date, and description

▶ **If logic**: The logic to trigger the rule

▶ **Then logic**: The logic to execute once the rule is triggered

In addition, multiple Else If logic and/or Else logic can be added, should the rule require it. They work in the same way as the If and Then logic. Figure 4.100 shows an example of a simple rule.

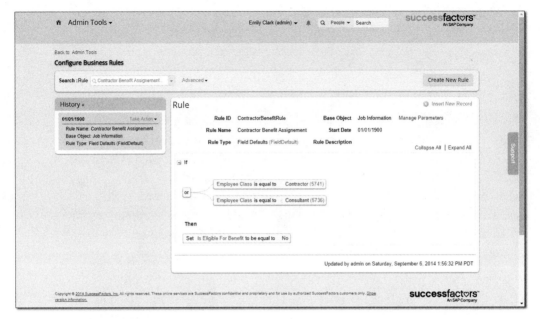

Figure 4.100 Example of a Rule

For IF logic, AND and OR conditions are used to model statements that can reference any object field or object field attribute of the base object that is selected. These statements determine the action to take, which is defined in the THEN logic. With THEN logic, an object field, object field attribute, or system variable can be set to a specific value. The If logic can be set to ALWAYS TRUE, which means that the Then logic is always executed when the rule is triggered.

In the example in Figure 4.100, the rule CONTRACTORBENEFITRULE is triggered if the EMPLOYEE CLASS field value is equal to CONTRACTOR or CONSULTANT. The logic to be executed sets the IS ELIGIBLE FOR BENEFIT field value to NO.

Once rules have been created, they need to be set to their trigger points. We'll now look at these trigger points.

Trigger Events

Rules can be triggered at the object or field level for Generic Objects, Employee Central Foundation Objects, Personal Information portlets, and Employment Information portlets. For rules triggered at the object level, the following trigger events are available:

▸ **OnInit**

Triggers the rule when a portlet or the New Hire transaction is loaded

▸ **OnSave**

Triggers the rule when the portlet or screen (e.g., ADD NEW EMPLOYEE, EMPLOYMENT INFORMATION, or PERSONAL INFORMATION) is saved after the user has modified it

▸ **OnView**

Triggers the rule for values that are calculated on the fly when a portlet or screen is loaded

▸ **OnEdit**

Triggers a rule to default the values for editable field in the *paymentInfo* object in Employee Central

▸ **saveAlert**

Triggers a rule for a workflow alert

At the field level, the *onChange* trigger is available. This triggers a rule when the field value is changed.

Assigning Rules

Rules are assigned to Employee Central objects either in the Data Model XML files or in the Manage Business Configuration UI. For Generic Objects, rules are assigned directly to the Generic Object definition.

More details about the Rules Engine can be found in the *Configuring Business Rules in SuccessFactors Implementation Guide* at *http://service.sap.com/sfsf* under PLATFORM.

4.16.5 Metadata Framework Picklists

MDF Picklists are similar to but configured differently from standard Picklists. You create them in OneAdmin, in CONFIGURE OBJECT DEFINITIONS under COMPANY SETTINGS by selecting PICKLIST in the CREATE NEW dropdown. MDF Picklists must be created before they can be assigned to Generic Object fields. Figure 4.101 shows the Picklist definition for the *State—USA* Picklist.

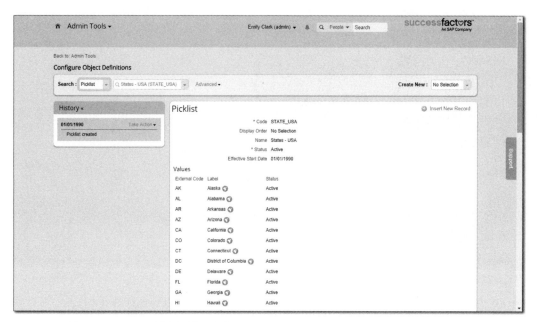

Figure 4.101 An MDF Picklist Definition

4.16.6 Data Import and Export

Through GENERIC OBJECTS IMPORT/EXPORT, it's possible to import or export Generic Object data, including Generic Object and rule definitions, as well as Generic Object data. You can also download a blank template file to populate with data.

4.17 Employee Central Extensions

With SAP HANA Cloud Platform, a Platform-as-a-Service (PaaS), it is possible to create custom applications to embed within SuccessFactors HCM suite solutions. At the time of writing, this is solely focused on adding new capabilities to Success-Factors Employee Central.

SAP HANA Cloud Platform is a cloud-based platform for developers to create scalable applications that can leverage the speed, power, and scale of SAP HANA and can integrate into cloud-based applications, such as SuccessFactors or applications within SAP's other cloud pillars. It also leverages the MDF and integrates with mobile and SAP Jam. One of the key platform services is the SAP HANA Cloud Portal, which enables the quick creation of mobile-ready, highly brandable sites without coding.

The Employee Central extension package was released to allow applications to be built for Employee Central on the SAP HANA Cloud Platform. Applications built on the platform integrate with Employee Central using SSO and leverage the SuccessFactors APIs to fetch employee details. These applications also integrate with the home screen (so they can be shown as tiles) and the theme and navigation of SuccessFactors HCM suite. Figure 4.102 shows the Networking Lunch application that has been created on the SAP HANA Cloud platform and is integrated into the SuccessFactors HCM suite.

Figure 4.102 Networking Lunch Application

SuccessFactors customers can access the Extensions Marketplace in OneAdmin by selecting EXTENSIONS under COMPANY SETTINGS. Here, customers can browse available applications and "test drive" applications in their instance to see how they work. Figure 4.103 shows the Extensions Marketplace.

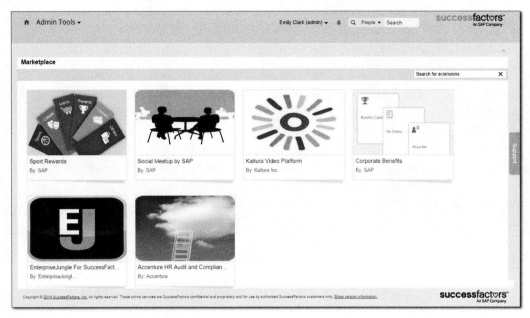

Figure 4.103 Extensions Marketplace in OneAdmin

More details about SuccessFactors extensions can be found in the *SAP HANA Cloud Platform, Extension Package for SuccessFactors Configuration Handbook* at *http://service.sap.com/sfsf* under EXTENSIONS.

4.18 Summary

We started this chapter with the technical architecture of SuccessFactors and the various layers of the architecture. Because this is a cloud solution, the architecture must be light, scalable, and powerful. SuccessFactors delivers this by using a dynamic backend technology, coupled with a JavaScript frontend that creates a very powerful architecture. Security is of the utmost importance to SuccessFactors. Therefore, every layer of technology within SuccessFactors contains its own strong security and is independently penetration-tested to ensure that the data, code, and connections are secured every step of the way.

We then covered the various features and components that are part of the SuccessFactors Platform before discussing the MDF. The MDF is a growing extensibility framework in SuccessFactors for creating data objects, screens, and rules that are future-proofed against future upgrades and releases.

Now that you understand some of the technology and functions that make SuccessFactors run, let's explore some of the common administration activities that can be performed in the system.

It's all good and well implementing SuccessFactors, but once you go live, you still need to continue maintaining the system. Common activities can be performed easily in the system and thus allow for painless ongoing administration.

5 Administering SuccessFactors

SuccessFactors—like any system—requires administration after implementation and go-live. The system is designed so that a business stakeholder, such as an HR business partner, can manage and maintain the system. It requires no special technical skill or programming ability. As the system landscape becomes slightly more complicated with integrations to SAP ERP HCM and other systems, some customers are sharing administration responsibility between IT and HR functions. There has been concerted effort over the last few years to put more control of the system in the hands of the customer via OneAdmin.

In this chapter, we will review some of the many administrative components of the SuccessFactors HCM suite that you will enable you to administer, update, and support the system. We'll go through a quick overview of general system configuration and administration (see Section 5.1) before looking at various administrative activities such as management of users (see Section 5.2). From there we'll identify the best method for administering necessary authentication and password policies to keep the system secure (see Section 5.3), and then move on to modifying email notifications (see Section 5.4) and managing Picklists (see Section 5.5). Then, we'll discuss the topic of data administration, from importing employee data (see Section 5.6) to purging unneeded data (see Section 5.7). We'll wrap things up by adding new files into Employee Central and the Employee Profile (see Section 5.9), and discussing a few Employee Central-specific administration tasks (see Section 5.10).

5.1   System Configuration and Administration

SuccessFactors HCM is a configurable system that is flexible and scalable. Much of the system is configured via the Provisioning tool, but there are also many things that can be done directly in the instance via the OneAdmin interface. Currently, customers do not have access to the Provisioning end of their instances and need to work with Customer Success or a Partner for anything that requires configuration in Provisioning. This includes making settings that impact the overall instance, such as enabling a module or turning on a language pack, as illustrated in Figure 5.1. Depending on the module, more of the configuration is done in Provisioning than in the instance. A good example is Recruiting Management—all of the recruiting templates that drive the system are configured via XML and need to be uploaded and managed in Provisioning. This is in contrast to Performance and Goal Management and Compensation, where templates can be created, updated, and copied right in OneAdmin.

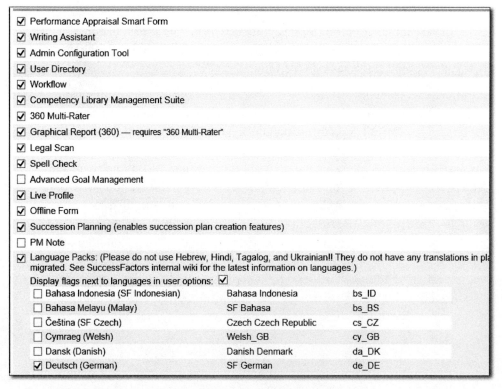

Figure 5.1 Company Settings Made in the Provisioning Interface

Some of the other features maintained in Provisioning include scheduled jobs that support data imports and exports and scheduled reports.

In contrast to Provisioning is the OneAdmin interface in the instance, which provides customers control over maintaining settings, data, and rules that govern their instance. The OneAdmin interface is intuitive and organized into module-specific activities, such as Performance Management, Recruiting, Compensation, Employee Files, and others. OneAdmin is pictured in Figure 5.2.

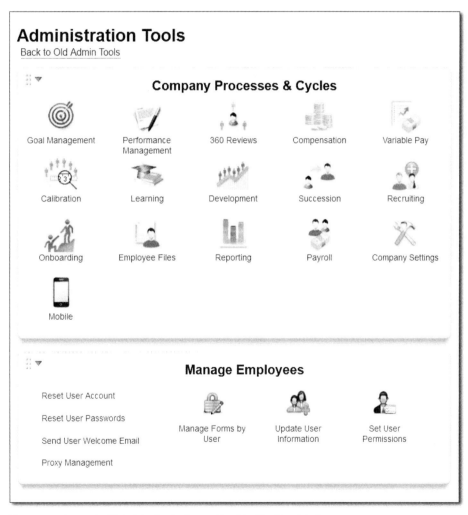

Figure 5.2 Access to Maintain the Instance, Provided by OneAdmin

There are several features in OneAdmin to help administrators find exactly what they are looking for. The TOOL SEARCH is an easy way to find actions you may not perform frequently. In addition, the MY FAVORITES section allows you to *bookmark* those actions you perform regularly for quick access. These features are illustrated in Figure 5.3.

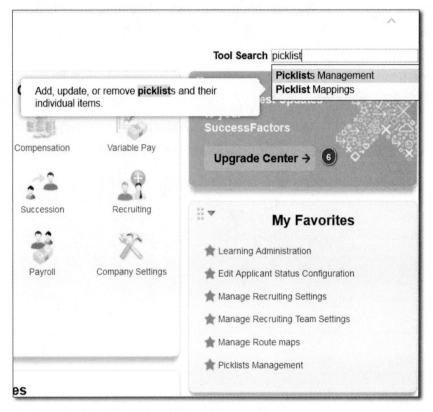

Figure 5.3 Tool Search and My Favorites

As with all parts of SuccessFactors HCM suite, OneAdmin features can be permissioned. Administrative roles can be created and managed in Role-Based Permissions to segment access to OneAdmin. For instance, it's common to have a role that provides access to the Recruiting administrative features but restricts access to the rest of the tool. The icons in OneAdmin are grayed out if a user's role does not allow access to that area of the system. We recommend that you have at least two users with full administrative access; many customers have more, depending on their employee size and needs.

Now that we've looked at the basics of using OneAdmin for system administration and configuration then we can take the first look at performing an activity. One of the most important of these activities is user management.

5.2   User Management

OneAdmin provides several features to administer and maintain users in the system. From importing data, resetting user passwords, and unlocking accounts to managing the proxy feature, administrators have a wide range of control over the users and related data in the system. Some of these features may not be accessible if a customer has an integration with SAP ERP HCM for user data.

5.2.1   Updating User Data

If you choose the UPDATE USER INFORMATION icon shown in the bottom-left of Figure 5.4, the system presents you with some of the tools that can be used to maintain user data.

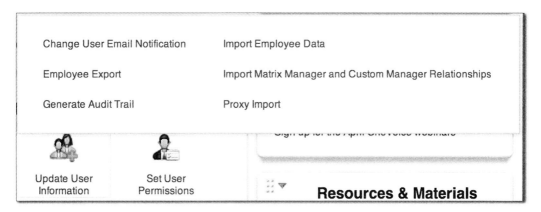

Figure 5.4 Update User Information Icon Tools

In this menu, an administrator is able to upload users using the IMPORT EMPLOYEE DATA function. This important function allows an administrator to upload a spreadsheet containing all of the users, user names, roles, and hierarchy. Figure

5.5 shows the IMPORT EMPLOYEE DATA screen and some of the useful options that administrators can use to populate users in the system.

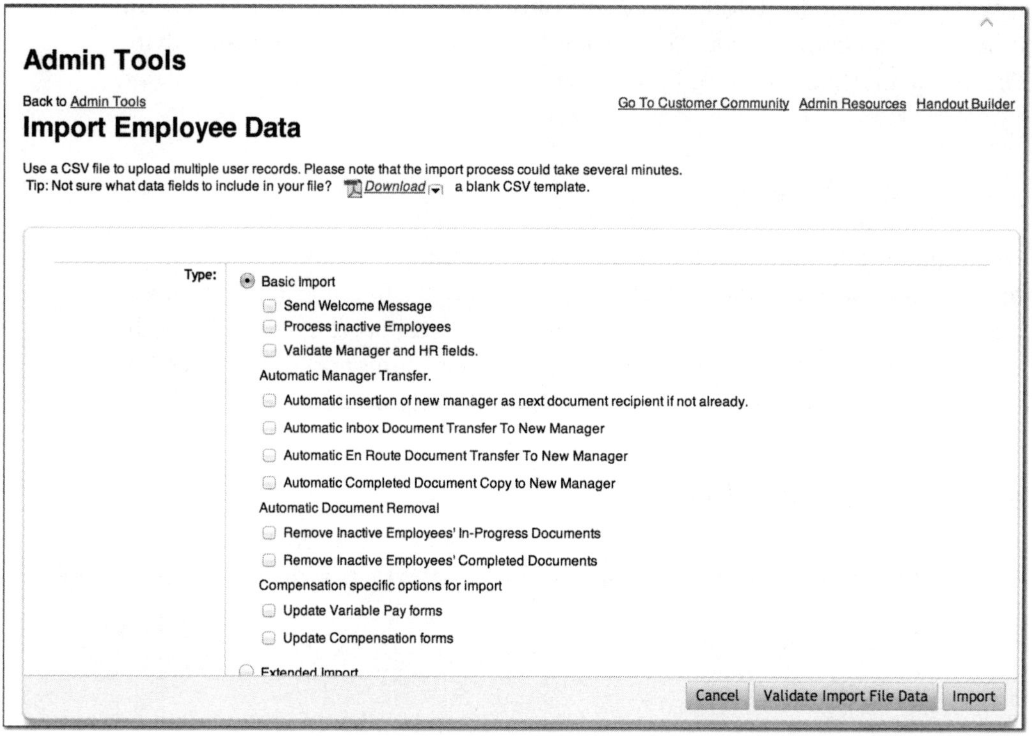

Figure 5.5 Import Employee Data

Here, administrators can easily import users into the system by downloading a CSV template directly from this page using the DOWNLOAD link and selecting a template.

5.2.2 Proxy Management

Also within the user administration tools is the ability to manage proxy users. *Proxy users* enable users to act as delegates for other users—for example, to access another user's data and functions. This, of course, needs to be carefully maintained because you are viewing sensitive data that belongs to others, but it is useful for troubleshooting issues for users. You can select a setting that allows users to nominate their own proxies, but most companies keep this powerful feature centralized for control and privacy of performance and compensation-related data (see Figure 5.6).

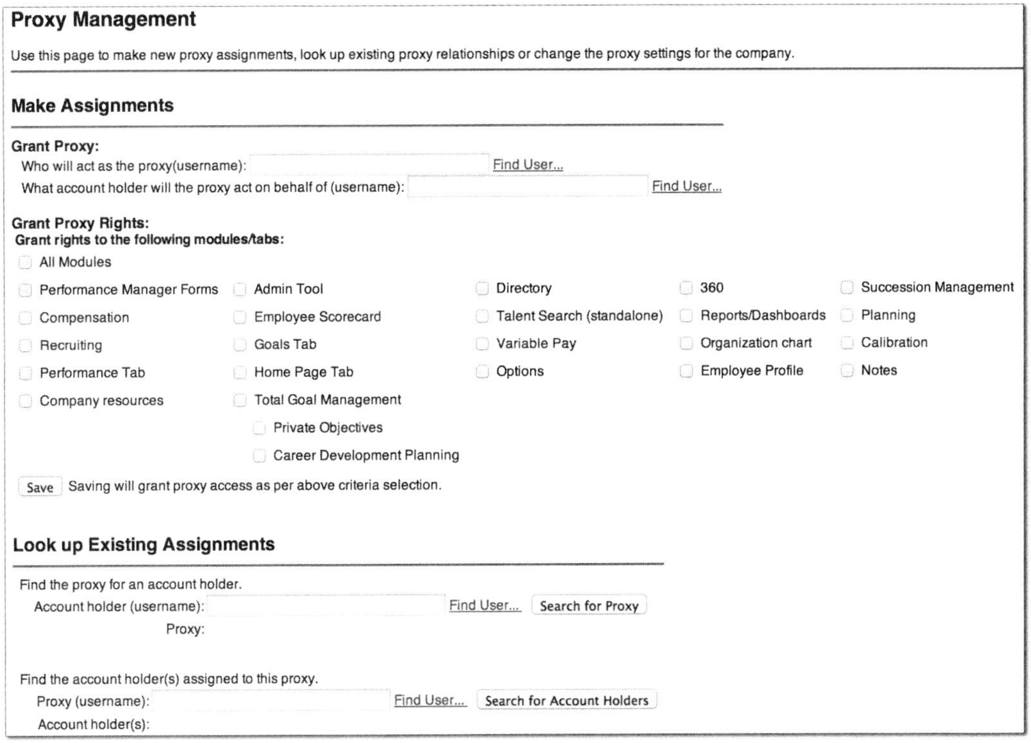

Proxy Management

Use this page to make new proxy assignments, look up existing proxy relationships or change the proxy settings for the company.

Make Assignments

Grant Proxy:
Who will act as the proxy(username):   Find User...
What account holder will the proxy act on behalf of (username):   Find User...

Grant Proxy Rights:
Grant rights to the following modules/tabs:

☐ All Modules

☐ Performance Manager Forms	☐ Admin Tool	☐ Directory	☐ 360	☐ Succession Management
☐ Compensation	☐ Employee Scorecard	☐ Talent Search (standalone)	☐ Reports/Dashboards	☐ Planning
☐ Recruiting	☐ Goals Tab	☐ Variable Pay	☐ Organization chart	☐ Calibration
☐ Performance Tab	☐ Home Page Tab	☐ Options	☐ Employee Profile	☐ Notes
☐ Company resources	☐ Total Goal Management			
	☐ Private Objectives			
	☐ Career Development Planning			

[Save] Saving will grant proxy access as per above criteria selection.

Look up Existing Assignments

Find the proxy for an account holder.
Account holder (username):   Find User... [Search for Proxy]
                       Proxy:

Find the account holder(s) assigned to this proxy.
Proxy (username):   Find User... [Search for Account Holders]
Account holder(s):

Figure 5.6 Proxy Management Screen

Another useful user administration tool is the ability to manage users' access and passwords. For customers that do not have Single Sign-On (SSO) enabled, administrators can unlock accounts of users who have attempted too many failed password attempts. Figure 5.7 shows the RESETTING USER ACCOUNTS tool, which allows an administrator to easily reset a user's account and information.

Along the same lines with user administration, administrators need to be able to set new passwords, reset passwords, and set password rules for users. Setting and resetting passwords can be done by all users, not just administrators. Figure 5.8 shows the PASSWORD RESET option for all users.

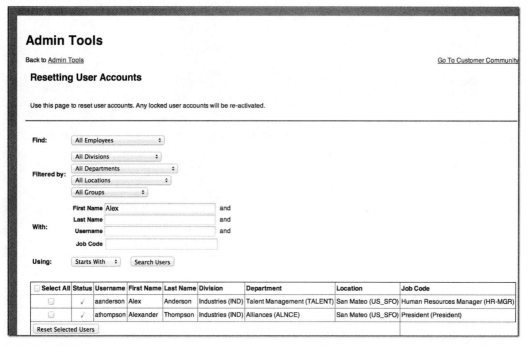

Figure 5.7 Resetting User Accounts Administrator Tool

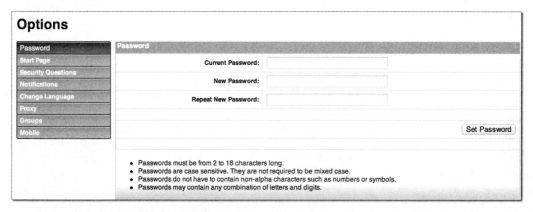

Figure 5.8 Password Reset

Continuing on the topic of passwords, the next section will discuss the administration of password policies and authentications.

5.3 Authentication and Password Policy

Unless SSO is enabled, users log on to the instance using a user name and password. Customers determine what the username for each user is during implementation and typically align this with network username or employee ID; however, anything can be used as a username. Password policies are maintained within OneAdmin in PASSWORD AND LOGIN POLICY SETTINGS, illustrated in Figure 5.9. Here, you can set minimum and maximum length and age of passwords, as well as enable case sensitivity and settings related to users' forgetting and resetting their own passwords.

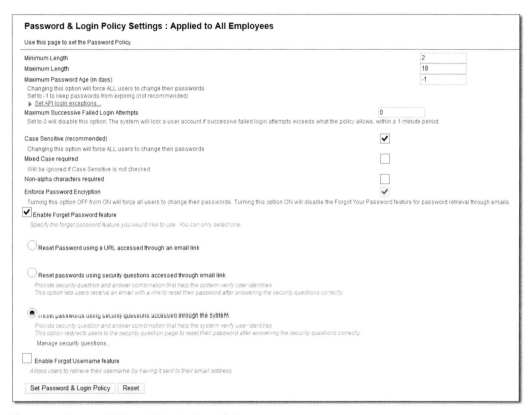

Figure 5.9 Password Policy Settings in OneAdmin

5.4 Email Notifications

Beyond general user management and maintenance, another important function that is used by all applications within SuccessFactors HCM suite is the *email notification*. Notifications are a powerful way to communicate system information to users. There are email templates provided with the application that can be enabled and disabled as appropriate with sample subject lines and text that can be modified by customers to suit their needs. These email notifications range from functions such as routing notifications that are sent each time a form is routed to a new user, when a goal has been created or deleted, to external recruiting candidates forgetting their password. Figure 5.10 shows a sample list of the system-wide EMAIL NOTIFICATIONS TEMPLATES that can be activated and customized. There are also additional ad hoc email templates and triggers that can be defined within the Recruiting Management module, but those sit within the Recruiting Administration area.

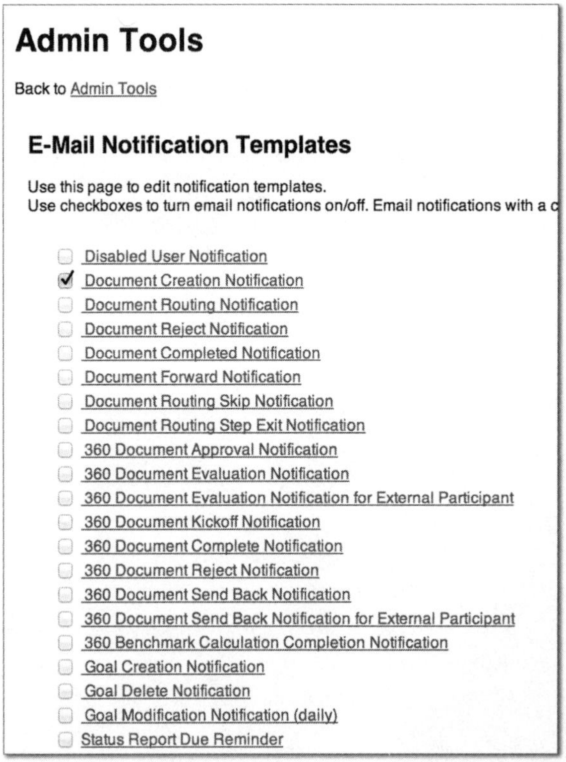

Admin Tools

Back to Admin Tools

E-Mail Notification Templates

Use this page to edit notification templates.
Use checkboxes to turn email notifications on/off. Email notifications with a

- [ ] Disabled User Notification
- [x] Document Creation Notification
- [ ] Document Routing Notification
- [ ] Document Reject Notification
- [ ] Document Completed Notification
- [ ] Document Forward Notification
- [ ] Document Routing Skip Notification
- [ ] Document Routing Step Exit Notification
- [ ] 360 Document Approval Notification
- [ ] 360 Document Evaluation Notification
- [ ] 360 Document Evaluation Notification for External Participant
- [ ] 360 Document Kickoff Notification
- [ ] 360 Document Complete Notification
- [ ] 360 Document Reject Notification
- [ ] 360 Document Send Back Notification
- [ ] 360 Document Send Back Notification for External Participant
- [ ] 360 Benchmark Calculation Completion Notification
- [ ] Goal Creation Notification
- [ ] Goal Delete Notification
- [ ] Goal Modification Notification (daily)
- [ ] Status Report Due Reminder

Figure 5.10 Sample List of Notification Activation

After you activate email notifications, the actual notification can be customized to change the text on the screen or add a logo. Each application has its own notifications that can be customized. Figure 5.11 shows the notification customization.

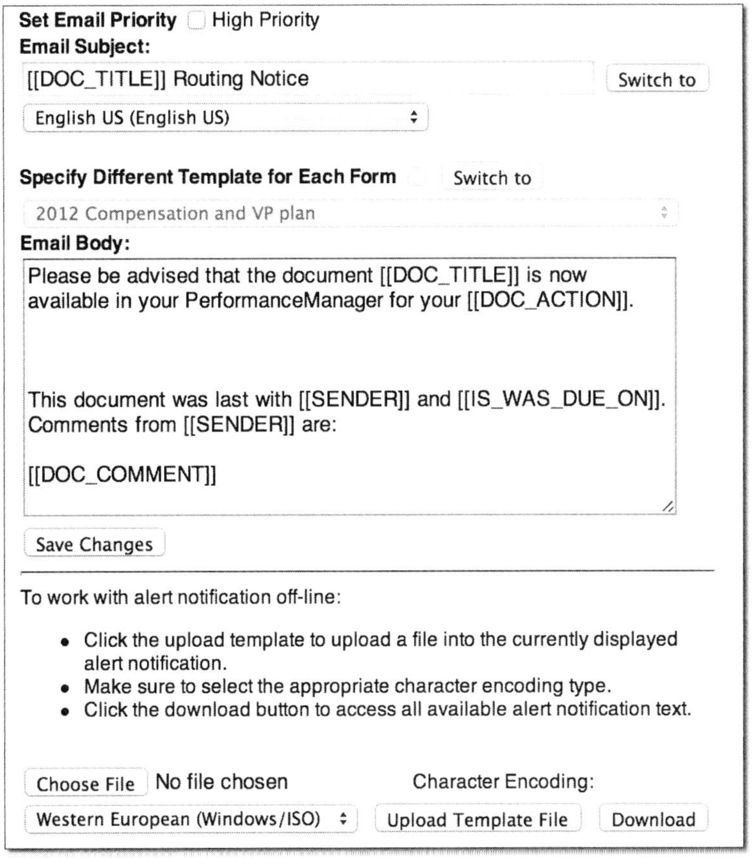

Figure 5.11 Notification Customization

We've seen how we can configure existing email notifications. In a similar vein, we'll now look at how we can configure and add Picklists.

5.5 Picklist Management

SuccessFactors HCM suite uses Picklists throughout the application. Picklists are fields that provide a list of values from which to select. Picklist values are maintained in OneAdmin under Picklist Management. From here, administrators can create new Picklists or update values in existing Picklists. These updates may include adding, reordering, or deleting values from the list. While it is necessary for the Picklists to be configured in XML templates, having the ability to create the Picklists and maintaining the values provides customers with a great amount of control over the data that makes up their configuration.

Picklists are managed in a .CSV file and imported into OneAdmin. To create a new Picklist, it is necessary to enter a few key elements of data, some of which are as follows:

▶ *PicklistID*
Is the value or key that is used to map the Picklists to fields in the configuration (data model, templates, etc.).

▶ *OptionID*
Is the value or key that is used to map edits to a previously established value. This value is assigned by the system, and you should leave the field blank when creating new Picklist values and not changes when editing existing Picklists.

▶ *Status*
Controls whether the Picklist value is displayed in the list of values in the interface; there are three options:

  ▷ *Active*: Means the value is available in the system

  ▷ *Deleted*: Means the value is disabled from use in the system

  ▷ *Obsoleted*: Means the value is disabled from the list of values but still available for reporting

▶ *en_US*
Is the default language coding and is required for all Picklist values. Other codes (such as fr_FR for French or de_DE for German) can be included for other languages, but each language code should be in its own column.

When you're working with Picklists, it's important to select the correct options in the import/export screen. The best practice is to first export the Picklist values and work with Picklist or Picklists that require updating. You can also use the template to create new Picklist values. Note that you cannot create a new Picklist and update an existing Picklist in the same file. Updates to Picklists are immediately rendered in the system (see Figure 5.12).

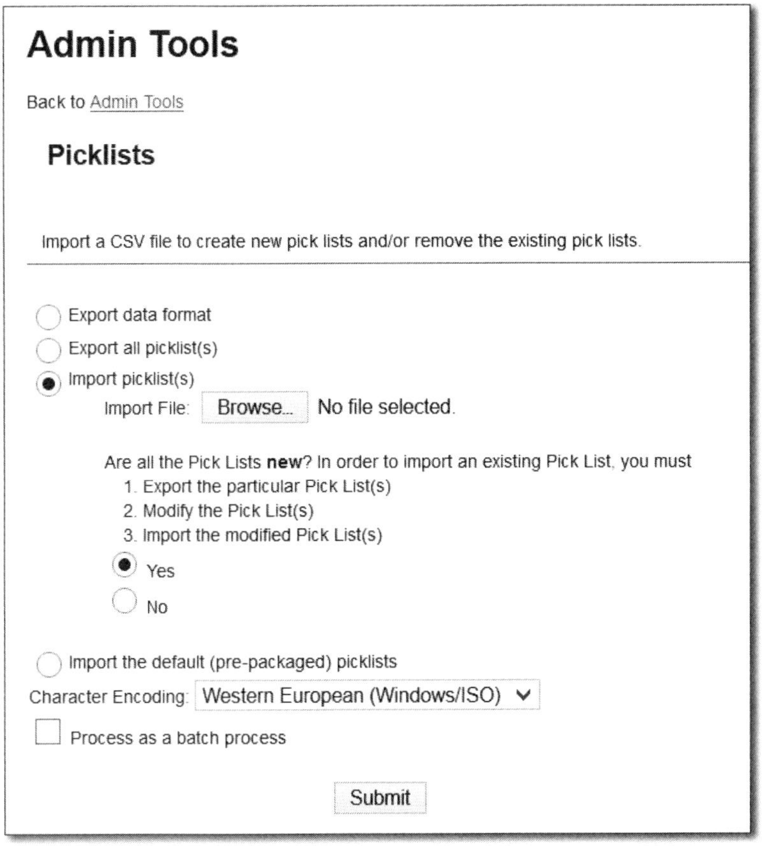

Admin Tools

Back to Admin Tools

Picklists

Import a CSV file to create new pick lists and/or remove the existing pick lists.

○ Export data format
○ Export all picklist(s)
● Import picklist(s)
  Import File: Browse… No file selected.

  Are all the Pick Lists **new**? In order to import an existing Pick List, you must
    1. Export the particular Pick List(s)
    2. Modify the Pick List(s)
    3. Import the modified Pick List(s)
  ● Yes
  ○ No

○ Import the default (pre-packaged) picklists
Character Encoding: Western European (Windows/ISO) ∨
☐ Process as a batch process

Submit

Figure 5.12 Picklist Import Options

We've seen how to maintain Picklists, but now we're going to switch our attention to data imports and look at how to get basic employee data in and out of the SuccessFactors system.

5.6 Employee Data Imports

Similar to the way employee data can be imported into the system, other employee-related data can also be imported into SuccessFactors HCM suite. Data may be imported into background elements in Employee Profile, as well as other data groupings within Employee Central. We recommend that you first export the appropriate template from the IMPORT EMPLOYEE DATA function in OneAdmin. When you select the arrow next to DOWNLOAD, a blank CSV template displays the available templates, as shown in Figure 5.13.

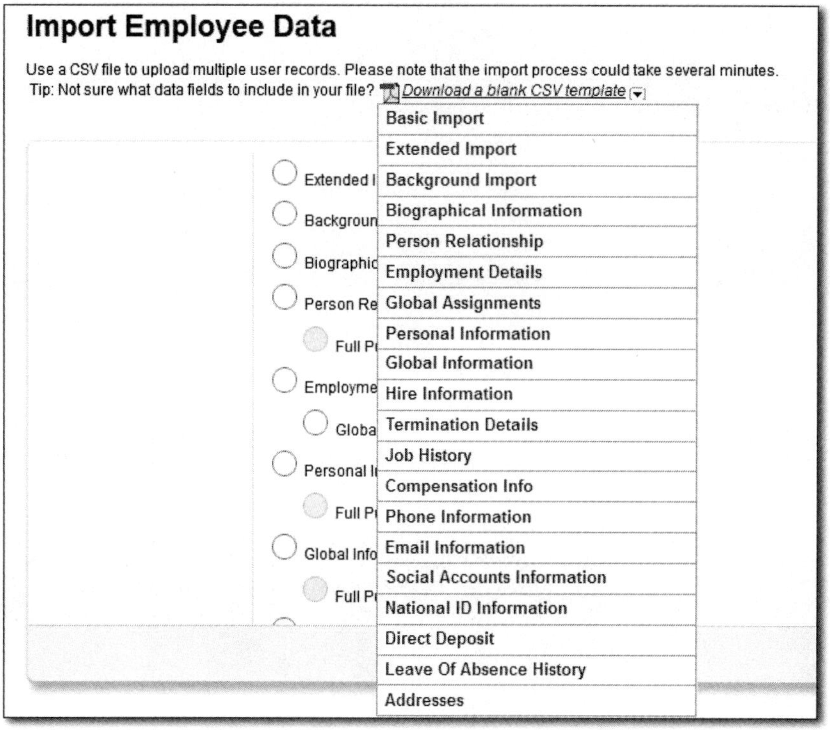

Import Employee Data

Use a CSV file to upload multiple user records. Please note that the import process could take several minutes.
Tip: Not sure what data fields to include in your file? ☒ *Download a blank CSV template* ⊡

| Basic Import |
| Extended Import |
| Background Import |
| Biographical Information |
| Person Relationship |
| Employment Details |
| Global Assignments |
| Personal Information |
| Global Information |
| Hire Information |
| Termination Details |
| Job History |
| Compensation Info |
| Phone Information |
| Email Information |
| Social Accounts Information |
| National ID Information |
| Direct Deposit |
| Leave Of Absence History |
| Addresses |

Figure 5.13 Export Template for Data Import

Once the data is added to the template, it can be imported into the system in the same screen. There is an option to select for each kind of employee data. It is important to select the corresponding radio button for the type of data being imported. The system validates the file and uploads the data into the system. Some files may be imported as a background process, and the user doing the import receives an email notification with the results of the import. The IMPORT EMPLOYEE DATA screen is provided in Figure 5.14.

Now that we've seen how to get data into the system, let's take a look at a related and equally import feature—the ability to purge data already in the system. Data retention management is possible with the Data Management feature.

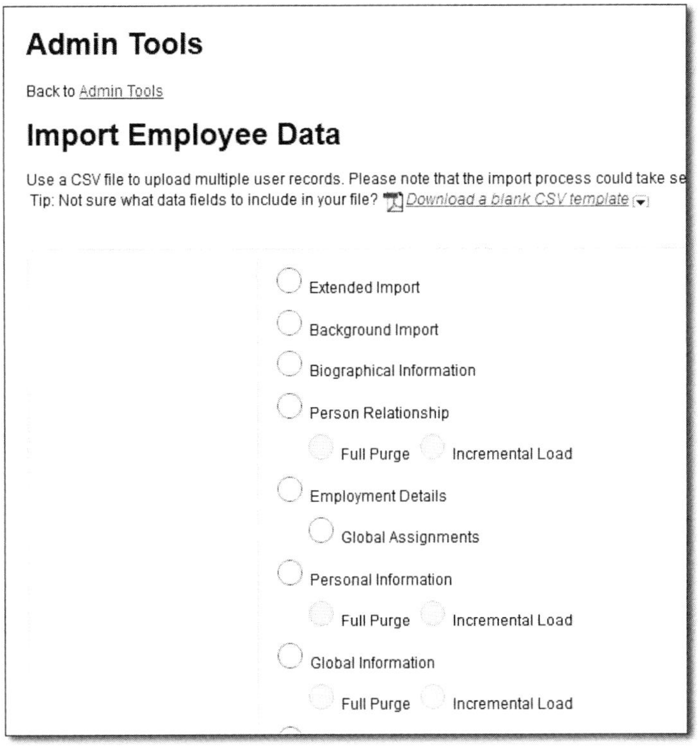

Figure 5.14 Importing Employee-Related Data

5.7 Data Retention Management

This feature allows for purging of obsolete data and users from the SuccessFactors HCM suite. This ensures that customers are compliant with local data privacy laws.

Data Management in SuccessFactors HCM suite requires a user (which in most cases would be the super admin) to submit a purge request that, upon approval, is executed. The following types of data purge requests can be submitted:

▶ Inactive User

▶ Performance Management or Succession Management

▶ Learning Activity

▶ Developmental Goal

▶ Career Worksheet

- Calibration

- Goal

- Inactive Job Applications

- Inactive Candidate

- Compensation/Variable Pay

- Inactive Employees in Employee Central

5.7.1 Create Request

To submit a request, click DATA MANAGEMENT under COMPANY SETTINGS in OneAdmin. Click CREATE NEW PURGE RULE (see Figure 5.15), and select the appropriate type of data purge to initiate.

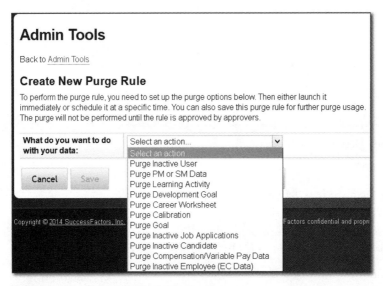

Figure 5.15 Create New Purge Rule

After clicking the type of data purge, you are requested to name the data purge request, fill out any relevant criteria for filtering, and identify one or multiple approvers for this request, as shown in Figure 5.16.

Upon submitting the data purge request for this data purge request, administrators that have approval rights and notified through email that the request is ready for approval.

Admin Tools

Back to Admin Tools

Edit Purge Rule

What do you want to do with your data:	Purge Development Goal ⌄
Name this purge request:	Purge Development Goal
Which template do you want to purge:	Development Goal ⌄ My Development Goals ⌄

Hire Date   from 09/02/2014 to 09/09/2014   Division   Select division...

Country   1 countries selected   Location   1 locations selected

Department   1 departments selected   Job Code   1 job codes selected

Select person who will review and approve the request:	adminaj 🗑
	admin1 🗑
	Add another approver ⊕

Cancel   Save   Delete...   Schedule...   Launch Now...

Figure 5.16 Purge Rule Criteria Setup

5.7.2 Maintenance Monitor

To view any data purge requests awaiting approval or approved requests, click MAINTENANCE MONITOR under COMPANY SETTINGS in OneAdmin, as shown in Figure 5.17.

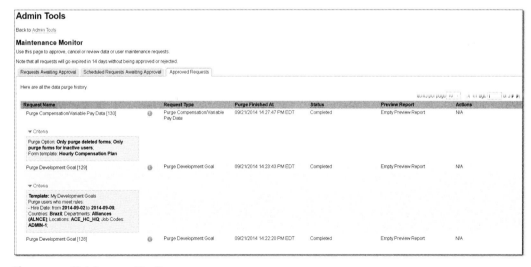

Figure 5.17 Maintenance Monitor

An administrator can download the preview report and ensure that valid objects are being requested to be purged. Once a request is approved or declined, the action cannot be reversed.

We just covered removing data and we'll now turn our attention to synchronizing data between different SuccessFactors instances.

5.8   Instance Synchronization Tool

This feature allows for synchronization of configuration objects between two SuccessFactors HCM suite instances. The feature behaves as a push model from the source instance to the target instance. As of the latest release, the following configuration objects are supported:

- Picklists
- Workflows
- Rating Scales
- Form Label
- Competency
- Families & Roles
- Goal Templates
- PM Templates
- System Properties
- Dashboard Settings

5.8.1   Configuration Sync Wizard

To launch the sync wizard, click SYNCHRONIZE INSTANCE CONFIGURATIONS under COMPANY SETTINGS in OneAdmin, as shown in Figure 5.18.

To initiate the sync, identify the target instance and configuration objects. The sync wizard then takes you through a series of criteria selection and confirmation screens per configuration object and presents a final summary of the instance sync request, as shown in Figure 5.19. Customers can choose to run the sync in test mode, which lets them preview the results of the sync process in a report format.

Figure 5.18 Instance Sync Configuration Wizard

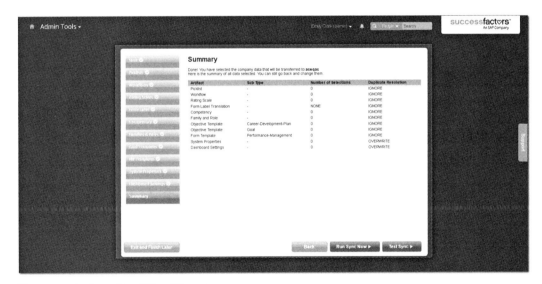

Figure 5.19 Instance Sync Wizard Summary

5.8.2 Instance Synchronization Monitor Tool

Once a configuration object sync is initiated in live or test mode, customers can monitor the progress of the sync process by going to INSTANCE SYNCHRONIZATION MONITOR TOOL under COMPANY SETTINGS in OneAdmin, as shown in Figure 5.20.

Figure 5.20 Instance Synchronization Monitor Tool

The sync monitoring tool allows for downloading of a detailed report of all actions that will be performed. Also, the tool has a hyperlink of the INSTANCE SYNCHRONIZATION RESPONSE CODES that provide a detailed explanation of the response code generated as part of the sync process, as shown in Figure 5.21.

Instance Synchronization Response Codes
Download Response Codes

Response Code	Response Message
SYNC-5002	This shall be updated Successfully in the actual sync.
SYNC-0806	Sender does not have a folder for the form
SYNC-5001	This shall be added Successfully in the actual sync.
SYNC-0700	Error adding competency.
SYNC-0807	Recipient does not have a folder for the form
SYNC-0701	Error adding sub competency.
SYNC-0808	The form has been added successfully [source ID, target ID]
SYNC-0702	Error updating sub competency.
SYNC-0703	Error updating competency.
SYNC-0600	Duplicate Rating Scale found.
SYNC-0601	Rating Scale does not exists.
SYNC-0500	source optionId ---> target optionId
SYNC-0501	No optionId was found on target instance for the picklist: {0}, optionId: {1}, locale: {2}, label: {3}
SYNC-0400	Route ID changed [from,to]:
SYNC-0100	Invalid Manager ID
SYNC-0103	Invalid Username
SYNC-0104	Duplicate Username
SYNC-0101	Invalid HR ID
SYNC-0102	Invalid User ID
SYNC-0004	Existing in target, ignored.
SYNC-0107	Invalid Second manager ID
SYNC-0108	Invalid Matrix Manager ID
SYNC-0002	Updated Successfully.
SYNC-0105	Manager Cycle Detected
SYNC-0003	No artifact with key found in source company

Figure 5.21 Instance Synchronization Response Codes

Before data is synchronized, it can be configured in the system. This is what we'll look at now when we discuss the *Business Configuration* feature.

5.9   Business Configuration

Being able to make changes to fields in Employee Central and Employee Profile is one of the key components of a system that needs to evolve along with your business. The MANAGE BUSINESS CONFIGURATION application enables you to do just that.

You access the MANAGE BUSINESS CONFIGURATION application in OneAdmin by selecting MANAGE BUSINESS CONFIGURATION in COMPANY SETTINGS. Figure 5.22 shows the application.

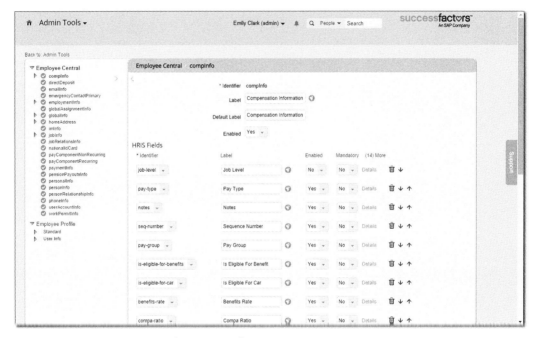

Figure 5.22 Manage Business Configuration Application

The application enables each of the portlets in Employee Central and both Standard and User Info elements of the Employee Profile to be configured using a simple UI. For Employee Central portlets, the portlet label and visibility can be changed, and fields can be added, removed, enabled or disabled, renamed, made required, changed to a Picklist, be masked, and so on. Figure 5.23 shows the types of changes that can be made to the job-level field on the COMPENSATION INFORMATION portlet.

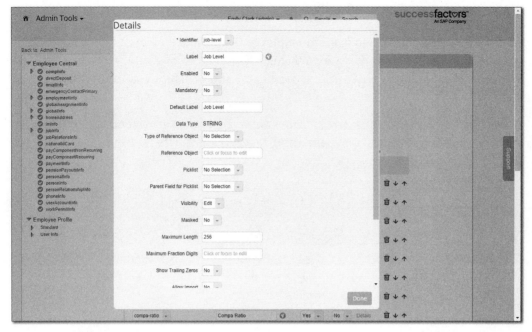

Figure 5.23 Field Details

For the Employee Profile elements, the label, visibility, Picklist, required, length, reportable, and masked attributes can all be set. For User Info elements, the field type (TEXT, DECIMAL NUMBER, NUMBER, BOOLEAN, or DATE) can also be configured. And you can also create new User Info elements here by clicking the CREATE NEW button at the bottom of the USER INFO list.

Next, we'll go through some of the common administration activities required when running Employee Central.

5.10 Employee Central Administration

In the next chapter, we'll look more deeply into SuccessFactors Employee Central and Employee Central Payroll. However, there are a number of key Employee Central administrative activities that may need to be performed on a regular basis, and thus should be addressed. We'll cover them now.

5.10.1   Invalid HR Data

Employees who have invalid data can be identified using the EMPLOYEES ASSOCIA-
TED WITH INVALID HR DATA application. You access this in OneAdmin by selecting
EMPLOYEES ASSOCIATED WITH INVALID HR DATA under EMPLOYEE FILES. Figure 5.24
shows the application.

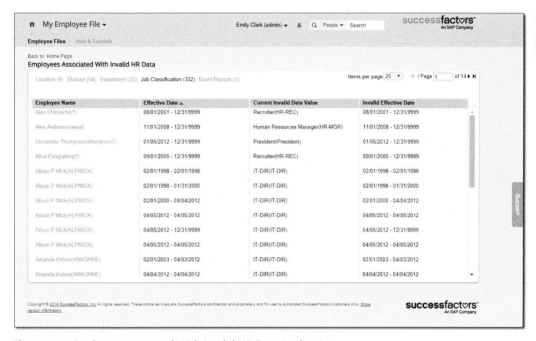

Figure 5.24 Employees Associated With Invalid HR Data Application

The application shows a horizontal list of fields at the top of the application portlet, with values in brackets next to them; these represent the different types of
invalid HR data that have been detected and how many instances have been
detected. The number of fields varies based on the amount of data issued in the
system. Each field is a hyperlink, and if you select one of them, you are shown a
complete list of employees with the effective date and invalid value.

Clicking an employee takes you to a screen showing the history screen and which
records and fields have invalid data. You can then correct this by using the TAKE
ACTION button and selecting MAKE CORRECTION. Figure 5.25 shows an invalid
LOCATION.

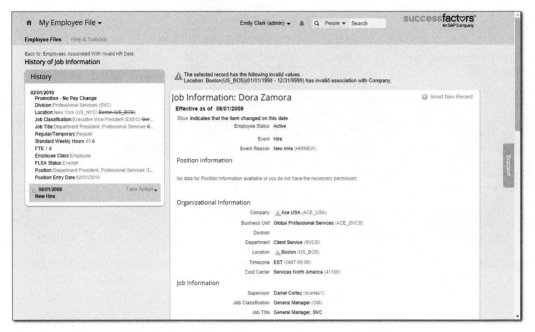

Figure 5.25 Invalid Data for an Employee

5.10.2 Manage Workflow Requests

There are two features available to allow the management of workflow requests. These are used to perform all sorts of activities on workflows, as well as identify workflows with invalid approvers. We'll take a brief look at each of these now.

Workflow requests can be managed through the option MANAGE WORKFLOW REQUESTS under EMPLOYEE FILES in OneAdmin. Here, workflow requests can be displayed based on a number of search criteria, including the initiator, subject employee, workflow configuration, workflow request status, effective date range, and requested date range. Figure 5.26 shows a list of workflow requests with status PENDING.

Each workflow can be displayed, as well as have one of the following options performed: lock the workflow request, add another approver, change approver(s), remove approver(s), re-route the request, or decline the request. You perform these by selecting the TAKE ACTION button in the ACTIONS column for the appropriate request. If the button does not exist, no actions can be performed on that particular workflow request.

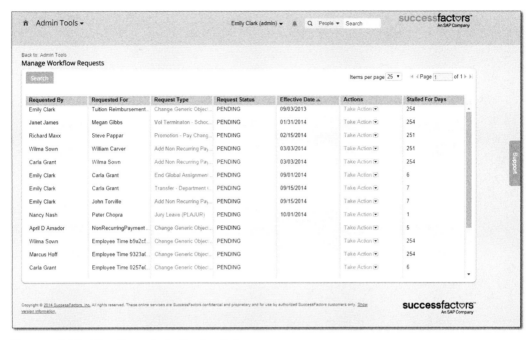

Figure 5.26 Workflow Requests for Pending Status

Workflow requests with invalid approvers can be managed through the option MANAGE WORKFLOW REQUESTS WITH INVALID APPROVERS under EMPLOYEE FILES in OneAdmin. This feature is very similar to the MANAGE WORKFLOW REQUESTS feature, although it does not have search criteria. In the list of workflows, the same columns are shown as in MANAGE WORKFLOW REQUESTS, with an additional column for the invalid approver. The same actions can be performed on these workflows as in MANAGE WORKFLOW REQUESTS.

5.10.3 Currency Conversion Table

When you use multiple currencies, a periodic activity for administrators is used to maintain the currency conversion table for Employee Central. You configure the currency conversion table in OneAdmin by selecting ACTIONS FOR ALL PLANS under COMPENSATION. In the ALL PLANS menu, select CURRENCY CONVERSION TABLE and then, once the list of currency conversion tables appears, select the currency conversion table ECT_CONV_TABLE. An example of a currency conversion table can be seen in Figure 5.27.

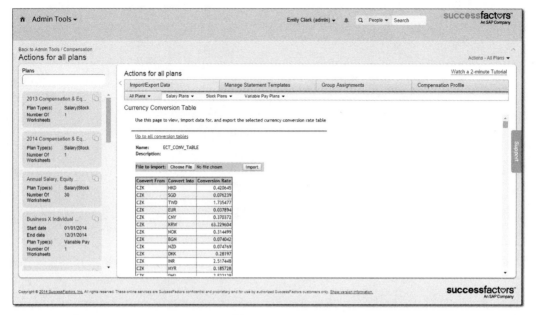

Figure 5.27 Currency Conversion table ECT_CONV_TABLE

The process for making changes is to export the table, update the exported CSV file, and import the modified CSV file. To export the currency conversion table, scroll to the bottom of the table and select the EXPORT button. Once you have modified the file, click the CHOOSE FILE button above the currency conversion table, locate the file, and then click the IMPORT button.

5.11   Summary

We've taken a look at a number of administrative activities that are required to continuously support the SuccessFactors system. After reading this chapter, you should be familiar with the different types of activities that administrators can perform to keep the system working. We've looked at user management and authentication, email notifications, Picklists, data imports, data retention and purging, instance synchronization, business configuration, and some of the various Employee Central administrative activities.

Next, we'll begin taking a look at each of the applications in the SuccessFactors HCM suite. We'll start off with Employee Central, the next generation core HRIS.

SAP's core HR system in the cloud is SuccessFactors Employee Central. Employee Central is a robust, innovative, and evolving solution for managing the enterprise. Coupled with its attractive user interface and Employee Central Payroll, Employee Central is an excellent foundation for the entire SuccessFactors HCM suite.

6   Employee Central

Organizations large and small are undergoing people and process transformations now more than ever before. They require a true Human Resource Information System (HRIS) that streamlines processes and data flows to achieve efficiencies while allowing them to build strategic HR programs and manage the enterprise efficiently and cost-effectively.

SuccessFactors Employee Central achieves all of this and more through its organic and robust design and superior user interface (UI). Built from the ground up with modern design principles and based on the needs of mature organizations, Employee Central is a continuously evolving HRIS based on the dynamically changing needs of global organizations and SAP's global co-innovation partners. Employee Central Payroll builds on SAP ERP Payroll to provide one of the many options that Employee Central customers have to run payroll within the convenience of the cloud.

In this chapter, we'll examine the Employee Central and Employee Central Payroll offerings, their key features, and the pivotal roles they play in transforming organizations with the value of an efficient people- and process-centric core HRIS. We'll look at the various business drivers that are making Employee Central a popular choice for cloud HRIS solutions (see Section 6.1), objects that lay the foundation of organizational and personnel data in Employee Central (see Section 6.2), HR processes and transactions supported by the system (see Section 6.5), and some of the key functionalities that can be implemented to further enhance the standard delivered product offering. Section 6.7 will walk you through the payroll offering in the cloud and how Employee Central Payroll complements Employee Central to provide customers with a true HRIS in the cloud.

> **Note**
>
> SAP has published upwards of 40 handbooks on Employee Central and Employee Central Payroll. These can be found on SAP Service Marketplace at *http://service.sap.com/ ec-ondemand*.

6.1 Employee Central Business Drivers

Employee Central is a genuine, 21st-century SaaS core HR system that offers flexibility, usability, and the principal functionality needed to manage the enterprise in a constantly challenging and changing world. HR professionals, managers, and executives can leverage these characteristics to more effectively manage personnel and organizational processes. Although it is lacking in the same depth of functionality as SAP ERP HCM, Employee Central does offer a broad range of features and functionalities that are user friendly and flexible enough to change however and whenever the business requires. In addition, Employee Central offers some functionality that cannot be found in SAP ERP HCM. There are some key drivers behind the use of Employee Central in addition to SAP ERP HCM, which we'll take a look at now.

6.1.1 "Glocalization"

One of the biggest advantages of Employee Central is its ability to function as a global system of record. A large number of customers that are evaluating a strategy to transition to the cloud are organizations that have disparate HR systems; with increased unification of business processes and revenue pools, they are looking to construct an HRIS that can serve as a global system of record with localized business processes.

Localizations for 71 countries (at the time of writing) include country-specific company and job fields, validations and dropdown values, localized regulatory compliance reporting, advances and deductions, global benefits, global assignments, and more. For example, National ID card options and validations are provided for each of these 71 countries, as well as country-specific address formats.

Currently, Employee Central supports 37 languages. Customers can switch on relevant language packs and enable translations for the required fields. The system provides standard translations that can be replaced with customer-specific translations, as required.

A current list of country localizations for Employee Central can be provided by SAP or found at *http://scn.sap.com/docs/DOC-48497*. A list of languages supported by Employee Central can be provided by SAP or found at *http://scn.sap.com/docs/DOC-48498*.

6.1.2 Self-Services

The drive for administrative efficiency is prompting companies to push more transactions to the lowest cost mode of execution, which is often via self-service, rather than a traditional HR business partner. The advent of Employee Self-Service (ESS) and Manager Self-Service (MSS) found its source in the need to decentralize administrative and service functions via HR solutions that enable employees and managers to handle most of their own processes and data maintenance activities. But, complex business needs require employees to understand myriad complex processes; having a modern core HRIS that leverages self-service capabilities with an intuitive UI simplifies the complex job functions performed by employees and managers and increases employee productivity and the profitability of an organization.

Employee Central offers both ESS and MSS capabilities built in, with no need for a separate portal or offering to provide these features to employees.

It is evident that self-service capabilities of a core HRIS are increasingly viewed in a more progressive dimension than in the past. The advent of Employee Self-Service (ESS) and Manager Self-Service (MSS) found its source in the need to decentralize administrative and service functions via HR solutions that enable employees and managers to handle most of their own processes and data maintenance activities. But complex business needs require employees to understand myriad complex processes; having a modern core HRIS that leverages self-service capabilities with an intuitive UI simplifies the complex job functions performed by employees and managers and increases employee productivity and the profitability of an organization.

Employee Central offers both ESS and MSS capabilities built in, with no need for a separate portal or offering to provide these features to employees.

6.1.3 Data Quality and Consistency

Sophisticated analytics and reporting are only as good as the data they are based on. How can you ensure that you don't suffer from poor data quality or data inconsistencies that affect critical, data-reliant processes such as payroll, talent management, or analytics? Bad data can be caused by user error, nonintegrated data, and poor system validations.

Picklists, rules, data propagations, event derivation, and associations are used to ensure that only correct values can be selected, and validations ensure that data selections are validated. *Propagations* ensure that one or more values are copied from the Foundation Objects (which we'll cover in Section 6.2.1) to the employee's Job Information, based on the selected Foundation Object. *Event Derivation* is where the system selects an Event and Event Reason based on the action or data change made by the user, which we'll cover in Section 6.4.2. *Associations* are relationships between objects that define what objects can be selected based on selection of another object.

6.1.4 Integration

As well as being integrated into the SuccessFactors HCM suite, SAP delivers several packaged integrations and standard integration templates to integrate Employee Central with SAP ERP, SAP Cloud applications, and third-party applications. To ensure a full cloud offering for Time and Attendance, Benefits, and Payroll, customers have the option of leveraging the open integration platform provided by Dell Boomi AtomSphere. Dell Boomi AtomSphere is the middleware included within the Employee Central subscription, and it is covered, along with the packaged integrations available, in Chapter 3.

6.1.5 Mobility

Mobility is an increasingly important part of an HR technology strategy, and the use of mobile devices for workplace activities is on the rise. Employee Central helps to facilitate mobility through functionality provided in the SuccessFactors HCM Mobile application. Although SAP's mobility platform—which comprises Sybase Unwired Platform and Gateway technology—scores high on scalability with the number of deployed applications and the heterogeneity of deployed application types, cost and required ROI can be prohibitive obstacles to rolling out mobility within the enterprise. SuccessFactors HCM Mobile is not only free, but also requires no additional infrastructure setup and is simple to download and activate.

We have seen the key business drivers that reiterate the need for a core HRIS that is not just a repository of employee and organizational data, but also truly enables business execution. Let's examine how in more detail in the upcoming sections.

6.2   Data Objects

Employee Central has an agile and easy-to-adapt design for customers' changing HR business requirements. It moves away from the structured design of SAP ERP HCM and the concept of infotypes and toward a free-flowing platform of flexible data models that allows you to store and manage data through simple and easy-to-configure attributes. The different types of objects allow data to be stored in a way that makes more sense to users and is flexible enough to be extended as required.

We'll now spend some time understanding the four data objects that comprise the architecture of the Employee Central data framework: Foundation Objects, Person Objects, and Employment Objects, and Generic Objects including how each can be used in Employee Central. After examining these objects, we'll see how they fit into the transactional aspect of Employee Central. Let's get started.

6.2.1   Foundation Objects

Foundation Objects define the company data for an organization. They are database objects that hold information about enterprise-level objects, such as a business unit or cost center. The Foundation Object tables capture detailed information about a company's organization, pay, and job structures. Each object has a set of standard fields, 80 available custom fields, and country-specific fields to house country-specific data. Of course, you are not expected to remember any table names or transactions to access the information housed in these objects! Let's look at each of these structures and understand their importance in building your core HR system through a few examples.

▶ **Organizational structures**
Organizational structures are the building blocks that organizations can use to structure their organizations to custom fit their needs. Eight standard organizational structures are delivered (Legal Entity, Business Unit, Division, Depart-

ment, Location Group, Geo Zone, Location, and Cost Center), but Generic Objects can also be created to act as custom Foundation Objects if the standard delivered objects need extending for your needs. For example, a division may have an additional level of subdivision in the organizational hierarchy.

▸ **Job structures**
Job structures' functionality can be used to create job codes and job functions in your organization. The two job structures objects are Job Classification and Job Function.

▸ **Pay structures**
Pay structures are used to store the compensation components of any employee. These objects include Pay Group, Pay Component, Pay Component Group, Pay Grade, Pay Range, Pay Calendar, and Frequency. Pay structure objects can be easily configured in the UI when elements of the structure change, such as new pay incentives or pay grades are introduced.

> **Note**
>
> Let's draw some similarities here to SAP ERP HCM. Pay group is the equivalent of a payroll area; pay components are analogous to wage types; and pay component groups comprise pay components, just like wage type groups are made up of wage types.

Now that we've covered the Foundation Objects, let's talk about what they do.

Foundation Objects, in addition to storing data about organizational elements, can also feed data to the employee's employment record using the propagation feature that we mentioned in Section 6.1.3.

An HR manager entering a new hire into the system must usually enter the following information into the system:

▸ **Job Code**: ENG00253

▸ **Job Title**: Java Engineer

▸ **Local Job Title**: Java Application Engineer

▸ **Standard Hours**: 40

▸ **FLSA Status**: Exempt

All of this information is also stored on Job Classification Foundation Object, so, instead of the HR manager's entering this data manually and possibly introducing errors, propagation can be used. Through the propagation configuration made during configuration, the HR manager can select the ENG00253 Job Classification in the Job Code field, and the remaining values are automatically populated on the screen. In SAP ERP HCM, this is similar to creating a job object and maintaining this data against that specific object. Figure 6.1 illustrates how data maintained at the job code level, such as standard hours and pay grade, can be populated on the employee record when that job code is assigned.

Country-specific data can also be stored on Foundation Objects. For example, perhaps you need to store country-specific fields such as FEDERAL EMPLOYER IDENTIFICATION NUMBER (FEIN) for a US-based legal entity or company code, but you need to keep the remaining fields applicable to all countries.

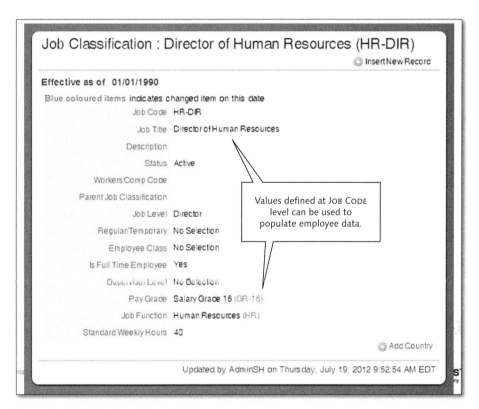

Figure 6.1 Job Code Foundation Object

Figure 6.2 shows an example of the country-specific fields configured for the United States on the legal entity Foundation Object ACE USA.

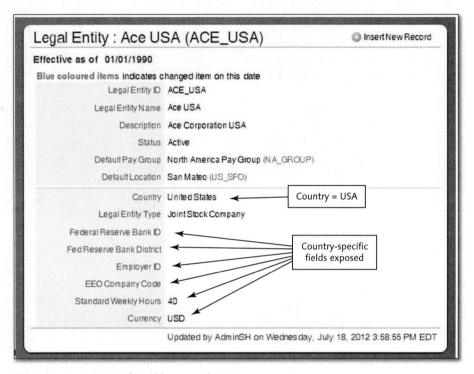

Figure 6.2 Country-Specific Fields on Legal Entity

6.2.2 HR Data Objects

HR data objects are separated into Person Objects and Employment Objects. Person Objects are found on the PERSONAL INFORMATION screen, and employment objects on the EMPLOYMENT INFORMATION screen.

Both Person Objects and Employment Objects appear as sections on the UI called *portlets*. In Figure 6.3, you can see the NATIONAL ID CARD, PERSONAL INFORMATION, ADDRESSES, and PERSON INFO portlets on the PERSONAL INFORMATION screen. You can rename these portlets, if you like, as well as add more fields.

Data captured in the HR data objects can be effective dated, although not all data is because it often does not change or no history is required. Effective dated information allows multiple time-dependent records to exist, along with the different EVENT and EVENT REASONS for that change in data. The portlets that contain effective dated data have a HISTORY link in the header if the user has permissions to view history. Figure 6.4 shows the history of JOB INFORMATION.

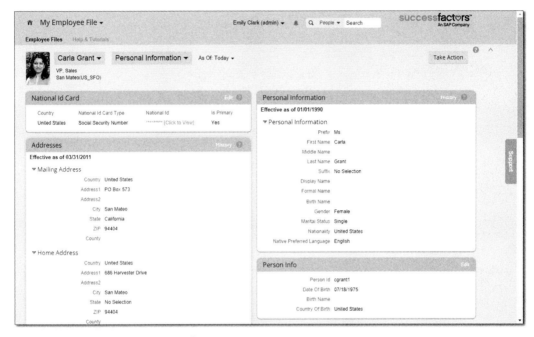

Figure 6.3 Portlets on the Personal Information Screen

Here, the user can view each record and see who was the last user to update that record, and when. On each record, the changes are highlighted in a different font color, and the previous values are displayed next to the new values with a strikethrough.

Depending on permissions, new records can be added with the INSERT NEW RECORD button, or existing records can be corrected or deleted via the MAKE COR-RECTION and PERMANENTLY DELETE RECORD options in the TAKE ACTION menu on the selected record. If the record was subject to workflow approval, you can also view the workflow approvers by selecting VIEW APPROVAL HISTORY in the TAKE ACTION menu.

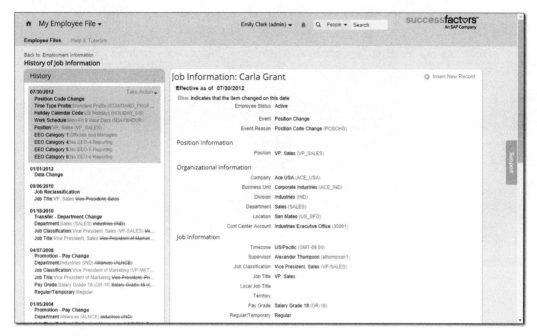

Figure 6.4 History of Job Information

6.2.3 Generic Objects

Generic Objects—which we covered in Chapter 4—are the foundation of custom objects and new functionality from SuccessFactors. They enable customers to add custom Foundation Objects and new objects and screens to cover their own requirements that aren't covered by the core product. In addition, SuccessFactors has used Generic Objects in functionality such as Position Management, Time Off, and Global Benefits. In the future, Foundation Objects and HR data objects will most likely be Generic Objects.

A prime example of a Generic Object used in Employee Central is the position object. The position object is natively integrated into Employee Central—as well as Succession and Recruiting—and appears in an employee's Job Information portlet. This can be seen at the top of the Job Information portlet in Figure 6.5.

Adding custom screens enables customers to add their own functionalities into Employee Central. This is especially useful for industry-specific capabilities. Figure 6.6 shows a GENERIC OBJECT screen.

Figure 6.5 Position Information in the Job Information Portlet

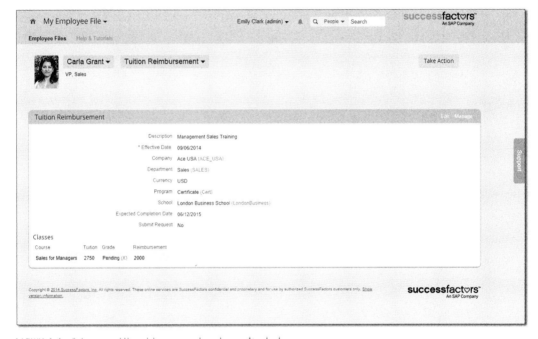

Figure 6.6 A Generic Object Screen in Employee Central

Now, let's take a look at what employee data is displayed and managed in Employee Central.

6.3 Employee Data

Employee data in Employee Central is accessed in Employee Files, just like the Employee Profile that we discussed in Chapter 4. Employee Central data is split into two main screens—called views—that are accessed from the EMPLOYEE FILES menu: PERSONAL INFORMATION and EMPLOYMENT INFORMATION. Other Employee Central views are accessed here, but we will cover them as we discuss the individual functionalities throughout the rest of this chapter.

All of the portlets can be extended with additional fields and have rules applied. However, additional portlets cannot be added to either of the views. Both views and all portlets can be renamed.

HR users—depending on the Role-Based Permissions configuration—can edit data in each portlet if they have been given permission to access the EDIT link in the portlet header. Users may also be given access to the additional HISTORY link that we discussed in Section 6.2.2. If these options are not available, users may have access to the TAKE ACTION button to make changes.

Additionally, you can display past or future data on screen by clicking TODAY next to As OF. This is illustrated in Figure 6.7.

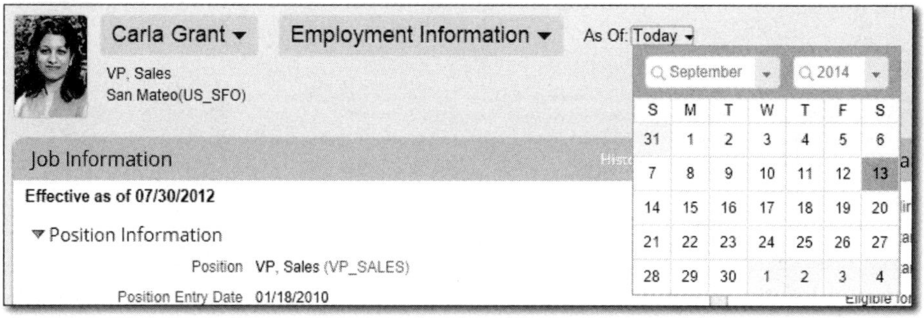

Figure 6.7 Changing the Effective Date of the Data on Screen

Now, let's take a look at the two views.

6.3.1 Personal Information

All person object data is displayed on the PERSONAL INFORMATION screen. In the standard configuration, it is made up of the following portlets:

▶ NATIONAL ID INFORMATION: Information about national IDs

▶ HOME ADDRESS: Home and other addresses of the employee

▸ PERSONAL INFORMATION: Information such as first name, last name, marital status, native language, and so on

▸ BIOGRAPHICAL INFORMATION: The employee's User ID, date of birth, country of birth, etc.

▸ WORK PERMIT INFO: Any work permits issued to the employee

▸ CONTACT INFORMATION: Email, phone, and social media contact information

▸ PRIMARY EMERGENCY CONTACT: Details about emergency contacts

▸ DEPENDENTS: Information about dependents of the employee

▸ PAYMENT INFORMATION: Direct deposit and payment details

We saw some of these in Figure 6.3. Figure 6.8 shows the CONTACT INFORMATION, PRIMARY EMERGENCY CONTACT, and DEPENDENTS portlets.

> **Note**
>
> Personal Information is the name of the view as well as a portlet in the view. Customers can rename views, as well as portlets, if required.

Figure 6.8 Contact Information, Primary Emergency Contact, and Dependents

The Personal Information, Home Address, and Dependents portlets store effective-dated data. These portlets can also store country-specific information. The address format in the Home Address portlet can vary depending on the country selected, as shown in Figure 6.9.

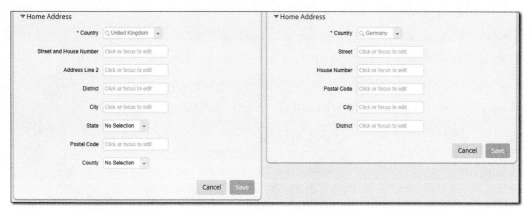

Figure 6.9 Country-Specific Address Formats

Now that we've looked at the Person Information screen, let's take a look at the Employment Information screen.

6.3.2 Employment Information

Employment objects include employment and job-related information, such as compensation information and hire date. The employment objects are displayed in the Employment Information screen, as shown in Figure 6.10. These objects are person-related and independent of the enterprise.

In the standard configuration and with all features enabled, the following portlets are displayed on the Employment Information screen:

- Job Information: All information about the organizational assignment, job, and position of the employee
- Employment Details: Details about hire date, service dates, stock options, etc.
- Alternative Cost Distribution: Any alternative cost distributions
- Job Relationships: Any job relationships, such as HR Manager or Matrix Manager

▶ COMPENSATION INFORMATION: All details relating to the employee's compensation

▶ ELIGIBILITY FOR ADVANCES: Any advances to the employee

▶ SPOT BONUS: Any one-off bonuses

▶ RECURRING DEDUCTION: Any recurring deductions

▶ ONE TIME DEDUCTION USER: Any one-off deductions

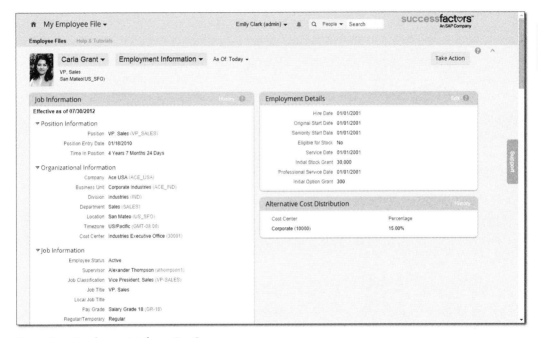

Figure 6.10 Employment Information Screen

Figure 6.11 shows the COMPENSATION INFORMATION, ELIGIBILITY FOR ADVANCES, and SPOT BONUS portlets.

In this section, we examined the two main views where employee data is displayed. We'll now scrutinize the different transactions, processes, and functionality available in Employee Central.

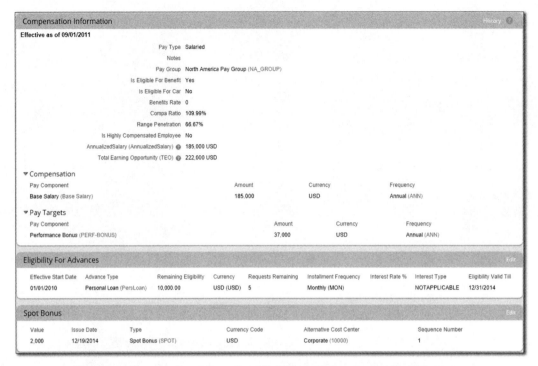

Figure 6.11 Compensation Information, Eligibility for Advances, and Spot Bonus

6.4 Events

Many events occur during the employee lifecycle, and Employee Central enables events and event reasons to be selected. The Event Reason Foundation Object is used to define the different reasons. A fixed set of events is provided with Employee Central, which cannot be modified. However, an unlimited number of Event Reason objects can be defined for each event.

Employee Central provides the following events in the system:

- ADD GLOBAL ASSIGNMENT
- ADDITIONAL JOB
- ASSIGNMENT
- ASSIGNMENT COMPLETION
- AWAY ON GLOBAL ASSIGNMENT

- ▶ BACK FROM GLOBAL ASSIGNMENT
- ▶ COMPLETION OF PROBATION
- ▶ DATA CHANGE
- ▶ DEMOTION
- ▶ DISCARD PENSION PAYOUT
- ▶ END GLOBAL ASSIGNMENT
- ▶ END PENSION PAYOUT
- ▶ FURLOUGH
- ▶ HIRE
- ▶ JOB CHANGE
- ▶ JOB RECLASSIFICATION
- ▶ LEAVE OF ABSENCE
- ▶ OBSOLETE
- ▶ PAY RATE CHANGE
- ▶ POSITION CHANGE
- ▶ PROBATION
- ▶ PROMOTION
- ▶ REHIRE
- ▶ RETURN FROM DISABILITY
- ▶ RETURN TO WORK
- ▶ START PENSION PAYOUT
- ▶ SUSPENSION
- ▶ TERMINATION
- ▶ TRANSFER

In the next two sections, we'll discuss Employee Status and Employee Derivation.

6.4.1 Employee Status

Employee Central enables the status of an employee to be controlled via Event Reasons. Event Reasons can have an employee status value assigned, to change the status of an employee when the associated Event takes place. For example, an Event Reason tied to the Hire event would have the employee status of ACTIVE.

Likewise, Event Reasons for the Termination event would have the employee status of TERMINATED.

Events do not have to have an employee status assigned. For example, a change in compensation does not change the status of an employee. Their existing status—whether ACTIVE, TERMINATED, PAID LEAVE, etc.—does not change based on the event that takes place and Event Reason selected. The following different employee status values are available in the system:

- ACTIVE
- UNPAID LEAVE
- PAID LEAVE
- RETIRED
- SUSPENDED
- TERMINATED
- FURLOUGH
- DISCARDED
- DORMANT

Occasionally, SuccessFactors introduces new events.

6.4.2 Event Derivation

Event Derivation enables the system to automatically select an event and Event Reason, based on the configuration during implementation. This significantly reduces user error, which can impact data accuracy and integrity, the JOB HISTORY portlet on the Employee Profile, and integration.

Event Reasons are used only for changes to the PERSONAL INFORMATION, JOB INFORMATION, and COMPENSATION INFORMATION portlets. Although the Event Reason is selected automatically with Event Derivation, it can be manually changed in the HISTORY screen of each portlet.

6.5 Processes, Transactions, and Features

Employee Central supports a wide range of HR processes and transactions, making it a complete HR system of record in the cloud. The following processes are supported in Employee Central:

- New hires and rehires

- Job Changes, Compensation Changes, and Transfers

- Employee Self-Service

- Mass Changes

- Global Benefits

- Time Off and Absence Management

- Global Assignments

- Advances and Deductions

- Alternative Cost Distribution

In addition to these processes, Employee Central also features the following:

- Position Management

- Event Derivation

- Workflows

- Concurrent Employment

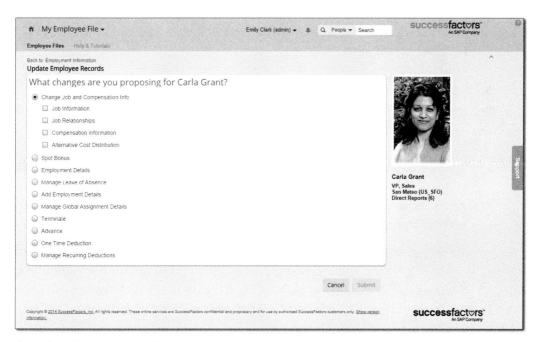

Figure 6.12 The Transactions Screen

Most transactions are initiated using the TAKE ACTION button on the PERSONAL INFORMATION or EMPLOYMENT INFORMATION screens. Typically, this would be the EMPLOYMENT INFORMATION screen. However, in an ESS scenario, many employees may have access to only the PERSONAL INFORMATION screen (see Figure 6.12).

These same transactions can also be launched from the employee quickcard via the People Search, which we discussed in Chapter 4. Figure 6.12 shows the TRANSACTIONS screen, which usually has the appropriate option defaulted.

Transactions can trigger workflows if the system is configured to trigger them. We will cover workflows in Section 6.5.13.

Let's look at a few examples of these processes to understand the value that Employee Central can add.

6.5.1 New Hires and Rehires

New hires can be added through the ADD NEW EMPLOYEE transaction. The transaction uses a four-step route map to enter details of the new employee. It can also match against previous employees who are not currently active in the system. The ADD NEW EMPLOYEE transaction leverages the configuration used on the PERSONAL INFORMATION and EMPLOYMENT INFORMATION screens. ADD NEW EMPLOYEE can be launched in two ways:

▸ Via OneAdmin using the ADD NEW EMPLOYEE option in UPDATE USER INFORMATION

▸ By clicking the ADD NEW EMPLOYEE button on the ORG CHART screen in COMPANY INFO

A rehire transaction can be launched using in OneAdmin using the REHIRE INACTIVE EMPLOYEE option in UPDATE USER INFORMATION. This allows an inactive employee to be selected before the ADD NEW EMPLOYEE transaction is launched with employee data pre-loaded into each of the screens.

If SuccessFactors Recruiting is used, you can use the MANAGE PENDING HIRES transaction in UPDATE USER INFORMATION in OneAdmin to launch the ADD NEW EMPLOYEE transaction for an employee who has accepted an offer. The ADD NEW EMPLOYEE transaction is launched with data from the requisition, application, and offer letter in SuccessFactors Recruiting.

The ADD NEW EMPLOYEE transaction—seen in Figure 6.13—is split into four parts: IDENTITY, PERSONAL INFORMATION, JOB INFORMATION, and COMPENSATION INFORMATION. The first thing you must do when launching the transaction is select the Legal Entity (Company) and the Event Reason. The Event Reasons are for the HIRE action, unless the REHIRE INACTIVE EMPLOYEE option is used, in which case the Event Reasons are for the REHIRE action.

The system walks you through each step, starting with setting up the IDENTITY, followed by entering PERSONAL INFORMATION and EMPLOYMENT INFORMATION, and finally, entering the COMPENSATION INFORMATION for the new hire.

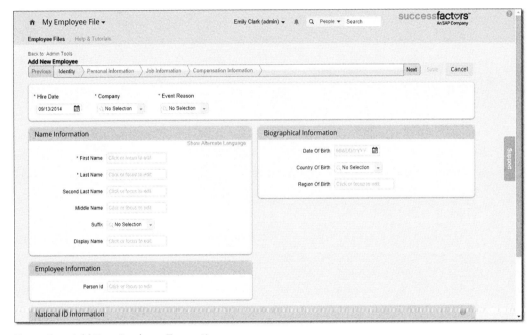

Figure 6.13 Add New Employee Transaction

PERSON ID can be generated automatically by the system or entered manually. If a PERSON ID or the FIRST NAME and LAST NAME combination entered on the IDENTITY screen already exists, the system validates it and informs the user of the duplicate entry, as shown in Figure 6.14. You can choose to go back and enter new credentials. If you click IGNORE MATCHES, the system gives you an error and prompts you to enter a unique value for the PERSON ID.

Once the process is completed, a workflow may be triggered. If this is the case, the new hire does not appear in the system until the workflow is approved.

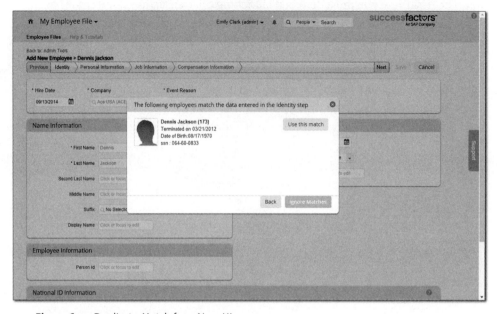

Figure 6.14 Duplicate Match for a New Hire

6.5.2 Terminations

As with any HRIS, employees who can be hired can also be terminated. Employees are terminated by navigating to the employee, clicking the TAKE ACTION button, and then clicking TERMINATE. Here, details about the termination can be included, such as termination date, event reason (which must be selected irrespective of whether Event Derivation is used), salary end date, and notes. If the employee has any direct reports, then once the termination date is selected, the option to select a new manager appears, along with the transfer date. The new manager is defaulted to the to-be-terminated employee's current manager. This can be seen in Figure 6.15.

Once the termination action is completed and the termination date is reached, the terminated employee's employment status changes to TERMINATED. On the EMPLOYMENT INFORMATION screen, the POSITION assignment is rendered unavailable and the EMPLOYMENT DETAILS portlet also shows the termination details. This can be seen in Figure 6.16.

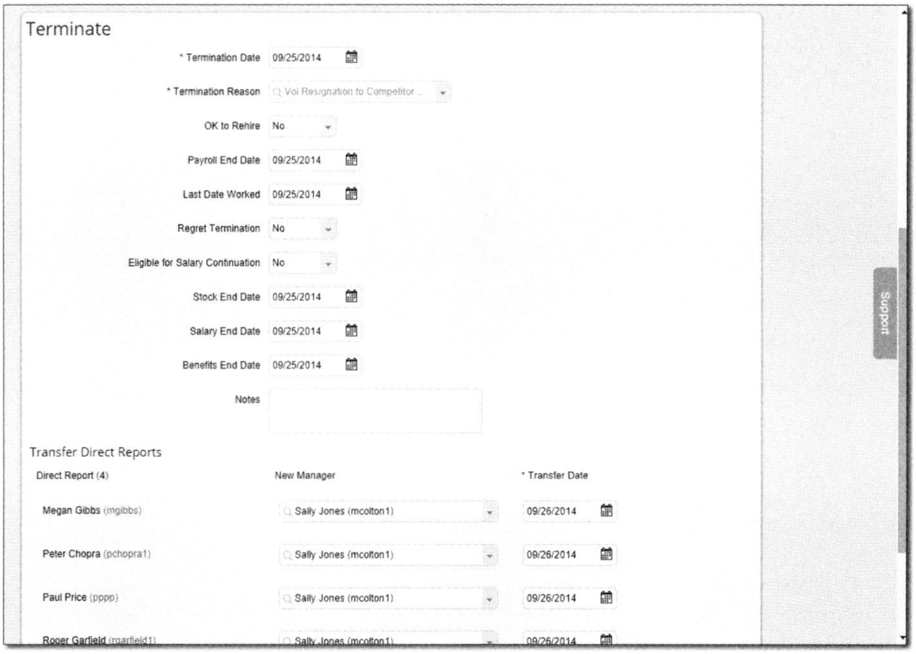

Figure 6.15 A Termination Transaction

Figure 6.16 Termination Details on the Employment Information Screen

If a user has permissions, they can search for terminated employees in Employee Files to view the Personal Information and Employment Information for a terminated employee. Terminated employees cannot be found using the People Search.

6.5.3 Job Changes, Compensation Changes, and Transfers

Managers and some HR professionals can initiate changes and transfers for their direct reports, such as a job change or compensation change. This would be considered Manager Self-Service (MSS) when performed by a manager. There are four primary actions that may be used in the TAKE ACTION button menu:

▸ CHANGE JOB & COMPENSATION INFO: Change data in the JOB INFORMATION, JOB RELATIONSHIPS, or COMPENSATION INFORMATION portlets

▸ SPOT BONUS: Award a one-off bonus

▸ EMPLOYMENT DETAILS: Change data in the EMPLOYMENT DETAILS portlet

▸ ADD EMPLOYMENT DETAILS: Add a concurrent employment

Once in the TRANSACTIONS screen, if the user selects CHANGE JOB & COMPENSATION INFO, then they have three other options corresponding to the three portlets in the EMPLOYMENT INFORMATION screen:

▸ JOB INFORMATION

▸ JOB RELATIONSHIPS

▸ COMPENSATION INFORMATION

There is also a fourth option (ALTERNATIVE COST DISTRIBUTION), which we will cover in Section 6.5.10.

Each of these changes—with the exception of JOB RELATIONSHIPS—is effective dated and, once approved, may require workflow approval prior to being visible on the employee's EMPLOYMENT INFORMATION screen. A manager is able to change any fields for which they have permission. It may even be that they do not have permission to see all of the above options, or your company may not use all of the functionalities (e.g., Spot Bonus or Concurrent Employment).

Figure 6.17 shows a SPOT BONUS being awarded.

Figure 6.17 Awarding a Spot Bonus

6.5.4 Employee Self-Service

Employees can make changes to their own data, such as address and dependents. This is called Employee Self-Service (ESS). These are typically changes on the PERSONAL INFORMATION screen and do not use the TAKE ACTION button; rather, the employee uses the EDIT button in the header of the portlet that they wish to change. It is possible that an employee sees some portlets, but cannot edit that data, such as national ID card.

Figure 6.18 shows an employee editing their home address in ESS.

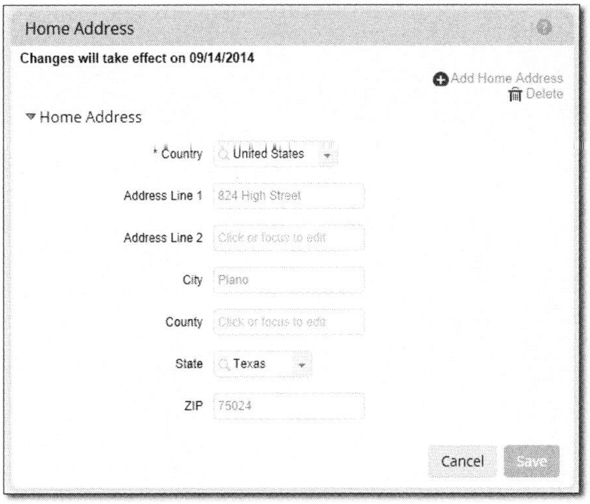

Figure 6.18 Editing Home Address in ESS

6.5.5 Mass Changes

Administrators can create mass data changes, such as organizational changes, job relationship changes, and so on. Mass changes are created in OneAdmin via MANAGE MASS CHANGES in EMPLOYEE FILES. They can be initiated for any field in the JOB INFORMATION or JOB RELATIONSHIPS portlets from the EMPLOYMENT INFORMATION screen.

Once the MASS CHANGES application is opened, a list of all created mass changes requests is shown. A new mass change can be created by clicking the CREATE NEW button. Existing mass changes can be viewed (and when viewed, executed) or copied.

Mass changes are created for specific employee groups—which are defined during the mass change creation process—on an effective date for one or more fields. For JOB INFORMATION changes, an Event Reason must always be defined, and this field displays in the list of fields automatically.

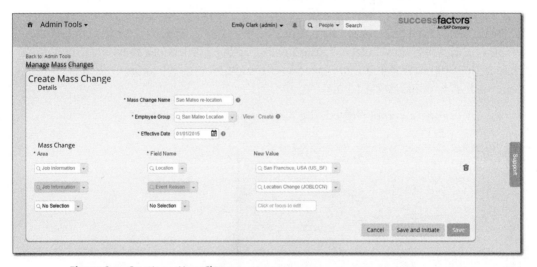

Figure 6.19 Creating a Mass Change

When you're creating a mass change, the name, employee group, effective date, and fields to be changed need to be defined. After a mass change action is created, the system gives you two buttons, SAVE and SAVE AND INITIATE, as shown in Figure 6.19. SAVE creates the mass change action but does not execute it, while SAVE AND INITIATE both saves the mass change and also executes it immediately. Once executed, the mass change shows in the list of mass changes on the main screen with status INITIATED. Once it starts, the status changes to STARTED until execution is completed; then, it changes to either COMPLETE SUCCESSFULLY or COMPLETED WITH ERRORS.

In the example in Figure 6.19, a mass change has been created for employees whose LOCATION is San Mateo. On January 1st, 2015, the LOCATION field value for all of these employees will change to San Francisco, United States.

6.5.6 Global Benefits

The Global Benefits functionality enables organizations to create country-specific and global benefits programs and benefits for employees. Employees can enroll in benefits programs, and HR, managers, and employees can manage benefits in the system. Although the solution is designed for global use use, it is currently focused on all countries except the United States, where one of SuccessFactors' partner solutions, such as Benefitfocus or AON Hewitt, is recommended. Some partners have also built US Benefits extensions on the SAP HANA Cloud Platform.

Global Benefits currently supports reimbursements, allowances, and benefits-in-kind benefits. Several pre-delivered benefits are delivered in the standard system that customers can leverage. Global Benefits is built on the Metadata Framework and leverages Generic Objects.

Creating and Managing Benefits and Benefit Programs

Benefit Programs and Benefits are managed in OneAdmin in BENEFITS ADMIN OVERVIEW in EMPLOYEE FILES. The UI is the same UI that is used to manage Generic Object data. Figure 6.20 shows a created Benefit Program that has four Benefits associated to it. Multiple benefit programs can be created.

As seen in Figure 6.20, benefits contain a number of details, such as BENEFIT TYPE, ENTITLEMENT AMOUNT, ENROLLMENT DETAILS, and an associated PAY COMPONENT. PAY COMPONENTS should be created prior to creating benefits. A benefit can be either a reimbursement or an allowance. Different rules can be created to manage eligibility to different benefits and benefit programs (see Figure 6.21).

Once Benefits and Benefit Programs are created, employees can enroll in or claim them. Auto-enrollment is also possible.

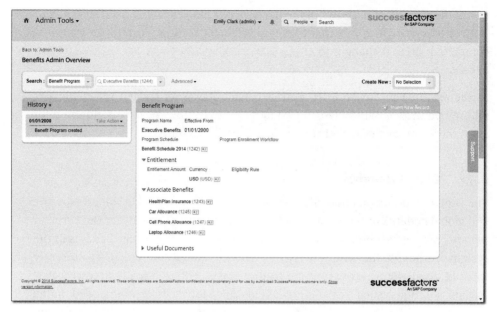

Figure 6.20 A Benefits Program in Benefits Admin Overview

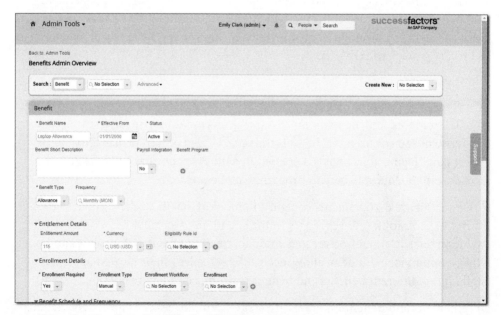

Figure 6.21 Creating a Benefit in Benefits Admin Overview

Employee Enrollment and Management

Employees can access their benefits, enroll in benefits or benefits programs, or claim a benefit by selecting EMPLOYEE BENEFITS in the menu in MY EMPLOYEE FILES. No other users can access this feature for another employee unless they proxy as that user. In this screen, users see an overview of their current benefits, claims, and enrollments. By using the TAKE ACTION button, they can select one of three actions: ENROLL BENEFIT, ENROLL BENEFIT PROGRAM, or CLAIM BENEFIT. Figure 6.22 shows the EMPLOYEE BENEFITS screen.

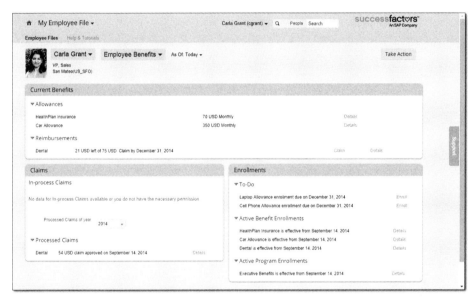

Figure 6.22 Employee Benefits Screen

Let's look at enrolling in a benefit program. By clicking the TAKE ACTION button and then the ENROLL BENEFIT PROGRAM option, we are taken to the transactions screen. Here, we can select the BENEFIT PROGRAM and enter the amount for each of the benefits for which we would like to enroll. This can be seen in Figure 6.23.

Once this is saved (and pending any workflow), the employee is taken back to the EMPLOYEE BENEFITS screen, where the new enrollment is visible. In Figure 6.22, this can be seen under the heading ACTIVE PROGRAM ENROLLMENTS in the ENROLL-MENTS portlet. If the employee is part of a benefits program then the employee can enroll in a benefit from that benefit program simply by clicking ENROLL next to the benefit in the ENROLLMENTS portlet.

We can repeat a similar process to enroll in benefits and make a claim against a Reimbursement benefit. Benefits that the employee has enrolled in are shown in the CURRENT BENEFITS portlet in the EMPLOYEE BENEFITS screen. These are separated by ALLOWANCES and REIMBURSEMENTS.

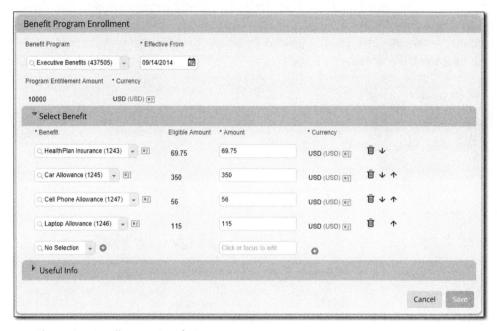

Figure 6.23 Enrolling in a Benefit Program

6.5.7 Time Off and Absence Management

In Employee Central, absence management enables companies to manage their employees' time off, whether this is planned leave or a leave of absence. To manage time off, the Time Off application is provided. Employees can request time off in SuccessFactors via the browser-based application or via a mobile or tablet device, and managers can approve time off requests in the same way. HR and managers can also create leave of absence requests for employees who may need to take unplanned or long-term absences outside of their vacation.

Time Off

Time Off, like Global Benefits, is based on the Metadata Framework and provides both administrative and employee screens to manage the Time Off processes.

Employees must have a Time Profile, Holiday Calendar, and Work Schedule assigned on their Job Information in order to use Time Off. These are Generic Objects, and data should be created in the system prior to providing access to Time Off. The Holiday Calendar must be maintained annually for each calendar year, while the Time Profile and Work Schedule can remain as is, unless the types of time or the work schedule of an employee changes.

Managing Time Off data

All of the Generic Objects used in Time Off are administered in OneAdmin via MANAGE TIME OFF STRUCTURES in COMPANY SETTINGS. This includes Time Types, Time Account Types, Holiday Calendars, Work Schedules, Accrual Rules Parameters, Accrual Rule Variables, and Period-End Processing Rule Parameters. Figure 6.24 shows an example of a TIME TYPE PROFILE.

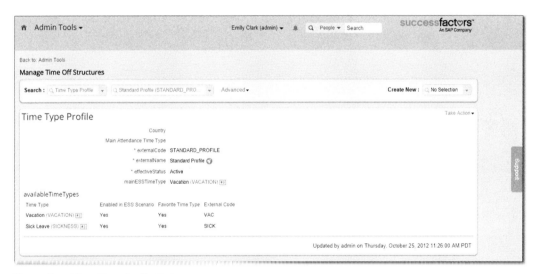

Figure 6.24 Time Type Profile Data

The different Time Off calendars are administered in OneAdmin via MANAGE TIME OFF CALENDARS in COMPANY SETTINGS. These enable period-end processing to take place.

The focus of Time Off is the Time Account, which represents a type of leave that the employee has and how much leave they are entitled to. This can be paid time off (PTO), vacation, sick leave, or another type of leave, per the employment contract.

HR and Manager Administration

HR and managers can view details of an employee's Time Off requests and remaining balances using MANAGE TIME OFF in the EMPLOYEE FILES menu of an employee or from the quickcard in the People Search. This is seen in Figure 6.25. Each of an employee's TIME ACCOUNTS—defined by the Time Profile assigned on the Job Information—can be viewed along with their balances and planned vacation in the TIME ACCOUNTS portlet at the top of the screen. This data can be viewed historically and in the future. Negative balances are allowed in Time Off. These can be used if an employee goes over their balance, is taking days against a future balance, or to clear old accounts at Period-End Processing. A limit can be placed on Time Accounts to prevent employees from going below a certain balance.

Any Time Off requests for forthcoming leave can be seen in the TIME OFF OVERVIEW portlet, and HR or a manager can create a request using the REQUEST TIME OFF button. This is a simple form that displays the TIME TYPE (e.g., vacation or sick leave), the start and end dates, and a COMMENTS field (see Figure 6.25).

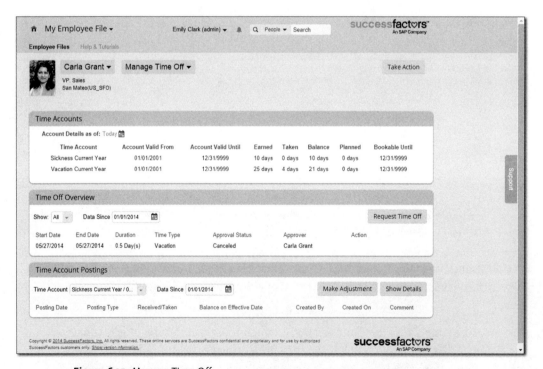

Figure 6.25 Manage Time Off

The TIME ACCOUNT POSTINGS portlet shows any TIME ACCOUNT balances that have been added manually to the employee. Manual adjustments to employees' Time Accounts can be made using the MAKE ADJUSTMENT button.

Employee Self-Service

Employees access Time Off by selecting TIME OFF in the menu in MY EMPLOYEE FILES. Like with Global Benefits, no other users can access this feature for another employee unless they proxy as that user (they should use MANAGE TIME OFF, as mentioned above).

The TIME OFF screen—shown in Figure 6.26—provides employees with an attractive and easy-to-use UI that allows them to access to their Time Account balances, a calendar, a link to access the TEAM CALENDAR, and a summary of any upcoming time off requests. Each Time Account can be selected to show further details, and the date can be adjusted to show previous or future balances. You can see an overview by clicking the INFORMATION icon to the right side of the TIME ACCOUNTS.

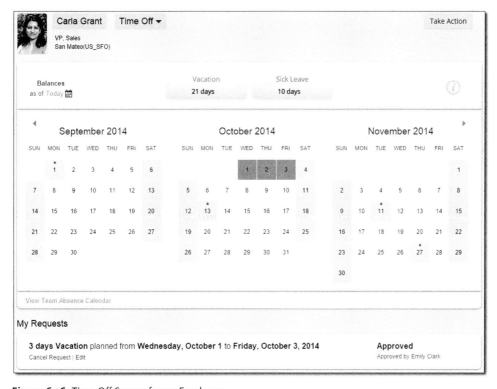

Figure 6.26 Time Off Screen for an Employee

A useful and intuitive feature for employees is the Calendar view. This shows each month in a calendar format, along with the weekends and public holidays greyed out. Public holidays are marked with an asterisk, and hovering over those days displays the name of the public holiday. These are defined in the Holiday Calendar. Any upcoming leave is highlighted on the calendar in the color of the Time Account that it represents. In Figure 6.26, there are three days of leave marked in green, which represents the VACATION TIME account.

The VIEW TEAM ABSENCE CALENDAR opens a pop-up that displays a month-by-month calendar showing the absences of each of the members of the employee's team. This can be very useful to avoid vacation conflicts across the team, as you can see in Figure 6.27. Managers can also access the TEAM ABSENCE CALENDAR from the MY TEAM portlet on the home page.

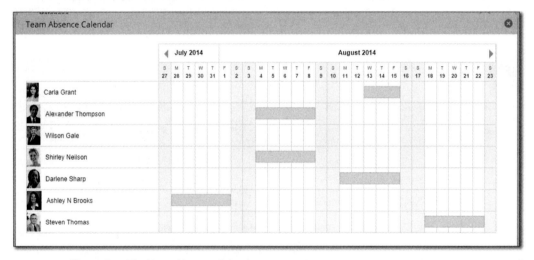

Figure 6.27 The Team Absence Calendar

Probably the most impressive feature of the TIME OFF screen is the calendar leave painter. When you select the appropriate Time Account and then move the mouse over the calendar, the pointer becomes a paint brush, and the employee can "paint" their vacation onto the calendar. This updates the Time Account balance in real time, shows an editable summary below the calendar, and shows a portlet that displays any other absences in the team (see Figure 6.28).

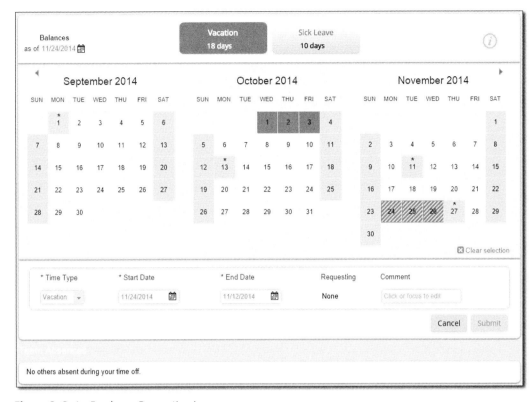

Figure 6.28 An Employee Requesting Leave

Positive Time Recording

Positive time recording is provisioned by SuccessFactors partners Workforce Software and Kronos, which offer standard integrations with Employee Central. "Lightweight" timesheet functionality will be introduced to Employee Central in 2014 and 2015.

Leave of Absence

You can manage Leave of Absence in SuccessFactors similarly to other types of transactions, through the TAKE ACTION button by selecting the MANAGE LEAVE OF ABSENCE option. Here, employees can have a Leave of Absence set or be set to return from a Leave of Absence. An employee can be assigned to only one Leave of Absence at any one time.

When entering the transactions screen to set an employee on a Leave of Absence, the user sees the ADD A LEAVE hyperlink in the MANAGE LEAVE OF ABSENCE portlet. Selecting this displays the Leave of Absence fields LEAVE START DATE, EXPECTED RETURN DATE, and LEAVE REASON, as seen in Figure 6.29.

Figure 6.29 Setting an Employee on Leave of Absence

Like with a Termination, an Event Reason must be selected manually when an employee is set to be on a Leave of Absence. If Event Derivation is used, then during implementation, the Event Reasons to use for Return to Work should be defined.

Once these details are entered and the TRANSACTION is saved, the employee's employment status changes from ACTIVE to either PAID LEAVE or UNPAID LEAVE, depending on the employee status configured in the Event Reason that was selected.

You set an employee as ACTIVE status again by navigating back to the MANAGE LEAVE OF ABSENCE transaction. The MANAGE LEAVE OF ABSENCE portlet shows the fields that were previously maintained, as well as the RETURN FROM LEAVE hyperlink on the right side. Selecting this displays the ACTUAL RETURN DATE field, as seen in Figure 6.30.

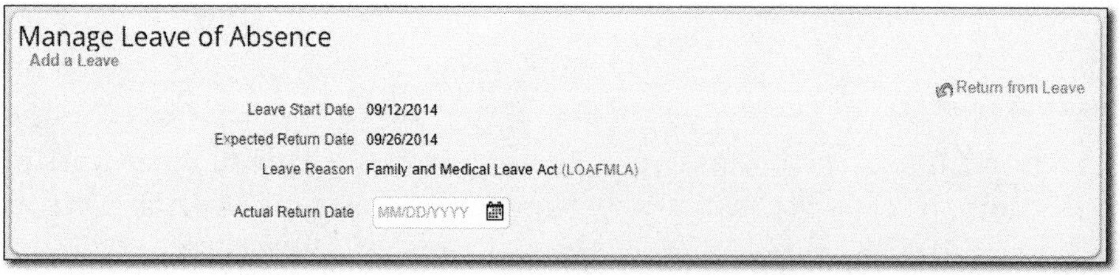

Figure 6.30 Return from Leave

Once the return date is entered, the action saved, and the date in the ACTUAL RETURN DATE field is reached, the employee status field updates. If this is in the past, the employee status change is back dated.

6.5.8 Global Assignment

Global Assignment enables employees to be sent on assignment to another company within their organization, with a home and host employment record to cover both the home employment and the expatriate employment.

Global Assignment works very similarly to the Leave of Absence process that we covered in the previous section. They are managed through the TAKE ACTION button by selecting the MANAGE GLOBAL ASSIGNMENT DETAILS option. Here, employees can have a global assignment set or set to return from a global assignment. An employee can be assigned to only one global assignment at any one time.

When entering the TRANSACTIONS screen to set an employee on a global assignment, the user sees the ADD GLOBAL ASSIGNMENT DETAILS hyperlink in the MANAGE GLOBAL ASSIGNMENT DETAILS portlet. Selecting this displays the global assignment fields EVENT REASON, ASSIGNMENT TYPE, START DATE, PLANNED END DATE, and COMPANY, as seen in Figure 6.31.

Figure 6.31 Setting an Employee on Global Assignment

Like with a Termination and Leave of Absence, an Event Reason must be selected manually when an employee is set to be on a global assignment. The ASSIGNMENT TYPE could be SHORT-TERM ASSIGNMENT, LONG-TERM ASSIGNMENT, or another type as defined by your company.

Once the COMPANY field value is selected, four further portlets appear below the MANAGE GLOBAL ASSIGNMENT DETAILS portlet: JOB INFORMATION, JOB RELATION-SHIPS, WORK PERMIT INFO, and COMPENSATION INFORMATION (which includes the information usually seen in the Spot Bonus portlet). Each of these portlets represents the expatriate (host) assignment details (see Figure 6.32).

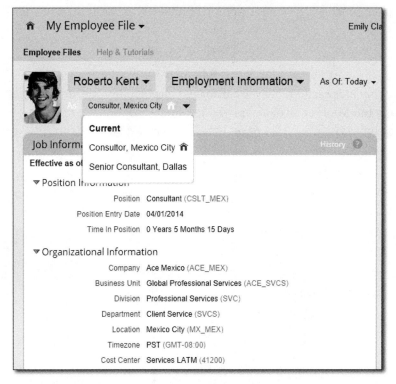

Figure 6.32 The Assignments Dropdown Button

Once these details are entered and the transaction is saved, the employee's EMP-LOYMENT INFORMATION screen displays a button showing the home assignment as the label, which can be used to select the home or host assignment. Past and future host assignments are also shown. Selecting the host assignment shows the EMPLOYMENT INFORMATION screen for that assignment. This button always remains on the EMPLOYMENT INFORMATION screen as long as there has been at least one global assignment in the past or there will be one in the future. This button can be seen in Figure 6.32.

The host assignment screen shows similar details to the standard Employment Information screen, but the EMPLOYMENT DETAILS portlet is replaced by the GLOBAL ASSIGNMENT DETAILS portlet for a host assignment. This is seen in Figure 6.33.

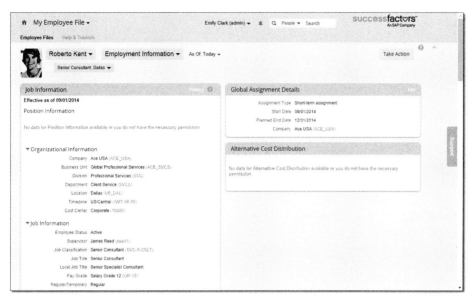

Figure 6.33 The Host Assignment

The global assignment can be edited or ended. To do so, select the host employment on the Employment Details screen followed by the TAKE ACTION BUTTON and the MANAGE GLOBAL ASSIGNMENT DETAILS option. Here, two options are presented to the user: EDIT GLOBAL ASSIGNMENT DETAILS and END OR DELETE GLOBAL ASSIGNMENT DETAILS. The first option allows you to change the ASSIGNMENT TYPE, START DATE, and END DATE of the assignment. The second option simply gives you the option to delete or end the global assignment. If you click the END button to end the global assignment, the END GLOBAL ASSIGNMENT DETAILS portlet is displayed under the MANAGE GLOBAL ASSIGNMENT DETAILS portlet. This is seen in Figure 6.34.

Once the ACTUAL END DATE, EVENT REASON, and PAYROLL END DATE (if required) fields are maintained, the global assignment can be ended. As mentioned above, the employment information of this global assignment can still be viewed from the EMPLOYMENT INFORMATION screen.

Figure 6.34 End Global Assignment Details Portlet

In GLOBAL ASSIGNMENTS, it is possible to set up automatic ending of global assignments using the rule engine. Additionally, alerts and notifications can be created to support the global assignments processes.

When employees who are on global assignment login to SuccessFactors then they will see their global assignment listed under their name in the header panel with a dropdown arrow. This enables them to switch between the each assignment so that they can perform different processes for each assignment.

6.5.9 Advances and Deductions

Employee Central provides functionality so that companies can give their employees advances against and make deductions from future compensation.

Advances

Advances can be made against an employee's future compensation and reclaimed over a number of installments over a period of time.

Advances are set up in OneAdmin in MANAGE ADVANCE OBJECTS under EMPLOYEE FILES. As with other features, Advances are built on the metadata framework, and the MANAGE ADVANCE OBJECTS screen will be familiar to users who have managed Generic Object data. The ELIGIBILITY FOR ADVANCES object is used to create the advances that employees can request. Figure 6.35 shows the data for an ELIGIBILITY FOR ADVANCES object for a personal loan in the United States.

When creating the ELIGIBILITY FOR ADVANCE record, automatic recovery of the advance can be selected. This requires the DEDUCTIONS feature to be enabled and for recurring and non-recurring PAY COMPONENTS to be created in the system.

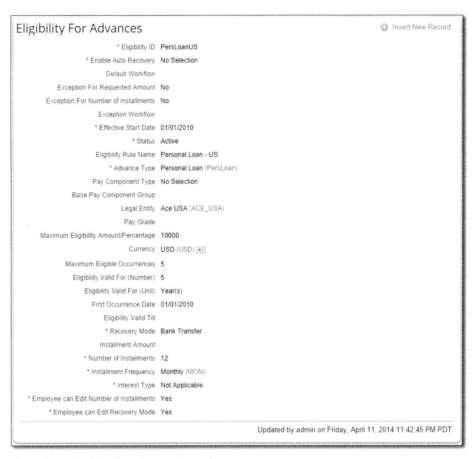

Figure 6.35 Eligibility for Advances Record

Eligibility for an advance is determined with a rule that is created in the Rules Engine in OneAdmin. This allows customers to use any criteria from the Job Information portlet to determine which employees are eligible to request advances.

For an advance to be requested, the TAKE ACTION button on the PERSONAL INFORMATION or EMPLOYMENT INFORMATION screens of the target employee should be used, and the option ADVANCE selected. The transactions screen shows the ADVANCE portlet, where the advance(s) that the employee is eligible for can be selected. Figure 6.36 shows the ADVANCE portlet with a request being made.

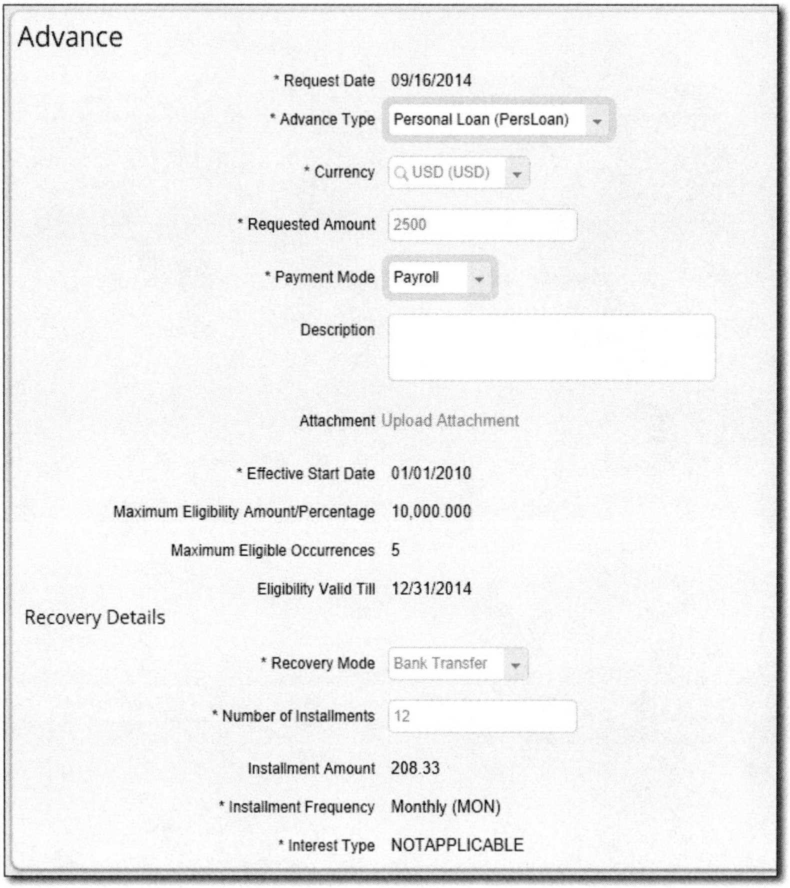

Figure 6.36 Requesting an Advance

The details of the advance can be entered, including the Advance type, requested amount, payment method, and description. When you enter the number of installments, the installment amount is automatically calculated. The number of installments cannot be higher than the amount defined when creating the ELIGIBILITY FOR ADVANCE record.

Once an advance has been submitted, it can be viewed on the employee's EMPLOYMENT INFORMATION screen in the SPOT BONUS portlet, and the remaining eligibility amount can be seen in the ELIGIBILITY FOR ADVANCES portlet, as seen in Figure 6.37.

Eligibility For Advances										Edit
Effective Start Date	Advance Type		Remaining Eligibility	Currency	Requests Remaining	Installment Frequency	Interest Rate %	Interest Type	Eligibility Valid Till	
01/01/2010	Personal Loan (PersLoan)		7,500.00	USD (USD)	4	Monthly (MON)		NOTAPPLICABLE	12/31/2014	

Spot Bonus									Edit
Value	Issue Date	Type		Currency Code		Alternative Cost Center		Sequence Number	
2.000	12/19/2014	Spot Bonus (SPOT)		USD		Corporate (10000)		1	
▼ Advance									
payDate		payComponentCode				currencyGO		payCompValue	
09/16/2014		Personal Loan (PersLoan)		-		USD (USD)		2,500.00	

Figure 6.37 Eligibility for Advances and Spot Bonus Portlets

Advances can either be recovered automatically as a deduction using the Deductions feature or be set up manually. Because we do not have automatic recovery enabled, we'll now look at setting up a recurring deduction to recover the advance.

Deductions

Deductions enable one-time or recurring deductions to be made from an employee's salary. This could be for a medical plan or to recover an advance.

Deductions are created for an employee by selecting TAKE ACTION and then either ONE TIME DEDUCTION or MANAGE RECURRING DEDUCTIONS on the PERSONAL INFORMATION or EMPLOYMENT INFORMATION screen, depending on the type of deduction that needs to be created.

For a recurring deduction, the RECURRING DEDUCTION portlet is shown on the TRANSACTIONS screen. This looks like the portlet seen in Figure 6.38. The effective date of the recurring deduction needs to be selected prior to entering the details of the deduction. If the recurring deduction is to recover an advance, selecting the advance in the ADVANCE dropdown auto-populates the AMOUNT/PERCENTAGE, CURRENCY, and FREQUENCY fields.

Once the recurring deduction is saved, it appears in the RECURRING DEDUCTION portlet on the EMPLOYMENT INFORMATION screen, which can be seen in Figure 6.39.

One time deductions can be created in a similar way. After selecting TAKE ACTION and then ONE TIME DEDUCTION, users are taken to the transactions screen and see the ONE TIME DEDUCTION portlet. Here, they can enter details of the deduction, as seen in Figure 6.40. If the deduction is to recover an advance with only a single repayment, selecting the advance in the ADVANCE dropdown auto-populates the AMOUNT/PERCENTAGE and CURRENCY fields.

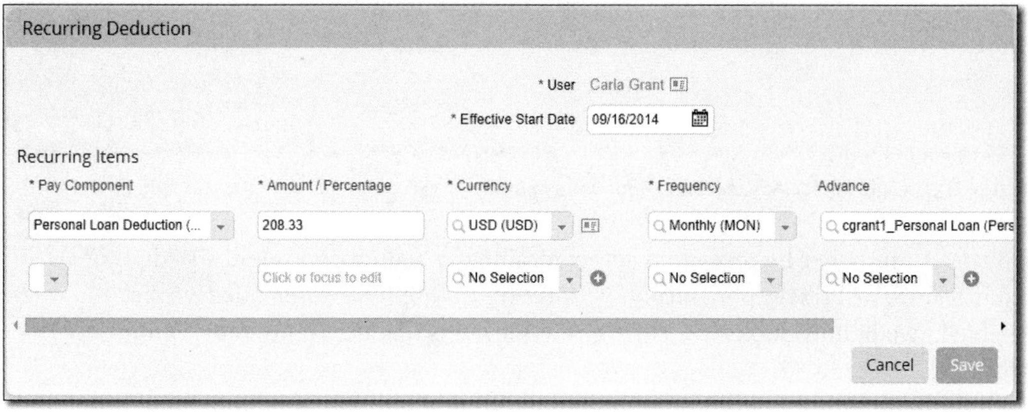

Figure 6.38 Creating a Recurring Deduction

Figure 6.39 Recurring Deduction Portlet

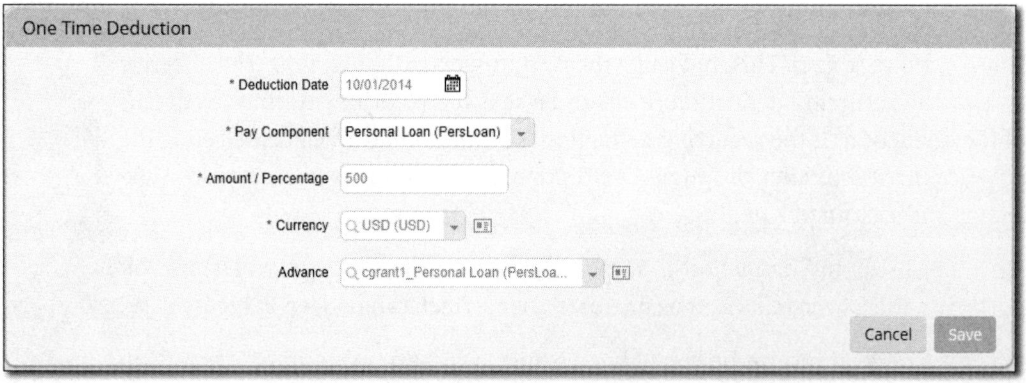

Figure 6.40 Creating a One-Time Deduction

Once saved, the deduction appears in the ONE TIME DEDUCTION USER portlet on the EMPLOYMENT INFORMATION screen.

6.5.10 Alternative Cost Distribution

Employees can have alternative cost distribution assigned to them, which can be used to divide costs across one or more cost centers in addition to the default cost center that is assigned to them. Up to 12 cost centers can be assigned to cover up to 100% of the employee's costs.

This is done by selecting TAKE ACTION and then CHANGE JOB AND COMPENSATION INFO. Once on the TRANSACTIONS screen, select the ALTERNATIVE COST DISTRIBUTION checkbox to open the ALTERNATIVE COST DISTRIBUTION portlet. This can be seen in Figure 6.41.

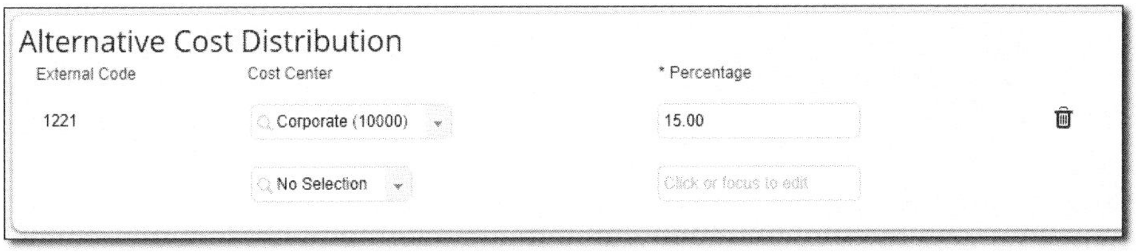

Alternative Cost Distribution

External Code	Cost Center	* Percentage	
1221	Corporate (10000) ▾	15.00	🗑
	No Selection ▾	Click or focus to edit	

Figure 6.41 Creating Alternative Cost Distribution

Once the effective date has been selected—should it differ from today's date—the cost center for the alternative cost distribution and the percentage of costs to be distributed should be selected. Once saved, it appears in the ALTERNATIVE COST DISTRIBUTION portlet on the EMPLOYMENT INFORMATION screen (see Figure 6.42).

Alternative Cost Distribution	
Cost Center	Percentage
Corporate (10000)	15.00%

Figure 6.42 Alternative Cost Distribution Portlet

6.5.11 Pension Payouts

Pension payouts can be created for employees and retired employees who are captured in the system as pensioners. If a pension payout is created for an active employee, they are set to employee status RETIRED and are no longer active in the company.

Pension payouts are created by selecting TAKE ACTION and then MANAGE PENSION PAYOUT DETAILS on the PERSONAL INFORMATION or EMPLOYMENT INFORMATION of the target employee/pensioned employee.

When entering the TRANSACTIONS screen, the user sees the ADD PENSION PAYOUT DETAILS hyperlink in the MANAGE PENSION PAYOUT DETAILS portlet. Selecting this displays the fields EVENT REASON, START DATE, END DATE, and PENSION PROVIDER, as seen in Figure 6.43.

Figure 6.43 Manage Pension Payout Details Transaction

The PENSION PROVIDER field provides a list of company Foundation Objects from which to select the pension provider. Once a company has been selected in the PENSION PROVIDER field, four further portlets appear below the MANAGE PENSION PAYOUT DETAILS portlet: Job Information (called PENSION PAYOUT DETAILS INFORMATION on-screen), Job Relationships (called RELATIONSHIPS on screen), COMPENSATION INFORMATION (which includes the information usually seen in the SPOT BONUS portlet), and DEPENDENTS.

Once these details are entered and the transaction is saved, the employee's EMPLOYMENT INFORMATION screen displays a button showing their current employment, similar to Global Assignment and Concurrent Employment. This button can be used to select the current or pensioned employment details. This button can be seen in Figure 6.44, along with the screen for the pensioned employment.

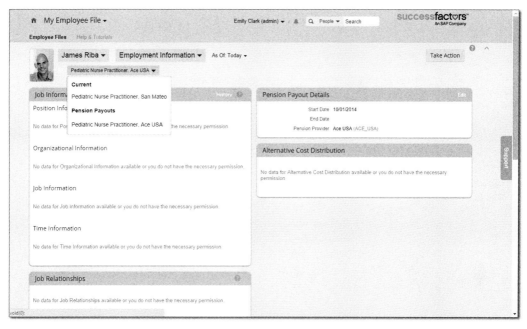

Figure 6.44 The Employment Information Screen for a Pensioned Employee

6.5.12 Position Management

Through the Position Management feature, you can manage the use of positions in Employee Central. These positions can also be used in other processes, such as recruiting and succession planning. There are a number of features when using Position Management, beyond configuring the position object. These include the following:

▶ Store and track position attributes, such as regular, part-time, job description, and related organizational entities

▶ Enable positions to inherit attributes from the assigned Job Code

▶ Enable employees to inherit attributes from the assigned Position

▶ Define an employee's manager when their direct manager leaves the organization or is transferred

▶ Configure headcount management (strict position control versus non-budget-driven process)

▶ For vacant/to-be-hired positions, launch requisitions in SuccessFactors Recruiting Execution with the required position information

▶ Use positions in the succession planning process so that the successors are planned based on the existing positions hierarchy

▶ View the position reporting structure in the Position Org Chart

The position object definition is configured as any other Generic Object, and position records are created in the same way that other Generic Object data is created. This means that various rules that enable field value defaulting, propagation, auto-generation of the position code, FTE management, workflows, and synchronizations can be applied to the position object. Figure 6.45 shows a position.

Position		◎ Insert New Record
Subject to Position Control	Yes
* Position ID	MGR_MAINT
* Status	Active
Change Reason	
Position Title	Maintenance Manager
* Start Date	07/01/2012
Comment	
Vacant	No
Company	Ace USA (ACE_USA)
Business Unit	Corporate Industries (ACE_IND)
Division	Industries (IND)
Department	Plant Maintenance (OPS-MAINT)
Cost Center	Plant & Equipment (33110)
Location	Denver (US_DEN)
Custom Counter	1342
Job Code	Maintenance Manager (PLANT-MAINT)
Job Title	Maintenance Manager
Job Level	Manager (MGR)
Employee Class	Employee (M)
Regular/Temporary	Regular (R)
Pay Grade	Salary Grade 5 (GR-5)
Target FTE	1
Parent Position	Director, Manufacturing (DIR_MFG)

Matrix Relationship

Type	Related Position
HR Manager (hr manager)	Business Partnership Manager, IND (HRAdmin1)
Matrix Manager (matrix manager)	VP, Operations (POS-VPOPS)

Updated by admin on Saturday, September 20, 2014 9:47:20 AM PDT

Figure 6.45 A Position

Part of the Position object is the ability to define matrix relationships, which cover each of the standard job relationship types (HR Manager, matrix manager, custom manager, etc.). These enable positions to be defined for each of these relationships, similar to how these are defined as employee relationships on the JOB RELATIONSHIPS portlet on the EMPLOYEE INFORMATION screen. This means that when an employee is assigned to a position, they inherit the relationship and holder of the position of that relationship in the JOB RELATIONSHIPS portlet on the EMPLOYMENT INFORMATION screen. This same logic applies to the manager when a Parent Position is assigned. For example, if position A is assigned as an HR Manager position for position B, and position A is assigned to an employee, then that employee's HR Manager becomes the holder of position A. Position matrix relationships can be seen in Figure 6.45.

Position Management settings are configured in OneAdmin in POSITION MANAGEMENT SETTINGS under EMPLOYEE FILES. This screen is shown in Figure 6.46.

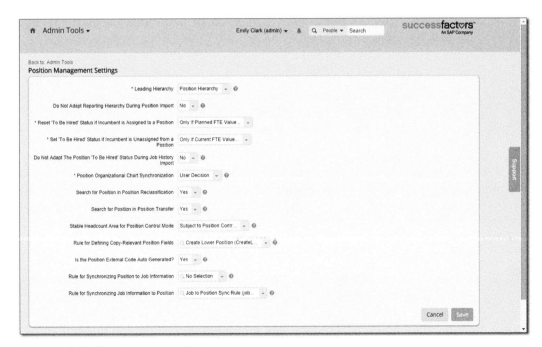

Figure 6.46 Position Management Settings

Specific settings enable the leading hierarchy to be selected:

- How the TO BE HIRED field is treated during assignment and transfer of employees
- Position searching during reclassifications and transfers
- The field for determining position headcount control
- If the position code is auto-generated
- The rules for defining fields during position copy and synchronizing position data position data with Job Information

The leading hierarchy is a concept that affects various actions in the system that involve positions. There are two options for leading hierarchy: POSITION HIERARCHY and REPORTING HIERARCHY. This selection affects how higher-level managers are selected for employees during position assignments, the new hire process, and position changes in the Position Org Chart. It also impacts how positions are found when a position reclassification takes place.

Positions are assigned to an employee's Job Information, usually during hire or when there is a position transfer. We saw this in Figure 6.5 in Section 6.2.3.

6.5.13 Workflows

Workflows enable actions and data changes to be approved or commented on, or for notifications to be provided. This ensures that the necessary approvals and authorizations are provided for important and sensitive data changes.

A workflow is a Foundation Object, so system administrators can easily create and maintain workflows in OneAdmin. However, workflow trigger rules are configured during implementation and can be changed only with access to Provisioning.

Workflow Foundation Object

The workflow Foundation Object contains all of the configurations to determine how a workflow operates, including the usual fields like the ID, name, and description. The workflow configuration also defines attributes of the workflow—such as how many days before a reminder is triggered, whether manual delegation is supported, what the alternative workflow is, and whether CC Role users are redirected to the workflow approval page—and each of the approver types. Figure 6.47 shows a typical workflow configuration.

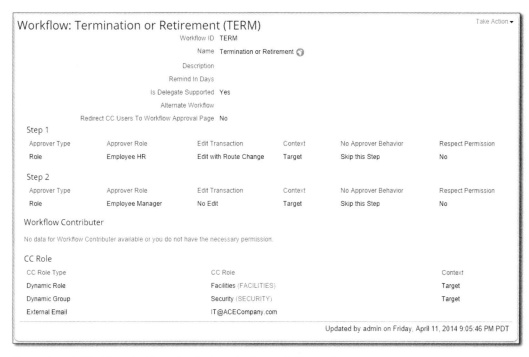

Figure 6.47 A Workflow Configuration for Termination or Retirement

Workflows have three types of participants:

▶ APPROVER: Users who are required to approve the workflow

▶ CONTRIBUTOR: Users who are able to add comments to an active workflow

▶ CC ROLES: Users who are notified once a workflow has been approved

Each type of participant can have multiple users assigned. However, for Approvers, the approval process is step-based, and each Approver must approve the workflow in the order they are assigned within the workflow configuration.

For each of the participants, there are different approver types that are used to determine the user. These are as follows:

▶ APPROVER: Role, Dynamic Role, Dynamic Group, Position

▶ CONTRIBUTOR: Role, Dynamic Role, Dynamic Group, Person, Position

▶ CC ROLE: Role, Dynamic Role, Dynamic Group, Person, External Email, Position

Let's briefly look at each approver types from the participants:

▶ ROLE

This is a fixed list of roles from which to choose the approver, all relating to the employee that is subject to the workflow. They comprise the employee, manager-based approvers, and possible relationships assigned in the JOB RELATIONSHIP portlet on the EMPLOYEE INFORMATION screen. These are as follows:

- ▶ Employee
- ▶ Employee's manager
- ▶ Employee's manager's manager
- ▶ Employee's HR Manager
- ▶ Employee's Matrix Manager
- ▶ Employee's Second Manager
- ▶ Employee's Custom Manager
- ▶ Employee's Additional Manager

▶ DYNAMIC ROLE

A DYNAMIC ROLE is a Foundation Object that allows the system to determine the participant based on foundation data assigned to an employee. For example, a DYNAMIC ROLE may have a different user assigned for every Business Unit in the system. Let's say that the employee who is the subject of the workflow is part of the Manufacturing Business Unit. The user assigned against the Manufacturing Business Unit in the DYNAMIC ROLE would be selected as the participant in the workflow. DYNAMIC ROLES must be defined before a workflow is created, and they are created in the same places as other Foundation Objects.

▶ DYNAMIC GROUP

A DYNAMIC GROUP is a group of several approvers who all receive the workflow. All members of the DYNAMIC GROUP are able to approve, contribute to, or receive the notification of the workflow approval. If the DYNAMIC GROUP is for an approval participant, once it is approved by a member of the DYNAMIC GROUP, it is not available for any other members of the DYNAMIC GROUP. DYNAMIC GROUPS must be defined before a workflow is created, and they are created in OneAdmin in MANAGE WORKFLOW GROUPS under EMPLOYEE FILES.

▶ POSITION

POSITION enables a position in the system whose holder can approve the workflow, contribute to the workflow, or receive a notification once the workflow is approved to be specified.

▶ PERSON
PERSON enables a user in the system who can contribute to the workflow or receive a notification once the workflow is approved to be specified.

▶ EXTERNAL EMAIL
EXTERNAL EMAIL enables any email address to receive a notification once the workflow is approved.

For the ROLE and DYNAMIC ROLE approver type, the CONTEXT field can be set to SOURCE or TARGET. When a data change occurs that can change one of the roles for an employee (e.g., a change in manager or change in HR Manager), this determines whether the workflow should route to the current or future role (e.g., the current manager or the future manager).

For the ROLE, DYNAMIC ROLE, DYNAMIC GROUP, and POSITION, there are other attributes that can be set:

▶ EDIT TRANSACTION
Determines whether the approver type can edit the workflow and—if they can edit the workflow—whether changes would re-route the workflow through all approvers or allow it to continue through the remaining approval steps of the workflow

▶ NO APPROVER BEHAVIOR
Determines whether the approval step skips or whether the workflow stops if the approver does not approve the workflow

▶ RESPECT PERMISSION
Determines whether RBPs should be respected for any data shown in the workflow approval page

Let's look at when workflows are triggers and what that looks like in the system.

Workflow Trigger Scenario

Should a workflow be configured to trigger based on a specific data change, one triggers when changes are made through the EDIT button on a portlet, through a transaction, when you make changes to a Foundation Object or Generic Object, or when the NEW HIRE transaction is completed (either for a Hire or Rehire). Making changes to data through the HISTORY button on a portlet does not trigger a work-flow.

When changes that trigger a workflow are being made, a pop-up window appears that shows the Event Reason for the workflow and a comments box. Selecting the SHOW WORKFLOW PARTICIPANTS hyperlink expands the window to show all the participants for the workflow. In the WORKFLOW pop-up window seen in Figure 6.48, the participants that were defined in the workflow configuration in Figure 6.47 can be seen.

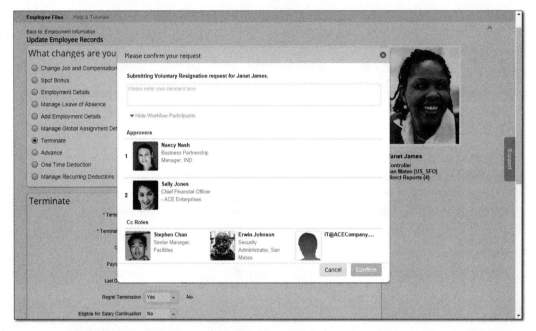

Figure 6.48 Workflow Pop-Up Window

Please note that the workflow window does not open if the employee does not have any users approvers assigned (e.g., they have no manager or no HR Manager) or the workflow has no approvers assigned. Also, the initiator of a workflow does not show if they are the first approver of a workflow.

Once a workflow is submitted (using the CONFIRM button in the workflow pop-up window), it is routed to the first approver and any contributors. If the user has permission, they see a pending approval notification within the appropriate port-let. For example, the termination transaction you saw in Figure 6.48 appears in the Job Information portlet on the Employment Information screen. Figure 6.49 shows this.

Figure 6.49 Pending Workflow Approval Notification

Approving a Workflow

Users who have workflows to approve can access them from the To Do tile on the home page, by navigating to Pending Requests in My Employee File, or from a link in the email notification they receive. Figure 6.50 shows the Pending Requests page.

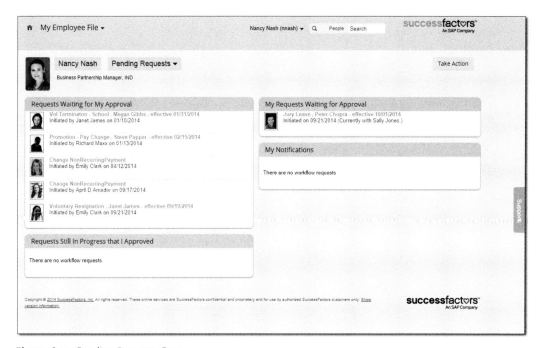

Figure 6.50 Pending Requests Page

Selecting a workflow opens the workflow approval page. Here, the details of the initiation, workflow participants, employee, data change, and workflow activity can be seen. A comments box is also available. The approver also sees the SEND BACK button next to the APPROVE button. The SEND BACK button enables the workflow to be rejected and returned to the initiator. If manual delegation has been configured on the workflow configuration, the approver sees the DELEGATE and hyperlink at the bottom of the screen. If the specific approver has been given edit rights, they see the UPDATE hyperlink. All of this can be seen in Figure 6.51.

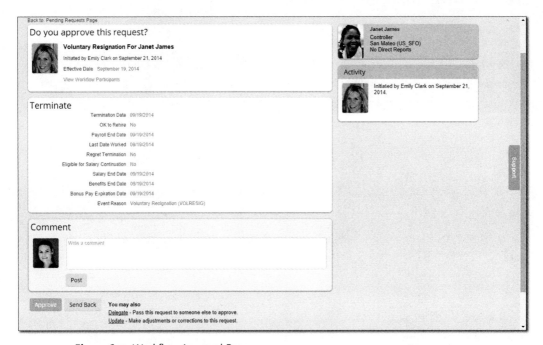

Figure 6.51 Workflow Approval Page

Once each approver has approved the workflow, the data becomes active in the system. For some Generic Objects, the data may become active instantly, although it still requires approval before additional edits can be made.

In the HISTORY page of an effective-dated portlet, the workflow approval history can be displayed by selecting TAKE ACTION and then VIEW APPROVAL HISTORY on the appropriate record. We can see this APPROVAL HISTORY in Figure 6.52.

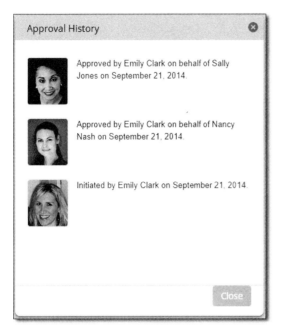

Figure 6.52 Workflow Approval History for a Record

6.5.14 Concurrent Employment

The Concurrent Employment feature enables employees to have multiple employments alongside each other. This may be if an employee has two or more roles in the organization that differ, for example, in location, responsibilities, and/or compensation. Concurrent Employment works very similar to the Leave of Absence and Global Assignment processes that we covered previously.

To add a concurrent employment, select Take Action and then select Add Employment Details. In the Transaction screen, the user sees the Add Employment Details hyperlink in the Add Employment Details portlet. Below this portlet is the Employment Details portlet, which shows the main employment details. Selecting the Add Employment Details hyperlink displays the Employment Detail fields to be maintained (as seen in Figure 6.53)—including the Event Reason, which is based on a Hire event, and the New Assignment Company—and the Employment Details portlet disappears. Figure 6.53 shows the Add Employment Details portlet.

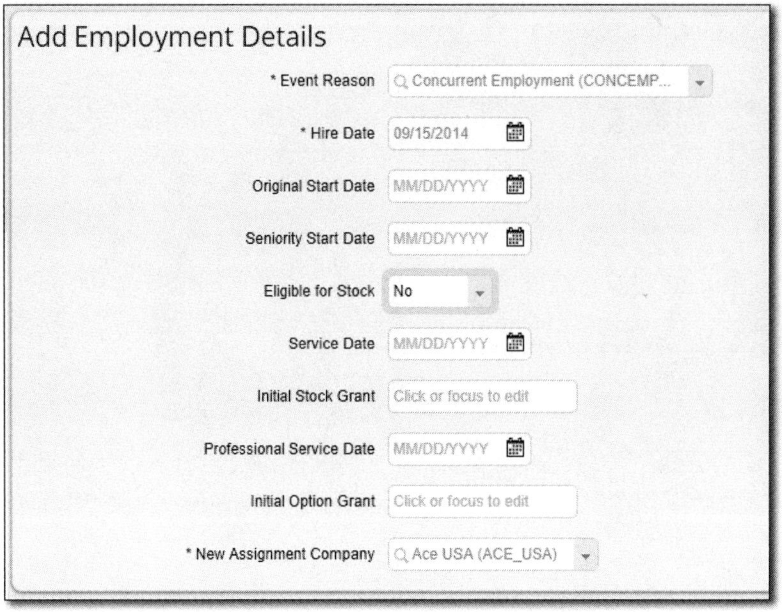

Figure 6.53 Add Employment Details Portlet

Once the NEW ASSIGNMENT COMPANY field value is selected, three further portlets appear below the MANAGE GLOBAL ASSIGNMENT DETAILS portlet: JOB INFORMATION, JOB RELATIONSHIPS, and COMPENSATION INFORMATION (which includes the information usually seen in the SPOT BONUS portlet). Each of these portlets represents the concurrent employment details.

Once these details are entered and the transaction is saved, the employee's EMPLOYMENT INFORMATION screen displays a button showing the main employment as the label, which can be used to select the main or concurrent employment. Selecting the CONCURRENT EMPLOYMENT shows the EMPLOYMENT INFORMATION screen for that employment. This button always remains on the EMPLOYMENT INFORMATION screen as long as there has been at least one concurrent employment either in the past or there will be one in the future. This button can be seen in Figure 6.54.

When employees who are on concurrent employment login to SuccessFactors then they will see their main employment listed under their name in the header panel, just as with a global assignment. As with that functionality, this enables the employee to switch between each of their employments to perform the different processes for each employment.

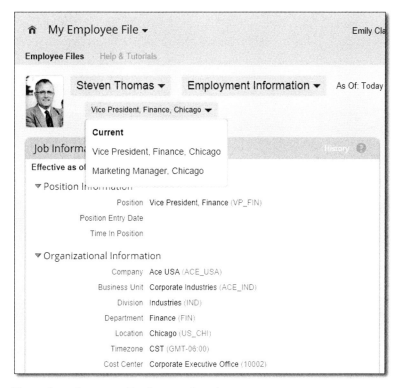

Figure 6.54 Concurrent Employment Dropdown

6.5.15 Employee Central Service Center

The Employee Central Service Center is a complete HR shared service hub for employees to raise HR-related tickets and have them centrally managed and processed. It also enables employees to ask HR questions and monitor their tickets and requests. Executives and managers of the service center process can view analytics. Employee Central Service Center is an optional extension to Employee Central, built on the SAP HANA Cloud Platform and available on mobile devices, so that it can be accessed anytime from anywhere.

Figure 6.55 demonstrates a typical front page from the Employee Central Service Center.

With the Employee Central Service Center, employees will see the Ask HR link on every page in Employee Central. This enables them to immediately find answers to any HR-related question.

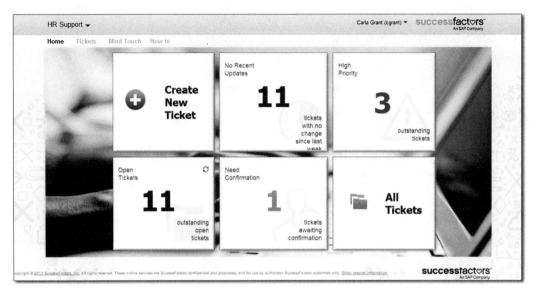

Figure 6.55 Employee Central Service Center

As might be expected, it has social collaboration features built-in so that teams can work on requests together and common solutions can be easily found by colleagues. This enables a knowledge repository to be created and accessed by all service center employees.

6.6 Reporting

Like with other applications, Employee Central data can be reported on with ad hoc reporting. However, Employee Central also features Employee Central Advanced Reporting. Employee Central Advanced Reporting provides more than 65 standard reports that can be used and adapted as required. These reports also include country-specific reports.

You access Employee Central Advanced Reporting in the Analytics module by selecting the ANALYTICS option. In the REPORTING tab in the box to the left of the screen, the option EC STANDARD REPORTING is available, which contains all of the report categories. Each of these categories contains the reports. Figure 6.56 shows the AGE RANGE REPORT.

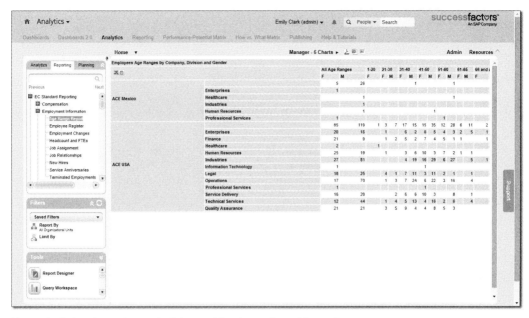

Figure 6.56 Age Range Report in Advanced Employee Central Reporting

The Report Designer can be used to create reports, based on the reports from Advanced Employee Central Reporting. Now that you've implemented Employee Central, and all your employee data resides in an intelligent and intuitive platform in the cloud, it's time to use that data to pay your employees, as well. This brings us to our next topic: Employee Central Payroll.

6.7   Employee Central Payroll

Employee Central Payroll is a cloud-hosted payroll system available for Employee Central customers *only*. It gives you the advantage of controlling your payroll within the convenience of the cloud. Employee Central Payroll is a hosted version of SAP ERP Payroll designed to work with Employee Central. It is hosted in the cloud by SAP. Upgrades, patches, legal changes, and tax updates are applied to the payroll engine without the customer ever having to experience the inconvenience of applying these upgrades, as is the case with on-premise SAP ERP Payroll. Figure 6.57 shows the Payroll Information view in Employee Files, where employees can view and/or maintain Employee Central Payroll information.

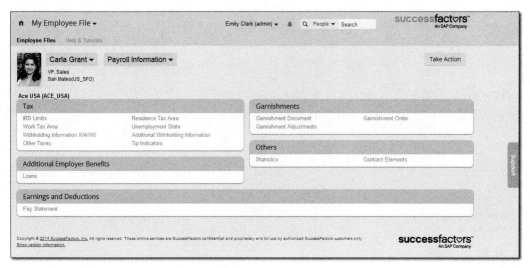

Figure 6.57 Payroll Information Screen

The customer has full control of the payroll implementation and processing. With Employee Central Payroll, customers have the world's most proven payroll solution, which currently supports 7,000 organizations in 90 countries. As of summer 2014, Employee Central Payroll is available for 28 countries, with a roadmap to build additional countries, depending on market demand.

A current list of country versions for Employee Central Payroll can be provided by SAP or found at *http://scn.sap.com/docs/DOC-45501*.

Employee Central Payroll Processes

You can execute the following processes in Employee Central Payroll:

▸ Gross pay calculation based on time entered

▸ Gross-to-net calculation of paychecks

▸ Retroactive pay calculation

▸ Garnishment calculation

▸ Paychecks and deposit advices

▸ Direct deposit of paychecks

▸ Payroll tax forms to be filed

▸ Quarterly and year-end reports and forms

▸ End-to-end payroll process interfacing with the General Ledger

6.7.1   Access and Data Replication

You can best understand access to Employee Central and Employee Central Payroll by viewing the roles of users who need to access the application. These roles can be divided into employees and managers, HR administrators, and payroll managers. The core HRIS data is maintained in Employee Central, while the payroll-related master data is maintained in Employee Central Payroll. Employees and managers maintain data and execute transactions in Employee Central, including viewing their pay slip (which is shown in Figure 6.58).

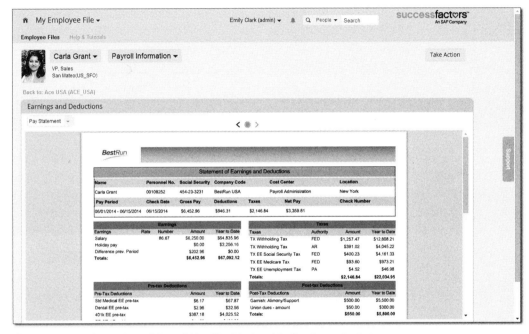

Figure 6.58 Employee Central Payroll Pay Slip Displayed in Employee Central

Mash-ups exist to allow Employee Central Payroll infotype data to be entered through Employee Central. Figure 6.59 shows a mash-up for Withholding Information W4/W5, which enables employees to enter withholding tax information for W-4 and W-5 tax forms.

Figure 6.59 Withholding Information W-4/W-5 Mash-up

Employee Central data is replicated to the payroll engine through delivered integration for the purposes of payroll processing. Figure 6.60 shows how access to Employee Central and Employee Central Payroll changes based on the role of the individual.

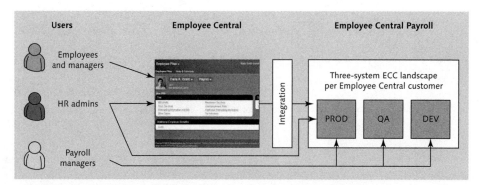

Figure 6.60 Employee Central Payroll Access Based on the Role of the User

The HR data objects (person and employment objects) that we covered in Section 6.2.3 are replicated to Employee Central Payroll:

- National ID Information
- Personal Information
- Address Information
- Biographical Information
- Payment Information
- Contact Information
- Job Information
- Employment Details
- Compensation Information

Any historical data items (including changes and deletions) are also replicated in Employee Central Payroll. Currently, integration between Employee Central and Employee Central Payroll is delivered using Dell Boomi AtomSphere. More details on integration can be found in Chapter 3.

6.8   Summary

SuccessFactors Employee Central is the foundation of the entire SuccessFactors HCM suite. Additionally, it's an excellent core HR system that can be used with or without SAP ERP HCM as the system of record.

In this chapter, we introduced the unique features and functionalities of Employee Central that offer a competitive advantage to customers looking for a global core HRIS integrated with the Talent Management solutions of the Success-Factors HCM suite. We explored the data models that form the spinal column of the Employee Central framework and the OneAdmin interface that empowers customers with a configurable UI. We also looked at the many transactions and processes that Employee Central supports, as well as the numerous other features included. Coupled with a robust global core HRIS in Employee Central, Employee Central Service Center enables shared services for employee HR requests, and Employee Central Payroll enables customers to control payroll processes, as well, thereby providing a complete HRIS in the cloud.

In the next chapter, we will look at the Performance Management and Goal Management modules available through SuccessFactors.

One characteristic of high-performing businesses is that they conduct multiple performance reviews each year. The Performance Management and Goal Management modules provide businesses with the tools to align their employees to corporate objectives and optimize workforce performance to achieve business execution results.

7   Performance and Goals

In today's competitive business environment, business execution is a key buzzword that corporations globally are striving to achieve. But many companies struggle to execute on their business strategies and never achieve the results they seek because they are unfocused or have either outdated or nonexistent technology to help them execute the strategies they do have.

SuccessFactors provides tools to align an organization to corporate objectives. Through the Performance Management (PM) and Goal Management (GM) modules in the SuccessFactors HCM suite, a company can drive alignment across the organization through a series of goals that are cascaded to every employee. Progress toward these goals can be tracked from the top; executives can be sure that their entire team of employees is aware of the corporate strategy and the role each individual plays in executing that strategy. This helps drive focus toward the right things, provides visibility of progress of the entire organization, and heightens accountability.

SuccessFactors HCM suite provides a series of robust tools to take performance and goal processes to the next level. One such tool is Stack Ranker, which lets managers rate their team at once against each other; with 360 Multi-Rater, they gain a well-rounded view of their employees' performance that serves as input to the overall performance assessment. New features of Team Rater take Stack Ranker to the next level, providing managers with a one-stop shop for completing their team's reviews. Calibration enables managers to level set ratings across their team for input to other performance processes, such as Compensation and Succession Planning.

While PM and GM are two separate modules within the SuccessFactors HCM solution, they work hand in hand to support talent development processes. In this chapter, we'll take a look at PM and GM. Performance reviews are incomplete without input from goal progress, and goals are only so meaningful in the absence of a formal performance review process. We'll discuss the tools available in the scope of the performance process. Specifically, we'll review the following PM and GM components:

► Goal Development and Execution

► Performance Reviews

► Team Rater

► 360 Multi-Rater

► Calibration

Let's begin by examining the performance process with Goal Management.

7.1 Goal Management

SuccessFactors is known for helping align an organization with company-wide goals. This is an area that remains critical to the development of the SuccessFactors HCM suite because of its foundational importance to business execution.

The performance process begins with goal setting and continues as employee's progress toward goals throughout the performance year. The SuccessFactors HCM suite facilitates the creation, alignment, monitoring, and measurement of both organizational and personal goals, as represented in Figure 7.1. The *goal plan* is the basis for GM in SuccessFactors. The goals that appear in the goal plan are easy to create and edit throughout the year, by both the employee and manager.

The goal plan comprises of the following elements:

► **Goal categories**
Categories are used to organize goals on the goal plan. Standard goal categories are based on the Balanced Scorecard methodology, but customers may configure additional or different goal categories to meet their tracking and reporting requirements.

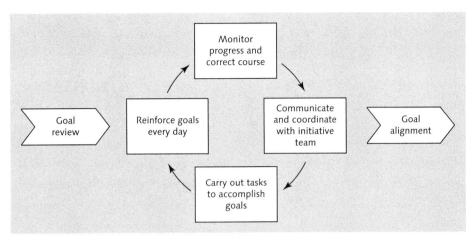

Figure 7.1 Goal Alignment through Execution

► **Align and Link**

This functionality encourages organizational goal adoption throughout business units, departments, and other organizational groups. Cascading goals from the top of the organization down through the organizational structure ensures company alignment to individual and group objectives. Linking goals allows alignment and tracking across the organization.

► **SMART Goal Wizard**

This powerful tool provides employees with a step-by-step wizard to walk through creating goals that are specific, measurable, attainable, relevant, and time bound—the tenets of SuccessFactors development.

► **Best-Practice Goal Library**

This best-practice collection of goals provides more than 500 ready-to-use, role-specific goals that customers can leverage as corporate or individual goals.

► **Goal Alignment Spotlight**

What use is goal alignment if you have no visibility? This feature provides full line-of-sight visibility to goals across and down through the organization.

► **Dashboards and spotlights**

This feature provides managers and other organizational leaders dashboard visibility into progression of the organization against corporate goals. From dashboards, managers can track how their team is performing against corporate strategies.

Goal plans, like the one shown in Figure 7.2, are structured for ease-of-use by employees and managers. Each category is clearly labeled with corresponding categorized goals that are numerically ordered under each category. Display options are user defined, so each user can display the information that is most pertinent and helpful to achieving the goals of that particular user. Managers may easily navigate to their team's goal plans with a single mouse click. You can track aligned (cascaded) goals directly from the user's goal plan by selecting the ALIGNED UP or ALIGNED DOWN display options to the left. Outlook calendar integration is available so that goal-related due dates can be added to a user's calendar. STATUS of the goal is clearly labeled with a colored bar to indicate goal progress.

A new user interface to the Goal Plan introduces Goal Management v12 and brings the Goal Plan look in line with Performance Management v12 forms.

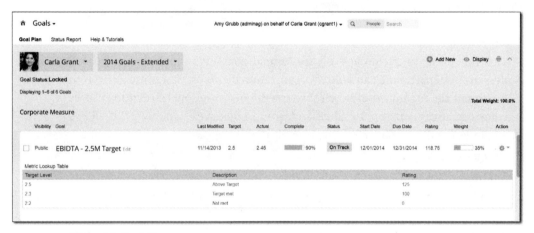

Figure 7.2 Goal Plan

7.1.1 Maintaining Goals

You can create or edit goals at any time. New or custom goals can be created in several ways:

- ▸ Create a custom goal
- ▸ Use the Goal Library
- ▸ Use the Goal Wizard
- ▸ Copy the goal from another goal plan

A user can create their own goal by selecting the ADD GOAL button (see Figure 7.3), which allows the user to populate all fields in the goal plan. Or, the user can choose CREATE A LIBRARY GOAL.

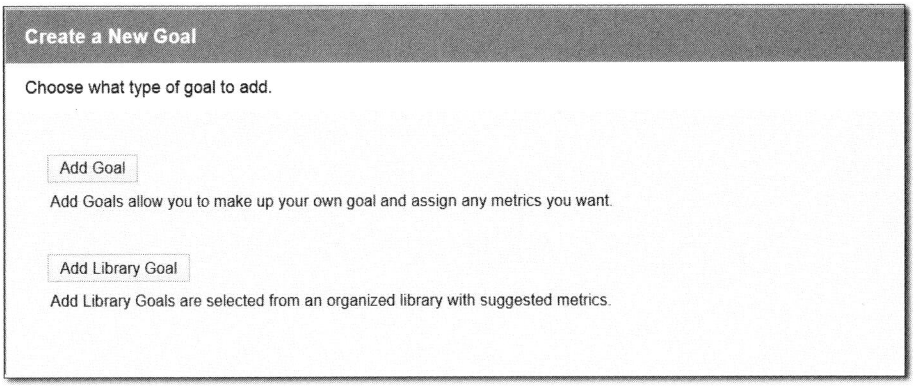

Create a New Goal

Choose what type of goal to add.

Add Goal

Add Goals allow you to make up your own goal and assign any metrics you want.

Add Library Goal

Add Library Goals are selected from an organized library with suggested metrics.

Figure 7.3 Create a New Goal Dialog

Regardless of which option a user chooses, the user ends up at the same screen. The appearance of the ADD GOAL dialog layout depends on the configuration decisions made during the design phase of implementation. The example in Figure 7.4 contains many fields, but customers can design a much more streamlined goal structure, if desired. Two critical features to note are the VISIBILITY and CATEGORY fields, which are boxed.

Visibility determines whether a goal is public (meaning anyone who can view the goal plan may also view the goal), or private (meaning only the employee; the employee's manager, and possibly second-level manager; and HR personnel may view the goal). This permission is determined in the configuration of the goal plan template to meet customer requirements. Default visibility is configured in the goal plan, but employees may choose to change this after the goal is created.

A category for each goal must be selected to correctly order the goals on the plan. The category can always be updated after the goal is created, but having goals incorrectly categorized could impact downstream reporting and alignment spotlights.

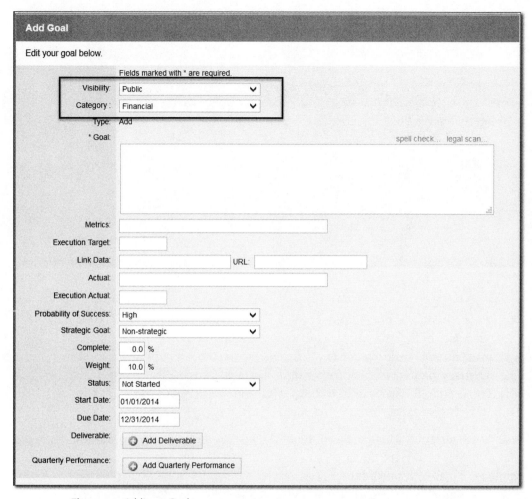

Figure 7.4 Adding a Goal

Users unfamiliar with SMART goals may opt to utilize the SMART Goal Wizard and have the system guide them through creating a SMART goal, as demonstrated in Figure 7.5. The Goal Library is also leveraged in the SMART Goal Wizard so users can select a library goal as a starting point by typing their goal in the GOAL NAME box. They are offered possible matches based on what they are typing. Users are taken through each step of a SMART goal until they have met all elements and are then presented the ADD GOAL dialog box, as displayed in Figure 7.4. Here, they can add any additional details that may be required and then save the goal (see Figure 7.5).

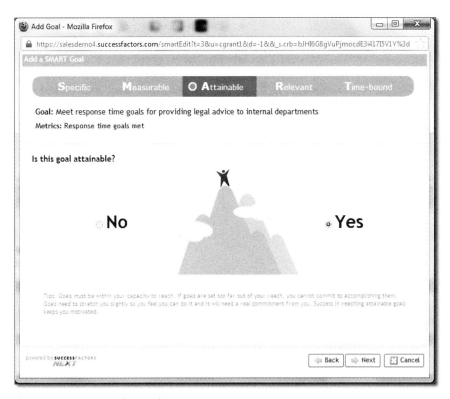

Figure 7.5 SMART Goal Wizard

7.1.2 Aligning and Cascading Goals

After goals are created, they can be cascaded up or down the reporting chain. Through this alignment of goals, a company has visibility to the goals that employees are working toward, as well as whether they are corporate or personal goals. Anyone with direct reports may cascade a goal down to their team or matrix reports. If goal plan permissions allow, goals may also be cascaded up. It's possible for mangers to cascade a goal up to themselves from their direct report's goal plan, or for employees to cascade a goal up to their managers.

Goals may be cascaded individually or in a group to one or more team members. The Cascade Goal Wizard walks through the steps necessary to cascade the goal(s) to the appropriate people, as shown in Figure 7.6. After they are cascaded, display options keep the user up to date on progress of aligned goals, as demonstrated in Figure 7.7.

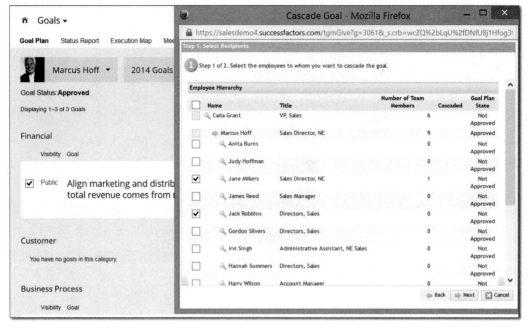

Figure 7.6 Cascade Goal Wizard

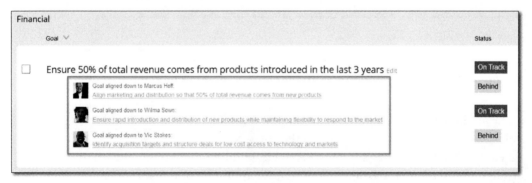

Figure 7.7 Aligned Goals Display

7.1.3 Goal Execution

Goal Execution is a part of GM that assists employees and managers in reinforcing goal progress and achievement. Through Goal Execution, managers have tools to help them ensure that their team is focused on the right goals and working toward achieving them on a daily basis.

Goal Execution is meant for companies that update and monitor goals on a regular basis. It's also intended for organizations that align goals by cascading them down through the reporting hierarchy. There are configuration considerations to be aware of when implementing Goal Execution; your implementation consultant will review those with you if you choose to roll out this powerful set of tools.

Goal Execution facilitates goal achievement by providing an interface to visualize goals and monitor progress every time a user logs in. Employees and managers, or executives at the highest level, can view individual goals and corporate goals to which they are aligned. Managers can track progress of goals and drill into each goal for more information on issues that may impede progress. The EXECUTION MAP illustrated in Figure 7.8 gives managers a visual representation of their team's goal progress. On-track goals are shown in green, while goals that are lagging are shown in red. From the EXECUTION MAP, the manager can drill into each goal to view details and determine what issues may be impeding progress.

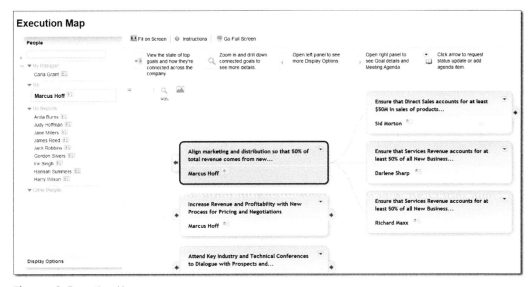

Figure 7.8 Execution Map

Workflows are available to allow employees to regularly update progress toward goals and level of effort, gauge the probability of success of each goal, and provide comments. This is visible via the status report shown in Figure 7.9.

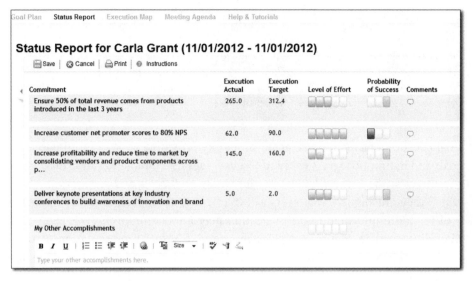

Figure 7.9 Goal Status Report

Additional tools available with Goal Execution assist managers in communicating with their teams on goal progress. The MEETING AGENDA subtab shown in Figure 7.10 provides an easy interface from which to build items for discussion with each employee about goal progress; it even provides Outlook integration so that managers can set up meetings with employees all from one place.

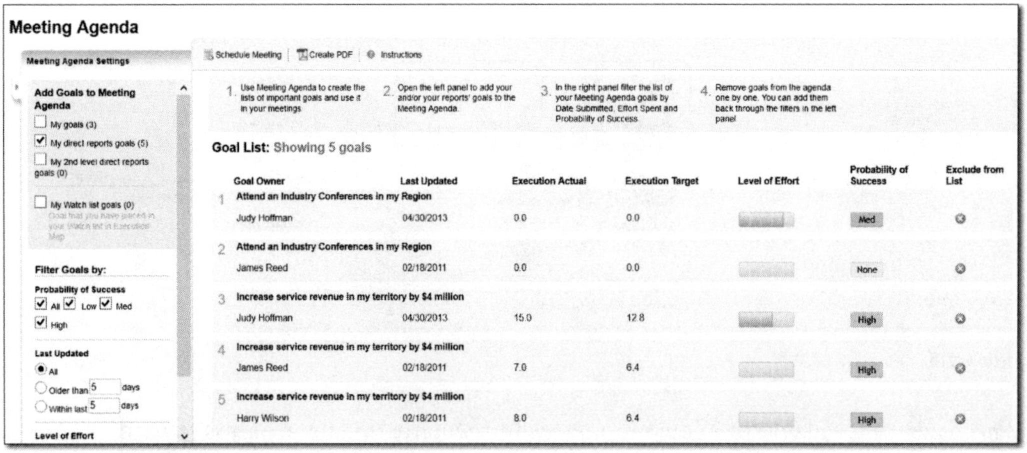

Figure 7.10 Meeting Agenda

7.2   Performance Management

As goals are established and tracked, they become part of the performance review process. Performance reviews in PM and GM assist companies in measuring individual performance against company objectives and competencies, as well as personal objectives and competencies. This information feeds into any number of other talent processes, such as SuccessFactors Compensation Management, Succession Planning, Learning, and Career Development. Performance reviews are designed on best practices and provide numerous tools to assist all participants in the process to produce the best possible performance feedback. Highlights of PM tools and functionality include the following:

▶ **Writing Assistant and Coaching Advisor**
This powerful tool provides best-practice content for commenting on competency feedback. It's available to both employees and managers and greatly increases the effectiveness of meaningful feedback in the performance process.

▶ **Flexible workflows**
Each form has a route map that determines who touches the performance review, what they can do with it, and when each step is due. Tools such as iterative steps to allow the form to go between two users before moving forward, and collaborative steps wherein the form resides in two users' inboxes simultaneously help increase completeness of performance reviews.

▶ **Legal Scan**
This tool works much like a spell check and reviews and flags potentially inappropriate language in a performance review.

▶ **Team overview**
A feature of Performance Management v12, this interface gives managers a dashboard-like view of their team's review status. Review feedback and workflow steps can be managed from this view.

▶ **Ask for Feedback**
Soliciting feedback from others as input to a performance review is effortless with the enhanced Ask for Feedback functionality. Requests are sent, and respondents can reply via email, and the responses are visible from within the performance review form.

7.2.1 Performance Review Structure

Although performance reviews can be configured to include items specific to customers' needs, the best practice performance review includes three main content sections:

- The goal plan
- Core competencies
- Role-specific competencies

Each section is given a weight of the overall performance score or selected to be excluded from the overall score. In the newest interface, ratings are as easy as hovering over the star icon and clicking to save the entry, as displayed in Figure 7.11; the form auto-saves as the reviewer moves through each item. Comments can be collected at the goal or competency item level, for the entire section, or both. The Writing Assistant is available for competencies. Each comment box can have spell check and Legal Scan available for use.

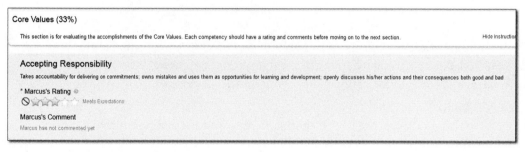

Figure 7.11 Sample Performance Review Section

Customers may choose to also include an INDIVIDUAL DEVELOPMENT PLAN section in the form; this is common for customers who are not implementing the Development module. Note that any development goals created in this section are available in the form only if linked to the *development plan* in the Development module. The Development module will be covered in detail in Chapter 12.

Finally, the form has an OVERALL PERFORMANCE SUMMARY section. This is visible to the manager and displays a summary of the rated items in the form. The OVERALL SCORE is also displayed at the top of the form in the SCORE POD, as shown in Figure 7.12. Other available pods track the number of incomplete items in the review and where the current employee ranks in the overall team.

2.67
Overall Score
*0
Incomplete Items
#3
Out of 3

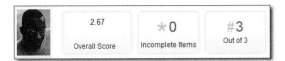

Figure 7.12 Manager View of Performance Form

7.2.2 Team Overview

Managers now have access to the TEAM OVERVIEW subtab, where they can manage all performance reviews in one view, which can be seen in Figure 7.13. In the TEAM OVERVIEW subtab, they can see who has completed a self-review and which team members still need to be rated, use the ASK FOR FEEDBACK function, and track the form along the workflow until it's completed.

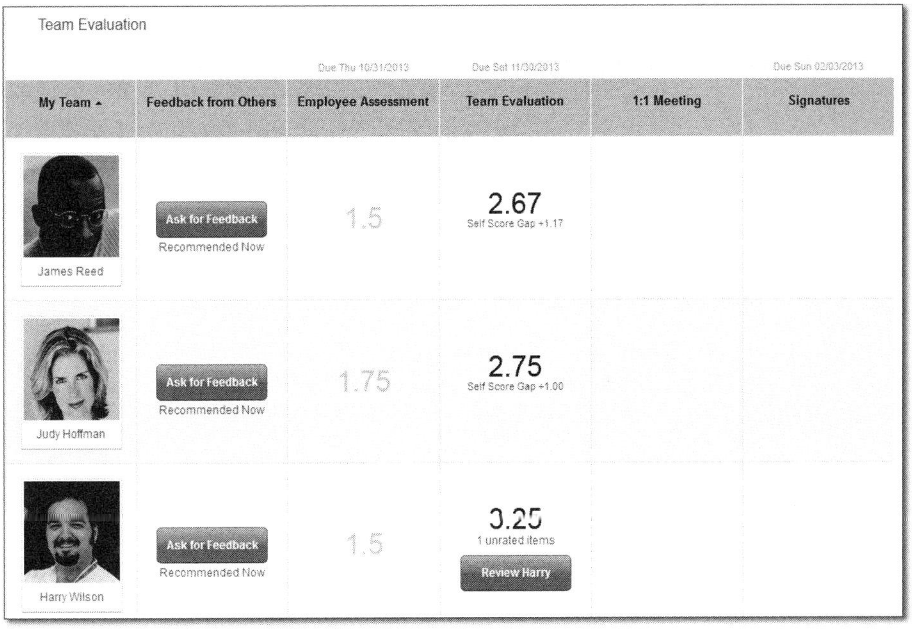
Team Evaluation
Due Thu 10/31/2013
Due Sat 11/30/2013
Due Sun 02/03/2013
My Team
Feedback from Others
Employee Assessment
Team Evaluation
1:1 Meeting
Signatures
James Reed
Ask for Feedback
Recommended Now
1.5
2.67
Self Score Gap +1.17
Judy Hoffman
Ask for Feedback
Recommended Now
1.75
2.75
Self Score Gap +1.00
Harry Wilson
Ask for Feedback
Recommended Now
1.5
3.25
1 unrated items
Review Harry

Figure 7.13 Team Overview

Team Rater

When self-reviews have been completed and all requested feedback has been received, managers can commence with rating their team's performance. The Team Rater feature builds on the Stack Ranker concept in SuccessFactors HCM to allow managers to rate all employees against the same competencies at the same time. This tool allows the managers to see how their team members stack up against each other, as demonstrated in Figure 7.14.

Figure 7.14 Team Rater

Managers can easily rate against each competency and add comments to each competency as they go along. Scores are summarized along the bottom, and managers have instant feedback on the employees' ratings. This information is also displayed along the right side of the screen, and each employee is given a ranking based on the employee's competency scores. The employees in Figure 7.15 have been ranked 1–3, according to their competency scores.

Figure 7.15 Stack-Ranked Employees

Ask for Feedback

As managers prepare to complete a performance review, they may find it helpful to have feedback from others who have worked with the employee throughout the year. Outside of a formal *360 Multi-Rater assessment*, managers can use the Ask for Feedback mechanism to solicit immediate feedback from others for the performance review. Feedback can be requested from internal employees or sent to those external to the organization. Responses are tracked from the Team Overview tab or within the performance form itself, in the Supporting Information pod. Recent enhancements have provided the ability to make multiple, distinct Ask for Feedback requests for different steps in the form route map. Requests are tracked separately, and one icon displays for each request. An example of the Ask for Feedback form can be seen in Figure 7.16.

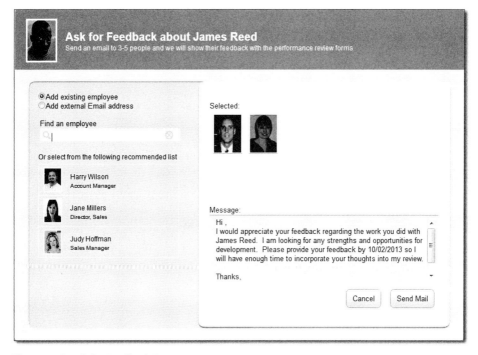

Figure 7.16 Ask for Feedback Form

7.2.3 Writing Assistant and Coaching Advisor

The Writing Assistant and Coaching Advisor tool helps managers provide accurate and meaningful feedback to their employees regarding their competency performance and coaching where needed. By offering suggested feedback that is tempered by the competency rating, this tool eliminates the age-old issue of "writer's block" when it comes time to provide feedback. The system begins with the competency description and rating and provides suggested statements to include as comments, as shown in Figure 7.17. The suggested statement can be used as a template, made more positive or less positive at the user's discretion, and then placed in the comment box. Comments can then be edited to be more personal, depending on the individual and situation. In this way, managers are giving competency-based feedback in such a way that employees can take action in developing in the future.

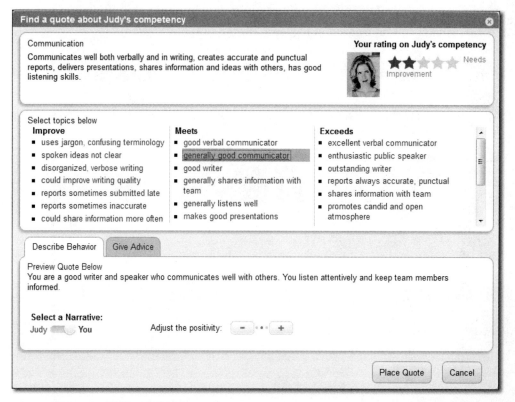

Figure 7.17 Writing Assistant

7.2.4 PM v12 Acceleration and Advanced Configuration

SuccessFactors has spent much of the last year focusing development efforts in Performance Management around providing one comprehensive product by enhancing PM v12 with many of the features available in Performance Management v11. The PM v12 Acceleration project provides most, but not all, of the features and configurations available in PM v11 to the PM v12 user interface. Many existing customers have not upgraded to PM v12 because it did not adequately support their processes.

With this much anticipated enhancement, more customers will be able to make the transition to PM v12; have support for their performance processes; and maintain features they are used to, such as HTML formatting in introduction sections of forms. Some of the enhancements from PM v11 now available in PM v12 include the following:

- Iterative and collaborative route map steps
- Matrix grid sections
- User Info section
- Viewing and rating by behavior
- Past form access for PM review and 360 Multi-Rater
- Reverse rating scale
- Compensation sections
- Archive and print support
- Maximum and minimum weight support
- Maximum and minimum item support
- PM v11 rating options
- Summary section additional configuration
- Goal field display support

Customers need to opt in for the Acceleration to use any of the features. Once available, the Validation tool allows for upgrading existing PM v11 form templates to PM v12.

Advanced configuration options were released for PM v12 early in 2014 and provide administrators with more control of configuration options on PM form templates from the Template Manager in OneAdmin. Configurations previously available only by modifying the XML template, such as setting required fields and configuring multiple languages, are now available via advance configuration.

SuccessFactors plans to extend the PM v12 Acceleration project through the end of 2014 and will continue to put more control into the hands of administrators via Advanced Configuration in OneAdmin.

7.3   360 Multi-Rater Assessment

The 360 Multi-Rater assessment facilitates gathering performance feedback on goals and competencies from everyone (i.e., both internal employees and personnel external to the organization). The 360 Multi-Rater assessment is different from the Ask for Feedback feature in that it's an actual form that allows raters to provide feedback and even rate an employee against the role-specific competencies assigned to that employee. This mechanism can collect quantitative and qualitative data from a wide range of respondents: the employee; the manager; peers; direct reports; and others, including external raters.

The 360 Multi-Rater assessment supports adding internal and external raters and has a configurable workflow, just like the performance review. Writing Assistant is available to help respondents provide meaningful feedback to the form subject. Recent enhancements have provided the Stack Ranker functionality to 360 forms so that raters can now evaluate multiple 360 participants against each other while providing feedback. This feature works exactly as it does in Performance Management, with one exception: the rater is always excluded from the list of those being evaluated. Detailed reporting that accompanies this feedback can be made available to the employee, the manager, or both.

If necessary, the 360 Multi-Rater evaluations can be made anonymously. Most customers solicit anonymous evaluations to encourage the most frank feedback from colleagues.

The detailed report, displayed in Figure 7.18, breaks down the ratings by rater and provides all raters' comments in one view, as well. This report can be permissioned, and it's the customer's decision to make this report available to the employee. This report can be accessed by managers from within the performance review form and can provide additional input into competency ratings and comments for performance review. Newer enhancements have made the DETAILED 360 REPORT button accessible from the FORM page, in the top toolbar section. This is helpful because it used to take quite a few mouse clicks to access the report.

Figure 7.18 Detailed 360 Multi-Rater Report View

Some other features released over the last few years include the following:

▶ **Validate Start Date**
The ability to validate that the start date of the form is earlier than the end date, and to prevent the start date from being edited erroneously after the form is launched.

▶ **Enforce Maximum Number of Raters**
The Forms Launch tool and Modify Participants interface now support enforcing the form setting limit for the number of times a user can be selected as a rater; administrators can choose to show a warning in the Modify Participants list or to disallow the addition of a user when the limit is reached.

▶ **Form Template Settings**
You can now automatically add the new manager as a 360 participant upon transfer to a new manager.

▶ **OneAdmin Features**
Now you can launch 360 forms and assign raters simultaneously via a CSV file; multiple documents can be sent to completion in the same manner.

7.4   Calibration

Many customers perform calibration of performance ratings across an organization to rationalize the rating distribution. Performance ratings are changed during the calibration exercise. The Calibration tool helps make employee calibration a simpler and more efficient exercise, bringing objectivity to a process that can often be too subjective. This is critical when the outcome influences an individual's career growth, compensation, and succession planning decisions.

To assess performance accurately, the Calibration feature shown in Figure 7.19 provides a visual comparison of employees, much like the Stack Ranker view for rating competencies. It allows managers in calibration sessions to see their team members against each other and make the most informed decisions, eliminating variability across managers. They can see performance ratings, compensation, and potential distributions in both bin and grid views.

The easy-to-use UI allows you to drag-and-drop employees from one bin to another to calibrate the ratings. This tool identifies a company's true high performers because all employees are viewed together. Managers are trained to assess performance more objectively and accurately when they see the results their ratings have on downstream processes, such as compensation and succession.

Figure 7.19 Calibration Session

7.5 Summary

SuccessFactors HCM Performance Management (PM) and Goals Management (GM) modules and the accompanying functionality in 360 Multi-Rater and Calibration provide a manager with a robust set of tools to accurately develop and track corporate, team, and individual goals and ensure that progress is on track and aligned with the overall corporate strategy. Goal Execution makes GM an easy daily task, rather than a chore. Performance reviews can become real avenues to development because tools such as the Writing Assistant help managers provide meaningful feedback that can be turned into action by employees.

Gathering informal feedback from others as input to the performance review is facilitated right from the TEAM OVERVIEW page. And tools such as 360 Multi-Rater provide another source of ratings against goals and competencies that managers can take into account when performing the year-end process. Finally, the Calibration sessions give visibility across the organization to ratings among managers and help restore objectivity to identifying and rewarding a company's true top performers.

In Chapter 8, we will look at SuccessFactors' Compensation module and how it facilitates managing merit, bonuses, and stock plans.

Designing an effective compensation system is crucial to an organization's talent management and total rewards strategy because compensation management plays a big factor in attracting and retaining talented employees. The SuccessFactors Compensation module provides the toolsets to design, automate, and launch a solid compensation program.

8 Compensation

Economic trends are forcing organizations to adopt pay-for-performance strategies because tying workers' pay to actual business results provides more visibility and control into the compensation payout, improves budget accuracy, and reduces risk. This helps enforce a culture in which everyone in the organization is awarded fairly according to individual contribution and organizational performance in areas such as teams, projects, and business units. It provides incentives for the workforce to align and deliver on the goals of an organization in a tangible way. This enables organizations to drive toward profitability and, thus, provide a bigger pool to reward employees who helped create that additional profitability.

SuccessFactors Compensation is a comprehensive solution that enables an organization to streamline the following planning components:

▸ **Base pay**
Merit, salary, promotion, and lump sum

▸ **Long-term incentive pay**
Restricted stock, stock options, performance units, and cash

▸ **Short-term incentive pay**
Bonus

▸ **Variable pay**
Bonus

Some common methods of calculating employee compensation are leveraging spreadsheet tools or deploying custom software. This complex and nonintegrated approach is inflexible to an organization's changing dynamics and introduces data inconsistencies between Human Resource Information Systems (HRISs) and Compensation systems.

SuccessFactors Compensation as a solution of the HCM suite provides a single source of all employee data to be utilized for calculation of compensation components. Data from SuccessFactors Employee Central or SAP ERP HCM is integrated, providing a single source of truth for the compensation process.

The SuccessFactors Compensation solution has the following two suite offerings:

▶ **Compensation (see Section 8.1)**
This is an engine for calculating merit, stock, and bonus data in relation to employee performance and guidelines.

▶ **Variable Pay (see Section 8.2)**
This complex and robust bonus calculation engine allows you to tie business goals and individual results to the payout amount.

Let's begin by taking a look at SuccessFactors Compensation.

8.1   Compensation Solution

SuccessFactors Compensation leverages standard HCM suite functionality that is essential in delivering a complete end-to-end compensation process:

▶ **Calibration**
"Nine-box" sessions review compensation data across teams, departments, and the entire organization to ensure fairness in the compensation process. Performance data from SuccessFactors Performance & Goal solutions can be leveraged to align performance and goals with compensation. Compensation data can be leveraged during the Succession Calibration session; Figure 8.1 shows an output of a Calibration session.

▶ **Live Metrics**
As shown in Figure 8.2, these offer graphical visibility into employee and compensation data, such as performance distribution by employees or pay versus performance matrix.

▶ **Rewards Statement**
You can generate compensation and variable pay statements for employees using standard fields and custom text.

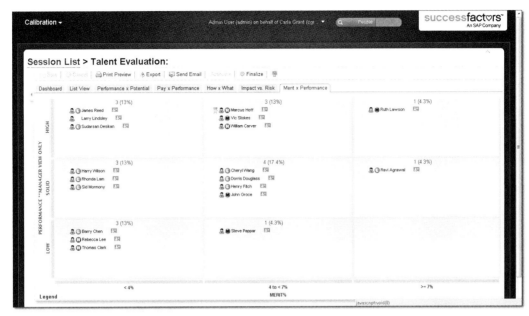

Figure 8.1 Calibration Session with Compensation, Performance, Succession, and Gender Data

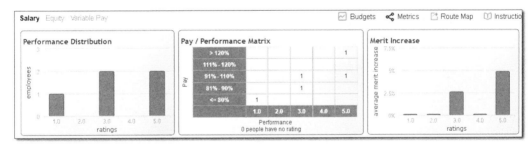

Figure 8.2 Live Metrics in Compensation Worksheet

▸ **Executive Review**

This provides visibility into all compensation and variable pay data. Employees can be viewed according to security permissions, reporting structure, organization levels, and views.

▸ **Compensation Profile**

This lets compensation planners make recommendations while viewing employee history and graphical views of positions. Figure 8.3 shows a planner's view of an employee compensation profile.

Figure 8.3 A Sample Employee Compensation Profile

SuccessFactors Compensation enables compensation planners and HR professionals to access information quickly, make required changes, and complete the compensation cycle in an efficient and simple manner.

An out-of-the-box and configurable workflow provides flexibility to launch the compensation cycle, whether you're using standard approval hierarchy or a custom compensation hierarchy. The OneAdmin tool provides configuration flexibility for each step of the compensation cycle. Approval of the compensation cycle is also a seamless process for both planners and HR professionals in the organization. As the compensation cycle progresses through the workflow steps, Compensation notifies the appropriate planner or administrator through emails and dashboard alerts if an action is required on their part.

To successfully launch a compensation cycle, you must set up a compensation plan template and perform the configuration and setup activities that meet the design needs of your organization. These activities are performed under the COMPENSATION HOME menu found under OneAdmin, as shown in Figure 8.4.

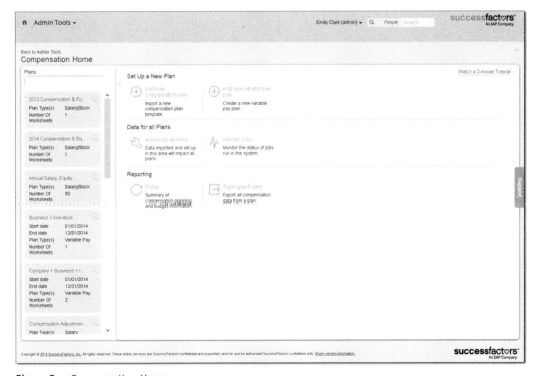

Figure 8.4 Compensation Home

The next step is to generate compensation worksheets (forms), which are created based on current data in the system. As the compensation cycle progresses toward completion, compensation forms require updates based on certain data elements that may have been updated during the compensation cycle.

The final step is to review and approve all of the compensation worksheets by the respective planners. Once this is completed, data is ready to be consumed by your HRIS for further action. Rewards statements and reports are generated after approval of the compensation forms.

With SuccessFactors Compensation, you can configure the following three compensation components:

- **Salary**
  You can configure any combination of merit increase, promotion, adjustment, lump sum, or bonus calculations. Performance ratings can be leveraged from the SuccessFactors Performance Management (PM) solution or uploaded into the solution as required per the compensation guidelines. You can prorate bonus calculations based on the employee hire date and end date for the year. Standard and custom fields set up for this component leverage the Lookup Tables, Salary Pay Matrix, and Job Code & Pay Grade Mapping tables to perform functions and calculations that are reflected on the compensation form.

- **Bonus**
  Management by Objective (MBO) can enforce a pay-for-performance bonus configuration, as opposed to a formula-based bonus. Goal attainment data is integrated from PM, and the bonus amount is calculated as a percentage of bonus targets.

- **Stock**
  You can configure stock options, restricted share units, performance units, and cash. Standard and custom fields set up for this component leverage the Lookup Tables, Stock Value, and Stock Factor tables to perform the calculations.

8.1.1 Compensation Plan

Most organizations have an annual compensation cycle; each compensation cycle should have a corresponding plan in the system. Figure 8.5 illustrates the summary of a sample compensation plan for all eligible employees. Plans are generally not personalized and represent an entire population of the organization under a specific hierarchy.

Figure 8.5 Summary View of the Compensation Plan

The PLAN STATUS section on the left provides a high-level summary about the plan; the ROUTE MAP PROGRESS section on the right illustrates the progress of the compensation cycle.

Figure 8.6 illustrates the BUDGET status for each compensation component within the plan, such as MERIT, PROMOTION, LUMP SUM, and so on.

Figure 8.6 Budget Overview of the Compensation Plan

Figure 8.7 illustrates the employee ELIGIBILITY statistics—comparing the number eligible and ineligible—for the plan components.

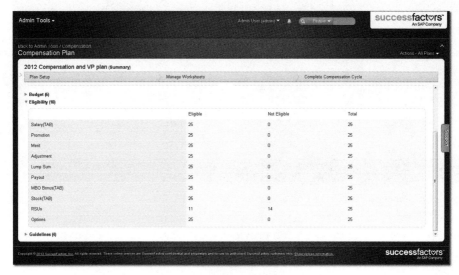

Figure 8.7 Eligibility Overview of the Compensation Plan

Figure 8.8 illustrates the GUIDELINES assignment statistics for employees. This provides a quick analysis of how many employees meet the guidelines configured for the compensation plan template.

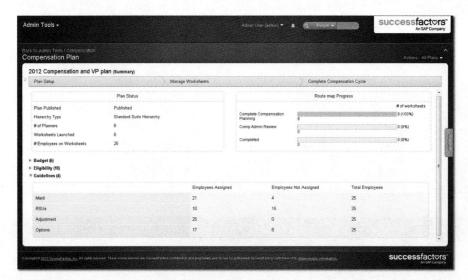

Figure 8.8 Guidelines Analysis of the Compensation Plan

8.1.2 Setup Data

Before you initiate the setup of the compensation plan, you must populate the required base setup tables with data. These data elements are in the IMPORT/EXPORT DATA section under the COMPENSATION HOME page, as shown in Figure 8.9.

Figure 8.9 Data Import, Export, and Setup Options for a Compensation Plan Template

All Plans

The ALL PLANS subsection of the IMPORT/EXPORT DATA section has the following options:

▸ EMPLOYEE DATA EXPORT
This option is very useful for troubleshooting employee data issues. You can use the export file as a basis for importing or updating employee data.

▸ CURRENCY CONVERSION TABLE
You can import currency conversion tables through this option. Figure 8.10 shows a sample table that charts the rates of conversion between U.S. dollars and other currencies.

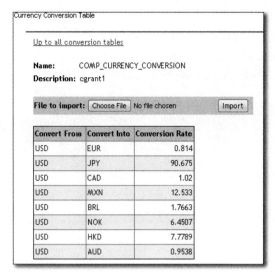

Figure 8.10 Currency Conversion Table

▶ LOOKUP TABLES

You can set up as many Lookup Tables (see Figure 8.11) as required under this option. Your compensation plan design includes gathering any requirements for setting these tables. Input and output columns form the structure of the lookup table, which is then referenced in the formula box of the compensation plan template.

Actions for all plans						
Import/Export Data			Manage Statement Templates			
All Plans ▼ Salary Plans ▼ Stock Plans ▼ Variable Pay Plans ▼						

Lookup Tables

Use this page to create, list lookup tables

Name	Description	Number Of Input	Number Of Output			Create

Name	Description	Number Of Input	Number Of Output	Last Modification	Last Modified By	Action
OMTARFET	TARGET	3	3	2013-05-07	admin	✗
PFACTOR	Company Performanc Factor for 2010 Comp plan	1	1	2010-09-13	admin	✗
ratecalc	Hourly calculation for salary Comprehensive Comp Plan	1	3	2010-09-09	admin	✗
prorate	Monthly proration for Comprehensive Comp Plan	1	1	2010-09-09	admin	✗

Figure 8.11 List of Lookup Tables

Salary Plans

The SALARY PLANS subsection of the IMPORT/EXPORT DATA section has the following options:

▶ SALARY RANGES

You can upload or export salary pay matrices, like the one shown in Figure 8.12 using this option. Salary pay matrices contain the salary ranges for each distinct value of pay grade. Values in the salary pay matrix are set up in functional currency and also drive the Compa-Ratio and Range Penetration calculation on the compensation form for each employee.

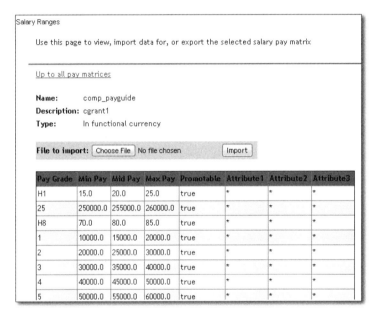

Figure 8.12 Salary Pay Matrix

The PROMOTABLE flag is used to define whether the pay grade is eligible for promotion. The ATTRIBUTE 1, ATTRIBUTE 2, and ATTRIBUTE 3 columns can be utilized to have different salary ranges for the same pay grade. At the bottom of this section, you have the option to upload a related MANAGER PROMOTION MAP, as shown in Figure 8.13.

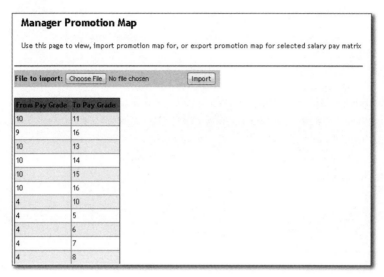

Figure 8.13 Promotion Map Table

▸ JOB CODE & PAY GRADE MAPPING

This area maintains the JOB CODE & PAY GRADE MAPPING table, which is shown in Figure 8.14.

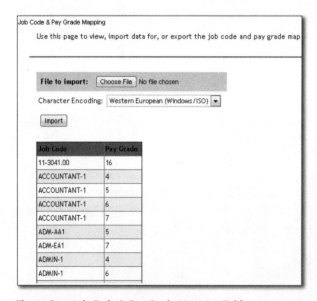

Figure 8.14 Job Code & Pay Grade Mapping Table

Stock Plans

The STOCK PLANS subsection of the IMPORT/EXPORT DATA section has the following options:

▶ STOCK VALUE TABLES

You can maintain this table (see Figure 8.15) with numerical values for each different type of stock. This numerical value can represent the purchase price of the stock or price per unit of a stock, depending on your design requirements.

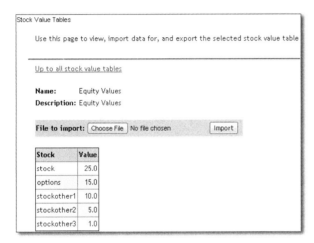

Figure 8.15 Stock Value Table

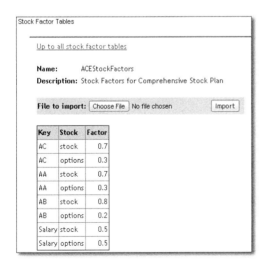

Figure 8.16 Stock Factor Table

369

▶ STOCK FACTOR TABLES

You can maintain this table (see Figure 8.16) to automatically calculate the appropriate mix of stock types for your employees. The KEY column represents the job level.

8.1.3 Plan Setup

The PLAN SETUP section of the COMPENSATION PLAN shown in Figure 8.17 contains the compensation plan template configuration and is where setup activities are performed.

Figure 8.17 Plan Setup Section of the Compensation Plan Template

Settings

The SETTINGS subsection is where the following details are visible and configurable:

▶ TEMPLATE NAME

As a best practice, choose a template name that reflects the year of the compensation cycle and the compensation components being planned against.

▶ UPDATED ON

This is the compensation plan template update date.

▶ FORMS USING THIS PLAN

This is the number of forms generated based on this compensation plan template.

▶ ENABLE GUIDELINE OPTIMIZATION

By default, this option isn't checked. If your organization has many compensation guidelines that are slowing down the performance of your system, check this option to improve performance.

▶ CURRENCY

This is the default functional currency of the form. If your organization has planners that plan in multiple currencies, the CURRENCY CONVERSION RATE TABLE converts the functional currency to the default currency of the form.

▶ ROUTE MAP

The route map is the sequence of workflow steps associated with all forms that have been generated based on this compensation plan template. Routing maps are configured to generate compensation forms with employees and their respective planners or HR administrators. Each route map has several steps; each step type can be assigned to a single role, be iterative between two people to exchange feedback, or be collaborative to allow for group review. Figure 8.18 shows a sample configuration screen for ROUTE MAP.

▶ CURRENCY CONVERSION TABLE

This is a mandatory currency conversion table per your organization's needs and setup.

▶ SALARY PAY MATRIX

If you are a SuccessFactors Employee Central customer, you can choose to use the salary pay matrix as defined in the Employee Central solution. For non–Employee Central customers, you must select a Salary Pay Matrix.

The ADVANCED SETTINGS subsection is the central location for managing the compensation plan template settings, such as form behavior, workflow, security, and functions. Figure 8.19 illustrates the ADVANCED SETTINGS area for the compensation template.

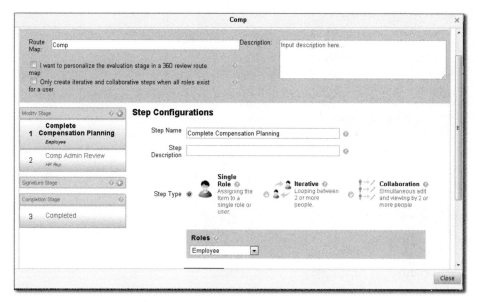

Figure 8.18 Route Map Configuration

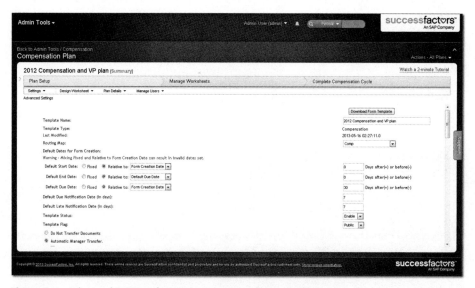

Figure 8.19 Advanced Settings for a Compensation Plan Template

Design Worksheet

The Design Worksheet subsection (see Figure 8.20) is where you design the layout of your compensation form and configure the fields for the compensation components that are required as part of the compensation plan template.

Figure 8.20 Compensation Plan Template Designer

Figure 8.21 illustrates the list of standard fields available when you select the Add Column option in the compensation plan template. These options are based on the instance configuration for your organization.

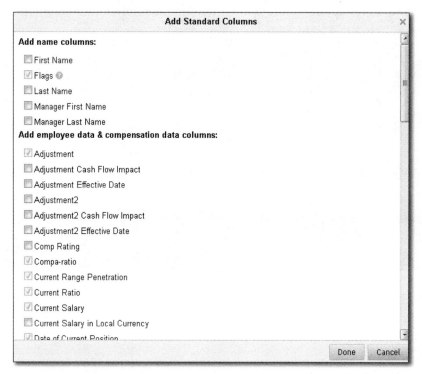

Figure 8.21 List of Standard Columns Available

Figure 8.22 shows how a custom column is added to the compensation plan template. The column properties such as title, read-only, visibility, type, format, and formula, among many others, can be adjusted. The FORMULA box is where you can enter mathematical calculations, If logic, conversions, and reference lookup statements pointing to the lookup tables. Each custom field can also be hidden if it is not required to be visible for the planner, be reloadable if data in this field will change frequently based on data import, be reportable to make available in reports and extracts, and have a unique import key associated with it, as shown in Figure 8.23.

After the STANDARD and CUSTOM columns have been configured, another logical step in the configuration process is to group relevant columns by selecting the ADD GROUPING option. You can visibly show each grouping separately on the compensation form by configuring it with its own HEX COLOR CODE, as shown at the bottom of Figure 8.24. This helps the planner identify employee and planning information easily on the compensation form.

Figure 8.22 Custom Column Configuration

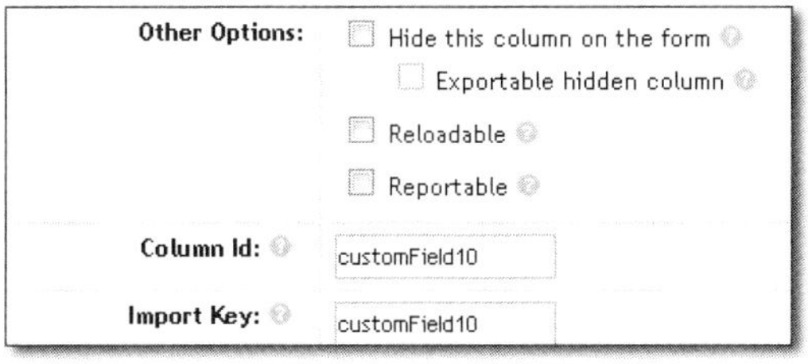

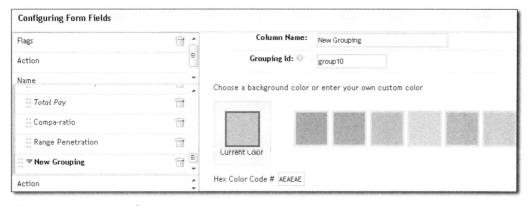

Figure 8.23 Custom Column Configuration Options

Figure 8.24 Grouping Configuration

> **Note**
>
> Compensation administrators can add restrictions to both standard and custom fields, which limit the field visibility and editability by enabling Field Permission Groups.

To add custom messages to be visible on the compensation form, the PLAN INSTRUCTION option under the DESIGN WORKSHEET subsection facilitates this process. Figure 8.25 illustrates the custom messages area available for the SALARY, BONUS, STOCK, and SUMMARY sections of the compensation form. These messages appear on top of the compensation form.

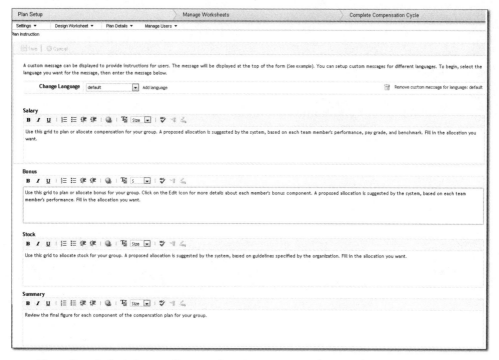

Figure 8.25 Default Custom Messages for a Compensation Plan Template

Plan Details

The PLAN DETAILS subsection allows for configuration of the following options:

▸ ADD BUDGET CALCULATION
This enables the planner to view the budget calculation status on the compensation form. Figure 8.26 shows the configuration options available for this section, such as the budget calculation mode shown on the form, the planning components the budget is used for, the default budget value, and whom to base the budget calculation on. Multiple budget calculation options can be configured within the compensation plan template shown in Figure 8.27.

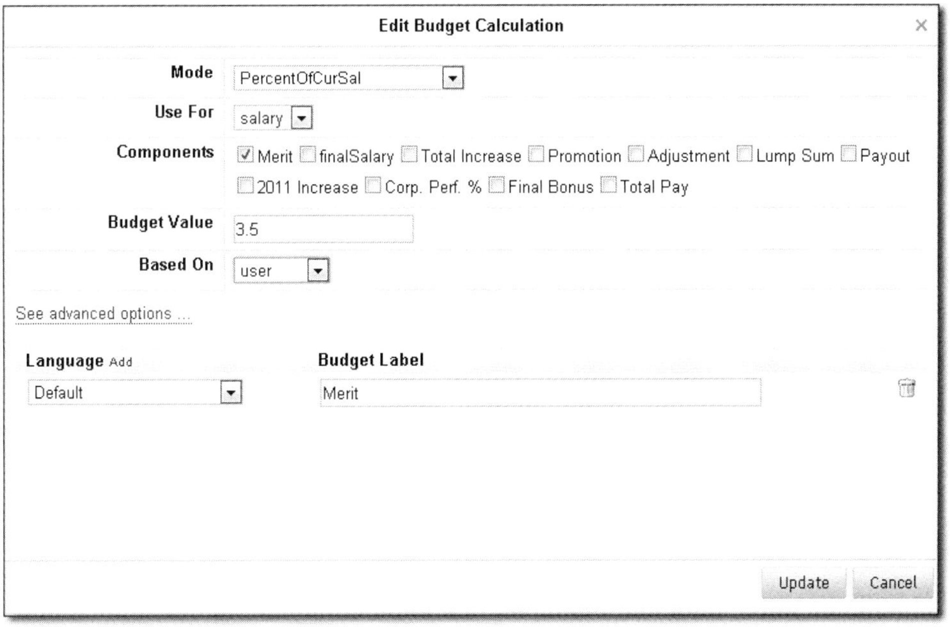

Figure 8.26 Budget Calculation Options

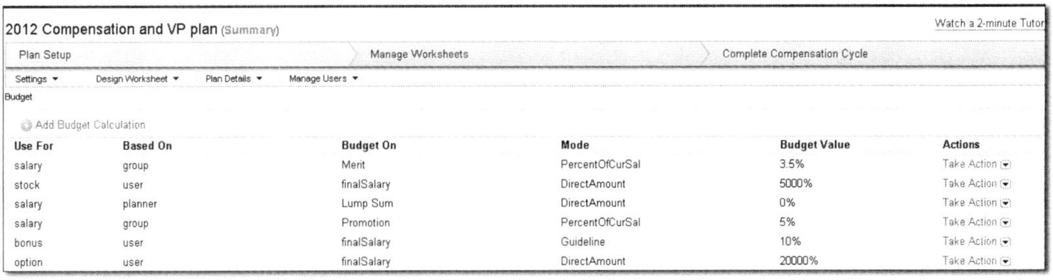

Figure 8.27 Budget Calculations Setup for a Compensation Plan Temple

▶ ADD BUDGET RULE

This option, shown in Figure 8.28, allows for the rule setup for budget calculations. You can choose to ALLOW, WARN, or DISALLOW planners to exceed budget calculations and whether to save the compensation form if the budget is exceeded. Options for entering warning messages are available in this area, as well. You can set up multiple rules for each compensation plan template.

Figure 8.28 Budget Enforcement Rule Configuration

▶ ELIGIBILITY
Multiple eligibility rules can be configured for the compensation plan template, as shown in Figure 8.29. Undertake designing each eligibility rule carefully because it affects the planner's ability to enter planning details against each employee on the compensation form. Rules can be anchored on standard fields available on the compensation plan template, such as pay grade or performance ratings.

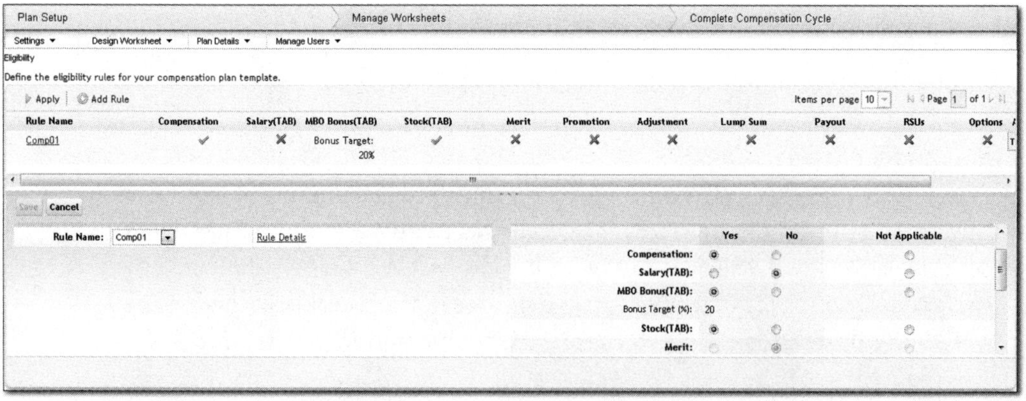

Figure 8.29 Eligibility Rules Setup

▶ GUIDELINES

Compensation guidelines, which are shown in Figure 8.30, are the rules a planner follows to effectively plan employee compensation for each component on the compensation form. Multiple rules can be set up per compensation plan template. As shown in Figure 8.31, each rule setup has much input: standard field criteria (RULE NAME, TYPE, FORMULA CRITERIA), MODE (AMOUNT or PERCENTAGE) for that rule, HARD LIMIT toggle, PRORATING toggle, FORCE DEFAULT ON RATING CHANGE toggle, and WARNING option if the planner exceeds or falls below the rule limit.

Figure 8.30 Guidelines for a Compensation Plan Template

Figure 8.31 Rule Setup

Each rule contains formulas that calculate the default planning component on the compensation form, as well as the MIN (minimum), LOW, DEFAULT, HIGH, and MAX (maximum) value for the component calculation. Figure 8.32 illustrates formulas set up for the rule; these can be imported, exported, or entered manually.

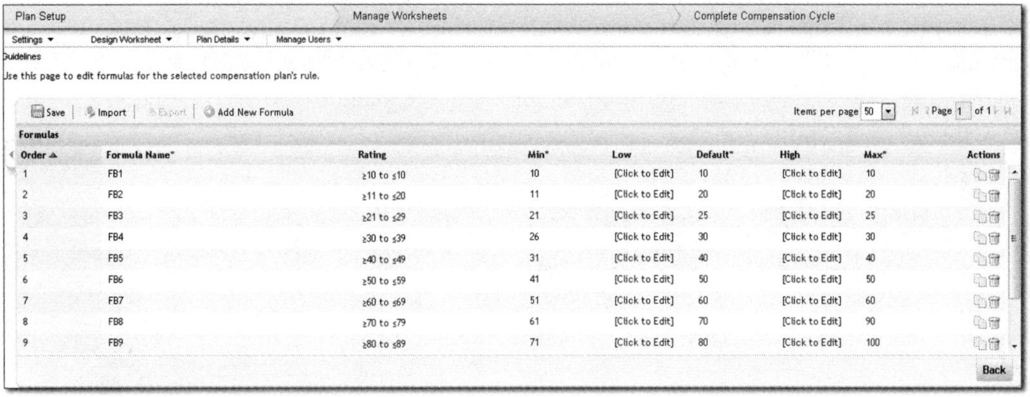

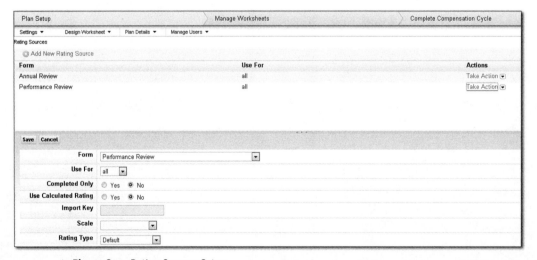

Figure 8.32 Formulas Grid

▶ RATING SOURCES
This option, as shown in Figure 8.33, allows for configuration of the employee performance rating source. You can import these ratings or leverage them from other SuccessFactors HCM suite solutions.

Figure 8.33 Rating Sources Setup

Manage Users

In the DEFINE PLANNERS subsection, shown in Figure 8.34, you define the hierarchy structure compensation forms that are generated for planners to plan employee compensation. The default option is to use the STANDARD SUITE HIERARCHY, which is based on the employee and the employee's manager, set up in the SuccessFactors HCM suite. Another option, the ROLLUP HIERARCHY, allows for planning responsibilities to be assigned to managers higher up in the organization. A custom hierarchy can also be configured as required to meet your organization's needs. This subsection is also leveraged for troubleshooting employee and planner hierarchy setup.

Figure 8.34 Standard Suite Hierarchy

8.1.4 Manage Compensation Forms

After all setup and configuration activities have been completed for the compensation plan template, the next step in the process is to generate compensation worksheets. Worksheets are forms that reside with the planners to enter compensation planning details and submit them for further action. The MANAGE WORKSHEETS section shown in Figure 8.35 is the central location to launch compensation forms and manage the lifecycle of the forms generated for the related compensation plan template.

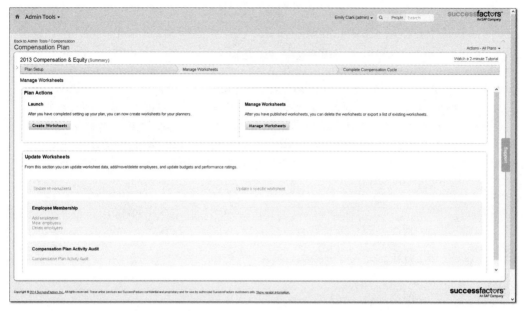

Figure 8.35 Manage Worksheets Section

Launch Forms

The CREATE WORKSHEET option under the PLAN ACTIONS subsection opens the panel, as shown in Figure 8.36, to provide step-by-step details for form generation.

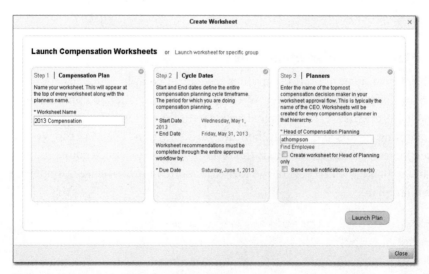

Figure 8.36 Launch Compensation Worksheets

The following steps are involved:

1. COMPENSATION PLAN

   Enter the form name visible to the planner. The planner's name is appended to this name automatically.

2. CYCLE DATES

   Choose the start and end dates of your organization's planning cycle. The DUE DATE controls the workflow activity of the form, such as when to notify planners based on date criteria.

3. PLANNERS

   Select the topmost planner in your organization hierarchy. This launches forms for all planners in the organization per the hierarchy configuration setting of the compensation template. If the requirement is to generate forms only for the specific planner, check the CREATE WORKSHEET FOR HEAD OF PLANNING ONLY option. You can choose to notify planners of compensation form availability by email. Planners can view the compensation form under the COMPENSATION section of SuccessFactors solution, as shown in Figure 8.37.

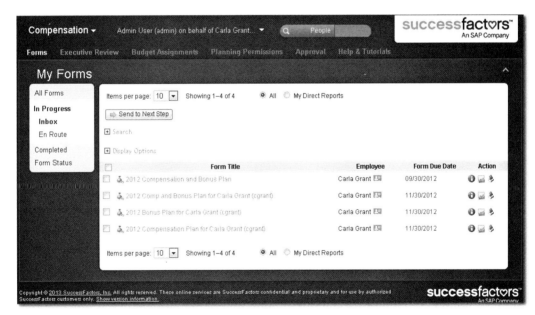

Figure 8.37 Manager's View of the Compensation Home Screen

After all of the details are entered, click the LAUNCH PLAN option to start the request for the form-generation process. Upon completion of the process, an email notification is sent with details about how many compensation forms were generated. At this stage, the compensation forms are considered in progress.

Manage Worksheets

The MANAGE WORKSHEETS option under the PLAN ACTIONS subsection, as shown in Figure 8.38, gives you visibility into the individual forms generated as part of the compensation plan template.

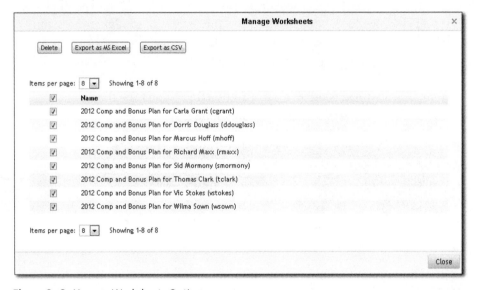

Figure 8.38 Manage Worksheets Options

In this example, there are forms for Carla Grant, Dorris Douglas, Marcus Hoff, and their colleagues. From this option, you can choose to DELETE the form, EXPORT AS MS EXCEL, or EXPORT AS CSV.

Update the Worksheets

After the compensation forms have been generated, you may need to periodically update data, update compensation form membership, or account for budget changes until the compensation planning cycle reaches completion. These activities are performed under the UPDATE THE WORKSHEETS subsection under the MANAGE WORKSHEETS section, as shown in Figure 8.39.

Figure 8.39 Update Worksheets Options

The following options are available in this subsection:

▶ APPLY DATA UPDATES
Clicking this option opens the panel shown in Figure 8.40. You can choose the settings that reflect the data change being applied, such as hire of a new employee, termination of an employee, budget changes, or change in organization hierarchy structure. Any changes in compensation eligibility criteria can be updated through this option. This option allows for updates to completed compensation forms, as well.

▶ ADD MEMBERS
Add members (employees) to existing compensation forms.

▶ MOVE MEMBERS
Move members (employees) from one compensation form to another existing compensation form.

▶ DELETE MEMBERS
Delete members (employees) from existing compensation forms.

▶ BUDGET ASSIGNMENT
Update the budget pool available for the compensation cycle. Additional budgets can be propagated and distributed to planners in the organization. Cascading budgets can't be propagated if the amount spent exceeds the new budget amount.

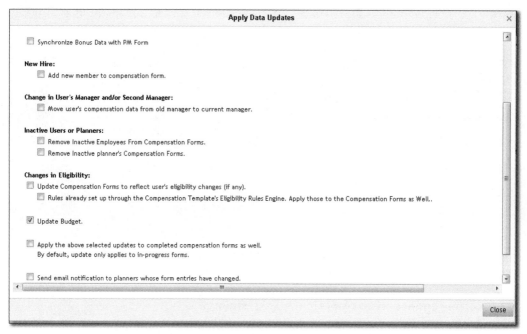

Figure 8.40 Apply Data Updates Options

8.1.5 Plan and Approve Recommendations

Each planner in the organization is responsible for timely recommendations for employees as part of the compensation planning cycle process. These activities are performed on the compensation forms generated for each planner. Figure 8.41 shows a sample compensation form with the salary compensation component configuration.

Planners can adjust the display options on the form to get the desired information about the employee by expanding the DISPLAY OPTIONS option, as shown in Figure 8.42.

Planners can filter employee information on the worksheet by clicking the FILTERS icon to FILTER BY EMPLOYEE NAME or FILTER BY CATEGORY, as shown on Figure 8.43 and Figure 8.44 respectively.

Figure 8.41 Planner's View of the Enhanced Compensation Worksheet

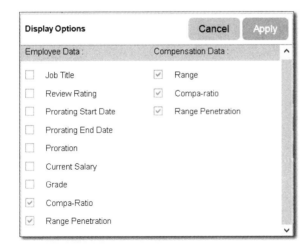

Figure 8.42 Display Options on the Enhanced Compensation Worksheet

Figure 8.43 Filter by Employee Name

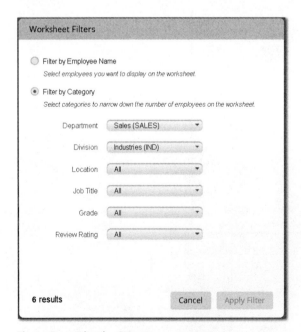

Figure 8.44 Filter by Category

Input Recommendation

Planners can choose to accept the calculated recommendations for the employees based on the compensation plan template setup or override the system-calculated recommendations. Planners also have the flexibility to view the compensation guidelines as a percentage value or numerical value by adjusting the toggle available in the appropriate column.

Depending on how the compensation plan template is configured, a planner can also view multiple compensation planning components as separate tabs by clicking the appropriate link on the top-left section of the compensation worksheet. The SUMMARY tab is shown in Figure 8.45.

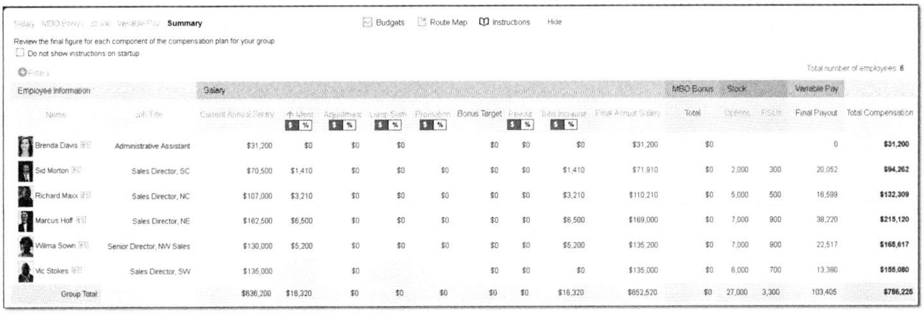

Figure 8.45 Summary Tab View on the Enhanced Compensation Worksheet

Figure 8.46 shows a sample compensation form with the bonus compensation component configuration.

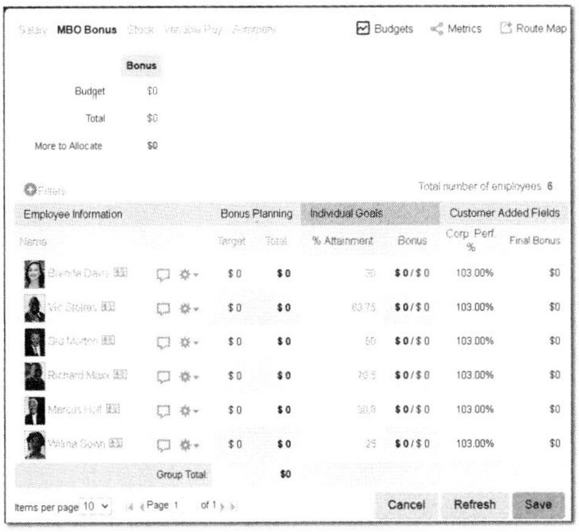

Figure 8.46 A Planner's View of the Bonus Component on the Enhanced Compensation Worksheet

Figure 8.47 shows a sample compensation form with stock compensation configuration.

Figure 8.47 A Planner's View of the Stock Component on the Enhanched Compensation Worksheet

Approval Workflow

After a planner has finished making their recommendations on the compensation form, the next step is to move the form to the next logical part in the workflow process. To perform this, a planner must click the SEND TO NEXT STEP button at the top of the compensation form, as shown in Figure 8.48.

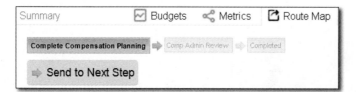

Figure 8.48 Compensation Form Workflow Steps

Hierarchy-Based Approval

Another option for approving the planner recommendations is to enable *hierarchy-based approval* as part of your solution design. It provides a simple approval model based on tree structure navigation that is built on the organization hierarchy. This configuration option eliminates the need to generate forms or send forms to the next step in the approval process. Figure 8.49 shows the planner view of the compensation components using hierarchy-based approval configuration.

Figure 8.49 Hierarchy-Based Approval Configuration

8.1.6   Reports

The two standard options for compensation reporting are ROLLUP and AGGREGATE EXPORT; these are available as part of the COMPENSATION HOME menu.

Compensation Aggregate Export

This is an export of all employee and planning data available within a specific compensation plan template. The extract includes all standard and custom fields (if marked as reportable) defined on the compensation plan template. A sample compensation aggregate export is shown in Figure 8.50.

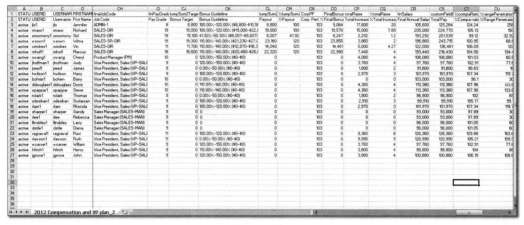

Figure 8.50 Compensation Aggregate Export

Compensation Rollup

This option allows for the generation of the compensation planning and budget information report based on a planner's hierarchy for the selected compensation plan template. Figure 8.51 illustrates the menu for generation of this report.

Back to Admin Tools / Compensation
Rollup
Actions - All Plans ▾

Compensation Rollup for Administrator

Watch a 2-minute Tutorial

Enter the username of the user as the head of the hierarchy to generate the Compensation Rollup Report

Planner: cgrant   [Find Plans] Find User...

Template Name	Name	Start Date	End Date	Due Date	Status	Last Modified	Action
2012 Compensation Plan	2012 Compensation Plan for Carla Grant (cgrant)	11/1/12	11/30/12	11/30/12	Modify Stage	5/19/13	🐾
2012 Compensation Plan	2012 Compensation and Bonus Plan	9/1/12	8/31/13	9/30/12	Modify Stage	12/11/12	🐾
2012 Compensation and VP plan	2012 Comp and Bonus Plan for Carla Grant (cgrant)	11/1/12	11/30/12	11/30/12	Modify Stage	5/19/13	🐾
Annual Individual Incentive Program : Corp x Individual Performance	2012 Bonus Plan for Carla Grant (cgrant)	11/1/12	11/30/12	11/30/12	Modify Stage	5/6/13	🐾

Figure 8.51 Compensation Rollup Generation Menu

8.1.7 Executive Review

The Executive Review functionality in the Compensation solution enables any active SuccessFactors user to review (read) or adjust (write) compensation recommendations made for all employees in the organization. The user must be granted this functionality as part of the RBP framework and assigned proper data access to the employee population. At any given time, data generated within a single compensation plan template can be accessed with EXECUTIVE REVIEW, as shown in Figure 8.52.

Figure 8.52 User Access to Executive Review

After the compensation plan template is chosen, the user is presented with a page that exactly matches the design and layout of the compensation plan template, as shown in Figure 8.53. This page isn't to be mistaken for the compensation form for a planner. Executive Review neither relies on a compensation form's workflow state nor behaves like a form. If compensation data is modified in Executive Review, you can send an email notification to the planners or reviewers of the affected underlying compensation form. Planners, HR Managers, and Administrators can filter data for employees they can edit or view.

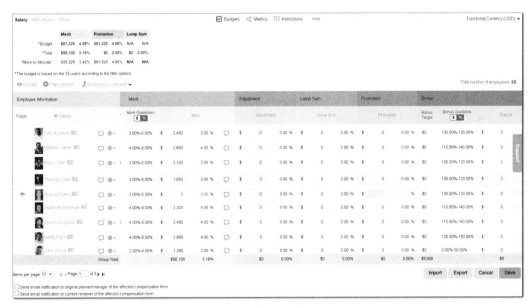

Figure 8.53 Executive Review for a Compensation Plan Template

The real advantage of using Executive Review is the ability to filter data by expanding the FILTER OPTIONS, as shown in Figure 8.54. This can provide for a detailed analysis and update of compensation data by the administrators, HR professionals, and managers in your organization. Data visible on the EXECUTIVE REVIEW screen can also be exported in CSV format.

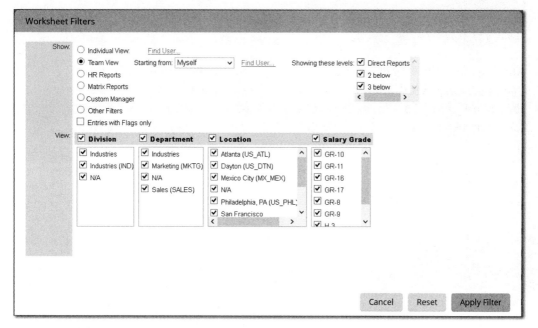

Figure 8.54 Filter Options for Executive Review

8.1.8   Reward Statements

Leading industry practices call for providing each employee with a Personal Compensation Statement highlighting the employee's compensation results at the end of the compensation planning cycle. The Compensation solution facilitates this process by providing the capability to create a PERSONAL COMPENSATION STATEMENT template, as shown in Figure 8.55. You can modify the template with your organization's text, logo, multiple sections, and standard fields on the compensation plan template.

After all compensation forms have been reviewed and marked completed, only then can a Personal Compensation Statement be generated for each employee.

The Personal Compensation Statement for an employee is available on the Employee Profile.

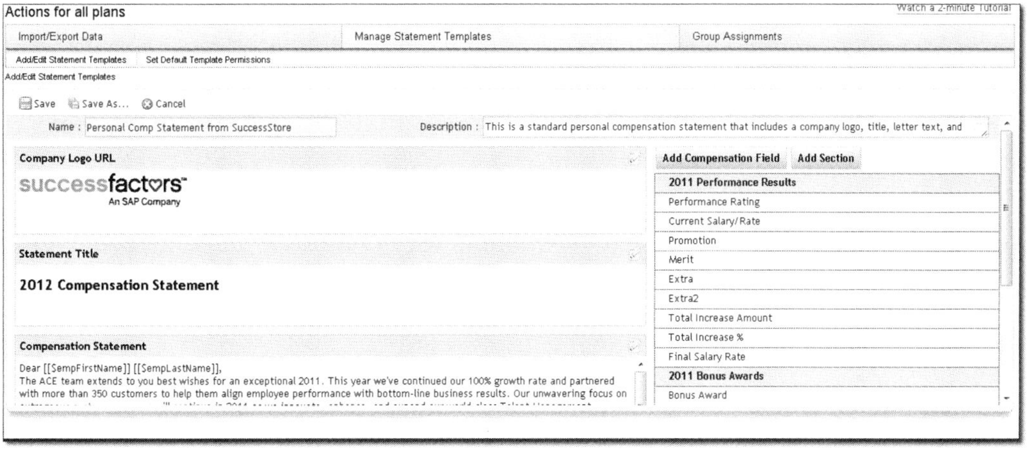

Figure 8.55 Personal Compensation Statement Template

8.2 Variable Pay Solution

SuccessFactors Variable Pay is a robust solution that calculates employee bonuses based on quantitative business performance and individual performance measures. An organization can decide whether to use the bonus calculation feature of the SuccessFactors Compensation solution or the Variable Pay solution as part of the compensation planning cycle design.

The following are key features of the Variable Pay solution:

- Proration of bonus calculation for an employee who has held two or more positions in the organization, has had two or more pay grades, has had a salary change, or is associated with multiple scorecards
- Management of several bonus plans with weighted business goals
- Modeling of "what-if" scenarios to forecast bonus payout
- Integration of employee performance in bonus calculation
- Support for additive or multiplicative formulas
- Multiple time-based payout cycles such as monthly, quarterly, and annually

Let's walk through the configuration steps required to create a Variable Pay program.

8.2.1 Plan Setup

The first step is to configure a variable pay plan within the PLAN SETUP section shown in Figure 8.56.

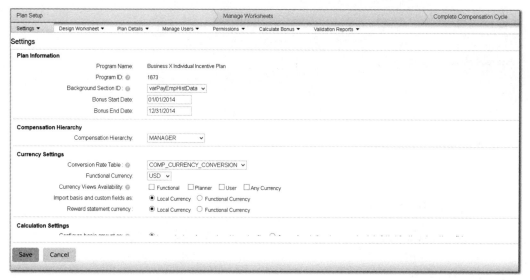

Figure 8.56 Variable Pay Plan Setup

The SET BONUS CALCULATION subsection has the following configuration options:

- IS THIS BONUS BASED ON ASSIGNMENTS?
  Select this option if the bonus calculation is based on employees' having different assignments in the year.

- BONUS CALCULATION EQUATION
  Select the appropriate bonus calculation for your organization's design of the variable pay program. The calculation options are shown in Figure 8.57.

- ENABLE MULTIPLE BONUS GOAL SECTIONS
  Check this option if you require tracking business performance at different levels in your organization.

- BUSINESS GOAL NAME
  Select the required business goal for the variable pay program.

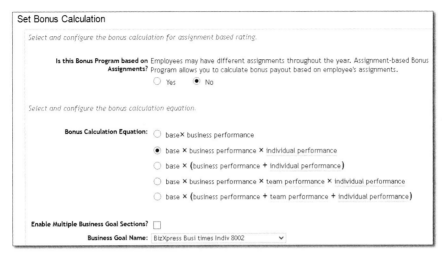

Figure 8.57 Bonus Calculation Setup for Variable Pay Template

▶ PERFORMANCE RATING SOURCE

Select the option to import performance rating by employee or assignment history. If integration with PM is required, select the TEMPLATE NAME and RATING option; see Figure 8.58.

▶ DEFINE BONUS CAPS

Select the option to apply bonus caps.

Figure 8.58 Performance Rating Source Configuration

The Set Number Format Rules subsection, as shown in Figure 8.59, enables the creation of number formatting rules. These rules are referenced for each value in the variable pay calculation.

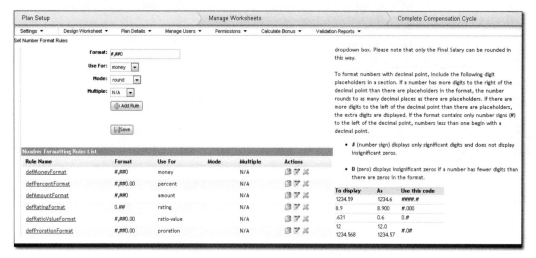

Figure 8.59 Set Number Format Rules Configuration

Design Worksheet

The Configure Label Names and Visibility subsection, as shown in Figure 8.60, controls the visibility of variable pay sections, fields, and label names.

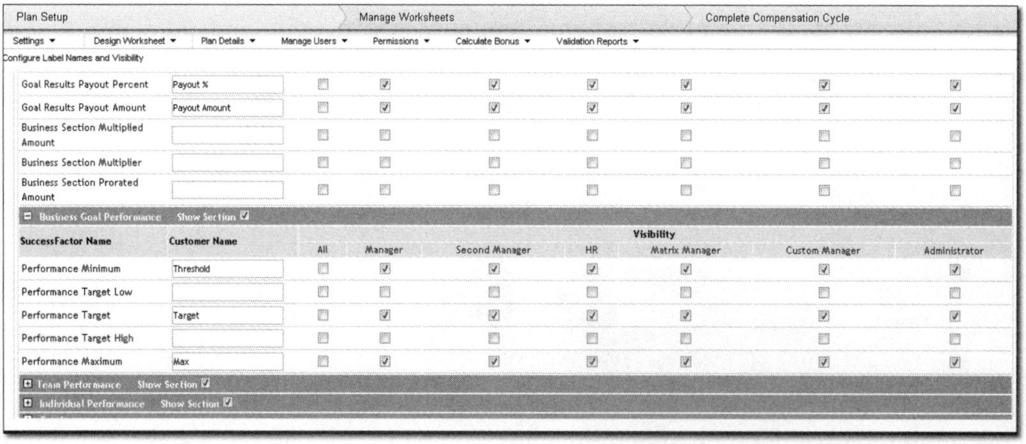

Figure 8.60 Configure Label Names and Visibility

The Column Designer subsection is very similar to the Design Worksheet option in the SuccessFactors Compensation solution. You can add standard or custom fields, as well as custom groups, to create the variable pay form layout.

The Set Number Formats subsection, shown in Figure 8.61, is where you set the number format for each value in the variable pay calculation.

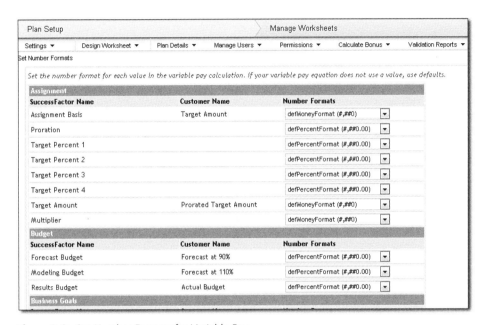

Figure 8.61 Set Number Formats for Variable Pay

Plan Details

The Plan Details subsection allows for configuration of the following options:

▶ Bonus Plans 1. Import Business Goals
Import a CSV file that contains the business goal definitions, goal forecasts, and goal results. This file is produced as part of the variable pay program design and is required for the configuration of the variable pay program.

▶ Bonus Plans 2. Import Bonus Plans
Import a CSV file that contains the bonus plan definition. This file is produced as part of the variable pay program design and is required for the configuration of the variable pay program.

▶ Bonus Plans 3. Configure Bonus Plans
Adjust the imported bonus plans parameters, as shown in Figure 8.62.

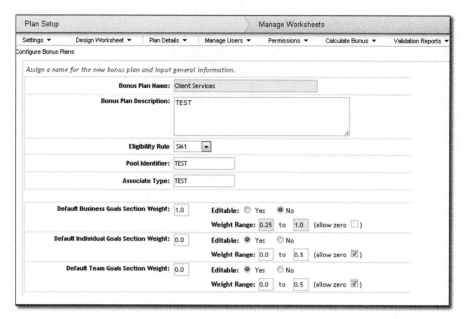

Figure 8.62 Configure Bonus Plans for Variable Pay

▶ IMPORT BUSINESS GOAL WEIGHTS
Import a CSV file that links the business goals to the bonus plans and assigns unique weighting. This file is produced as part of the variable pay program design and is required for the configuration of the variable pay program.

▶ ELIGIBILITY
Import a CSV file that contains the eligibility rule for the bonus plans. This file is produced as part of the variable pay program design and is required for the configuration of the variable pay program.

▶ BUDGET
Configure budget visibility and percentages, as shown in Figure 8.63.

▶ INDIVIDUAL GUIDELINE
Configure the mapping of employee performance rating sources to input guidelines, as shown in Figure 8.64.

▶ TEAM GUIDELINE
Configure the mapping of team performance rating sources to input guidelines.

▶ ADVANCED GUIDELINES
Configure the formulas for individual guidelines.

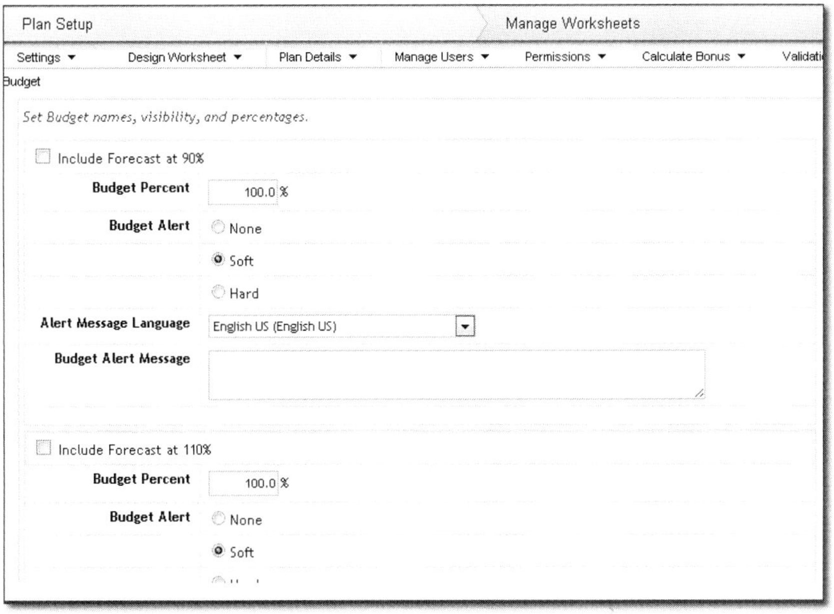

Figure 8.63 Budget in Variable Pay

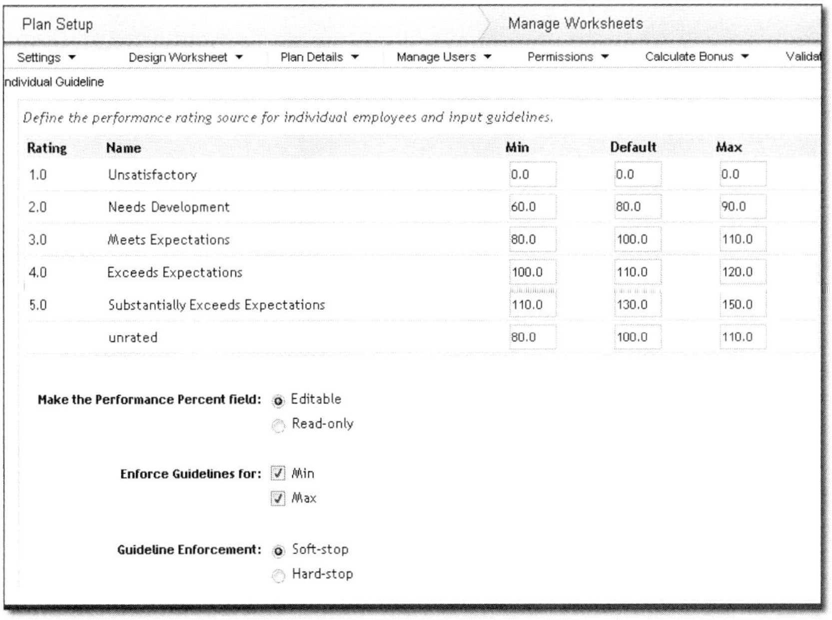

Figure 8.64 Individual Guideline for Variable Pay

Manage Users

The MANAGER USERS subsection is where you import the employee's date-effective history file in a CSV format. This is a required file for variable pay plan setup and calculation. This subsection is also used for performing an online edit of the employee history rows. Figure 8.65 shows the EDIT EMPLOYEE HISTORY screen with rows uploaded in the system.

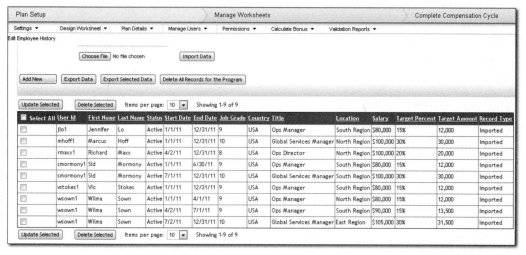

Figure 8.65 Employee History File for Variable Pay

The employee history can also be processed from the PM solution, if required.

Calculate Bonus

After all setup activities have been performed and employee history data is uploaded into the system, the next step is to trigger the BONUS PAYOUT calculation process, as shown in Figure 8.66. The calculation can be made for one of the bonus plans, a manager, and an employee.

The user who initiated the process is notified by email of the successful completion of the bonus payout calculation.

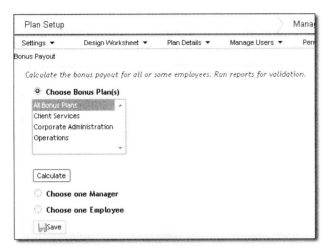

Figure 8.66 Bonus Payout Calculation

Validation Reports

The Variable Pay solution is delivered with the reports shown in Figure 8.67, which help validate the variable pay program setup.

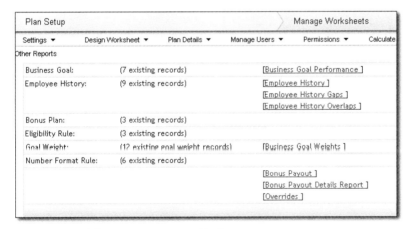

Figure 8.67 Validation Reports in Variable Pay

8.2.2 Manage Variable Pay Forms

After the Variable Pay setup is complete, the process to generate variable pay forms is exactly the same as for generation of compensation forms discussed in Section 8.1.4. After the forms are generated, the planner can review them, as shown in Figure 8.68.

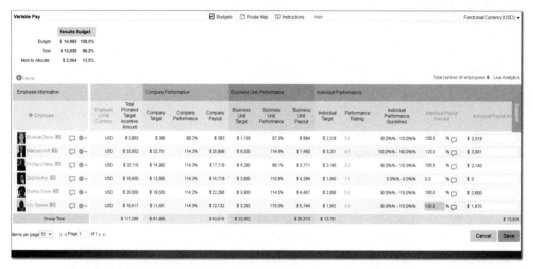

Figure 8.68 Enhanced Variable Pay Worksheet

If the planner wants to view detailed calculations instead of this overview, the planner can click the Action icon to access the View Details sub-selection next to the employee's name. The plan details include, for example, target amounts, proration, goals, weighting, and payout amounts, as shown in Figure 8.69.

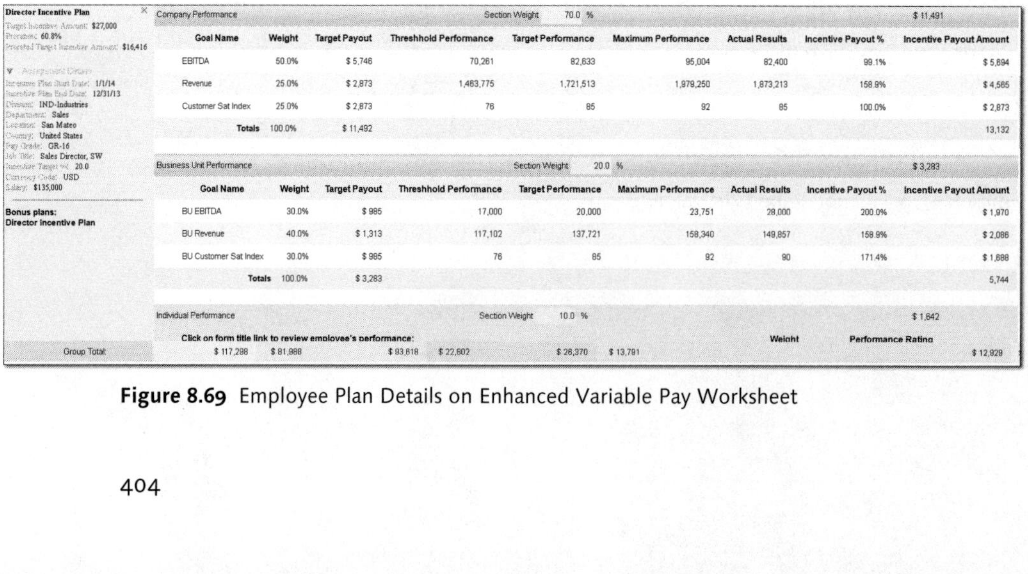

Figure 8.69 Employee Plan Details on Enhanced Variable Pay Worksheet

Alternatively, the planner can expand the Compensation Profile to conduct further analysis on the employee result, as shown in Figure 8.70.

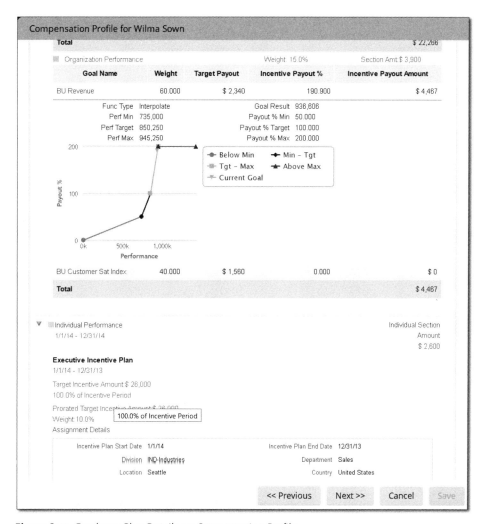

Figure 8.70 Employee Plan Details on Compensation Profile

The planner can also view summary results of the Enhanced Variable Pay Worksheet by clicking the Live Analytics link located on the top-right section, as shown in Figure 8.71.

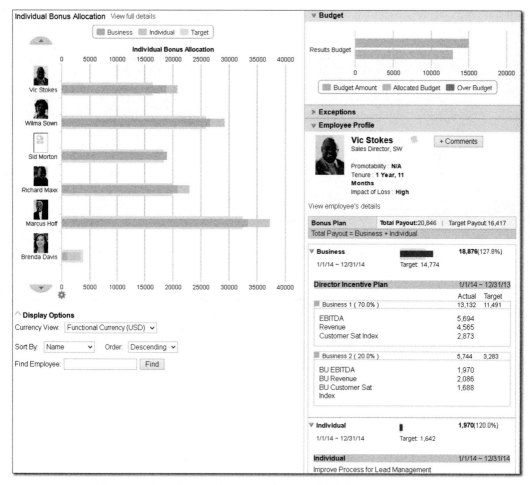

Figure 8.71 Live Analytics on Enhanced Variable Pay Worksheet

8.2.3 Approve Recommendations

After the planner is satisfied with the calculations on the variable pay form, clicking the SEND TO NEXT STEP button at the top of the variable pay form moves it into the next step in the workflow.

> **Note**
>
> The hierarchy-based approval configuration for approving compensation forms isn't available for the Variable Pay solution.

8.2.4 Executive Review

The Executive Review functionality in the Variable Pay solution behaves exactly the same way as the SuccessFactors Compensation solution discussed in Section 8.1.7.

8.2.5 Reward Statements

The Variable Pay solution provides the capability to create a Personal Variable Pay Statement template. You can modify the template with your organization's text, logo, multiple sections, and standard fields available on the variable pay program.

8.3 Decentralized Administration

Global companies with unique local requirements for compensation components can administer their plans in the Success Factors Compensation and Variable Pay solution by leveraging the Decentralized Administration functionality. This is achieved by enabling local administration with governance provided by the centralized administration team. The elements currently available for decentralized administration are as follows:

- Compensation and Variable Pay Guidelines
- Variable Pay Bonus Plans, Business Goals, and Business Goal Weights

Figure 8.72 displays how Compensation Guidelines can be administered by various local administrator Groups.

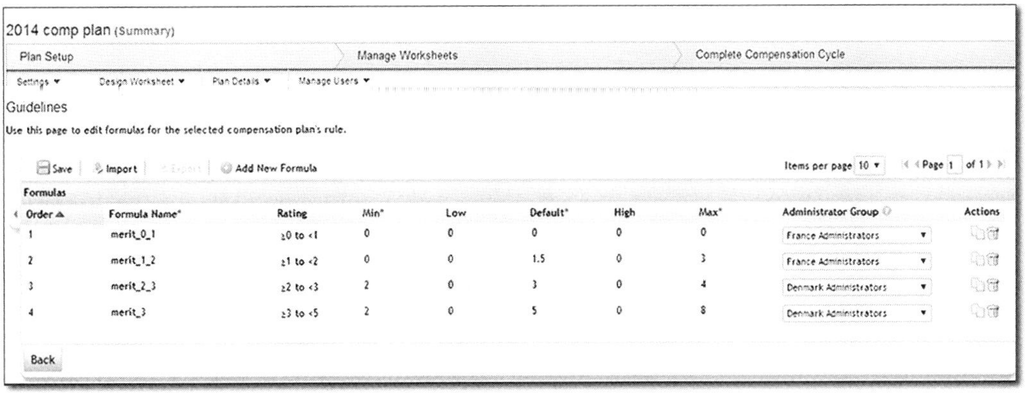

Figure 8.72 Decentralized Administration of Compensation Guidelines

8.4   Summary

The SuccessFactors Compensation and Variable Pay solutions provide a robust platform to meet the complex needs of an organization's compensation design and truly enforce a pay-for-performance culture. The solution offerings in SuccessFactors Compensation provide the organization the agility needed to effectively manage a successful compensation cycle by streamlining the planning process. Integration capabilities with SAP ERP HCM and Employee Central provide the benefit of not having to manage multiple data points.

In this chapter, you learned what is required for the setup of the yearly compensation forms and how to design your compensation worksheets. You also learned how to execute a compensation review and complete the compensation process. We covered the SuccessFactors Variable Pay module and how it can offer you the ability to perform compensation reviews for individuals whose pay varies based on different business factors.

In the next chapter, we'll look at the SuccessFactors Recruiting Execution solution and how it can support recruiting management, applicant tracking, and recruiting marketing activities.

Recruiting in today's competitive environment encompasses three phases that are all critically important to ensuring that you hire the right candidates to drive business results. SuccessFactors Recruiting Execution provides all the tools to attract, engage, and select the best talent for your organization.

9   Recruiting Execution

Legacy Applicant Tracking Systems (ATS) have focused almost exclusively on selecting candidates. While many tools are now available on the market to help companies find and engage candidates, most aren't connected to the application and selection processes and tools. But, in today's competitive hiring environment, finding the best candidates isn't enough. You need to get them engaged and moving through your hiring process quickly so you don't risk losing them to a different opportunity.

The SuccessFactors Recruiting Execution module (hereafter, RX) brings together Recruiting Marketing (RMK) and Recruiting Management (RCM) to combine the best features of an ATS, application processing and candidate management features, and high-powered tools to attract and engage candidates in one solution. This complete recruiting solution sits inside the SuccessFactors HCM suite, enabling customers to connect it to their other modules, such as SuccessFactors Workforce Analytics, Workforce Planning, Succession Planning, Learning, Performance Management, Goal Management, Compensation, and other collaboration solutions. As shown in Figure 9.1, RX is an integral piece of a complete HCM solution that drives business execution results and is the first step for customers to optimize their workforces—finding the right people for the right jobs.

RX not only manages the transactional components of a traditional ATS from a requisition and application perspective, but also goes beyond that, providing tools that ensure that customers can attract and engage the best candidates in their recruiting process.

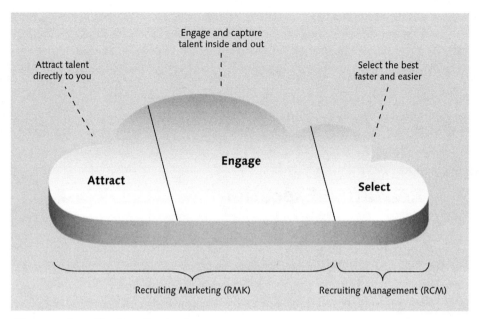

Figure 9.1 Recruiting Execution Landscape

The recruiting process with RX is driven by collaboration. It allows different players in the process—recruiters, hiring managers, coordinators, and others—to actively participate in managing an open position, reviewing and assessing candidates, and eventually selecting the right candidate for hire.

The system is intuitive and easy to use; any player in the process can log in and understand what to do and where to do it with very little training. For recruiters who spend all day in the system, RX saves time and frustration by reducing the number of mouse clicks to complete an action, from maintaining a requisition to moving candidates through the Talent Pipeline and eventually processing the successful candidate for hire.

RMK features introduce the concepts of Search Engine Optimization (SEO) and social media integration to attract top talent and help them find the jobs customers are sourcing. Advanced RMK analytics provide never-before-available insight into how marketing strategies and dollars are being utilized and facilitate real-time adjustment.

Other tools, such as the Requisition dashboard, give recruiters an overview of critical pieces of data on their open positions. The Candidate Workbench provides many tools for recruiters to evaluate and communicate with candidates and share qualified candidates with other colleagues.

Interview Central facilitates competency-based assessment of candidates. It leverages the SuccessFactors HCM Stack Ranker functionality to allow interviewers to evaluate candidates against each other and give an overall rating and comments. Recruiters can build interviewer teams for requisitions and assign the same team to each candidate being interviewed, saving time and increasing recruiter efficiency. Candidates can now schedule themselves into interview times online and manage these appointments based on what fits best with their schedules.

RX provides one of the most comprehensive metrics engine in the industry. Providing metrics such as cost per hire; time to hire; and candidate quality by source, location, and other criteria, RX provides the raw data customers need to evaluate the effectiveness of their recruiting processes and tools.

As with the rest of the SuccessFactors HCM suite, RX is highly configurable. It offers more than 30 standard fields available for use on the requisition and application and supports unlimited custom fields. The customer's branding and messaging is supported by SuccessFactors' best practices and platform.

9.1   Recruiting Execution Foundation

Before we look at the features of RX, let's outline some helpful foundational concepts.

9.1.1   Recruiting Roles

Roles associated with the recruiting process are identified by each customer, based on who needs to approve requisitions and view candidates. These process roles are then associated with the standard RX roles, which define the following:

- Field, button, and feature permissions on the requisition
- Field, button, and feature permissions on the candidate application
- Which role creates the approval workflow for the requisition and reviews the requisition

Within the RX module, seven roles can be permissioned. These roles are separate from roles created in Role-Based Permissions (RBP) and are defined and permissioned directly in the requisition template configuration. Roles correspond to operator fields on the requisition (for example, the RECRUITER in the example provided in Figure 9.2). The following recruiting roles are available:

- ORIGINATOR
- RECRUITER
- HIRING MANAGER
- SOURCER
- COORDINATOR
- SECOND RECRUITER
- VP OF STAFFING
- APPROVER

Figure 9.2 Requisition Operator Roles

Unless an operator field is tied to a Dynamic Group, limiting the users who can be selected as an operator in that field, any user in the system can be selected as an operator on the requisition. This provides a great amount of flexibility in who can participate in the recruiting process.

9.1.2   Recruiting Templates

There are three main components of configurable templates within RX: the Job Requisition Data Model, the Candidate Data Model template, and the Candidate Profile Template. For customers who use Offer Approval, there is also an Offer Details Template that is configured.

Job Requisition Data Model

A requisition defines the requirements of the position being filled. Requisitions are created from a template that is configured during implementation. The template is called the Job Requisition Data Model (JRDM) and specifies the fields on the requisition and who has permissions to read and write to each field. Requisitions are created manually by operators in the recruiting process, such as a hiring manager or recruiter. Integration now supports open positions in SAP ERP HCM triggering the creation of a requisition in Recruiting Management. Requisitions are tied to a route map (or workflow) for approval before they are open and can be posted to the Career site. The JRDM is completely configurable to meet customer requirements using either the standard fields for requisitions or any number of custom fields that may be required.

Candidate Data Model

The Candidate Data Model (CDM) is RX's application. It defines information about a candidate who is applying for a position and contains identifying information, such as name and contact data; job-specific requirements the candidate possesses; and other demographic data the customer needs to capture, such as Equal Employment Opportunity (EEO) status. The application template is also completely configurable and can utilize the standard application fields or any custom fields required to support the customer's needs.

Candidate Profile Template

The Candidate Profile Template (CPT) is the candidate's online résumé. It leverages Employee Profile functionality and can be designed to capture static information about a candidate, such as education, work experience, and references. The CPT can be synced to the Employee Profile for internal candidates so that this information is entered only once.

Offer Details Template

The Offer Details Template defines the data elements of a candidate offer sent through the system for approval. It can pull data from fields on the requisition or application, or data can be entered directly onto the template. The approvers can be added ad hoc or leverage a pre-defined workflow that is configured into the template. This supports defining recruiting roles, recruiting groups, or specified users.

Now that we've laid a foundation to discuss RX, let's take a look at the recruiting process.

9.2 Requisition Creation and Approval

The recruiting process in RX begins with creating a requisition and sending it through the approval workflow, or route map. This gives each operator in the approval workflow an opportunity to review the position requirements, make additions or correct data, and send it back if there is an issue that needs to be addressed. After the requisition is approved, it can be posted to the internal and external career portals, job boards, or agency portal.

9.2.1 Requisition Creation

Requisitions can be created in two ways: an open position in SAP ERP HCM triggers the requisition, or a recruiting operator manually creates a requisition. For manually created requisitions, any user who has been granted permissions to create the requisition form can start the requisition process. The user who creates a requisition, like the one shown in Figure 9.3, is known as the originator and has permissions on the requisition that have been granted in the requisition configuration for the originator role. The originator role completes the operators who need to approve the requisition and any other fields for which they have permissions.

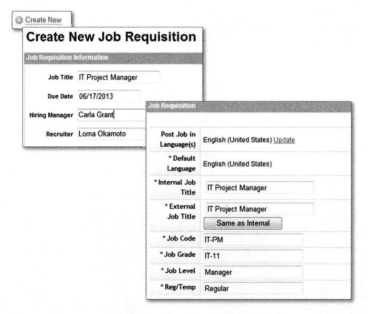

Figure 9.3 Creating a New Requisition

Requisitions created via the integration with SAP ERP HCM appear as pre-approved requisitions in the RECRUITING dashboard. Fields of data may be updated or completed as needed, and the requisition sent through the route map for approval.

9.2.2 Requisition Approval Workflow

Each job requisition template can be associated with one approval workflow, called a route map. A route map electronically moves a requisition from one user to the next until all appropriate approvals have been received (see Figure 9.4).

Figure 9.4 Requisition Route Map

While the route map defines which users touch the requisition, the permissions assigned to each role in the route map define what the users can see and do to the data in the requisition. Steps in the route map can be linear or iterative. Iterative steps involve two or more parties and allow the requisition to be sent back and forth between the two parties until it's ready to move forward. After the requisition is approved, it can be posted, and candidates can view it on the career portal. We'll cover this step next.

9.3 Job Posting and Sourcing

Open requisitions can be posted so candidates can search for them and apply. Job posting is where the power of RX's marketing capabilities come into play and illustrate SuccessFactors' dedication to candidate engagement. SuccessFactors is committed to delivering data-driven and user-centric best practices that optimize site conversion rates and maximize the user's experience.

The power of SuccessFactors Recruiting Marketing (RMK) is making job postings available to the brightest and best talent possible. A common problem facing talent acquisition professionals is that their jobs aren't easy to find. RMK leverages proven marketing techniques such as SEO, social media integration, and customized landing pages while applying them to talent sourcing in new ways to drive applicant flow. Talent communities capture passive candidates who may have been previously lost to recruiters. SuccessFactors implemented RMK internally in early 2012, and within 10 months of implementation, visitors to its career site increased from 10,000 to more than 80,000, resulting in more than 150 hires. Now, the company can track more than 50% of its hires directly back to the source.

Easily accessible sourcing analytics provide new visibility to marketing strategies and their effectiveness at any given time. Dashboards on recruiting marketing sources provide real-time data on where candidates are coming from, enabling customers to evaluate and adjust recruiting marketing strategies and dollars in an agile manner. These advanced analytics support tracking candidates from sourcing to hire to retire.

SuccessFactors treats every job as a campaign to attract candidates to your sites based on their interests and skill sets. Customized landing pages attract candidates based on their particular interests and drive them to the main career site within RCM. Talent communities are candidate-centric, automated recruiting pools that grow over time. They connect talent with the company's brand, store contacts in a centralized place, and track visitors to a customer's site who begin the application process but don't complete it. Talent communities open communication channels with candidates who would not otherwise exist.

Jobs are posted through the JOB POSTINGS page and, from there, are picked up and distributed to the predetermined channels based on the criteria established during implementation.

As shown in Figure 9.5, approved requisitions are available for posting in various places within RCM:

▸ Internal posting (internal career site)
▸ External posting (external career sites)
▸ Job board postings (via eQuest integration)
▸ Agency listings (SuccessFactors' Agency Portal)

Jobs posted to the intranet appear on the CAREERS tab within the SuccessFactors HCM Platform and are available to all employees. Corporate postings are those made to the microsite created for external candidates. Customers have one default microsite but can create additional sites as requirements dictate. This flexibility enables sites to focus on certain populations or target candidates. However, the decision to create additional microsites should be made in the context of the RCM strategy employed by each customer. Microsites are most powerful for companies that choose to implement RCM before RMK or opt not to implement RMK at all.

Jobs can be posted for a specific period of time by providing a Posting Start Date and a Posting End Date. If a job should be posted indefinitely, no Posting End Date is provided, and it stays posted until the posting is removed by the recruiter.

Figure 9.5 Job Postings in RX

Job board postings are an add-on service provided by SuccessFactors' partner eQuest. The job boards available depend on a customer's separate contract and subscription with eQuest. This aggregator allows recruiters to post jobs to multiple places via one interface. Specific fields must be configured on the requisition template to support the fields eQuest requires to post.

SuccessFactors supports working with agencies using its Agency Portal. There is one Agency Portal that is shared by all customers, and each customer sets up individual agency accounts for those agencies they want to post jobs for, as shown in Figure 9.6. The Agency Portal functionality has increased significantly in the last year and now allows agency users to track the progress of the candidates they submit to requisitions. There are also email triggers that can be set up to communicate with agency users.

Figure 9.6 Setting Up Agency Access in OneAdmin

After agencies have been set up in OneAdmin and granted access to the Agency Portal (see Figure 9.7), recruiters can post jobs to the portal, and agency users can submit candidates for open positions. Agency candidates are easily identifiable from the Candidate Workbench, as well as within the Candidate Snapshot.

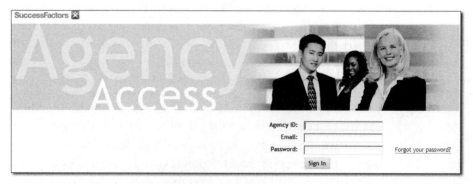

Figure 9.7 The SuccessFactors Agency Portal

9.4   Candidate Experience

Candidates interact with the system in several ways. They can search for open positions and set up a Candidate Profile, apply for jobs, manage job applications already submitted, and set up job alerts to be notified of future positions that become available.

The Candidate Profile and Candidate Data Model are two major elements of the candidate's job search experience, and they work together to provide recruiters and hiring managers a complete picture of the candidate. This picture is used to evaluate the candidate against the job requirements, leading to the selection of a qualified candidate. This section looks at how the two elements of the candidate experience—the Candidate Profile and Candidate Data Model—work together to provide recruiters and hiring managers with a complete picture of a candidate's background and qualifications for a position.

9.4.1   Career Sites

As we saw in Section 9.3, jobs are posted in two places within RX: an internal careers page (where internal employees go to find open positions for which to apply through SuccessFactors HCM) and microsites (where external candidates can view jobs and set up an account via one or more external career sites).

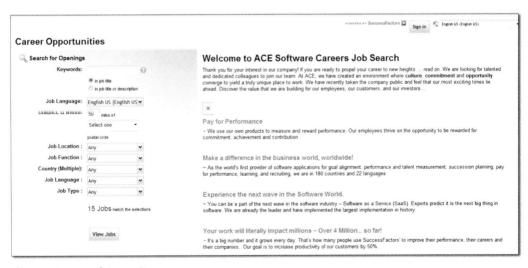

Figure 9.8 External Career Site

External sites like the one in Figure 9.8 are generated in OneAdmin, and a customer can have multiple microsites within its RX system. Each site has its own URL and can be used for marketing jobs to specific audiences. This is irrespective of other channels that funnel jobs in RMK.

Search Criteria

From the CAREER page, candidates can use search criteria to find positions that interest them. By clicking the VIEW JOBS button, they can display more detail on each position before drilling into job descriptions to view the requirements of each position, as shown in Figure 9.9. Customers can define welcome messages in the right two-thirds of the CAREER page. This is also done in OneAdmin, and it supports graphics, hyperlinks, and deep links to other URLs.

Figure 9.9 View Job Search Results

Search criteria are defined by the customer during implementation. There are standard search criteria that can be activated, such as keyword search and radial search. And customers may define unique search criteria that use data from the requisition to help candidates find positions of interest.

Candidates can create an account to set up a Candidate Profile and apply for jobs. External candidates are identified by their email address, which is also their user ID.

Candidate Home Page

After candidates log on to the Career site, they are taken to a HOME page like the one shown in Figure 9.10. This provides additional space for the company to communicate with candidates and gives candidates an easy way to jump to actions they want to perform, such as searching for a job or maintaining their profile. Whether to use a HOME page is a configuration decision, and the HOME page can be turned on and off depending on the customer's requirements.

Figure 9.10 Career Page Home Page

9.4.2 Candidate Profile

The Candidate Profile serves as a candidate's online résumé. It leverages Employee Profile functionality to capture static candidate information such as name and contact information, work history, education, languages spoken, and geographic mobility, among others, as shown in Figure 9.11. It serves to capture all of the information about a candidate that isn't job specific and applies to any position to which the candidate applies. Candidates enter this data just once in a central location that is visible to and searchable by recruiters. The Candidate Profile exists for all potential candidates, including all existing employees with access to SuccessFactors HCM and external candidates who create an account.

Data collected on the Candidate Profile is searchable by recruiters who may be sourcing positions and others who have been permissioned to conduct candidate searches. To ensure consistency for internal employees between Employee Profile and Candidate Profile, the system supports mapping of the data elements configured on each Profile template. Fields that reside on both the Employee Profile and Candidate Profile can be synced so that internal employees need to maintain information in only one place. The trend is moving toward capturing more information on the Candidate Profile, rather than the application (or CDM), so candidates have one place to update information that remains fairly constant from one position to another.

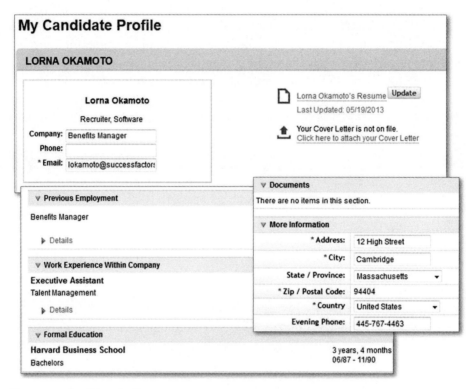

Figure 9.11 Candidate Profile

There is only one CPT that is used for both internal and external candidates. This is critical to keep in mind during design because both types of candidates need to use the same template but often have varying data needs. RX supports configuration for internal and external audiences to assist with this situation.

It's possible to have fields configured on the CPT that are visible only to internal candidates; likewise, fields that apply and are visible only to external candidates can also be configured. For internal candidates, background elements on the Candidate Profile that are duplicates of Employee Profile background elements can be mapped so that data is synced between the two. This alleviates the internal candidate from having to maintain the same data in two places in the system.

9.5 Candidate Data Model

The CDM shown in Figure 9.12 defines the data that the applicant submits to apply for a job. The CDM captures job-specific information, such as special qualifications and skills that are applicable to the position for which the candidate is applying.

The CDM and Candidate Profile can be configured so that data entered into one is mapped to the other. So, for example, if the candidate opens the application and completes the Candidate Profile first, information such as name, address, email, and phone number are populated on the application. Any documents such as résumé and cover letter uploaded to the Candidate Profile are also available on the CDM. Updates to documents made on the CDM are updated on the Candidate Profile, as well.

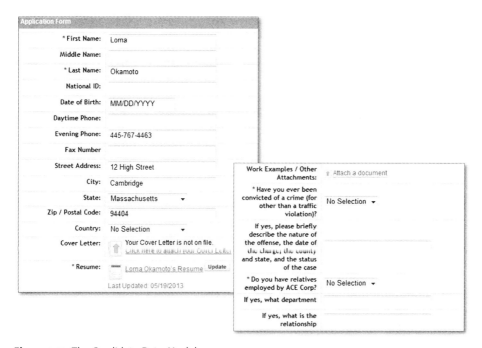

Figure 9.12 The Candidate Data Model

The CDM also controls what individuals in the recruiting process see when viewing candidates who have applied to positions. For example, the hiring manager may be permissioned to see all fields on the CDM except self-identification fields such as gender and veteran status, while the recruiter can see all fields.

Country-specific field configuration is also supported if a customer has a need to display certain fields only to candidates in a certain country. For example, a customer that sources jobs in the United States often collects EEO data from candidates. Of course, they would not want these fields to be displayed to a candidate applying for a job in Canada or the United Kingdom because they aren't applicable. Country-specific configuration can be applied to these fields so that they appear only for positions based in the United States.

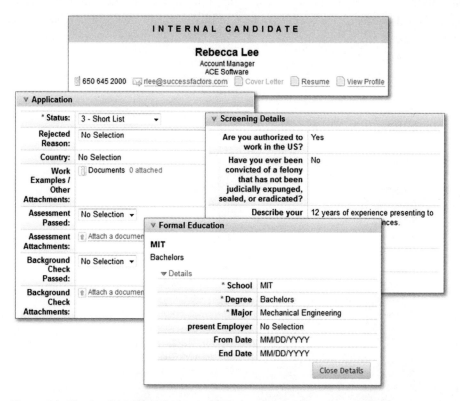

Figure 9.13 The Candidate Snapshot

Together, the Candidate Profile and CDM present the complete picture of the candidate to the recruiter and others evaluating them for a position. This complete picture is presented in the Candidate Snapshot (see Figure 9.13) and gives the recruiter the full view of a candidate's experience, qualifications, and interests.

From the Candidate Snapshot, recruiters can view the résumé, cover letter, Candidate Profile, Candidate Profile elements, and any screening details from questions added to the requisition. Every type of candidate is identified by the banner across the top as internal candidate, external candidate, or agency candidate.

By default, the system is configured so that a candidate may choose to complete the Candidate Profile before or after submitting an application. However, there is a setting that mandates that the Candidate Profile be completed prior to submitting the application. This recommended setting requires candidates to provide as much background information as possible for recruiters and hiring managers to use to evaluate the candidate for the position. With the trend being toward a more robust Candidate Profile and streamlined CDM, the required fields on the application may be very few, so without completing the Candidate Profile before applying for a job, candidates wouldn't otherwise be providing a well-rounded representation of their skills and experience. The CPT view provided to recruiters in the CANDIDATE DETAIL view is a "snapshot" of the CPT at the time the candidate submits an application. If the candidate has not yet completed the Candidate Profile, much data about the candidate's education, experience, and other qualifications isn't available in this view.

The advantage of setting up this configuration is that customers can ensure that candidates have completed all required fields on the Candidate Profile before submitting an application. Any subsequent applications follow the same process of taking the candidate to the Candidate Profile to update any necessary information or provide an updated résumé before continuing with the application submission.

9.6   Candidate Selection Management

After jobs are posted and candidates begin applying, the recruiter has numerous tools available for evaluating candidates and making sure the best quality candidates are identified and ushered through the hiring process quickly. The two main tools are the Candidate Workbench and Interview Central.

9.6.1   Candidate Workbench

The Candidate Workbench is the place recruiters spend most of their time. It gives them access to the applications and profiles of candidates who have applied to each position and shows how candidates rate against the requirements estab-

lished in the requisition (see Figure 9.14). From here, recruiters begin dispositioning candidates—or moving them through the Talent Pipeline—in multiple ways:

▶ Selecting one or more candidates and using the ACTION column to perform any
  number of actions on a candidate, such as changing their status or emailing
  them

▶ Updating the STATUS field within the Candidate Snapshot

▶ Using the MOVE CANDIDATE button to update the candidate status in the Candidate Snapshot

▶ Dragging and dropping a candidate into the appropriate status

Name	New	Status	Rating ▾	Source	Phone Number	Source:
Caroline Clark		3 - Short List	100.0	Internal Referred		
Aaron Allen	New	1 - New Application	50.0	Corporate Site	(713) 382-7188	Corporate Website
Tiffany Peters	New	1 - New Application	50.0	Corporate Site	303-888-8888	Hot Jobs
Gina Walker		Hireable	50.0	Internal Referred	408-555-1214	
Jonathan Burns		Hireable	50.0	Corporate Site	303-333-3030	Corporate Website
Brad Jones		Auto Disqualified	0.0	Corporate Site		Corporate Website

Figure 9.14 The Candidate Workbench

The TALENT PIPELINE contains all of the statuses in the hiring process, as well as
some system default statuses (see Figure 9.15). It organizes the candidates as they
are evaluated against job requirements and moved through the process. It is
divided into three sections:

▶ **Default statuses**
  The FORWARDED and INVITED TO APPLY statuses are tied to specific functionalities in the system whereby a user can forward a candidate to a job through
  Candidate Search and then invite the candidate to apply via an email link to the
  job posting, if their qualifications match up to the those of the position. These
  statuses can't be edited or disabled.

▶ **In-progress statuses**
  This section of the pipeline contains all new applications and is configured to
  represent all of the stages of a customer's hiring process, such as résumé
  review, interview, background check, offer, and hire. In-progress statuses
  should encompass all stages of a customer's hiring process for candidates who
  remain under consideration until they are disqualified for any reason.

▶ **Disqualified statuses**

These statuses capture the reasons that candidates aren't selected to move through the process, including the system status of AUTO-DISQUALIFIED, which is tied to a candidate answering required questions on the requisition incorrectly.

Figure 9.15 The Talent Pipeline

Statuses in the Talent Pipeline are completely configurable by the customer, with the exception of the system statuses FORWARDED, INVITE TO APPLY, and AUTO-DISQUALIFIED. The customer can create any number of statuses required for assessing candidates for hire or dispositioning them to a disqualified status that is reportable. While the number of statuses dictates the length of the pipeline visually, the system scrolls through the pipeline using the left and right arrows on each end of the pipeline, making navigation quick and easy.

Several of the actions recruiters can make against candidates, such as scheduling interviews or generating offer approvals and letters, are controlled by a Features Permissions functionality that is configured within the requisition template. This means that customers can decide when they want recruiters to have access to the Set Up Interviewers portlet or the Offer functionality, as an example. These decisions are made during implementation and are configured directly into the requisition. Customers can also decide which roles can perform certain actions. So if they want recruiting coordinators to set up interviews but not generate offers, they can use the Feature Permissions functionality.

9.6.2 Interview Central

Interview Central is where the interview team can evaluate candidates. RX is based on competency evaluation and leverages the competency library within the SuccessFactors HCM platform. Customers can define a competency library that contains interview-related competencies that are added to the requisition and are then available to rate candidates against in Interview Central.

Setting Up Interviews

Setting up interviews is a Feature Permission functionality that can be configured against one or more in-progress statuses in the Talent Pipeline. When a candidate is moved into one of these statuses, such as INTERVIEWING, the SET UP INTERVIEWERS portlet shown in Figure 9.16 is available within the Candidate Snapshot. Recruiters can define the interview team and set dates and times for each interviewer to evaluate the candidate. The recruiter also has the option of emailing this information to the interview team and including the candidate's résumé and cover letter.

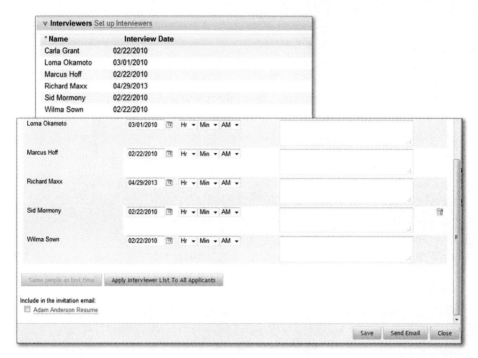

Figure 9.16 Set Up Interviewers

Note that this option does not put a calendar entry on the interviewers' calendar. To do this, the recruiter needs to use the CREATE MEETING button to use email to send a meeting invitation via that avenue.

One of the newest features of RX is the online interview scheduling interface. This has two facets: online scheduling of interviewers and allowing candidates to book themselves into interview blocks via the Candidate portal. First, recruiting operators need to set up the interview blocks with the interviewers who are available in each time block. This feature will include Outlook integration in future releases and will replace the Set Up Interview portlet that customers may be used to. Once the interview blocks are established, candidates who are move into interview statuses are able to view the open times and schedule themselves into the blocks of time that best suit their schedules. They can also cancel and reschedule interviews as needed. Giving candidates this capability and control over the interview schedule should eliminate much of the back-and-forth of emails and phone calls of interview scheduling!

Evaluating Candidates

Interview Central is where competencies added to the requisition come into play. It provides tools for interviewers to provide feedback and rate candidates against those requisition competencies. They can access all candidates they are scheduled to interview, by job. From the main screen, shown in Figure 9.17, they can see who has been evaluated, who has yet to be evaluated, and how all candidates stack against each other. Notes from the hiring manager about the particular job, if provided on the requisition, are displayed to all interviewers, and they can choose to use the PRINT AND GO feature to print a hard copy of the candidate's résumé, cover letter, and the job description with competencies to be rated.

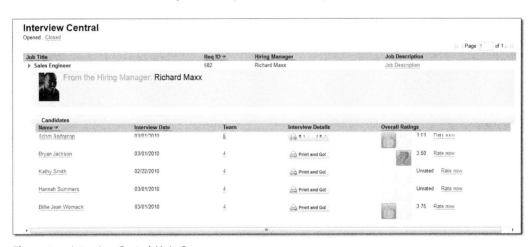

Figure 9.17 Interview Central Main Screen

Evaluating candidates is as easy as selecting the RATE NOW link to see all candidates evaluated for that job. Interview Central utilizes the Stack Ranker functionality to give a visual of all candidates against each other. This also makes rating quick and easy and can be done for all competencies and all candidates at the same time. As ratings are given, an overall score is generated based on the rating scale defined for the requisition.

Interviewers can provide comments on each competency and overall comments on their rating. They can also upload a document if they take notes electronically. These notes are available to recruiters managing the position. Finally, interviewers provide an overall rating of THUMBS UP or THUMBS DOWN on each candidate for a dashboard-like view of how the candidates rate against each other (see Figure 9.18).

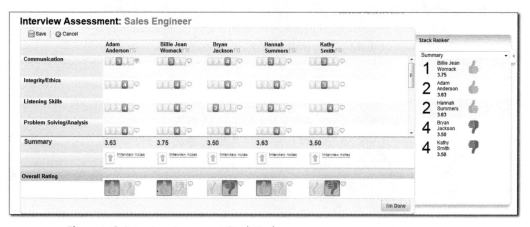

Figure 9.18 Interview Assessment Stack Ranker

9.7 Offer Management

Offer Management in RX offers two alternatives for customers. Offer letters can be generated from the system and sent to candidates, or the offer can be formally approved in the system before the offer letter is created.

RX enables customers to create and maintain multiple offer letter templates to meet a variety of requirements. Recruiting administrators can create or edit offer letter templates at any time in OneAdmin (see Figure 9.19). Tokens are available to embed in each template so that information can be dynamically populated into each offer letter.

Figure 9.19 Offer Letter Template in OneAdmin

Offer letter functionality is tied to statuses in the Talent Pipeline. Offer letters can be made available in one status or several statuses, depending on the customer requirements. Recruiters have the option of generating PDF versions of the offer letter or sending them as text embedded in an email. This is illustrated in Figure 9.20. The offer letter and verbal offer are captured in the audit trail for each candidate.

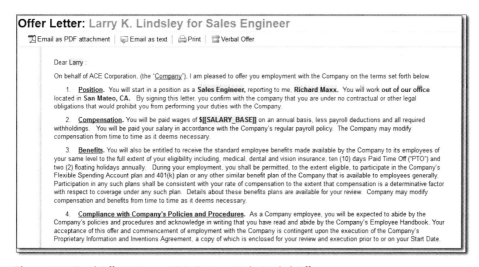

Figure 9.20 Send Offer Letter as PDF, Text, or Make Verbal Offer

Online offer acceptance is also now available. This method sends candidates a link to view and accept their offers electronically, rather than printing an offer letter, signing it, and trying to return it to the recruiter. The offer letter process also supports documenting a verbal offer that may occur. And, with the most recent release of SuccessFactors, customers can now integrate with DocuSign for e-signature of offer letters. This requires a separate agreement with DocuSign. With both online acceptance and e-signature, results are tracked and available from within the Offer portlet in the Candidate Details.

For customers who have a more formal approval process for offers, the system supports defining an OFFER DETAILS template, like the one shown in Figure 9.21.

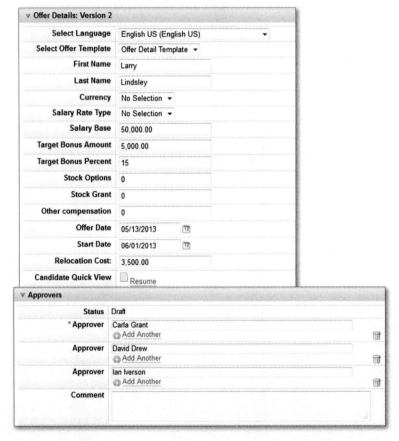

Figure 9.21 Offer Approval Detail Template

This template captures the particulars of each specific offer, such as job title, salary offered, vacation, and bonus details, among others. Information can be mapped from the requisition, application, and Candidate Profile, so this is already on the offer details at creation. Recruiters can then enter any additional data related to the offer for each candidate.

The approval chain for an offer detail may be completely ad hoc or pre-defined in the Offer Details Template. This pre-defined workflow can support recruiting roles, recruiting groups, or defined users. This workflow can be modified to add additional ad hoc approvers, as well. Ad hoc approvers can be anyone from the user database. The approval process is defined by the users in the order they are added as approvers. After one user approves the offer, it is available for the next approver until all approvers have approved the offer. Each approver has the option to decline the offer and add comments for the recruiter about what needs attention before the offer is approved.

After the offer detail is approved, the offer letter may be generated and sent to the candidate as discussed.

9.8 Hiring and Onboarding

After a candidate is identified and an offer is made, RX offers several options for transferring the candidate to Employee Central or core HR and getting them onboarded as employees.

If a customer is running Employee Central as their HRIS, RX has standard functionality to transfer candidates to Employee Central after they are moved into a status with the type of HIRABLE. This status is unique to Employee Central and tells the system to send them over to the Employee Central module as a pending hire.

A configured template defines the data from the recruiting process that should be transferred over to Employee Central in order to complete the hiring process. Data such as job title, job grade, level, salary, and others can be sent directly from RX to pre-populate the foundation objects in Employee Central to ease the hiring process.

SAP provides new hire integration for clients using both SAP ERP HCM and SuccessFactors RX via an integration pack that allows you to transfer applicant data from RX into SAP ERP HCM using SAP Process Integration (SAP PI).

To facilitate this integration, SAP ERP HCM and RX must include certain prescribed configurations. Configuration for both RX and SAP ERP HCM, plus additional details on the add-on, can be found in Chapter 3.

RX offers *onboarding services* through the SuccessFactors Onboarding module, discussed in Chapter 10.

9.9 Employee Referral

Employee referral functionality enables customers to increase employee engagement in the recruiting process by providing them with an avenue to participate in building the potential talent pool within the company. While there is existing Employee referral functionality in RMK, this new release is housed within RCM and leverages LinkedIn and Facebook profiles to allow employees to match their friends and professional contacts to jobs. Existing employees can do the following:

- ▸ Match jobs to contacts
- ▸ Refer a contact to a recruiter
- ▸ Track the progress of their referrals
- ▸ Determine what referral bonuses they have earned

9.10 Summary

With RX, customers have all of the transactional components of traditional Applicant Tracking Systems combined with powerful tools to market their jobs to attract and engage the best possible candidates. The players in the recruiting process are actively involved in creating open positions and reviewing candidates, including approving critical recruiting documents and providing candidate feedback on their mobile devices. RX's intuitive features allow users to log in, understand what to do with very little training, and get up to speed and using the system immediately. This enables companies to accelerate their recruiting processes while ensuring that only the most qualified candidates are selected for hire.

In this chapter, we've looked at the foundation for and components of SuccessFactors Recruiting Execution. We've explored creating and approving requisitions, as well as job postings and sourcing. In addition, we've looked at the candidate experience, the selection process of those candidates, and managing offers to candidates. We've also discussed the hiring and onboarding processes that are offered in the solution.

Now you should understand how the SuccessFactors Recruiting Execution solution can provide value for your recruiting, candidate, and application tracking processes. In the next chapter, we will examine Onboarding, which supports the onboarding of new employees into your organization, as well as cross-boarding and offboarding.

Onboarding new employees into any organization can be a complex process with a significant impact on time to productivity and first-year employee retention. Being able to quickly educate, integrate, and prepare new starters for their new roles can significantly reduce costs and improve engagement, retention, and time to contribution.

10   Onboarding

SuccessFactors Onboarding, which is the most recent addition to the SuccessFactors HCM Suite, supports the onboarding of new employees into your organization, as well as offboarding and cross-boarding (transfers).

Onboarding is an automated solution that supports the workflows associated with the onboarding process and provides a one-stop-shop of resources, activities, and required documentation for new joiners. It addresses the compliance-driven activities associated with onboarding, as well as a more strategic set of activities: connecting, informing, and empowering new hires even before their first day on the job with the right tools, content, and connections to start driving business results faster.

It leverages the SuccessFactors HCM suite platform, as well as existing functionality found in solutions such as Employee Central and SAP Jam and is therefore easy to use and intuitive for individuals to quickly begin onboarding activities. It significantly reduces the time and effort required by managers and HR professionals to manually manage the onboarding process and ensure that forms are completed correctly. SuccessFactors Onboarding also provides a complete set of new hire activities specifically designed to help them assimilate as quickly as possible.

In addition, it acts as a starting point for other HR and talent processes, such as Goal Management, Performance Management, and Learning. And with the possibility to provide access even before the new employee has started with your company, new hires can hit the ground running and begin making a meaningful contribution as soon as they arrive on their first day.

The Onboarding solution is based on a structured yet configurable onboarding process and contains functionality to suit this type of process. The Onboarding process involves several players, including the hiring manager, new hire, HR business partner, new hire buddy, and possibly others. The solution features the following functionalities:

- Introduction wizard
- Pre-hire verification steps
- Introductory information
- Activities
- Paperwork
- Configurable workflows
- Email notifications
- Integration with Goal Management, Learning, Development, Recruiting Execution, and Employee Central
- Tracking of manager's onboarding process to identify best processes

Now, let's run through the key features.

10.1   Pre-hire Verification Steps

Onboarding starts with an email to the new hire, who is invited to begin the onboarding process before they begin with the company. This pre-hire verification step allows the company the option to collect additional information from new hires that may not have been collected during the hiring process, without waiting until employees arrive on their first day. When accessing the system through the email link, new employees are presented with information they have previously provided so that they can verify or update this information, which feeds back into the talent/core HR systems. With a few simple steps, they are guided through a short wizard to provide this information in which they see a welcome message and the key features of Onboarding. They can then follow the wizard steps to set a preferred name, upload a photo, and create an introduction message that is shared with the team, with the manager, and on the employee's profile.

Figure 10.1 shows the step of the wizard whereby employees can define their preferred name, make a recording of it, and upload a profile picture.

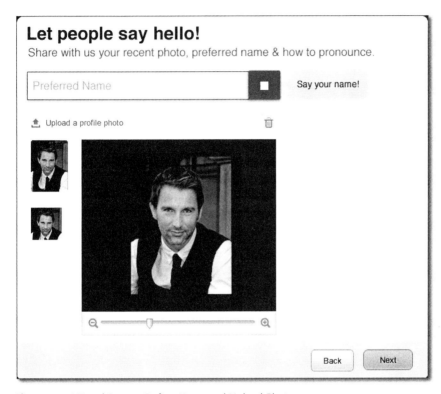

Figure 10.1 Wizard Step to Define Name and Upload Photo

10.2   Introductory Information

The WELCOME page for new hires (see Figure 10.2) provides employees with general introductory information to help them get started with the process. The content on this page is fully configurable and can feature the following types of information:

▶ WELCOME

▶ CEO'S WELCOME LETTER

▶ ORIENTATION ROADMAP

▶ GETTING TO KNOW US

▶ BENEFITS INFORMATION

▶ POLICIES

Employees can click the GET STARTED button on the WELCOME page to begin completing the prerequisite paperwork. Any paperwork they do not complete can be completed later. This is accessed via their ACTIVITIES page, which we'll cover next.

Figure 10.2 Home Page

10.3 Activities

By clicking the ACTIVITIES link at the top of the page, employees can access the ACTIVITIES page, which contains a host of activities that the new starter can perform, all of which are configured specifically for that employee (see Figure 10.3). Here, the employee has a number of tiles that provide information or allow the employee to perform an activity. The following tiles are set up by the employee's manager as part of the step-by-step setup wizard:

▶ INTRODUCTION POSTCARD
Displays a message from the manager

▶ PAPERWORK
Allows the employee to start the process of completing the prerequisite paperwork for employment

▶ UPCOMING MEETINGS
Displays upcoming events and meetings arranged for the employee (such as an orientation day), which displays the agenda of a meeting when the mouse is hovered over it

▶ LINKS
Contains links provided by the manager

▶ LEARNING
Contains links to the Learning Plan in SuccessFactors Learning

▶ JAM GROUPS
Displays the SAP Jam groups that the employee has been assigned to, either manually by the manager or automatically (with Auto Groups)

▶ MEETING YOUR BUDDY
Shows the "buddy" who has been assigned by the manager and displays details when the mouse is hovered over the buddy

▶ MEET YOUR TEAM
Shows the peers of the employee's team and displays details when the mouse is hovered over a team member

▶ RECOMMENDED PEOPLE
Shows recommended people to follow, again with further details when the mouse is hovered over one of the people

The hover-over details for the last three tiles display the person's name, their position and location, their telephone number and email address, their manager, the size of their team, a button to launch the Org Chart, and a menu to take further actions. From here, employees can email their "buddy" or other team members to introduce themselves.

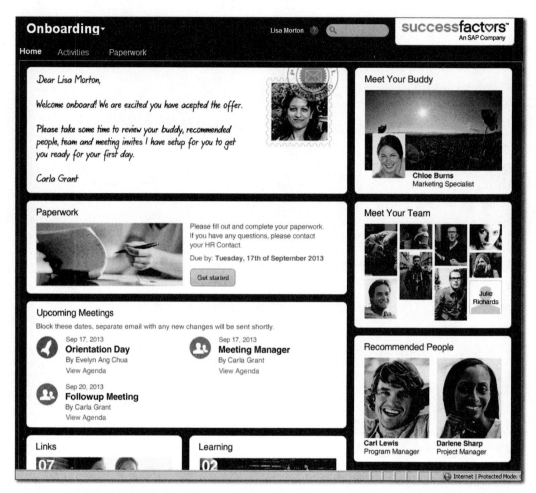

Figure 10.3 Activities Page

10.4 Paperwork

The PAPERWORK page contains the necessary forms for completing prerequisite employment paperwork, such as e-Verify, I-9, or W-4 in the United States. This part of the process is configurable to include whatever forms the company and local government require. It is a menu-guided wizard that takes the employee through each form.

Like the ACTIVITIES page, the PAPERWORK page can be accessed from the PAPER-WORK link at the top of the page (see Figure 10.4) or from the HOME page, if configured.

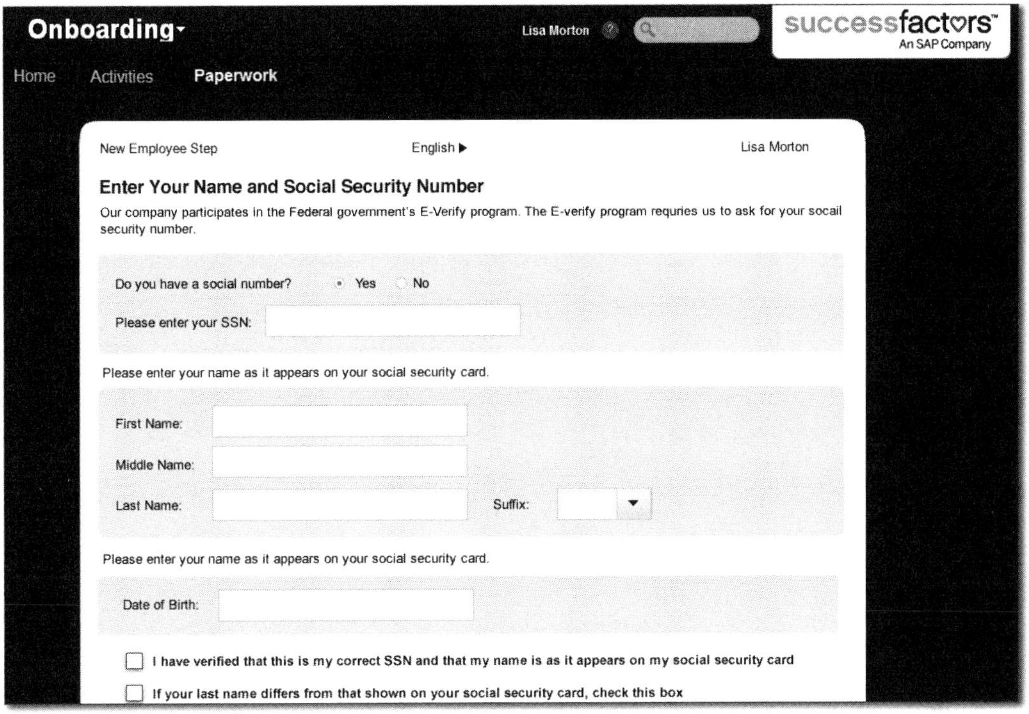

Figure 10.4 Paperwork Page

10.5 Integration

Onboarding features integration with a number of solutions in the SuccessFactors HCM suite. It features employee data used across the suite and integrates with SAP Jam for groups and SuccessFactors Learning for the Learning Plan. It integrates with Recruiting Execution to begin the Onboarding process from the Candidate Workbench, pulling information from the requisition and candidate profile. Onboarding also integrates with Employee Central to create users and complete the hiring process. Enhancements over the last year have made many features in Onboarding available in the SuccessFactors HCM mobile app. Refer to Chapter 15 for more information on the mobile-capable features of Onboarding.

10.6 Summary

Onboarding is a value-adding and time-saving solution to enable quick and efficient onboarding of new employees, designed to also improve time to productivity, employee engagement, and employee retention. It removes the manual effort required by managers and HR professionals during the onboarding process and allows employees to become oriented with their new colleagues and working environment before they even set foot in the office.

We've looked at the features and functionality that support this and discussed the integration that exists. You should now have an overview of what the solution offers and what the process is for onboarding an employee with the solution.

In the next chapter, we will take a look at SuccessFactors Learning.

*SuccessFactors Learning is a robust, state-of-the-art learning manage-
ment system that can accommodate any organization's learning process
and requirements. Its intuitive interface is easy to navigate and highly
configurable to provide employees, managers, and administrators with
the best learning experience possible.*

11   SuccessFactors Learning

SuccessFactors Learning manages the entire learning life cycle. As users progress
through their development cycle, they search for learning to add to their Learning
Plans, complete online training, and manage their other development requirements. Managers can access their teams and manage their learning, as well as their
own. If a user is also an administrator, the user has access to the administrator
interface to complete tasks such as maintaining catalogs, assignment profiles, master data, and running reports.

SuccessFactors Learning is highly configurable — and the majority of the configuration occurs in the interface itself. In this way, customer administrators are
heavily involved in the implementation; they learn how to "configure" the solution as the project progresses and take ownership of the system configuration
almost from the beginning of the project. The functionality delivered by Success-
Factors Learning is enough to fill a book on its own, so this chapter will provide
a high-level overview of the features of SuccessFactors Learning and how users of
all types can interact with the system.

SuccessFactors Learning can be approached from two directions: the user interface and the administrator interface. SuccessFactors Learning is a user-based system that allows employees and managers to take an active role in assigning and
completing learning items. As users, employees can browse the catalog and add
items to their Learning Plans. If items require approval, these remain in a pending
status until approved by their manager. Users can also complete online learning
and register for classroom-based or virtual learning.

Users who are managers can manage both their own learning and the Learning
Plans of their teams. Managers can assign learning directly to their employees'

Learning Plans, record learning events (if permissioned), and run reports on the progress of their teams.

Then there is the administrator interface, which we'll cover in Section 11.3. Administrators have access to all of the tools and data items that comprise the system "configuration." Administrators are also users, in which case, they have two interfaces to work within.

However, before we begin, we want to introduce a few foundational concepts that you should understand before diving into the solution:

▶ An *administrator* has privileges to create master data, set up catalogs, manage assignment profiles, set user permissions, launch forms, and run reports. Administrators access SuccessFactors Learning via the administrator's interface.

▶ A *user* is the end user of SuccessFactors Learning and includes managers and employees. Users log in to the user interface to perform activities such as adding courses to their Learning Plans, participating in courses, and managing their team members' Learning Plans.

▶ *Domains* control administrative access to records; *catalogs* control what training items are available to employees for self-assignment and enrollment. Users are assigned one or more catalogs from which to choose learning, and they can't see any items that don't appear in one of the catalogs they are assigned.

▶ *Organizations* are other groups of users that are managed by organization owners; they have corresponding dashboards that display pertinent information about the organization's learning activities. Organizations can have slots in scheduled offerings reserved for them and can purchase training.

Let's begin by looking at the user interface that supports employees and managers in their learning needs.

11.1 User Interface

Users access the system from their SuccessFactors HCM HOME page, as with other solutions. The LEARNING tile on the HOME page displays the five items on a user's Learning Plan that are due the soonest. It also displays a link that takes the user to their MY LEARNING ASSIGNMENTS page in SuccessFactors Learning.

What a user can access in the Learning module is dictated by which catalogs have been assigned to them. User roles can be defined to grant varying levels of access to different kinds of users. For example, a company may have contractors that require access to complete some learning, but they should not have the same level of system access as employees. You can define user roles for employees and contractors to differentiate the levels of access and then assign them to users accordingly.

11.1.1 User Interface Home Page

When users land on their LEARNING HOME page (see Figure 11.1), they are presented with their LEARNING PLAN, as described in this section. The MY LEARNING ASSIGNMENTS area displays items assigned to the user by the user's manager, an automatic assignment, or self-assignment from the catalog. Catalog searches can be accessed from the FIND LEARNING tile. THE LINKS tile provides quick access to other parts of the system. The MY CURRICULA tile provides a snapshot view for assigned curricula, and completed learning items can be accessed from the HISTORY tile. With the new SCHEDULED OFFERING tile, users can see the first few offerings that are scheduled to start in the future: those they are not already enrolled in or that are not in their catalog. As with the HOME page in the SuccessFactors HCM suite, the tiles on the LEARNING HOME page can be rearranged by users according to their needs.

Figure 11.1 User Home Page

Learning Plan

The Learning Plan to-do list items listed on the MY LEARNING ASSIGNMENTS tile can be broken down into buckets of due dates. An administrator can configure these, but the following default values are available:

▶ OVERDUE

▶ DUE WITHIN A WEEK

▶ DUE WITHIN A MONTH

▶ DUE LATER

▶ NO DUE DATE

Users can view details of items on the Learning Plan by clicking the link in the item name or by clicking MORE to display a quick view of the course description, delivery method, and duration. The MY LEARNING ASSIGNMENTS tile can be seen in Figure 11.2. It displays items that have been assigned to the user by the user's manager, an administrator, or the user themselves. Some items may have due dates, and others may not. As items are completed, they drop off the to-do list and are moved to the LEARNING HISTORY pod.

Figure 11.2 Item Details from To-Do List

From the Learning Plan, users can perform a variety of tasks:

▶ Launch online content

▶ Launch an online exam

▶ Register for a learning offering

▶ Request approval to register for an offering

- ▸ Request a schedule for an offering when it's not available
- ▸ Launch an evaluation survey

You can filter the Learning Plan to show only certain types of items or all learning, as shown in Figure 11.3. This is a helpful feature for users who have many items on their MY LEARNING ASSIGNMENTS page. As tasks are completed, they drop off the LEARNING PLAN and are instead available on the LEARNING HISTORY pod.

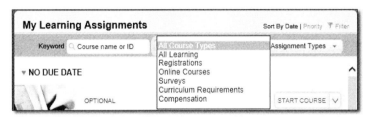

Figure 11.3 Filter My Learning Assignments

Catalog Search

Users can perform a quick catalog search from the search dialog box on the HOME page. Entering a keyword returns items that match in the item title or description, as you can see in Figure 11.4.

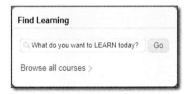

Figure 11.4 Catalog Search

As shown in Figure 11.5, users can also browse the catalog if they choose. Browsing the catalog takes users to a screen where they can select categories of training such as INSTRUCTOR-LED and ONLINE courses, as well as filter training offerings by the SUBJECT AREAS that have been configured in the administrator interface.

One of the nicest features of the catalog search is the CALENDAR view, shown in Figure 11.6, which users can use to browse course offerings by dates on a calendar. Days that have offerings scheduled display links. Clicking the links takes the user to the offering details, where they can register or add to their Learning Plan.

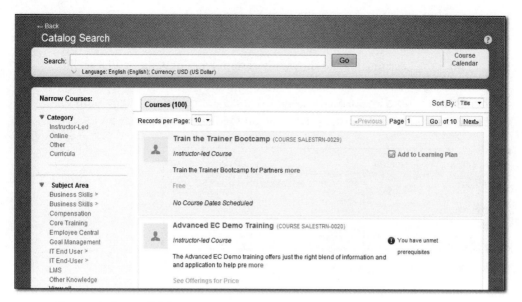

Figure 11.5 Browse Catalog

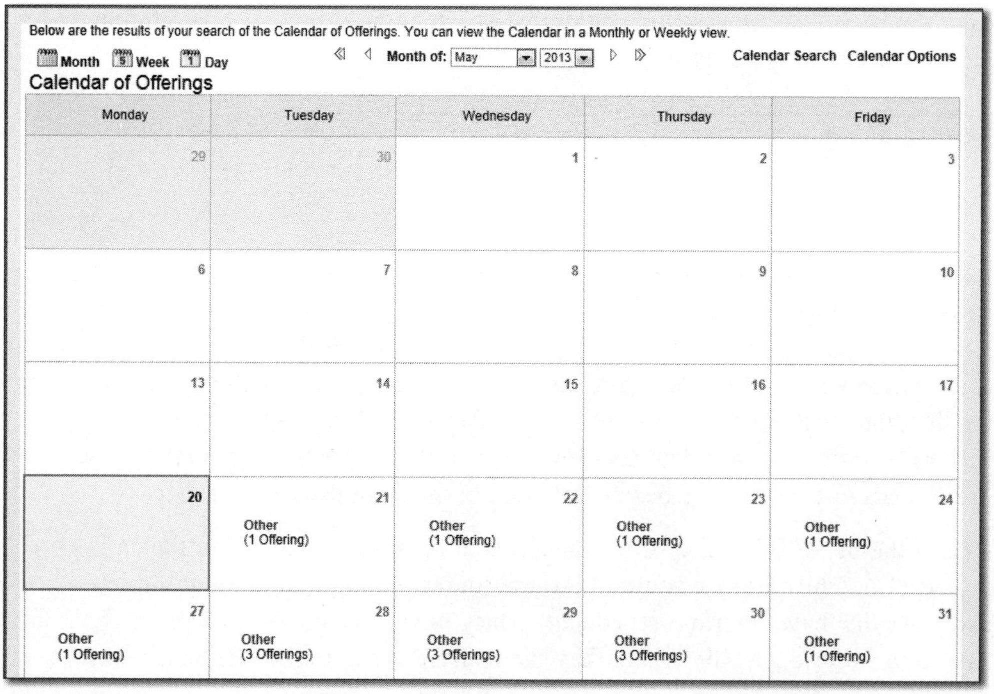

Below are the results of your search of the Calendar of Offerings. You can view the Calendar in a Monthly or Weekly view.

📅 Month 📅 Week 📅 Day   ⟪ ◁ **Month of:** May ▾ 2013 ▾ ▷ ⟫   Calendar Search Calendar Options

Calendar of Offerings

Monday	Tuesday	Wednesday	Thursday	Friday
29	30	1	2	3
6	7	8	9	10
13	14	15	16	17
20	21 Other (1 Offering)	22 Other (1 Offering)	23 Other (1 Offering)	24 Other (1 Offering)
27 Other (1 Offering)	28 Other (3 Offerings)	29 Other (3 Offerings)	30 Other (3 Offerings)	31 Other (1 Offering)

Figure 11.6 Calendar View of Learning Offerings

Easy Links and Learning Status

Also available from the HOME page, users have access to helpful LINKS that jump them to other parts of the system. There are LINKS provided by default, but administrators can also define up to 10 additional internal or external URLs. The default LINKS include the following:

▶ APPROVALS
Managers can jump to the APPROVALS page to manage their team's approvals.

▶ NEWS PAGE
This area can be used to promote learning-related news in the company or provide tips on how to better utilize the system (see Figure 11.7).

▶ OPTIONS AND SETTINGS
Users can change their passwords, set delegates, set notification preferences, and set locale and time zone settings.

▶ REPORTS
Reports can be run that provide managers with information on their teams' enrollments, learning progress, and completions.

LINKS can be limited to groups of users based on user roles that are defined by the administrator.

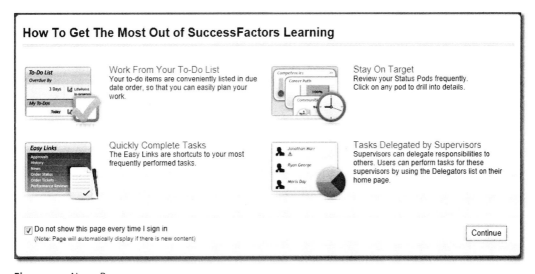

Figure 11.7 News Page

The My Curricula pod shown in Figure 11.8 displays where a user is against curricula and displays completed items. This dashboard view gives users an overview of critical items related to their progress against their assigned learning activities. The Curricula status displays a color-coded picture of the status for all assigned curricula. Clicking the pod drills down to the details of the related items. It also displays a green checkmark if a user is up-to-date with all curricula on their Learning Plan.

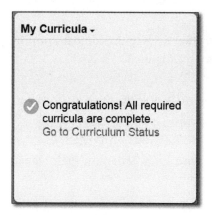

Figure 11.8 My Curricula Pod

11.1.2 Learning History

After users have completed learning items on their Learning Plans, they are moved to Learning History. Online items such as courses and documents can be accessed again and again from the Learning History pod to enable continuous, just-in-time learning.

Learning History fed from SuccessFactors is also available to display in a background element in Employee Profile. Some companies prefer to make this information available in Employee Profile in addition to the Learning History in SuccessFactors Learning because it can be critical data input to other talent development processes, such as Career Development Planning and Succession Planning. An example of the Learning History background element is provided in Figure 11.9. Data in this portlet is fed directly from the LMS and is not editable by any user in Employee Profile.

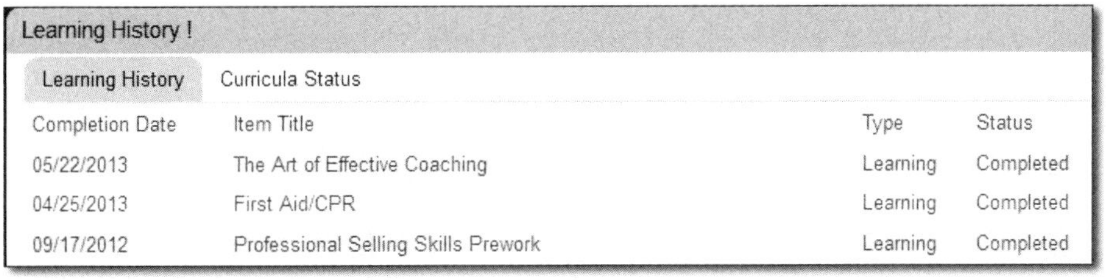

Learning History !			
Learning History	Curricula Status		
Completion Date	Item Title	Type	Status
05/22/2013	The Art of Effective Coaching	Learning	Completed
04/25/2013	First Aid/CPR	Learning	Completed
09/17/2012	Professional Selling Skills Prework	Learning	Completed

Figure 11.9 LMS Portlet

Users can always access online content for repeated viewing from their Learning History (see the REVIEW CONTENT button in Figure 11.10). This provides continuous, just-in-time learning to support a user's training and development needs as they arise.

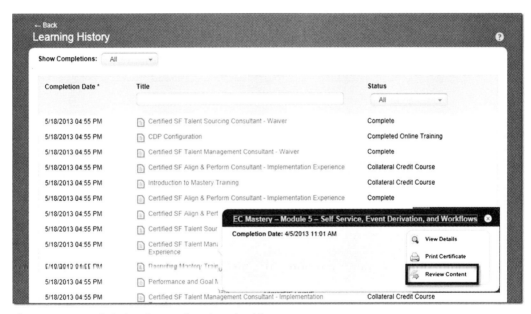

Figure 11.10 Launch Online Content from Learning History

11.2 Supervisor Interface

Anyone who has direct reports in SuccessFactors is recognized as a supervisor in SuccessFactors Learning and automatically has access to their employees' records. Supervisors have access to view all information related to their team members' learning information. The scope of supervisor actions is determined during implementation, at which time customers can determine which actions they would like supervisors to complete, such as the following:

▸ View assigned learning, the curriculum status, and overdue learning for all team members

▸ Assign learning items and curricula to their teams

▸ Register team members into scheduled offerings

▸ Record learning events/completions for their teams

▸ Run reports for direct and indirect team members (second level of reporting)

▸ Delegate responsibilities to other users

▸ Assign alternate supervisors for their teams

Managers can also get a bird's-eye view of their teams' learning status under MY EMPLOYEES. This is a jump-to link to a view of their teams' Learning Plans, where they can assign and remove learning, grant approvals for registrations, get a dashboard view of their employees, and run reports. These functions are available in the SUPERVISOR LINKS pod, as displayed in Figure 11.11.

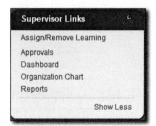

Figure 11.11 Supervisor Links

11.2.1 Manage Team Member Learning Plan

Supervisors are able to add items to and remove items from their team members' Learning Plans. The system walks them through the process using a wizard. It's possible to select one or more users to assign or remove learning in five easy steps, as numbered in Figure 11.12:

❶ Choose ADD ITEMS AND CURRICULA or REMOVE ITEMS.

❷ Select the team member(s) for whom to perform the action.

❸ Search the catalog for the appropriate items to add.

❹ Select the items to add from the search results.

❺ Set required dates, if applicable.

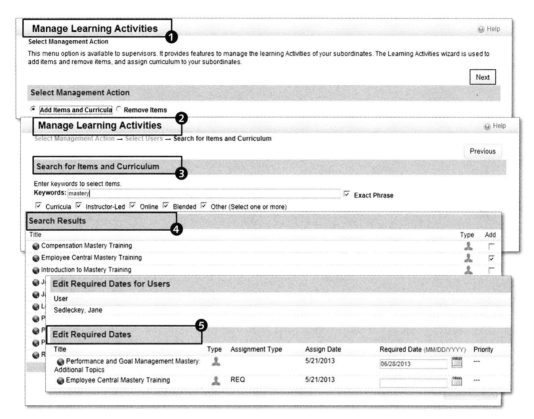

Figure 11.12 A Manager Adding Items to Learning Plan

11.2.2 Manage Training Approvals

Supervisors can approve or deny requests from their teams to attend or complete training, including scheduled offerings and online content. Administrators can establish approval workflows to include others besides the direct supervisor. This is a configuration decision and can be set up at any time in the administrator interface.

When a user registers for an offering that requires approval, they see a status of PENDING APPROVAL. This status remains until action is taken on the request. The supervisor and other approvers can view the request, approve or deny it, or skip the request for later action. When a request is approved or denied, the user receives email confirmation that action has been taken on the request, along with any comments on the action. For example, if the request is denied, the email includes any reason the approver chose for denial.

If an approval workflow contains more than one approval, it must go through all levels of approval before the user can register for a seat in the offering or launch the online content.

11.2.3 Other Supervisor Actions

Supervisors can complete numerous other actions for their teams, as shown in Figure 11.13. These are accessible from the callout that appears when you hover over the team member's name. From here, links are available to manage an alternate supervisor and generate reports on this user. Supervisors can also view profile information. Note that this isn't a link to the Employee Profile and displays only minimal information that is maintained within SuccessFactors Learning.

Figure 11.13 Other Supervisor Actions

11.3 Administrator Interface

Recall from earlier in the chapter that administrators access administrative functions via the administrator interface. While the user and administrator interfaces are integrated, a user who is also an administrator has different access and is able to perform pre-defined and permissioned tasks within the administrative interface. This section will review a sample of the administrator capabilities in the system. Please note that the administrator capabilities of the system are vast, so this is a very high-level view.

11.3.1 Administrative Home Page

The ADMIN page is organized with menus across the top navigation bar and QUICK LINKS in the middle of the screen (see Figure 11.14). Six different layouts are available to organize the HOME page: USERS, PERFORMANCE, LEARNING, CONTENT, COMMERCE, and SYSTEM ADMIN. The slide bar between the two sections can also be moved to adjust the size of each area.

Figure 11.14 Administrative Home Page

As shown in Figure 11.15, administrators can set up their own Quick Links or use the default links and choose the layout of their HOME page. Administrators utilize Quick Links often for their common tasks, and it's quite helpful to modify these based on an administrator's role and the tasks that they routinely perform in the system.

Quick Links are an easy way for administrators to get working on the things they need to complete. Hovering over a Quick Link displays the options available within that particular link. The callout box also gives some perspective on where in the process that action should occur. For example, in Figure 11.16, the description for CREATE INSTRUCTOR-LED COURSE tells the administrator that this action is undertaken after the user and item have been created. It then explains what can occur after completing this action: learning completions can be recorded.

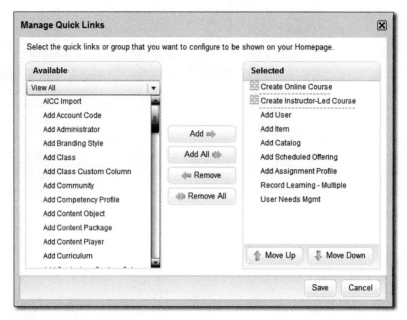

Figure 11.15 Manage Quick Links

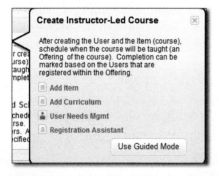

Figure 11.16 Actions Available from Quick Links

Also available in the QUICK LINK dialog box is the option USE GUIDED MODE. This is a wizard that walks the administrator through each step in the process CREATING AN INSTRUCTOR-LED COURSE. More information on administrative actions that can be done in SuccessFactors HCM suite can be found in Chapter 5.

11.3.2 Users Menu

The Users menu contains all of the actions an administrator can perform related to user records and related information. From the Users menu, administrators can create and modify the following records, as shown in Figure 11.17:

▶ Users

▶ Assignment Profiles (used to assign learning automatically)

▶ Job Codes

▶ Job Families

▶ Positions

▶ Organizations

▶ Organization Groups

▶ Regions

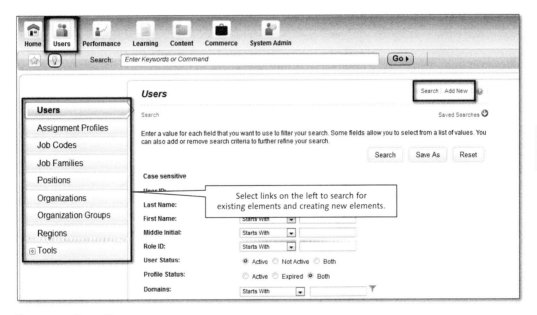

Figure 11.17 Users Menu

Select a link from the left column of Figure 11.17 to search for or create a new element on it.

Note that several of these elements, such as users and job codes, are defined in Employee Central and may have been transferred into SuccessFactors via the user integration from core HR, so it's likely that only a super administrator has access to all of these functions.

11.3.3 Performance Menu

This menu is a legacy system functionality related to performance. This is superseded by SuccessFactors Performance & Goals.

11.3.4 Learning Menu

The LEARNING menu actions control the creation and modification of learning items that reside in the catalog(s) and all of their derivations (see Figure 11.18). Here, administrators maintain items, group them into curricula, create new catalogs, and add scheduled offerings to the calendar, among other things. You can also create or modify instructors and maintain tasks.

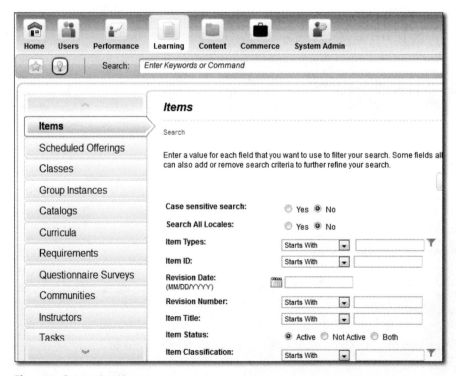

Figure 11.18 Learning Menu

The TOOLS option under the LEARNING menu controls actions related to scheduled offerings such as closing and cancelling, editing required dates, and using the Registration Assistant, which allows an administrator to register, withdraw, or hold seats for users.

11.3.5 Content Menu

As the name implies, the CONTENT menu organizes all of the functions related to online content (see Figure 11.19). An important note about SuccessFactors Learning and online content is that the system points to content that is stored elsewhere. No online content is housed within SuccessFactors Learning. Online content can be a web-based training course or online exam that is attached to an item in the catalog. These are the various content-related elements that can be maintained in the system:

▶ **Content objects**
Content objects are records that provide the system instructions to find and launch a unit of online content. Each content object references one launchable file. Content objects in the system can be reused multiple times. Content objects are assigned to items; they aren't in themselves assigned to learning plans, nor are they recorded as completed in the Learning History.

▶ **Content packages**
This is a grouping of multiple content objects. Packages are a way to organize all relevant content for an item. Content packages can be created manually or imported via an Aviation Industry Computer-Based Training Committee (AICC) or Sharable Content Object Reference Model (SCORM) import tool.

▶ **AICC and SCORM wrappers**
A feature of SuccessFactors Learning is the "wrapper," which is available for AICC and SCORM standards. This allows an administrator to create a content object in the system to "wrap" a document and requires users to read and acknowledge that they either accept or reject it. Users can simply click a button to complete the item rather than launching and completing an entire online course. This is an excellent way to put "read and understand" training in the system and automate the completion and tracking of this type of training.

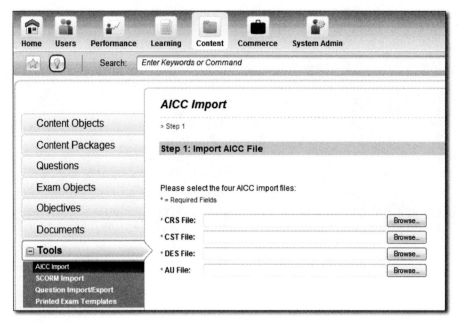

Figure 11.19 Content Menu

▶ **Content import tools**

The system provides utilities to facilitate import content that is either AICC or SCORM compliant. The AICC IMPORT button is for a single content object. After the import, the administrator needs to search for the object, add the domain and assignment type ID, and add it to the applicable catalog(s).

The SCORM IMPORT button imports a single SCORM file, either as a ZIP file or via a URL (for files larger than 1 MB). Finally, the SCORM IMPORT utility can be used to import one or more content packages and deploy them to a content server. They can then be configured to an item through the wizard in the system.

11.3.6 System Administration Menu

The last menu, SYSTEM ADMIN, is where all system administration functions occur (see Figure 11.20). This menu should be granted only to "true" system administrators who understand the power of these features. This is where configuration occurs in the system in setting up connectors, creating automatic processes, configuring custom columns, and configuring background jobs.

Security is also a main feature of this menu. This is where domains and domain restrictions are managed. Roles are also created here. Administrators create multiple roles and then assign these roles to users or groups of users.

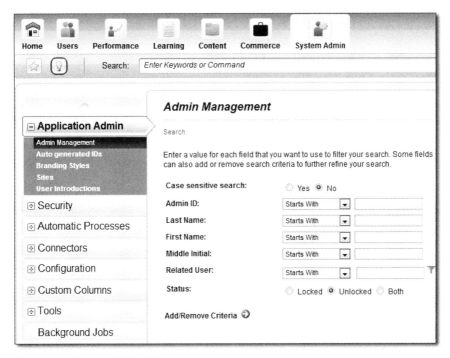

Figure 11.20 System Admin Menu

11.4 Security and Access

SuccessFactors Learning has a multilevel security model that allows administrators access to various functions related to specific data sets in the system. Security in the system can be set up to restrict what information administrators can access and what they can do with it. This is accomplished through domains.

11.4.1 Domains

Recall that domains restrict what administrators have access to; they also act as filters for data. Domains can be built in a hierarchical, or parent-child, structure. A domain can have many children, but only one parent. This structure permits access to data within organizational structures with minimal administrative setup. The domain structure required for a customer's system is discussed and determined during implementation. However, domains can be maintained by a system administrator, and it's important that these users understand the domains' function and purpose in the system, as well as how to maintain them.

A *domain restriction* is a group of domains defined to fit a specific need. Domain restrictions provide a more granular level of security than at an administrator account level. Rather, they are applied to individual data types within a domain to which administrators have access. They can even be applied to operations such as view, add, delete, and so on.

11.4.2 Workflows

Workflows define what administrators can do within SuccessFactors Learning. A *workflow* is comprised of a function that is related to an entity, which can be a user, an item, or a scheduled offering. A *function* is an action such as view, edit, or delete. Example workflows include viewing user data and recording learning events. Administrators can have any number of workflows assigned to them to allow them to perform their required tasks in the system.

11.4.3 Roles

A role is created by a combination of workflows and domain restrictions. The system supports any number of roles required, and they can be broad, finite, or both to suit customer requirements. Roles are assigned to users, and each user can have multiple role assignments.

11.4.4 Admin Accounts

Any user who logs in to the administrator interface needs an admin account. This account has one or more administrative roles assigned to it, depending on the functions the administrator needs to complete in the system. If an administrator is also a user, it's possible to link the user ID and admin account together so that the user can toggle back and forth between the user interface and the administrator interface.

11.4.5   Organizations

An *organization* is an entity that is used to group users. Organizations can be designed and maintained to completely meet the customer's requirements. They can be designed along functional lines, represent business units, or have any other basis that makes sense in the customer's environment. Organizations can be used as follows:

▸ Users within an organization can use the account code to pay for learning items that have a cost.

▸ Organizations can reserve space in scheduled offerings.

▸ Organizations can have their own branding of the interface.

▸ Organizations can control multilevel approval workflows (rather than using domains).

▸ Organizations can be used as search criteria to locate users and as an attribute to assign learning.

▸ Organizations can have owners identified who can have access to the organization dashboards mentioned earlier in this chapter.

When designing organizations, it's important to keep reporting in mind. These elements can increase the value of assigning learning and generating reports, as well as make searching easier.

Organizations are elements that can be used to group and identify users in the system. They provide another level of structure in the system.

Organization dashboards provide a graphical representation of learning-related information that assists organization owners in analyzing metrics within the organization(s) they own. You can filter data based on core attributes, and drill-down capability is available to gain a deeper view of the data behind the attributes. Dashboards are available for the following, as shown in Figure 11.21:

▸ **Learning item completions**
Shows the number of items and learning hours completed by each organization within a given time period.

▸ **Learning projections**
Displays the number of items and learning hours predicted for delivery within a given time frame.

- **Curriculum status**
  Provides the status of the organization's employees' assigned curricula.

- **Registration status**
  Displays the registration status of all users in the organization.

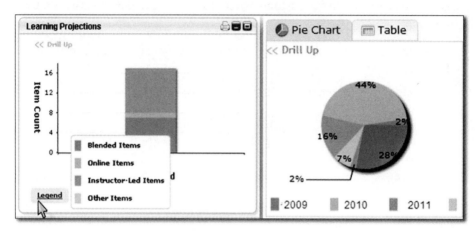

Figure 11.21 Sample Organization Dashboards

11.5 Summary

SuccessFactors Learning's two interfaces—the user interface and administrative interface—and robust functionality provide employees, managers, and administrators with a plethora of tools to manage learning needs for organizational, team, and individual development. It's a best-in-class system that is capable of meeting nearly any business requirement. The user interface puts learning needs and requirements at the fingertips of the individual learners and gives their supervisors the necessary tools to monitor and participate in their teams' learning activities. It's a critical piece of the SuccessFactors HCM talent management picture.

Administrators have a completely flexible system that can be mostly configured directly from the administrator interface. As an active part of implementation, system administrators learn by doing, from the beginning, how to maintain the system configuration to meet growing and changing requirements within the company.

In this chapter, we've touched on what SuccessFactors Learning can offer an organization from a very high level. We've discussed the types of users of the system, the different interfaces they have, and what actions they have. We've looked at how content can be created and imported into the system, as well as the security and access functionality that is available. You should now have a comprehensive understanding of how SuccessFactors Learning can work for you and your organization.

We'll now turn our attention to Succession & Development in the next chapter.

Managing succession plans and employee career development is critical to maintaining organizational sustainability and protecting against unmitigated losses. Personal development provides engagement across the workforce and increases competency, productivity, and leadership in critical positions.

12 Succession & Development

Managing succession plans is a crucial exercise, and being able to develop high-performing and high-potential employees into future leaders and holders of your most critical positions is of utmost importance. Hiring and onboarding are costly exercises, and key talent can be difficult, if not impossible, to replace, particularly at the senior and board-room levels. Studies have shown that employees value non-tangible benefits, such as development and career advancement, more than financial benefits, which means employee retention can be directly impacted by ensuring that you offer employees the possibility to develop their careers within your organization.

SuccessFactors Succession & Development is a comprehensive and easy-to-use solution that offers all of the core features and functionality of a best-practice succession management and career development planning solution. It allows the management of key positions, successors, career plans, and development plans and enables a talent manager or HR professional to view bench strengths, nominated and assigned successors, and key talent data, such as performance, potential, and risks. In addition, it features classic features such as the nine-box grid, organizational chart, talent search, and reports.

The Development Planning functionality provides management of development activities that integrate with the SuccessFactors Learning module and leads to the development of competencies. It also gives employees a platform to manage their careers and make choices about where they want to go in your organization.

In short, SuccessFactors Succession and Development features the type of functionality that you would expect in a comprehensive succession planning and career development planning solution. The solution is split into two core modules that are accessed from the module navigation menu: the Succession module and the Development module.

The Succession module focuses on the succession planning process. We'll run through how the Succession module supports it in Section 12.1.

The Development module, which is also known as *Career Development Planning* (CDP), provides development planning, career planning, and learning activities management. In Section 12.2, we'll explore how these support the growth of an employee's competencies and career within your organization and how they can be used to develop successors into the leaders of tomorrow.

12.1 Succession

The succession management process typically kicks off after the annual performance appraisal process has been completed, either in SuccessFactors Performance & Goals or an external performance management system, such as Employee Performance Management in SAP ERP HCM. If the succession management process begins before the annual performance process has completed, then Succession & Development offers the opportunity to maintain performance ratings ad hoc. Quite often, employees are reviewed and calibrated before the process so that they can be assigned to talent pools. These talent pools are used to supply talent to the succession plans of key positions. During the process of assigning successors, you can evaluate and rate the potential and possible risks of employees.

After successors have been assigned to succession plans, their Development Plan can be updated to reflect the competency gaps identified during assignment. Learning activities can be assigned to the Development Plan to obtain the required competency. Employees should maintain their career plans on a periodic basis to help inform managers and talent professionals of how they want to move within the organization, because this will have an impact on the decision to make them a successor.

Management of key positions is an ongoing activity and isn't generally confined to just the core of the succession planning process. Generally, most key positions are identified during implementation and set as such, but sometimes, new requirements or organizational changes may necessitate the assignment of new key positions or removal of key statuses of existing positions.

Now, let's look at some key functionality that supports this process and how it supports the management of succession plans.

12.1.1 Organizational Charts

Succession is focused on leveraging one or more org charts to support visualization of succession plans across areas of the organization. These charts provide greater breadth of visibility of succession plans, risks, and coverage over teams.

Succession Org Chart

The main focus of the Succession module is the *Succession Org Chart*. The SUCCESSION ORG CHART, which is shown in Figure 12.1, provides the foundation of organizational-based succession planning and allows an overview of succession plans across different departments within the enterprise.

Figure 12.1 Succession Org Chart

The Succession Org Chart displays the logged-in user and all of the user's direct reports. Each of the direct reports of each direct report can also be viewed, and so forth. In addition, there are several options to search within, display, and sort the Org Chart, as well as display the Org Chart and the contents of each box.

Most of the data within the position boxes can be switched on or off, such as photo, risk of loss, impact of loss, newness to company, bench strength, successors, nine-box placement, and successor details. You can also highlight key positions. There are also three modes that can be selected to change the layout of the Org Chart:

▶ HIERARCHY VIEW
Displays the "classic" Org Chart, as shown in Figure 12.1

▶ TEAM VIEW
Displays all of the reports and their direct reports

▶ KEY POSITION VIEW
Displays only the key positions

Each box represents a position and has a lot of information and options. As with the standard Org Chart, there is a business card available to get an overview of the employee and go to different pages within the SuccessFactors HCM suite. However, the key differences between the two business cards are the Current Nominations for succession plans, and talent pools instead of the employment information and personal information links. Figure 12.2 shows the CURRENT NOMINATIONS box from the business card.

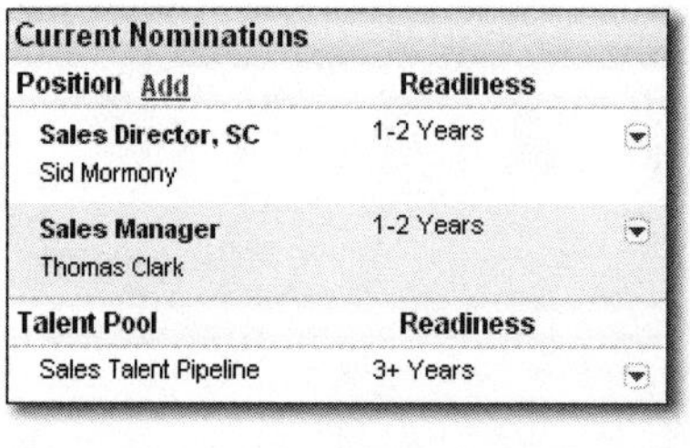

Current Nominations		
Position Add	**Readiness**	
Sales Director, SC Sid Mormony	1-2 Years	▾
Sales Manager Thomas Clark	1-2 Years	▾
Talent Pool	**Readiness**	
Sales Talent Pipeline	3+ Years	▾

Figure 12.2 Current Nominations

Using the ADD link in the CURRENT NOMINATIONS box, you can assign an individual as a successor for a position. We'll cover this in more detail in Section 12.1.7.

The position box action dropdown menu (located in the top-right corner of a position box) provides a number of options that include editing, deleting, and hiding the position; adding a peer or direct report; finding successors; viewing the position in the Lineage Chart; viewing the nomination history; and creating a Job Requisition in SuccessFactors Recruiting Execution. The EDITING A POSITION option refers to setting a position as a *key position*. However, the most interesting feature of the Succession Org Chart is the information available within the position boxes.

The wealth of information that can be either shown in or hidden from the boxes as required provides the opportunity to get an overview of the status of succession across your team and, if required, their reports below. For example, it can be very easy to see the overall risk of loss for each of your team members or get the total coverage of successors and bench strength.

> **Bench Strength**
>
> Bench strength is a subject evaluation of the succession plan and the cascaded succession plans (chain of succession). It provides a way of measuring the readiness of the succession plan of the position so that managers and HR professionals can understand whether the position is adequately covered and how "deep" the bench is.

As with the holder of the position, each nominated successor has a BUSINESS CARD icon; you can view details about the person and select options to view the person's nomination details, delete their nomination, and evaluate their readiness from SuccessFactors Performance & Goals from the action dropdown menu.

Lineage Chart

Succession also offers the Lineage Chart, which shows the chain of successors. That is, it shows the user's successors and that user's successors in turn. Use the EXPAND button to expand your view to the next level of successors, and so forth, as shown in Figure 12.3. This provides a quick overview of how well covered a position is and the positions of the nominated successors—something measured with bench strength.

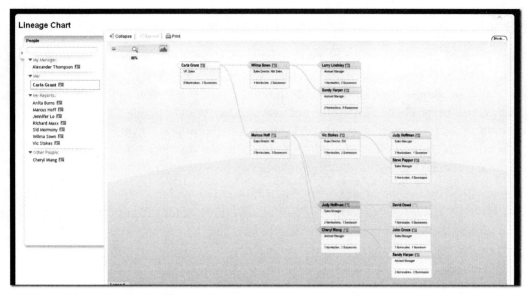

Figure 12.3 Lineage Chart

Now that we've covered the Org Charts that are used in Succession, let's look at the different matrices that can be used for reviewing and identifying the talent that will be used to nominate successors.

12.1.2 Matrices

The performance-versus-potential nine-box grid is commonly used within a best-practice succession planning process. Succession & Development features not only the *Performance-Potential Matrix*, but also the *How vs. What Matrix* grid. Both matrices can be used to source talent for succession plans and feature a host of filter options for the search that can encompass large areas of the organization. They are also both separately configurable in OneAdmin, including components such as labels, ratings, and icons. They are both accessed from the options at the top of the page of the Succession module.

For filter options, both matrices allow you to report by your team or the team of a direct report for up to three levels below, the Succession Management and Matrix Report Permissions, or a group. Groups are custom made based on specific characteristics, such as job code, department, division, location, and so on. The matrices allow you to view data based on any department, division, or location for any date range.

Performance-Potential Matrix

The Performance-Potential Matrix is used to help identify the high-performing, high-potential individuals who are the most likely to progress through the ranks of your organization. It plots individuals into a grid based on their performance and potential ratings so that it's easy and quick to identify not only which individuals are the top talent within your organization, but also which individuals are in need of support to improve their performance. Essentially, this helps provide an overview of how development activities can be focused to ensure that individuals are performing to the level required by your organization.

Figure 12.4 shows the PERFORMANCE-POTENTIAL MATRIX with a number of employees plotted within each square, called a quadrant. Each quadrant on the matrix has a name (e.g., STAR EMPLOYEES or EMERGING STARS) and lists the number of employees; percentage of the total employees in that quadrant; and employees themselves, with an icon for their business card and historical trend of performance and potential ratings. The HISTORICAL TREND icon opens a pop-up window with a graph showing the history of both the performance and potential rating, as shown in Figure 12.5.

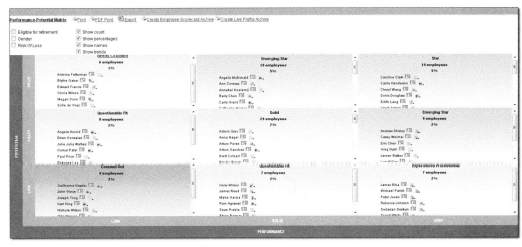

Figure 12.4 Performance-Potential Matrix

The matrix can also have icons displayed for those eligible for retirement, gender, and risk of loss to enable balanced and informed decision making to be made. You can also print or export the matrix to a PDF or Microsoft Excel file to be used in talent review meetings or calibration sessions. Below the matrix, you can display the employees who are too new to rate or are unrated.

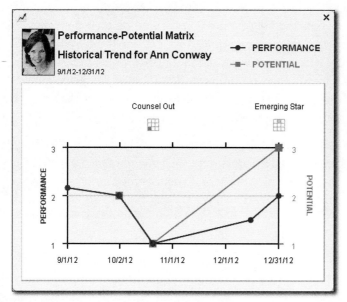

Figure 12.5 Historical Trend Pop-Up Window

After employees have been reviewed, you can nominate an employee for a succession plan or a talent pool by selecting the employee's BUSINESS CARD icon, selecting SCORECARD, and taking the necessary action. These will be covered in Section 12.1.3 and Section 12.1.7.

How vs. What Matrix

A unique feature in the Succession & Development solution is the HOW VS. WHAT MATRIX, shown in Figure 12.6. This grid plots employees based on their competencies ("How") and their objective ratings ("What") so that individuals who are higher achievers and regularly meet their objectives with distinction can be easily identified. Although the outcome of using this matrix is the same as the Performance-Potential Matrix, it provides a different method of achieving it through objectives, rather than solely job performance and future potential.

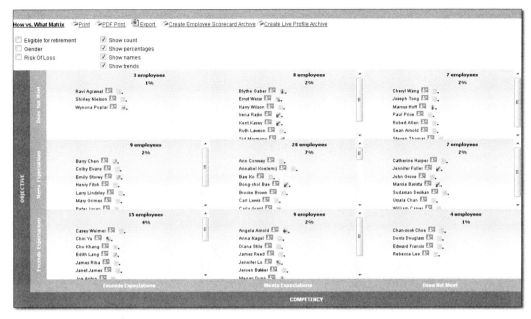

Figure 12.6 How vs. What Matrix

12.1.3 Portlets in Employee Profile, Talent Info, and Scorecard

Although the Employee Profile and Scorecard are covered in Chapter 4, there are some portlets that are available by default or can be added to these views to show succession planning–specific information.

The Nomination Portlet and Talent Information portlet can display and maintain specific succession planning information.

The Nomination Portlet displays nominations for succession plans for talent pools, as shown in Figure 12.7. By selecting the Add Nomination link in the top-right corner, the user can make additional nominations for succession plans and Talent Pools.

The Talent Information portlet contains the Risk of Loss, Impact of Loss, Reason for Leaving, New to Position, and Future Leader attributes. This portlet is visible only to the manager or HR specialists, and not to the employee. You can maintain each of these attributes here by clicking the Edit link.

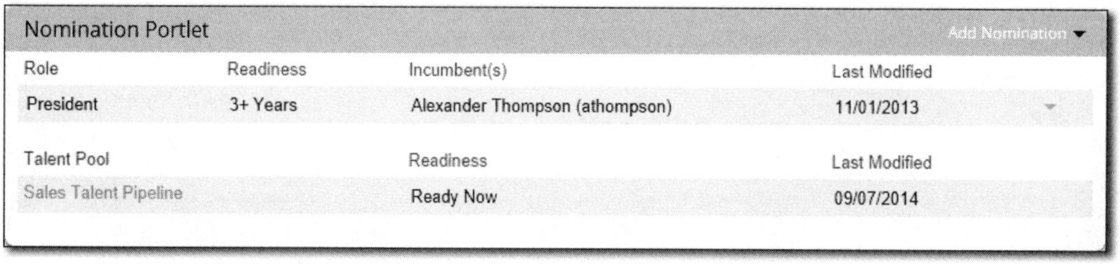

Nomination Portlet
Add Nomination
Role
Readiness
Incumbent(s)
Last Modified
President
3+ Years
Alexander Thompson (athompson)
11/01/2013
Talent Pool
Readiness
Last Modified
Sales Talent Pipeline
Ready Now
09/07/2014

Figure 12.7 Nomination Portlet

The TALENT MANAGEMENT SNAPSHOT portlet displays FUTURE LEADER, RISK OF LOSS, and IMPACT OF LOSS fields for the individual, as shown in Figure 12.8. You can maintain this data by clicking the EDIT link.

Talent Management Snapshot
Edit
Talent Pool
Future Leader No
Risk of Loss High
Impact of Loss High

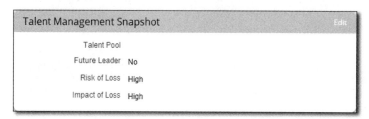

Figure 12.8 Talent Management Snapshot

The SUCCESSOR portlet shows all of the succession plans that the individual is nominated to. Nominations can be added or deleted from here, and details of each nomination displayed. Figure 12.9 shows this portlet.

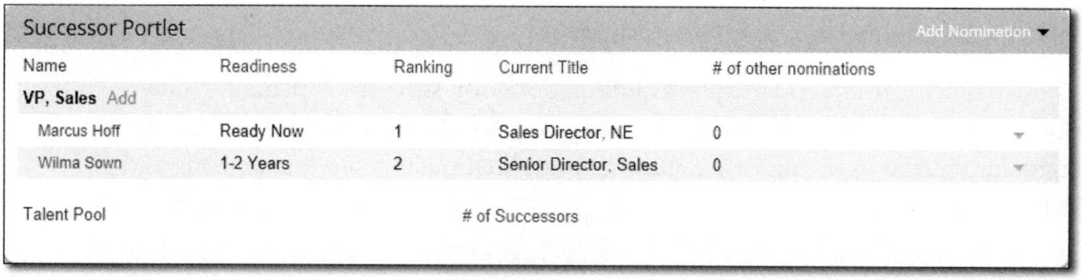

Successor Portlet
Add Nomination
Name
Readiness
Ranking
Current Title
# of other nominations
VP, Sales Add
Marcus Hoff
Ready Now
1
Sales Director, NE
0
Wilma Sown
1-2 Years
2
Senior Director, Sales
0
Talent Pool
# of Successors

Figure 12.9 Successor Portlet

12.1.4 Talent Search

Talent Search provides a powerful interface for finding, filtering, and matching employees for key positions and talent pools. It provides managers and HR with the ability to search for individuals by numerous criteria, such as job role, background criteria, and competencies. Search criteria can be saved so that it can be reused again, or even created specifically to be used by certain teams or departments within your organization.

> **Note**
>
> When you are searching for talent, you may have to use a number of different searches with different criteria to find the right candidates. Make sure to use all of the search criteria to ensure the best possible results.

Searching

You access the Talent Search by selecting Talent Search from the options at the top of the page of the Succession application. By default, it opens to the Keyword Search, which allows you to enter any search term and execute the search. Below this, you can open the Advanced Options section by clicking the Expand button.

The Advanced Options include a host of criteria that can be used to find the right talent, whether you're searching to populate a talent pool or to find a successor. The first part of the Advanced Options section includes criteria fields such as Title, Job Code, Division, Department, Location, Diversity Candidate, Hire Date, Risk of Loss, Impact of Loss, and Reason for Leaving. Below these options, you can select the Background Criteria. The dropdown list of background criteria provides 15 options, three of which are available within the Manager view only. These fields include Work Experience within Company, Previous Employment, Formal Education, Language Skills, Leadership Experience, Career Goals, Geographic Mobility, Performance, and Potential, among others.

When one of these criteria has been selected from the dropdown, additional criteria that differ for each selected criterion become available. For example, selecting Leadership Experience provides a dropdown to select the Area of Leadership, and then text boxes for Years of Experience, Number of People Managed, and Dollars Managed. Clicking the Add Criteria button or green arrow adds this to the criteria list, and then additional background criteria can be added. Within the overall search, you can assign each background criterion a weight so that, for example, years of experience weigh more than number of employees managed.

The third part of the ADVANCED OPTIONS section provides the ability to search by competencies from the competency libraries available in the system. After a competency has been selected from one of the available libraries, click the green arrow to add it to the list of criteria, just as you did for BACKGROUND CRITERIA. However, for competencies, it's possible to enter a range for the score, select whether the competency is required, and weight these criteria relative to the overall search.

Figure 12.10 shows an example of the possible search criteria that can be selected in TALENT SEARCH.

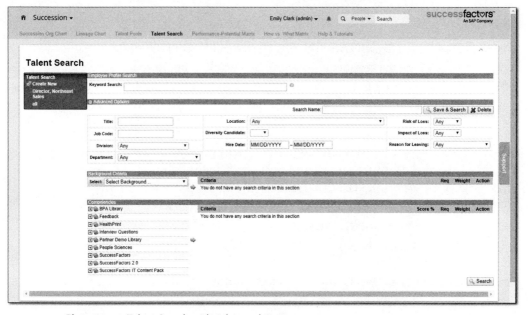

Figure 12.10 Talent Search with Advanced Options

After you've entered search criteria, you can either search using the SEARCH button or enter a name for the search and select SAVE & SEARCH to save this criterion for future use before you execute the search.

> **Note**
>
> The maximum number of search results that Succession can return is 400, although the default maximum is set to 50. It's possible for the system to return 50, 100, 200, or 400 maximum records.

Results

After the search has executed, the results are displayed on a new screen. Each record in the results displays the name, photo, business card icon, background criteria match, competency match, total match, and performance and potential grid icon, as shown in Figure 12.11. The results list can be exported to Excel.

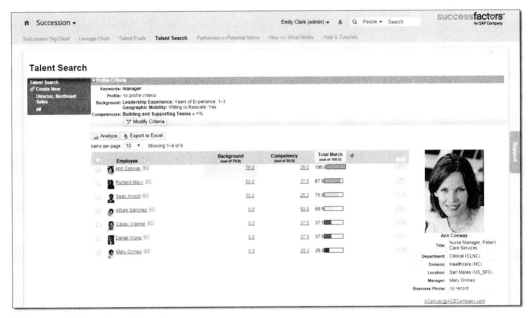

Figure 12.11 Talent Search Results

The most interesting feature of the search results is the Compare Successors analysis report. This option allows individuals selected in the search results to be compared for a variety of different attributes. By comparing multiple individuals, you ensure that the best possible candidates can be chosen.

To open the COMPARE SUCCESSORS window, check the checkbox next to each employee to include them, and click the ANALYZE button. Figure 12.12 compares three employees' competencies.

After candidates have been identified, they can be nominated to talent pools or succession plans, as we'll discuss in the next two sections.

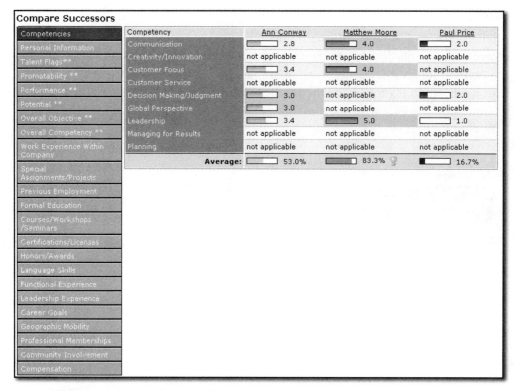

Compare Successors				
Competencies	Competency	Ann Conway	Matthew Moore	Paul Price
Personal Information	Communication	2.8	4.0	2.0
Talent Flags**	Creativity/Innovation	not applicable	not applicable	not applicable
Promotability **	Customer Focus	3.4	4.0	not applicable
Performance **	Customer Service	not applicable	not applicable	not applicable
Potential **	Decision Making/Judgment	3.0	not applicable	2.0
Overall Objective **	Global Perspective	3.0	not applicable	not applicable
Overall Competency **	Leadership	3.4	5.0	1.0
Work Experience Within Company	Managing for Results	not applicable	not applicable	not applicable
Special Assignments/Projects	Planning	not applicable	not applicable	not applicable
Previous Employment	**Average:**	53.0%	83.3%	16.7%
Formal Education				
Courses/Workshops /Seminars				
Certifications/Licenses				
Honors/Awards				
Language Skills				
Functional Experience				
Leadership Experience				
Career Goals				
Geographic Mobility				
Professional Memberships				
Community Involvement				
Compensation				

Figure 12.12 Compare Successors Feature

12.1.5 Position Tile View

The Position Tile view is an alternative to the Succession Org Chart that provides a tile-based list view of positions for succession planning. You access it by selecting POSITION TILE from the options at the top of the page of the Succession application.

The Position Tile view provides a more visual method of performing succession planning by showing all positions and successors, rather than using a hierarchy. This can be useful for succession planners of the entire organization, specific groups of positions, or teams. Figure 12.13 shows the POSITION TILE view.

Clicking a position shows an overview of the Position where any assigned successors are displayed and their succession details (e.g., readiness) edited. Successors can also be added and removed, and the Talent Card of any assigned successors can be viewed. Figure 12.14 shows the POSITION overview.

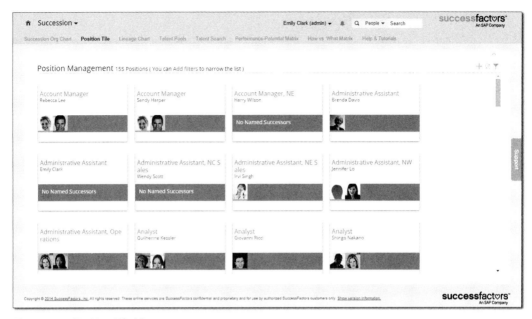

Figure 12.13 Position Tile View

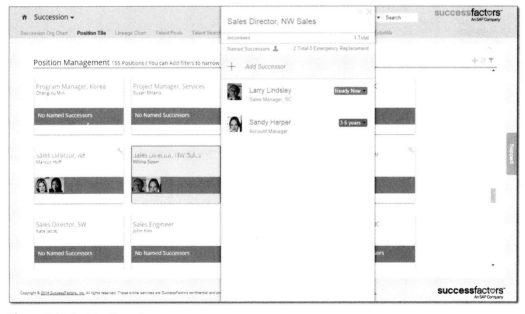

Figure 12.14 Position Overview

12.1.6 Talent Pools

Talent pools provide a way of classifying and aggregating individuals to groups so that they can be sourced for succession plans and talent searches. This enables organizations to scale their succession planning effort and begin identifying, tracking, and preparing candidates for future roles even though they may not be nominated as a successor to a position yet.

Talent Pools are accessed by selecting TALENT POOLS from the options at the top of the page of the SUCCESSION application. The TALENT POOLS screen shows all of the Talent Pools that have been created, with an overview of the individuals assigned to each Talent Pool. You can create new Talent Pools by clicking the ADD A POOL button. Figure 12.15 shows the TALENT POOLS screen.

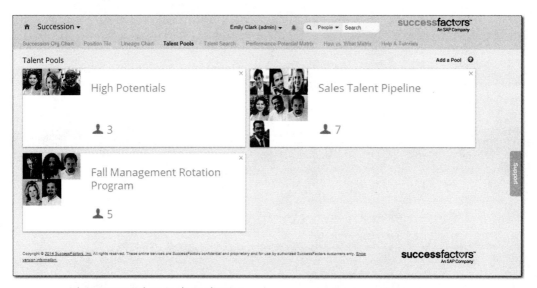

Figure 12.15 Talent Pools Application

Selecting a Talent Pool takes the user to that TALENT POOL screen. You can also open a talent pool from the NOMINATION PORTLET in the Talent Profile or Scorecard and from the Succession Org Chart from the Quickcard of any employee who is a member of that Talent Pool. In Figure 12.16, you can see the SALES TALENT PIPELINE TALENT POOL screen.

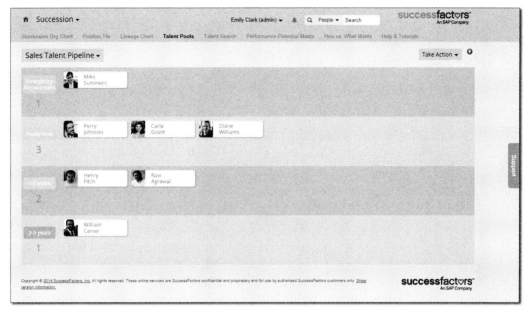

Figure 12.16 Sales Talent Pipeline Talent Pool Screen

On this screen, the TAKE ACTION button can be used to add employees to the Talent Pool or view the Talent Pool information. When adding an employee, the readiness is selected and optionally a description can be entered.

Talent Pools can be mapped to Job Roles in Job Profile Builder and to Legacy Job Roles in Manage Families & Roles.

12.1.7 Nominating Successors

After you've identified the supply of talent, you can begin the process of nominating successors. In Succession & Development, nominating successors is form based; you must configure and assign a template in OneAdmin before nominating can begin.

In the Succession module, functionality is provided to seek and nominate individuals *for* a specific position (i.e., from the position perspective) or nominate a specific individual *to* a position (i.e., from the employee perspective). Managers are responsible for nominating successors for positions within their teams, and they can also nominate their direct reports as successors for other positions.

Successors can be nominated to positions in a number of different ways:

- ▸ Succession Org Chart
- ▸ Lineage Chart
- ▸ Scorecard
- ▸ Talent Profile

In the Succession Org Chart and Lineage Chart, an individual can be nominated as a successor to the position via the CURRENT NOMINATIONS box on the business card by selecting the ADD link. From the position box action dropdown menu, you can nominate a successor using the FIND SUCCESSORS option. In the Scorecard and Talent Profile, you can nominate an individual to a position by selecting the ADD NOMINATION link in the NOMINATION PORTLET. The process of nominating a successor doesn't differ greatly from the position perspective or from the employee perspective. Now, let's walk through an example in which you are nominating a successor for the VP of Sales position.

First, you locate the VP, SALES position box in the SUCCESSION ORG CHART and select FIND SUCCESSORS from the actions dropdown menu. This opens the FIND A SUCCESSOR window, where you can search for an employee or add an external candidate. You can either enter a name into the text box or click the ADVANCED TALENT SEARCH link to open the TALENT SEARCH in an external window. In this example, enter "Richard Maxx" into the text box and click GO.

On the next screen, which is shown in Figure 12.17, you can see your nominee RICHARD MAXX and the existing nominated successors. You also have the option to compare the nominee and existing nominated successors using the COMPARE SUCCESSORS feature in the Talent Search by selecting the COMPARE THE NOMINEES link.

After reviewing the successors, click NEXT to go to the screen to select the READINESS and RANKING for your nominee, and add any NOTES. You see that Richard Maxx is a competent successor, but still needs some time to develop. Therefore, you select the readiness as READY IN 1-2 YEARS from the dropdown and enter a ranking of "3". In the NOTES text box, you add some notes about Richard Maxx's needing some competency development before being ready to take the role. After this is done, you select the NOMINATE button to close the window and confirm the nomination. If you now take a look at the VP, SALES position box in the SUCCESSION ORG CHART, you'll see RICHARD MAXX is now listed as a successor.

Figure 12.17 Find a Successor Window with the Nominees for VP, Sales

A useful feature of Succession & Development is your ability to nominate an external candidate as a successor. This can be a job candidate from SuccessFactors Recruiting Execution or a defined individual, such as a candidate that has been headhunted outside of the standard recruitment process. External candidates are nominated by selecting either FIND EXTERNAL CANDIDATE or ADD A NEW EXTERNAL CANDIDATE in the FIND A SUCCESSOR window (which is the same place where an employee is searched for).

Nomination history can be viewed for a position by selecting NOMINATION HISTORY in the action dropdown menu of a position box in the SUCCESSION ORG CHART. Figure 12.18 shows the nomination history to the VP, SALES position held by CARLA GRANT.

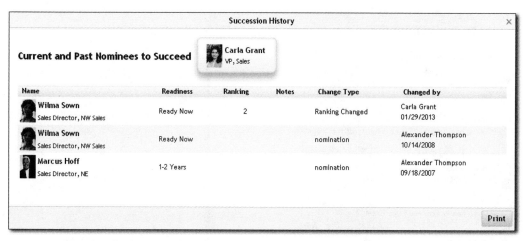

Figure 12.18 Nomination History

12.1.8 Position Management

Succession & Development leverages Position Management, which considers positions as a separate entity from a job code and an employee. Position Management is part of the Metadata Framework (MDF). Because succession planning is focused on positions and you may not use these objects in your SuccessFactors system, it's necessary to have these objects within the MDF.

If MDF is not used for Positions, it is still possible to use position data. Positions can be created by synchronizing employee data using the option SYNC POSITION MODEL WITH EMPLOYEE DATA option under POSITION MANAGEMENT in OneAdmin. This creates both the positions and the reporting relationships between the positions. Data can be imported in OneAdmin using the IMPORT POSITIONS option under POSITION MANAGEMENT. The import file must include the position code, employee's ID, reporting position, and job code for vacant positions. Positions can also be marked as a key position within the import file.

Creating Positions

SuccessFactors offers various ways of creating position objects if they don't exist, including the following:

▶ **Using the Succession Org Chart**
  Within the Succession Org Chart, you can create new positions by selecting the

ADD DIRECT REPORT option in the ACTIONS dropdown menu on the position box of the parent position.

▸ **Importing position data**
In OneAdmin, you can import position data by using the MDF data import/export option IMPORT AND EXPORT DATA under EMPLOYEE FILES.

▸ **In OneAdmin**
In OneAdmin, the option MANAGE POSITIONS under EMPLOYEE FILES is used to both create and manage position objects.

Maintaining Positions

Positions can also be maintained through the Succession Org Chart and the MDF. Within the Succession Org Chart, the EDIT POSITION option in the actions dropdown of a position box allows the user to maintain information about that position (shown in Figure 12.19), while the DELETE POSITION option from the same menu deletes that position. The MDF can also be used to edit position objects, as described above.

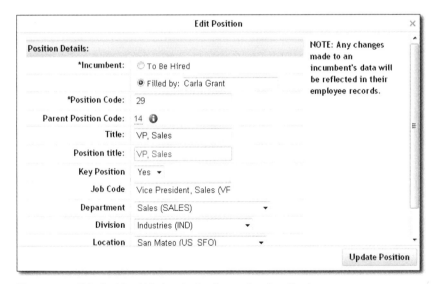

Figure 12.19 Edit Position Window in the Succession Org Chart

More details about Position Management can be found in the *Position Management Implementation Guide* at *http://service.sap.com/sfsf* under EMPLOYEE CENTRAL.

12.1.9 Reporting and Analytics

We've already covered a number of tools within Succession that can be used for reporting, such as Talent Search, Scorecard, and Nomination History. In addition to these tools, Succession offers powerful ad hoc reporting. It's important to note that Succession doesn't offer any predefined analytics.

The ad-hoc reporting feature in SuccessFactors allow you to combine specific succession data with demographic or other organizational data to produce your own meaningful reports. They are accessed in the ANALYTICS module by selecting AD HOC REPORTS in the REPORTING tab. From here, users can create their own ad hoc reports based on criteria chosen from a list of more than 250 different fields for each of the succession planning domains:

- Succession (incumbent-based nominations)
- Inclusive succession (position-based nominations)
- Succession history (incumbent-based nominations)
- Succession history (position-based nominations)

Figure 12.20 shows an example of an ad hoc report for *inclusive succession* (position-based nominations).

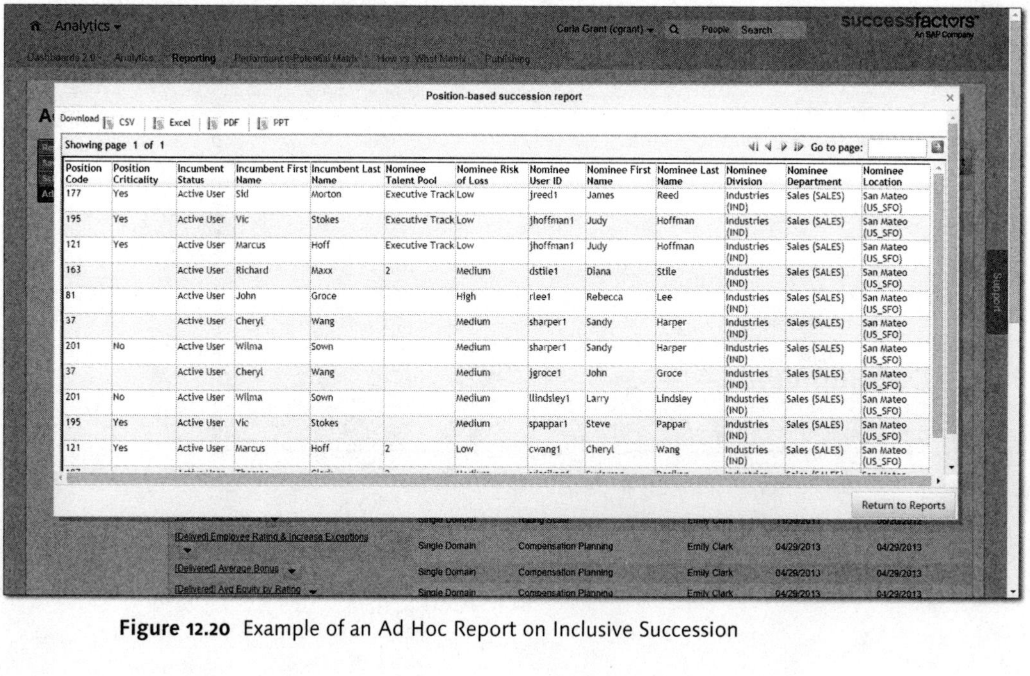

Position Code	Position Criticality	Incumbent Status	Incumbent First Name	Incumbent Last Name	Nominee Talent Pool	Nominee Risk of Loss	Nominee User ID	Nominee First Name	Nominee Last Name	Nominee Division	Nominee Department	Nominee Location
177	Yes	Active User	Sid	Morton	Executive Track	Low	jreed1	James	Reed	Industries (IND)	Sales (SALES)	San Mateo (US_SFO)
195	Yes	Active User	Vic	Stokes	Executive Track	Low	jhoffman1	Judy	Hoffman	Industries (IND)	Sales (SALES)	San Mateo (US_SFO)
121	Yes	Active User	Marcus	Hoff	Executive Track	Low	jhoffman1	Judy	Hoffman	Industries (IND)	Sales (SALES)	San Mateo (US_SFO)
163		Active User	Richard	Maxx	2	Medium	dstile1	Diana	Stile	Industries (IND)	Sales (SALES)	San Mateo (US_SFO)
81		Active User	John	Groce		High	rlee1	Rebecca	Lee	Industries (IND)	Sales (SALES)	San Mateo (US_SFO)
37		Active User	Cheryl	Wang		Medium	sharper1	Sandy	Harper	Industries (IND)	Sales (SALES)	San Mateo (US_SFO)
201	No	Active User	Wilma	Sown		Medium	sharper1	Sandy	Harper	Industries (IND)	Sales (SALES)	San Mateo (US_SFO)
37		Active User	Cheryl	Wang		Medium	jgroce1	John	Groce	Industries (IND)	Sales (SALES)	San Mateo (US_SFO)
201	No	Active User	Wilma	Sown		Medium	llindsley1	Larry	Lindsley	Industries (IND)	Sales (SALES)	San Mateo (US_SFO)
195	Yes	Active User	Vic	Stokes		Medium	spappar1	Steve	Pappar	Industries (IND)	Sales (SALES)	San Mateo (US_SFO)
121	Yes	Active User	Marcus	Hoff	2	Low	cwang1	Cheryl	Wang	Industries (IND)	Sales (SALES)	San Mateo (US_SFO)

Figure 12.20 Example of an Ad Hoc Report on Inclusive Succession

We've examined how Succession empowers organizations to identify key talent and nominate that talent to critical positions with the help of the Succession Org Chart. The next step is to develop the identified talent to ensure readiness for the succession plans to which they have been assigned. We'll now examine the Development module and how it supports these activities.

A number of analytical dashboards are available in DASHBOARDS 2.0 in the ANALYTICS application. They are viewable by selecting SUCCESSION from the dropdown menu and entering the desired filters. Figure 12.21 shows the SUCCESSION READINESS dashboard.

Figure 12.21 Succession Readiness Dashboard

12.2   Development

The Career Development Planning (CDP), or just Development, module provides the ability to create Development Plans, link them to career plans, and plan learning activities to support them. This makes the CDP an actionable and powerful tool for companies to close the talent gap and utilize and retain talent with high merit for succession planning and overall personnel development activities.

There are three core components to the CDP module:

- Development Plan
- Career Worksheet
- Learning Activities

Now, let's take a look at how each component supports these activities.

12.2.1 Development Plan

After successors have been assigned to succession plans, a suitable Development Plan is required to ensure the development and readiness of the successors. The Development Plans are accessible by the individuals, as well as their managers.

Development Plans comprise *development goals*, which are oriented toward developing skills and competencies in the chosen direction for career progression. Unlike goal plans in SuccessFactors Performance & Goals, these plans can span multiple years. The CDP module comes with a comprehensive and integrated design that enables organizations to accomplish this very important aspect of ensuring that they have the right talent in the right position.

Figure 12.22 illustrates the Development Plan and its various goals.

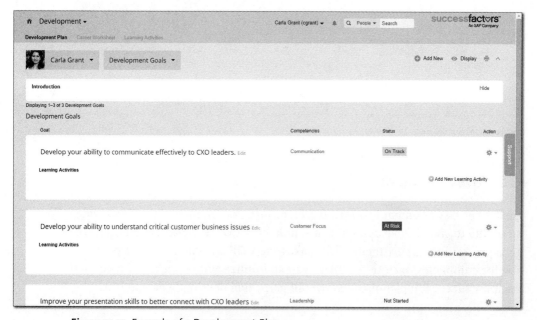

Figure 12.22 Example of a Development Plan

However, like the goal plan in the SuccessFactors Performance & Goals (covered in detail in Chapter 7), the Development Plan can be created from a template and configured according to the needs of the organization. Various information of a development goal can be displayed or hidden by selecting it in the DISPLAY OPTIONS section. This includes ALERTS, VISIBILITY, MEASURE OF SUCCESS, COMPETENCIES, START DATE, DUE DATE, STATUS, and LEARNING ACTIVITIES.

> **Note**
>
> Although largely an integrated solution, the Development Plan within the CDP module does not integrate with the goal plan in Performance & Goals.

Within each Development Plan, it's also possible for a manager to select their own Development Plan or the Development Plan for any of their direct or matrix reports.

Creating Development Goals

Development goals are added to a Development Plan by clicking the ADD NEW button in the top-right and selecting CREATE A NEW DEVELOPMENT GOAL from the dropdown menu. This opens the ADD DEVELOPMENT GOAL window (see Figure 12.23), where details of the new development goal can be defined.

Several different attributes can be chosen for a development goal, but only the GOAL description and COMPETENCIES fields are compulsory:

- ▶ VISIBILITY
  Defines whether the development goal is publicly visible or visible only to the individual and the corresponding manager

- ▶ GOAL
  Freeform text box to describe the development goal

- ▶ MEASURE OF SUCCESS
  Freeform text box to describe the measure of success for the development goal

- ▶ START DATE
  The start date of the development goal

- ▶ DUE DATE
  The date by which the development goal should be completed

▶ STATUS

The status of the development goal, which can be set and changed throughout its lifecycle to one of the different predefined statuses

▶ COMPETENCIES

The one or more competencies from the competency library that is gained after the development goal is completed.

▶ PURPOSE

Whether the development goal is for a current role, future role, or general skill set

The GOAL and MEASURE OF SUCCESS fields feature both a spell checker and the Legal Scan feature. The values for STATUS are defined in the Development Plan template.

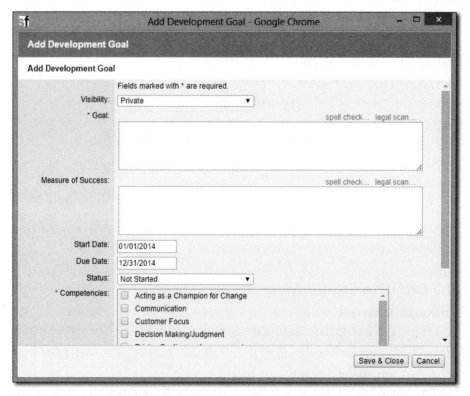

Figure 12.23 Add Development Goal Window

You can also copy development goals from another Development Goal template by clicking the ADD NEW button in the top-right and selecting COPY FROM OTHER DEVELOPMENT GOAL PLAN from the dropdown menu.

Assigning Learning Activities

After you've created a development goal, you can assign one or more learning activities to it via the ADD NEW LEARNING ACTIVITY button, located to the side of the development goal. Learning activities can be selected from the learning catalog, or custom learning activities can be created. This provides organizations with the possibility to assign learning to aid the development of the required competencies of a position for which the individual is a successor, or just to increase their productivity within their existing role. Figure 12.24 shows the addition of a LEARNING ACTIVITY to the development goal.

Figure 12.24 Adding a Learning Activity to a Development Goal

After a LEARNING ACTIVITY has been added, it can be removed by clicking the DELETE icon under ACTION. Clicking the name of the Learning Activity displays its details.

Maintaining and Tracking Goals

Development goals can be edited, removed, or added to Outlook as required. Editing a development goal—including changing its status—can be done freely at any time. This enables development goals to be altered as an employee develops or changes roles and supports tracking of the current status.

By selecting VIEW DEVELOPMENT GOAL DETAIL in the ACTIONS menu of the development goal, you can see the detail view of the development goal (see Figure 12.25). Although the information is largely the same from that provided when a development goal is created or edited, the detail view screen does show the AUDIT HISTORY of the development goal.

Figure 12.25 Detail View of a Development Goal

You can remove development goals from the Development Plan by selecting them and clicking DELETE DEVELOPMENT GOAL in the ACTIONS menu.

Publishing to the Scorecard

Managers and employees can view the development goals on the Scorecard, which increases visibility and actionable analytics to the career development processes. This is done by selecting the ADD DEVELOPMENT GOAL IN SCORECARD icon in the ACTIONS menu. After the goal is added, this icon switches to the REMOVE DEVELOPMENT GOAL FROM SCORECARD icon, which can be used to remove the development goal from the Succession Scorecard.

> **Note**
>
> Private development goals can't be published on the Scorecard. They are visible only within the Development Plan by the manager and the employee.

Development Objectives Portlet

The Development Objectives Portlet can be added to the Employee Profile to show all of an employee's development goals, as shown in Figure 12.26.

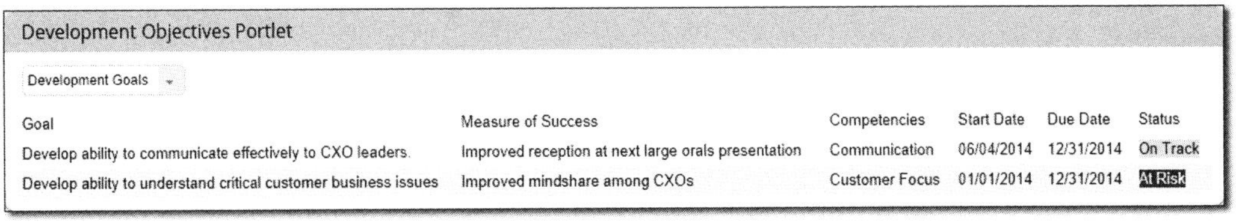
Development Objectives Portlet

Development Goals

Goal	Measure of Success	Competencies	Start Date	Due Date	Status
Develop ability to communicate effectively to CXO leaders.	Improved reception at next large orals presentation	Communication	06/04/2014	12/31/2014	On Track
Develop ability to understand critical customer business issues	Improved mindshare among CXOs	Customer Focus	01/01/2014	12/31/2014	At Risk

Figure 12.26 Development Objectives Portlet

To maximize returns from a Development Plan, it's imperative that you also align it with the individual's career plan. We'll explore the Career Worksheet and how it enables organizations to integrate the Development Plan with the career path of its talent next.

12.2.2 Career Worksheet

The *Career Worksheet* is the main focus of the CDP module and serves as an actionable view of an employee's career path, current and future roles, and existing and required competencies. Because it's linked to the Development Plan, it's a powerful tool to align your talent's development goals with the planned career progression for current and/or future goals. You can assess the readiness of your talent for a particular role that they have been nominated for using the Career Worksheet (see Figure 12.27). If no Career Worksheet exists, the user can perform a self-assessment of their current Job Role.

The Career Worksheet allows an individual or the individual's manager to map out the individual's career by adding potential jobs, viewing competency gaps, and adding development goals aligned with the competencies required to ensure the readiness of the future role. This is based on the assumption that a prior activity has been performed to add competencies for various job roles for your organization. New competencies added to a job role are immediately available for consumption in the CDP module.

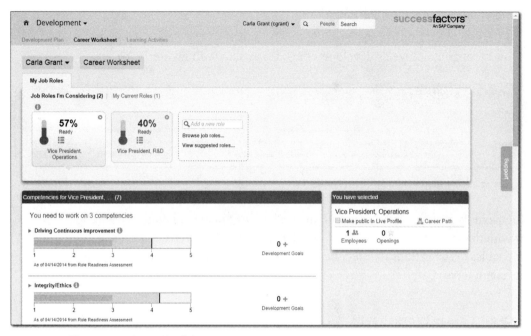

Figure 12.27 Career Worksheet

The MY JOB ROLES tab on the CAREER WORKSHEET page displays the Job Roles that the individual is considering. You can switch between the Job Roles being considered and current Job Roles using the hyperlinked options at the top of this area. For each Job Role that is being considered, a readiness percentage is displayed alongside a color-coded measurement. The ROLE DETAILS icon—located below the percentage—shows a pop-up with details about the Job Role, which you can see in Figure 12.28. Additional Job Roles to be considered can be added by searching for them in the search box. You can also browse Job Roles or display suggested roles, both by selecting the relevant hyperlink options under the search box.

The portlet immediately below the MY JOB ROLES tab shows the competencies for the current selected Job Role. The competencies for each Job Role can be switched by selecting the hyperlink of the Job Role in the MY JOB ROLES tab. Competencies are listed by groupings. The first group is the competencies of the Job Role that require development activities (e.g., those wherein the employee has not yet met the competency requirement). The second group is those competencies for which the employee has met the requirements.

Each competency is displayed with the individual's current and expected rating. You can view details of each competency as a pop-up by hovering the mouse over the COMPETENCY DESCRIPTION icon to the right of the competency name. You can add development goals for each competency by selecting the ADD DEVELOPMENT GOAL icon above the words DEVELOPMENT GOALS to the right of the competency rating. The development goals added here also get reflected in the Development Plan. All of these features can be seen in Figure 12.27.

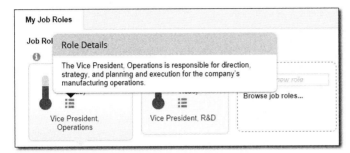

Figure 12.28 Job Role Details

One of the useful features of the Career Worksheet is the ability to view the Career Path of the Job Role, which you display by selecting the CAREER PATH option in the YOU HAVE SELECTED portlet below the MY JOB ROLES tab and to the right of the COMPETENCIES portlet. Figure 12.29 shows the Career Path.

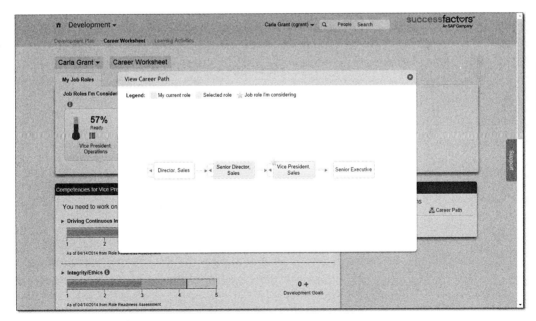

Figure 12.29 Career Path

You saw in the preceding sections how the Development Plan and Career Worksheet work in tandem to help organizations assess competency gaps for their talent to craft a suitable Development Plan. For your talent to fill the competency gaps, they need to be registered to a learning plan. This brings us to the next feature of the CDP module: Learning Activities.

12.2.3 Learning Activities

Let's look at the LEARNING ACTIVITIES section of the CDP module. The LEARNING ACTIVITIES section allows you to add a training course, certification, and so on to the Development Plan so that employees can achieve their development goals.

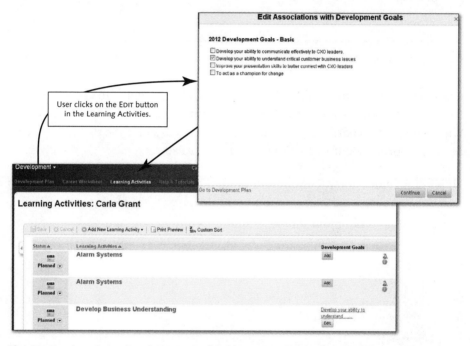

Figure 12.30 Associating Development Goals with a Learning Activity

Although learning activities can be added directly in the Development Plan itself, as discussed in Section 12.2.1, the LEARNING ACTIVITIES page also allows employees or their manager to view all of the learning activities that are assigned to them from a development and career perspective and take actions for each of them. For example, a learning activity can have development goals added or edited, be associated with a development goal, or be launched. You can create a printable version of the learning activities list using the PRINT PREVIEW button.

Figure 12.30 shows how you can link a learning activity to one or more development goals. The system recognizes that a particular learning activity can help you accomplish some of the development goals in your Development Plan that don't require a one-to-one relationship between a learning activity and a development goal.

12.2.4 Analytics

A Career Worksheet dashboard is available in DASHBOARDS 2.0 in the ANALYTICS application. You view it by selecting CAREER WORKSHEET from the dropdown menu and entering the desired filters. Figure 12.31 shows the dashboard.

Figure 12.31 Career Worksheet Dashboard

12.3 Summary

SuccessFactors Succession & Development is a two-fold solution for managing organizational sustainability through succession planning and career development planning. Its core functionality enables full management of the succession planning process and of employee career paths. It also enables employees to make choices about their own careers and actively develop their own skills and competencies.

In this chapter, we've learned how the Succession module supports the full succession planning process through the Succession Org Chart, matrices, Talent Search, and talent pools, as well as by leveraging Position Management. We also covered the reporting possibilities that exist in the solution.

We explored the Career Development Planning module and how it supports competency growth and career planning for all employees, as well as those planned for critical or leadership positions. We looked at how all of this integrates with other solutions within the SuccessFactors HCM suite.

In the next chapter, we'll take a deep dive into SuccessFactors Workforce Analytics and how it provides real-time analytical insight and the foundation for SuccessFactors Workforce Planning.

There is a growing trend for organizations to understand the constantly changing dynamics of their human capital and its impact on business outcomes. SuccessFactors Workforce Analytics provides insight into workforce issues, risks, and opportunities and links HR initiatives to organizational strategy through standardized HR metrics, key performance indicators, and analytic investigations.

13 Workforce Analytics

Compared to its predecessors and contemporaries, SuccessFactors Workforce Analytics (WFA) is on the cutting edge of the HR transformation, making it a key differentiator in the SuccessFactors product suite. By empowering companies to analyze the myriad of data they are already collecting about their people and processes, organizations can obtain a more holistic picture of their workforce, as well as identify areas of opportunity to drive actions resulting in either cost savings or increased revenue.

The SuccessFactors WFA solution clears the hurdles commonly experienced in launching and sustaining a WFA program by guiding you in what to measure and how to verify the accuracy and validity of your data. It also provides methods for utilizing the analysis, visualizing results, and recommending actions. The process of telling stories with data enables HR to transform the decision making process from being based on gut feelings to data-driven insights. Additionally, companies that utilize WFA can leverage a standardized metrics catalog to compare individual results against various categories of benchmarks, such as industry, geographic region, organization size, or revenue.

In this chapter, we'll provide you with an understanding of the multitude of analytic capabilities delivered by SuccessFactors WFA, including standardized metrics (see Section 13.1), the benchmarking program (see Section 13.2), and reporting functionality and advanced analytical tools (see Section 13.3). The modular design is followed by a detailed description of the metrics methodology, associated metrics packs, and common WFA data sources. The chapter concludes with the Headlines functionality (see Section 13.4), which is fully integrated into the SuccessFactors HCM suite and with SuccessFactors HCM Mobile.

13.1   The Foundation of Workforce Analytics

In this section, we'll examine the foundation of the WFA application. All WFA implementations begin with the base Metrics Pack, known as Core Workforce & Mobility, which is used as a foundation to extend into more specific functional areas (e.g., Learning, Performance, Recruiting Execution, etc.) through additional *Metrics Packs*.

The standards for each Metrics Pack have been defined by the legacy Infohrm group, which was acquired by SuccessFactors in 2010. Based on more than 30 years of consulting experience in the field of Workforce Analytics, Infohrm (and now SuccessFactors) is an influential global presence in the space. By working with hundreds of organizations across industries around the globe, Infohrm standardized an implementation and ongoing consultative process designed to ensure successful client experiences. This proven methodology was quickly adopted by SuccessFactors to maintain global leadership in the WFA field.

13.1.1   Implementing Core Workforce & Mobility

The first phase of any WFA implementation begins with the Core Workforce & Mobility Metrics Pack, which takes between three and four months to complete. The base Metrics Pack is sourced from your Human Resource Information System (HRIS) and consists of more than 150 metrics for headcount, staffing rates, terminations, movements, and hires. In addition, the core implementation typically includes at least 20 analysis options (also referred to as dimensions, analysis options, or dimension hierarchies), which are used to slice and dice your core workforce and mobility metrics. Examples include gender, diversity, job level, pay band, and so on. The final component of the core implementation includes an organizational structure, which typically represents the roll-up of business units (by cost center, supervisor, location, etc.). We will delve deeper into both analysis options and organizational structures at the end of this section.

Let's begin by deconstructing the base Metrics Pack, which forms the foundation of WFA. The Core Workforce & Mobility Metrics Pack supports the necessary data items required to generate measures and reporting structures for a comprehensive HR reporting solution.

Note

The Core Workforce & Mobility Metrics Pack primarily consists of measures in the Workforce Profile and Workforce Mobility categories and includes a limited number of measures in the Workforce Productivity, Workforce Compensation & Benefits, and Staffing Function categories. If clients choose to purchase additional Metrics Packs, such as the Payroll & Benefits Metrics Pack or Financial Metrics Pack, these categories become more comprehensive.

The standard metrics included in the Core Workforce & Mobility Metrics Pack are bucketed into operational measure categories and associated subcategories:

▸ **Workforce Profile**
Describe and compare an organization's workforce using a range of organizational and personal characteristics, such as organizational structure, age, employment status, occupational group, tenure, gender, and diversity groupings. These measures provide insight into workforce demographics and their implications on workforce skill and experience levels.

▸ **Workforce Productivity**
Provide macro indicators that are helpful in the first step of the diagnostic process. This section combines a range of input and output/outcome measures that can be considered together in an examination of organizational effectiveness. The Termination Value per Termination metric is included in the subcategory called Workforce Costs.

▸ **Workforce Mobility**
Monitor and compare the flow of the workforce into and out of the organization. These include measures of staff recruitment, transfer/promotion, and separations. Subcategories include Recruitment, Movement, and Termination.

▸ **Workforce Compensation and Benefits**
Monitor and compare the remuneration to reward and motivate employees. For example, the Average Annual Salary metric is included in the subcategory called Compensation.

▸ **Staffing Function**
Provide an overview of the effectiveness of the staffing function from a turn-

over standpoint. For example, the Quick Quits metric Turnover Rate <30/90 Days is included in the subcategory called Staffing Effectiveness.

Note

The full-time equivalent (FTE), external hires, termination, and retirement measures included within the Core Workforce & Mobility Metrics Pack are all requirements for the SuccessFactors Workforce Planning (WFP) solution. The WFP solution allows organizations to create forecasts using either headcount or FTE metrics and leverages the underlying analytics engine to include projected retirements, terminations, and hires into the forecast. We will study WFP in more detail in Chapter 14.

13.1.2 Metrics Packs

Despite the availability of systems that are continuously collecting workforce data, deriving insights that can be used to make informed business decisions remains a challenge. The following are some of the common reasons hindering the decision making process; if any of these resonate with you, consider evaluating the WFA product for your organization:

▸ **Data accessibility**
IT alone has access to the required data, and HR is still waiting for key data that will be used to facilitate discussions with the business.

▸ **Incomplete view**
Business intelligence (BI) tools often lack a holistic view of the workforce, meaning that total workforce issues are not addressed. BI tools are built for finance and IT departments, and they are typically not targeted at analyzing employee issues.

▸ **Analytical capability**
HR lacks analytical skills and is not well equipped to interpret data and generate compelling stories.

▸ **Data quality**
The business questions the validity and credibility of data provided by HR, due in part to the lack of standardization around HR metrics.

SuccessFactors WFA is designed to address each of these challenges, and Metrics Packs play a key role in minimizing the effects of these issues. Metrics Packs can be defined as standardized sets of metrics sourced from your HR or business systems, such as SAP ERP HCM, Employee Central, Recruiting Execution, Performance Management, Finance, Sales, and so on. In effect, each functional area has an associated Metrics Pack and includes standards for sourcing the data, formulas used to calculate metrics, and benchmarks.

The following Metrics Packs are available for you to analyze in conjunction with your core workforce data:

▶ Core Workforce & Mobility/Workforce Planning

▶ Absence Management

▶ Compensation Planning

▶ Payroll and Benefits

▶ Employee Relations

▶ Finance Management

▶ Health and Safety

▶ HR Delivery

▶ Leave Accrual

▶ Performance Management

▶ Recruitment

▶ Succession Management

▶ Survey

▶ Talent Flow Analytics

▶ Learning and Development

▶ Custom Data Source (e.g., custom Metrics Pack sourced from a system not listed here)

After the Core Workforce & Mobility Metrics Pack is implemented, you can begin to map in additional Metrics Packs from other data sources (e.g., Recruiting Execution, Learning, Finance, etc.). Note that you can use virtually any data source, including homegrown systems and Excel worksheets, as the source of data for any Metrics Pack. The preferred, and most common, method is to extract raw data from a source system because this mitigates the risk of importing incorrect data often held in Excel or other similar data files. Depending on the complexity of the Metrics Pack, the typical length of time to implement ranges between 3 and 12 weeks. By integrating data from your core HRIS with other systems, you can yield more powerful insights and analyses than a singular view would allow.

For example, the integration of learning data with sales data can allow you to analyze the effect of specific training courses on sales output. Essentially acting as a data warehouse, WFA provides you with a tool to move beyond operational reporting and counting of things (e.g., how many employees took a specific training course) to become a more strategic partner to the business (e.g., sales went up 30% for employees who took the training course).

To provide another example, the Absence Management Metrics Pack helps derive absence measures that can be used to gain insights into an organization's productivity and the profitability per employee. For example, the Absence Management Metrics Pack includes the following metrics:

- Unscheduled Absence Rate
- Total Cost of Sick Leave per FTE
- Absence Duration Days per FTE

When you cross these metrics with your core workforce data, you can begin to answer questions like the following:

- What percentage of our absence days is unscheduled, versus scheduled?
- How do our sick leave occurrences differ according to employee generations (baby boomers, Generation X, etc.)?
- What is the remuneration value of unscheduled absence per employee? How does it vary across lines of business or geographies?

In summary, each Metrics Pack is based on a highly structured framework that does the following:

- Defines the SuccessFactors standard set of core metrics for each respective functional area (e.g., Core HRIS, Learning & Development, Recruiting Execution, Sales, etc.)
- Defines a standard set of dimensions/hierarchies to support further analysis of results
- Maps requirements to a source set of base data items
- Includes template extract programs and scripts for common and large enterprise HRISs/HRMSs
- Includes common business logic that can be customized for customer-specific requirements

- ▶ Includes benchmarks
- ▶ Includes logical groupings within categories and subcategories to minimize effort searching for specific metrics

We have examined what constitutes a Metrics Pack and how metrics enable organizations to analyze their workforce issues and organization-wide trends. While the Metrics Packs are based on standardized formulas that represent the most frequently analyzed metrics by function, it is important to note that clients have the ability to add custom metrics or calculations at any time. In the next section, we will cover how the Metrics Packs are used as building blocks to implement the *Metric Methodology*.

13.1.3 Metric Methodology

Now that we've built the case for WFA and defined Metrics Packs, let's take a deeper look at the metric methodology. If we were to ask you what the starting point is for workforce analytics, of course, your answer would be data. However, the tricky part is advancing from mere data points to full-fledged analytics.

The metric methodology is the same for all Metrics Packs, so we'll use the Core Workforce & Mobility Metrics Pack to illustrate the process. The first step is to define the metrics sourcing logic, which are the data fields sourced from the HRIS (e.g., SAP ERP HCM or Employee Central). Data from the core HRIS is mapped to standardized formulas by the SuccessFactors data transformation engine to generate what are called *base input measures* (e.g., FTE) and *dimension hierarchies* (e.g., gender). These base input measures are filtered through the dimension hierarchies to generate a rich set of *derived input measures* (e.g., # of FTE—Female).

Lastly, the derived input measures are combined in formulas to generate *result measures* (e.g., male to female staffing ratio) commonly used in analysis and reporting and are displayed in the form of rates, ratios, percentages, averages, and so on. In other words, the derived input measures and the base input measures are the numerators and denominators making up each rate or ratio, respectively. Figure 13.1 shows the metric methodology.

All measures (base input, derived input, or result) and dimension hierarchies represented by the dotted box are available to support a customer's reporting and analytics agenda.

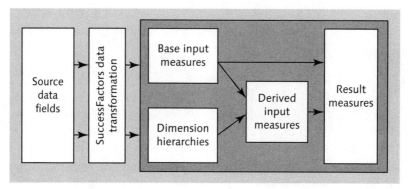

Figure 13.1 Metric Methodology

Now that we've examined how the metric methodology is structured and defined, we'll review the analysis options, organizational structures, and other tools for analyzing the data.

13.1.4 Analyzing Your Data

As data analysts, we often use the phrases "slicing and dicing" or "drilling through the data" to describe the process of dissecting the total organizational result to identify patterns, trends, and insights. Often, this can be a challenging task that requires a high level of manual effort because data is usually available only in an aggregate form. WFA includes numerous analysis options for easy slicing and dicing of data results, all located within the ANALYZE BY tab in the FILTERS pane, as shown in Figure 13.2. This list is often referred to as the Dimensions list, and it's organized in alphabetical order.

In effect, analysis by dimensions allows for greater insight into the characteristics or performance of a metric by looking at results across different subgroups, which is often referred to as "segmenting the workforce." By segmenting the workforce, we can break down the organizational result and start to see which employee populations or areas of the organization are driving the total result for the organization.

Let's take a look at the example in Figure 13.3, which shows VOLUNTARY TERMINATION RATES BY TENURE. In this example, we can see that, at nearly 40%, the 1-<2 year tenure band has considerably higher voluntary turnover than other tenure groups. This may indicate a low tenure turnover problem, which could warrant further investigation, and ultimately, targeted interventions.

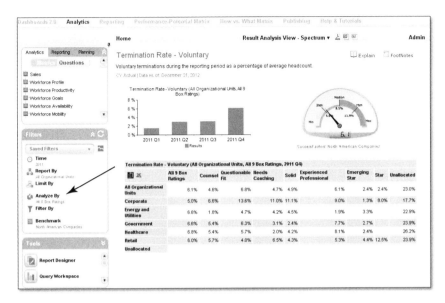

Figure 13.2 Analyze By

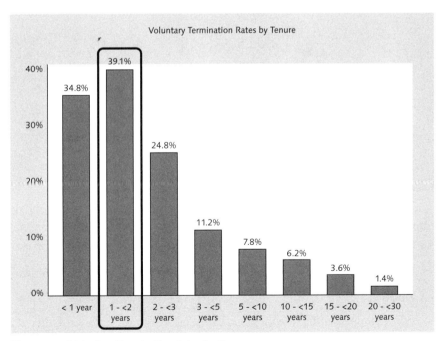

Figure 13.3 Voluntary Termination Rates by Tenure

Organizational Structures

The next logical step in the analytics process is to determine where in the organization the low tenure turnover problem is occurring. To do this, we need to drill through the organizational structure to identify locations where voluntary turnover rates are highest for the 1-<2 year tenure band. Organizational structures represent the hierarchical relationship of business units, cost centers, reporting relationships, or geographic locations. The most common organizational structure is the cost center structure, or business unit roll-up.

In Figure 13.4, we can clearly see that the HEALTHCARE business unit has significantly higher low-tenure voluntary turnover rates (78%) than the rest of the organization.

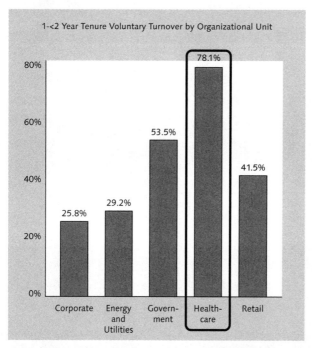

Figure 13.4 1-<2 Year Tenure Voluntary Turnover by Organizational Unit

Analysis Options

Now that we've identified the business unit with a low tenure turnover issue, we can continue to slice and dice our results to understand which populations within the Healthcare business unit are of particular concern. This can be done by applying additional analysis options, such as job family, gender, ethnic group, age group, and so on.

In Figure 13.5, we've analyzed low-tenure voluntary turnover within the Healthcare business unit by gender, and you can see that almost all women (almost 84%) have left within the first 2 years of employment.

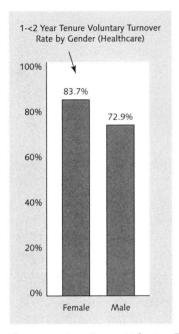

Figure 13.5 Low-Tenure Voluntary Turnover by Gender (Healthcare)

Filtering

Sometimes, it can be useful to apply a second level of analysis when you're trying to pinpoint the hot spot in your data, and this is done by using the FILTER BY option (also located in the ANALYTICS pane and shown in Figure 13.2). This feature effectively allows you to go one level deeper into your analysis by limiting the data to one specific node of an ANALYSIS OPTION. For example, we've already sliced the 1-<2 year tenure voluntary turnover in the Healthcare business unit by gender. However, perhaps we want to look at only employees who left that were 20–29 years old. By filtering by the 20–29 year old age group, we can see in Figure 13.6 that 70.2% of employees who left the HEALTHCARE business unit were 20–29 year old females with 1-<2 years' tenure.

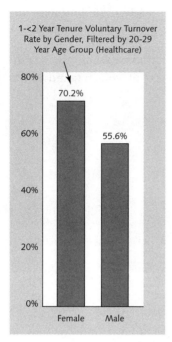

Figure 13.6 Low-Tenure Voluntary Turnover by Gender Filtered by 20–29 Age Group (Health Care)

Now that we've identified a low-tenure turnover issue in the Healthcare business unit for females in the 20–29 year old age group, we may want to view the employee-level details that make up this population.

Drill to Detail

The Drill to Detail functionality is embedded within the WFA application and allows users to click any hyperlinked result (e.g., percentage or raw count). As a result, the tool generates the details of the individual records represented in the result in a transactional list-based view. Customers can limit what is returned in the Drill to Detail view, but in theory, they can choose to show any of the fields that are included in the data file that is sent as part of the monthly data refresh cycle. Figure 13.7 shows the hyperlinked result (70.2%) that we can click to activate the DRILL TO DETAIL functionality.

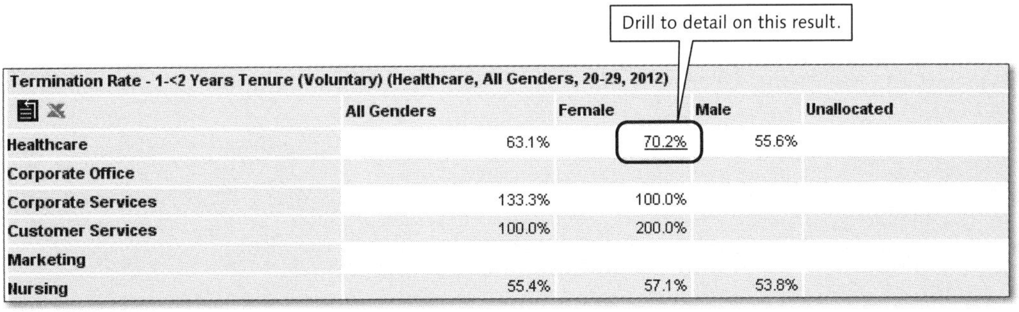

Termination Rate - 1-<2 Years Tenure (Voluntary) (Healthcare, All Genders, 20-29, 2012)	All Genders	Female	Male	Unallocated
Healthcare	63.1%	70.2%	55.6%	
Corporate Office				
Corporate Services	133.3%	100.0%		
Customer Services	100.0%	200.0%		
Marketing				
Nursing	55.4%	57.1%	53.8%	

Figure 13.7 Hyperlinked Result for Drill to Detail

If you click the hyperlink, the system generates a transactional list of the specific employees that make up the result, as shown in Figure 13.8. Also, note that clicking the EXCEL icon in the upper-left corner of the table allows a user to export the table for further analysis or distribution. One tip is that, if you're accessing WFA through Single Sign-On (SSO) and your organization also utilizes SuccessFactors Employee Profile, you can click the boxed PERSON icon next to any Drill to Detail record to see that individual's profile.

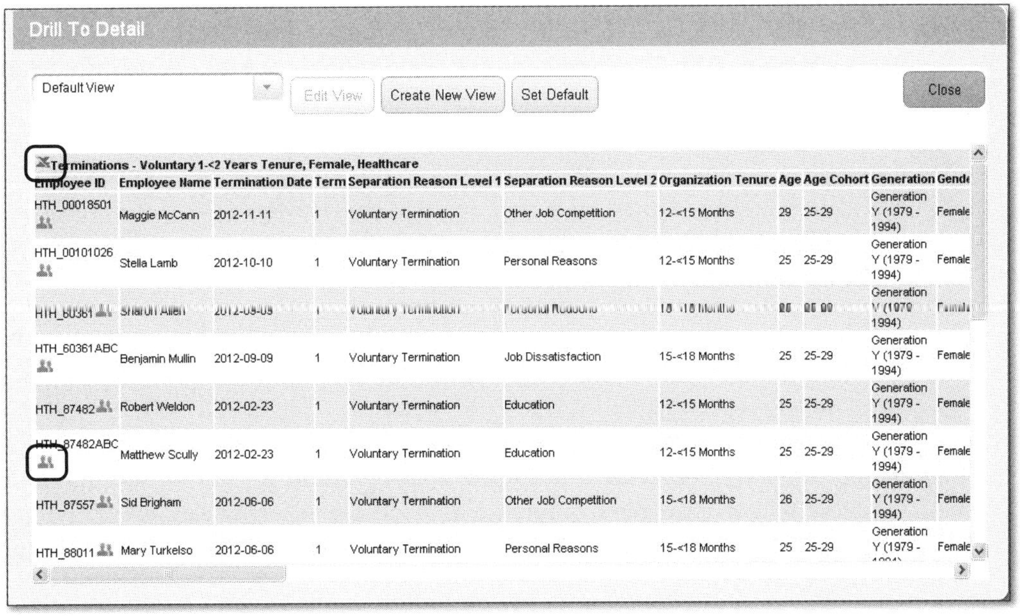

Employee ID	Employee Name	Termination Date	Term	Separation Reason Level 1	Separation Reason Level 2	Organization Tenure	Age	Age Cohort	Generation	Gende
HTH_00018501	Maggie McCann	2012-11-11	1	Voluntary Termination	Other Job Competition	12-<15 Months	29	25-29	Generation Y (1979 - 1994)	Female
HTH_00101026	Stella Lamb	2012-10-10	1	Voluntary Termination	Personal Reasons	12-<15 Months	25	25-29	Generation Y (1979 - 1994)	Female
HTH_60361	Sharon Allen	2012-09-09	1	Voluntary Termination	Personal Reasons	15-<18 Months	25	25-29	Generation Y (1979 - 1994)	Female
HTH_60361ABC	Benjamin Mullin	2012-09-09	1	Voluntary Termination	Job Dissatisfaction	15-<18 Months	25	25-29	Generation Y (1979 - 1994)	Female
HTH_87482	Robert Weldon	2012-02-23	1	Voluntary Termination	Education	12-<15 Months	25	25-29	Generation Y (1979 - 1994)	Female
HTH_87482ABC	Matthew Scully	2012-02-23	1	Voluntary Termination	Education	12-<15 Months	25	25-29	Generation Y (1979 - 1994)	Female
HTH_87557	Sid Brigham	2012-06-06	1	Voluntary Termination	Other Job Competition	15-<18 Months	26	25-29	Generation Y (1979 - 1994)	Female
HTH_88011	Mary Turkelso	2012-06-06	1	Voluntary Termination	Personal Reasons	15-<18 Months	25	25-29	Generation Y (1979 -	Female

Figure 13.8 Drill to Detail Result

In summary, Drill to Detail enables users to verify which employees are included within a particular result. This customer-driven enhancement is a tool for validating the quality of the data to gain credibility with the business.

In the next section, we'll discuss the Benchmarking program in depth.

13.2   The Benchmarking Program

External benchmarks are extremely useful for organizations to utilize as a reference point to gauge performance against competitors. Additionally, you can leverage benchmarks as an input in the target-setting process or to understand whether your organization is following or deviating from macroeconomic trends over time. Many clients find the Benchmarking program to be a key value-add from their SuccessFactors WFA investment.

In this section, we'll examine the Benchmarking program methodology, the categories and subcategories for viewing benchmarks, and how to access benchmarks in WFA.

13.2.1   Benchmarking Methodology

Every customer using SuccessFactors WFA contractually agrees to share their data for benchmarking purposes. Unlike other popular benchmarking programs (e.g., Saratoga or Watson Wyatt), SuccessFactors does not use a survey methodology to collect data for benchmarking purposes. Instead, SuccessFactors accesses clients' raw data to calculate the benchmarks using standard formulas and definitions. This ensures that all data is being viewed in an apples-to-apples comparison and increases the quality of the benchmark figures.

Another quality assurance check embedded in the Benchmarking program is the minimum sample size criteria. For a benchmark to be calculated, there must be a minimum of eight organizations providing the data elements necessary to generate a benchmark result. This rule also acts as a safeguard for organizational anonymity. Because benchmarks are always reported in aggregates, the minimum sample size also provides confidence that no single organization's individual results are identifiable. The benchmarks are published once a year, usually during the first quarter after year-end data has become available.

Now, we'll look at the various categories of benchmarks available for analysis purposes.

13.2.2 Benchmarking Categories

As the number of SuccessFactors WFA clients grows, so does the Benchmarking program's capability to provide benchmarks for more metrics in the metrics catalog. The total benchmark database is called the SuccessFactors North American Companies; for organizations based in North America, this is your best bet for finding an acceptable sample size for the metrics you're interested in benchmarking.

However, sometimes it's helpful to look at specific slices of the database, such as by industry, organization size, or revenue. The Benchmarking program provides clients with seven main categories of benchmarks to choose from in addition to the total North American Companies results. Figure 13.9 shows the main categories available to clients for benchmarking purposes.

Figure 13.9 Benchmarking Categories

When you select one of the benchmark categories, a list of subcategories appears for you to choose from to further refine your selection. Note that as you restrict your selection, the sample size criteria may not be met, and therefore no benchmark result is displayed. Now, we'll look at how to navigate through the WFA application to apply benchmarks to specific metrics.

13.2.3 Applying Benchmarks

Benchmarks are embedded within the WFA technology and, therefore, cannot be turned "off" on your specific instance. There are a few different methods for accessing the benchmarks, the easiest of which is to navigate to a specific measure page where the benchmark result for that measure is displayed as a component of the standard page layout. For example, if you were interested in seeing the benchmark for voluntary termination rate, you would see the standard page layout as depicted in Figure 13.10.

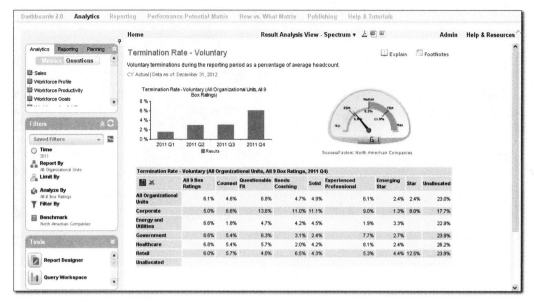

Figure 13.10 Benchmarks on a Measure Page

As you can see, each measure page shows a gauge image for the benchmark result, including breakdowns for the 25th, 50th, and 75th percentiles. The title below the spectrum denotes the benchmark group you're viewing—in this case, the default SuccessFactors: North American Companies. Please note that clients can choose to set their default benchmark group to any of the categories or subcategories available.

The benchmark spectrum also utilizes the stoplight methodology (i.e., red/yellow/green color coding) to indicate where desirable and undesirable results fall within the provided ranges. Clients can view their organizations' results by either reading the digital result in the bottom of the gauge or hovering on the needle.

If you want to see how your organization's result compares to a different benchmark group, you can easily make this selection in the Filters pane. Figure 13.11 illustrates how to make your benchmark selection by clicking Benchmark.

You can see that the current selection is North American Companies, but let's say you want to view benchmarks for the Healthcare industry instead. After clicking Benchmark, a new window pops up that allows you to select the Industry category in the Dimension window, and then a list of subcategories appears in the Selection window. Figure 13.12 shows how to change the benchmark selection.

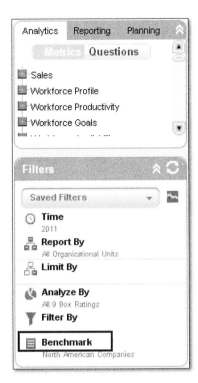

Figure 13.11 Changing the Benchmark Group in the Filters Pane

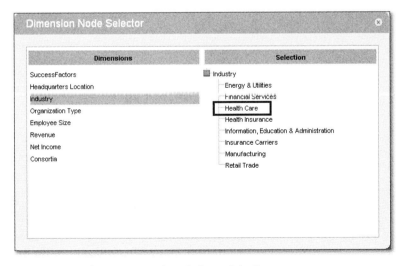

Figure 13.12 Applying Your Benchmark Group Selection

After you click HEALTH CARE, the window closes, and the benchmark image, title, and percentile ranges change to reflect this selection, as displayed in Figure 13.13.

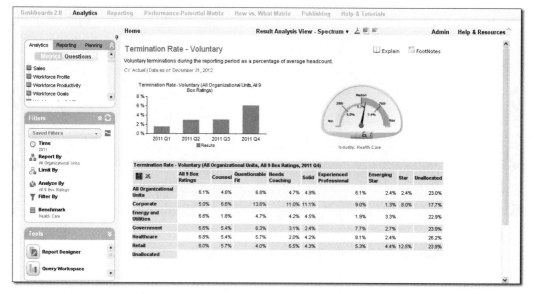

Figure 13.13 Health Care Benchmark Selection on a Measure Page

There are a few additional methods for viewing benchmarks in the WFA application, including the Benchmark View, Benchmark Scorecard, and Benchmark Chart. We'll review each of these in detail, beginning with the Benchmark View.

Benchmark View

Several *views* are available that allow users to change the measure page layout for any measure on the site. The VIEW dropdown is located at the top of any measure page and includes various options such as RESULT ANALYSIS VIEW (default), RESULT TREND VIEW, RESULT INPUT VIEW, and RESULT BENCHMARK VIEW. The view you're currently in is denoted by a * symbol. To switch a view, simply hover over the dropdown arrow, and a list of available views appears. Note, that the viewing options are different for result measure pages and input measure pages.

In Figure 13.14, we've selected the RESULT BENCHMARK VIEW in the dropdown list. In this particular view, users are given additional breakdowns of the benchmark result, including the year-over-year benchmark trend and more granular slices of results by percentiles.

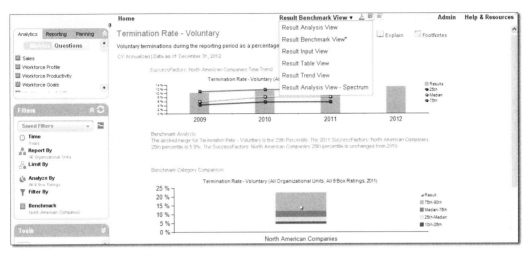

Figure 13.14 Result Benchmark View

Benchmark Chart

The Benchmark Chart is a component of the Benchmark View, as shown in Figure 13.14, and it can also be selected as a charting option in Report Designer. The Benchmark Chart differs from a regular chart in that it shows the benchmark result for the previous four years, provided there are benchmark results for that time period. This trend view shows users how the 25th, 50th, and 75th percentiles have changed from year to year, allowing clients to see where their organization's results fell within the percentiles for a specific year. Lastly, the Result Trend View can help organizations understand whether they have been following or deviating from the benchmark trend over the past four years.

Benchmark Scorecard

The final method for viewing benchmarks is the Benchmark Scorecard, which can be found on the REPORTING menu (see Figure 13.15) or in the Report Designer library.

The Benchmark Scorecard is a standard SuccessFactors dashboard (e.g., out-of-the-box report) that is available to all clients, and it provides a table list of all measures on the site and the corresponding benchmark results. The measures are arranged in the same categories found in the ANALYTICS tab and show the current organizational result; the past four years' benchmark results; and the 25th, 50th, and 75th percentile results for the current year. There is also a column denoting the color-coding associated with your organization's result and a sample size of the number of organizations making up the benchmark result. Figure 13.16 shows a sample of the Benchmark Scorecard.

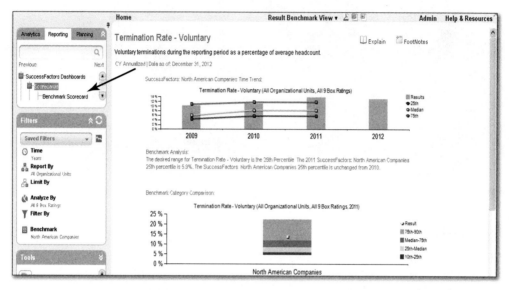

Figure 13.15 Benchmark Scorecard

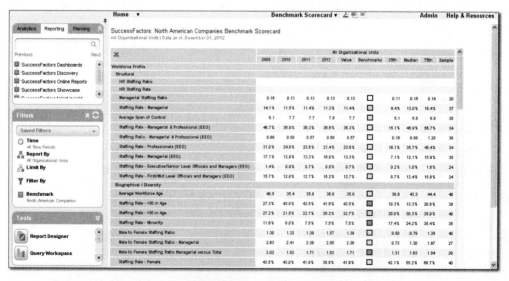

Figure 13.16 Sample Benchmark Scorecard

We've now covered the Benchmarking program in detail, so let's shift our attention to the analytical tools embedded in the WFA application.

13.3   Analytical Tools

The WFA solution includes multiple analytical tools located in the Tools section of the Analytics pane, and their purpose is to help to simplify the data analysis and reporting process. Acting as a complement to the standard measure pages and portal pages, the tool includes both basic and advanced analytical tools. Mainly aimed at the power users of the system, all tools are user friendly and intuitive and play an integral role in creating a repeatable and scalable WFA program.

This section will cover the main querying, statistical analysis, and reporting tools that are the crux of the power user's toolkit.

13.3.1   Query Workspace

The querying tool embedded in the WFA application—known as Query Workspace—utilizes a drag-and-drop interface similar to a pivot table in Excel. Users can build custom queries ranging from basic lists to complex combinations of multiple measures and dimensions. This powerful tool is controlled by role-based security, and administrators of the system can determine which user roles should be given access to the querying tool. Typically, access is limited to power users in the HR field, as well as the core WFA team. To access the Query Workspace tool, first locate the tab in the Tools section of the Analytics pane (refer to Figure 13.16). After you click the Query Workspace button, a new page loads, and a query displays the data you were last viewing. From here, you can modify the existing query, create a new query, or open an existing query in the Folder menu.

Let's look at an example of how to create a new query. Using our example from earlier, we'll create a query for Termination Rate—Voluntary. Figure 13.17 illustrates how to start a new query—by clicking File • New Query.

After you click New Query, a window appears that allows you to build a custom query. Locate the measure in the metrics catalog on the Measures tab, which in this example is located under Workforce Mobility • Terminations • Termination Rate—Voluntary. After selecting the measure, drag it onto the rows and drop it when the ROWS column turns blue, as depicted in Figure 13.18.

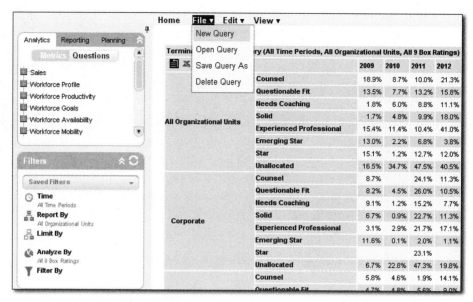

Figure 13.17 Create a New Query

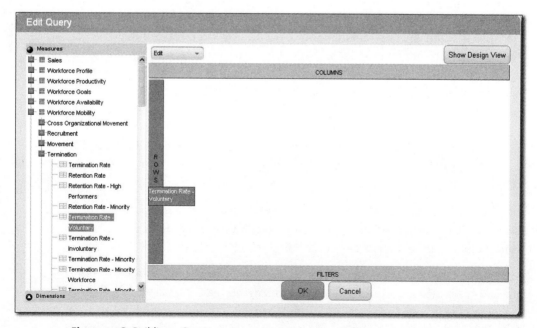

Figure 13.18 Building a Query

After you drop the measure, the data populates for the most current year of data, which in this case is year-end 2012. As soon as you drop the measure on the rows (see the basic query in Figure 13.19), the MEASURES list is replaced by the DIMENSIONS list on the left side of the window, and you see your result for TERMINATION RATE—VOLUNTARY in 2012.

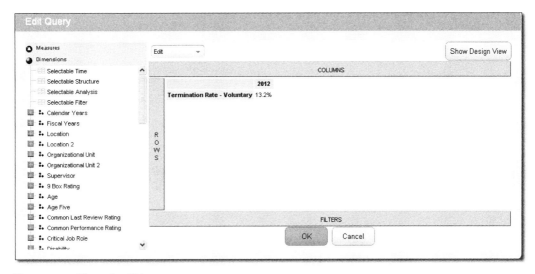

Figure 13.19 Dimension List

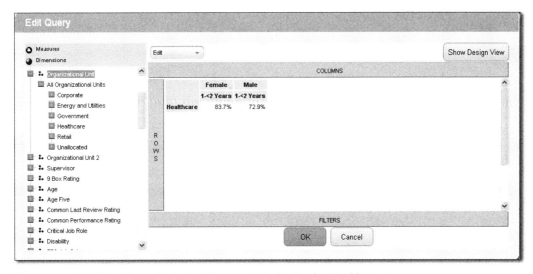

Figure 13.20 1-<2 Year Tenure Voluntary Turnover Rate by Gender (Health Care)

Now that the basic query is built, you have limitless options to expand your query. However, the most common additions are to add slices of analysis from the DIMENSIONS list, add additional measures to the rows, or filter by a specific dimension node. Using the example from earlier, let's quickly walk through how to build on this basic query to show 1-<2 year tenure voluntary termination rates by gender in the Healthcare business unit (see Figure 13.20).

By clicking the SHOW DESIGN VIEW button in the top-right corner, you can see the parameters for the query you've defined so far. Note that the drag-and-drop functionality is still applicable in the design view. Use of the design view allows you to construct a richer, more complex query that enables even closer analysis of the targeted measure. Figure 13.21 shows the design view for your current query; you can toggle back to the table view by clicking the SHOW TABLE VIEW button in this right corner.

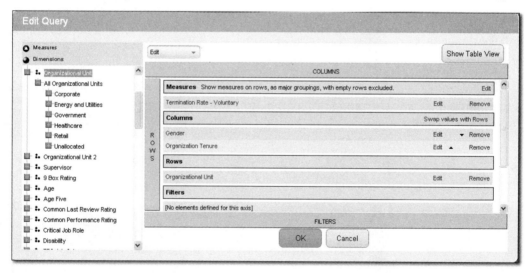

Figure 13.21 Design View

When you're happy with your query, click the OK button, and the query is displayed on the page in a table format. You can export the query by clicking the EXCEL icon on the table (make sure you have clicked OK first!), or you can chart the query by clicking the VIEW dropdown arrow. Some queries may not be suitable for a chart if there are multiple measures and dimensions on the rows/columns. Lastly, the Drill to Detail functionality does work in queries built in the Query

Workspace. However, you must make sure to include a measure on both the rows and columns.

The Query Workspace tool also houses the customer-driven enhancement called Custom Members/Sets (also known as Custom Dimensions). This functionality provides users with the ability to create specific dimension views to be used for analysis and reporting purposes. This is especially useful when there is an ongoing need to view either parts or aggregates of existing dimensions in a custom view. An example of a custom member is if you want to report on directors and above as a group, but your current ANALYSIS OPTION displays results for each individual manager level.

Custom Members/Sets makes it possible to group together the nodes you want to see results for in an aggregate form, and you can apply it to future queries or reports without having to recreate the view. To access a Custom Member/Set when building a query in Query Workspace, locate the SPECIAL FUNCTIONS folder on the DIMENSIONS list (refer to Figure 13.19). A quick tip is that, to see your Custom Member/Set in the SPECIAL FUNCTIONS folder, you must first make it public by clicking the STATUS button in the MANAGE CUSTOM MEMBERS pane.

In addition to creating custom views for dimensions, you can create custom measures (also known as custom calculations). You create custom measures by dragging and dropping inputs and formula operators (e.g., divided by, plus/minus, etc.) into a designer, and the measure builds itself in real time. All custom measures can be saved for future use in queries and reports by enabling the custom measure to be public (you can also do this by clicking SHARE in the MANAGE CUSTOM CALCULATIONS pane). After your custom measure is public, you can access it in a folder called CUSTOM CALCULATIONS in the QUERY WORKSPACE MEASURE list. One quick tip is to always make sure to validate your formula, which you can do by clicking the VALIDATE button in the MANAGE CUSTOM CALCULATIONS pane. If no errors are detected, the system displays an ALL IS VALID message. Validation becomes an increasingly necessary function throughout the life cycle of the cube and portal as measures and dimensions are added, modified, and occasionally removed as part of the refresh process.

The final component of query workspace we'll cover is folder management, which allows queries to be saved in user-specific folders. It's important to note that all users can edit or access other users' queries, so proper folder management is critical. Queries saved in folders can also be linked to reports in Report Designer, which we'll cover next.

13.3.2 Report Designer

One of the key components of any WFA program is a reporting strategy designed to get key information into decision makers' hands on a regular basis. The WFA tool enables the reporting process by making the creation of reports, and subsequent distribution, much easier to manage than typical reporting tools. The drag-and-drop interface we saw in Query Workspace is also utilized in Report Designer, making the tool very user-friendly. Additionally, clients find that the reporting process is significantly more efficient because the data is automatically refreshed in every report on a monthly basis. Essentially, clients can build one master report and send it pre-sliced to each different business unit every month with minimal effort. The reduced manual effort through this approach can save a significant amount of money in your organization, as well as free up your WFA team to do more strategic analyses. Let's now review the key functionality within the Report Designer.

Accessing Report Designer and Existing Reports

To access the Report Designer tool, a user role must have access granted through the Role-Based Permissions (RBP) framework. Similar to other power user tools, the primary users of Report Designer are the core WFA team. To access the Report Designer, click the REPORT DESIGNER button found on the TOOLS menu in the ANALYTICS pane (refer to Figure 13.16). A new page refreshes, displaying the Report Designer Library, which utilizes a similar folder management system to Query Workspace. All users can create as many reports and folders as they wish; however, report "owners" can restrict other users from modifying your existing reports.

In the Report Designer, you are prompted to select a report from the folders or create a new report. The ANALYTICS pane is replaced with a MANAGE REPORTS section, which is where you find the NEW REPORT button. Figure 13.22 illustrates the initial access page for Report Designer.

The MANAGE REPORTS section in the ANALYTICS pane houses all of the main reporting functions. Beginning with the FILE dropdown menu, you can choose to link reports to the reporting menu, edit ownership of reports, delete reports (either permanently, or put them in the recycle bin if you want to access certain pages again in the future), and edit headers and footers. Next, you can choose to either add a blank page to your report or copy a page from any existing report. The FOL-DER dropdown allows you to manage your folders by creating new folders, naming them, or deleting existing folders.

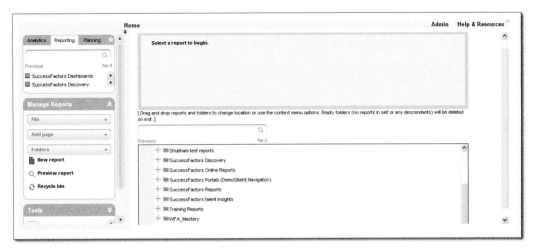

Figure 13.22 Report Designer Access Page

The final button we'll cover in the MANAGE FOLDERS pane is the PREVIEW button, which allows you to view a report on the main site as an end user would experience. This functionality temporarily moves the report out of design mode and allows the report builder to check that the report features are working as expected.

When you click an existing report in a folder, the gray box above the folders populates with key information about the selected report, such as the report owner's name, the number of pages in the report, the last date/time the report was modified and by whom, and whether the report is currently linked to the REPORTING menu. In this view, you can also modify any existing pages in the report you've selected, add new pages to the report, or reorder the pages in the report.

Report Designer Components

Users have complete flexibility in Report Designer to create a multitude of data visualizations, known as components. Components are the building blocks of a report page and can be charts, tables, text, images, or composite queries. All components can be edited to fit a user's preferences, including the font, size, color scheme, and so on. Each of the components has a different purpose that can be used on Report Designer pages, ranging from basic tables to complex queries utilizing formulas and conditional formatting. If you can imagine it, you can build it in Report Designer.

When you add a blank page or copy of an existing page to the report you're building, a new menu appears in the ANALYTICS pane with one tab to add components and a second tab to edit components. Accessing the choices for components is simple because they are all arranged by type in the ADD COMPONENT window, as shown in Figure 13.23.

You'll also notice that there is a new pane below the ADD COMPONENT pane called PAGE PROPERTIES. This is where you can modify the page margins, switch to landscape view, validate that the components on the page are working properly, and enable a grid view to ensure that components are properly aligned.

To edit a component, you must first drag and drop one of the component options onto the page. After you do so, a default image shows up in the component box with demo data to illustrate the type of component you've chosen (e.g., table vs. chart). After you drop the new component onto your page canvas, the ADD COMPONENT menu is replaced by the EDIT COMPONENT menu.

Now you have several options for editing your component, all of which can also be accessed by right-clicking on the component as a shortcut. The EDIT COMPONENT menu, shown in Figure 13.24, allows users to do all normal editing activities, such as changing the chart type (e.g., pie vs. bar chart), changing the color scheme, adding data labels or a legend, and adding a chart/table title. You can create a custom color palette utilizing your corporate colors, which you can later incorporate into charts, reports, and so on.

In addition, you'll notice a [CLICK FOR FULL EDITOR] link. Clicking this link opens a new edit window that includes an option to link your component to an existing query in Query Workspace. This is a great time saver because you don't need to rebuild all queries from scratch for reporting purposes. Also, in the full edit window, you have the option to PREVIEW your component to avoid repeatedly clicking in and out of the editor to make changes. Finally, the copy-and-paste right-click feature works nicely in Report Designer, which can save time editing and formatting components.

Figure 13.23 Add Component Menu

Figure 13.24 Edit Component Menu

Report Distributor

Half the battle of establishing a regular reporting process is automating the report schedule. To eliminate this challenge, the WFA solution has an embedded Report Distributor tool that allows clients to set up "bundles" to be delivered on a regular basis.

The WFA team can determine what information the end user should receive and how often. For example, you may want the CFO to receive a report via email already drilled down to the finance organization on a monthly basis. This feature, which can be found on the TOOLS menu, is a key piece of delivering WFA in a scalable manner across the organization.

Reports can be distributed via FTP or email, or run offline. Word, PowerPoint, and Excel file formats are supported.

In the next section, we'll cover the more advanced analytical tools available in the WFA application.

13.3.3 Analytics Workspace

As your WFA program begins to mature, some analyses might require more powerful statistical analysis tools. The Analytics Workspace feature of the WFA product includes several additional data analysis tools that can be extremely useful for identifying, refining, and visualizing your key findings. Analytics Workspace is controlled through role-based security and is located on the TOOLS menu in the ANALYTICS pane. Note that all queries built in Analytics Workspace can be included in reports built in Report Designer. In this section, we'll give a brief overview of the various tools accessible in Analytics Workspace.

Scatterplots

A scatterplot is a data visualization tool that quantifies a relationship between two measures, or one measure over two time periods, while also analyzing the strength of that relationship through correlation and regression. To access the Scatterplot tool, you must first click the ANALYTICS WORKSPACE tab in the TOOLS menu and then click the SCATTERPLOT graphic. A new page displays a sample scatterplot and, similarly, to other tools within the WFA solution, a user can choose to open an existing query or build a new scatterplot from scratch. When using the Scatterplot tool, you can view only two measures from the same data cube in one query, meaning that measures from different data sources cannot be analyzed together.

Data Highlighting

Data Highlighting is an effective tool for searching through the large amounts of data in WFA. Essentially, this analytical tool allows you to define the parameters of your search, and it returns the results that meet your criteria in a list-based table. The results in the table are drillable, meaning that you can quickly navigate to the measure page for the result you're interested in investigating further.

The data-highlighting functionality is particularly useful when there is a specific issue you're trying to hone in on within your data (e.g., business units with voluntary turnover rates greater than 20%). Additionally, you can add expressions using and/or logic that enables more complex searches and, thus, more refined results.

Significance Testing

While WFA does not require sophisticated statistics to be effective, sometimes there is a need to perform more advanced statistical tests to ensure that the data results are significant. For those well versed in statistics, there is a tool called Significance Testing in the Analytics Workspace that allows users to perform *chi-squared* and *z-tests*. The chi-squared test is used to determine the probability that results are due to chance or whether your results are significant according to the significance level you define (usually 5%). After you have the chi-squared test results, you can choose to perform a z-test to determine whether the results are statistically equivalent for two groups.

Predictive Models

While the Predictive Models tool sits within the Analytics Workspace of the WFA solution, the output is typically leveraged for Strategic Workforce Planning purposes. Essentially, the Predictive Models analytical tool allows organizations to model the relationship of two variables across time, both from a historical perspective and to predict future trends. For example, if you want to determine the impact of sales roles on profitability, the tool shows the historical performance of these metrics against each other, as well as leveraging an underlying algorithm to predict future performance. This becomes useful during the action planning phase of Strategic Workforce Planning to determine which strategies should be implemented to drive specific organizational outcomes.

In addition, the SuccessFactors Workforce Planning solution allows custom demand models to be built in the Predictive Models tool and then uploaded into demand forecasts for more sophisticated analyses. Demand forecasting is covered in more depth in Chapter 14.

Career Trajectory

The newest tool to be added to the suite of tools in Analytics Workspace is Career Trajectory, which maps the path, progression, or line of development for individual employees or groups of employees (e.g., organizational unit or location). The upward mobility or succession of employees can then be set against the desired career path to determine whether they are within the Career Target Zone (where the organization expects people to be at that tenure level). The goal of this analytical tool is to give greater focus for managing career trajectories as part of the succession management and employee development process.

All tools within the WFA solution have associated product documentation and can be found in the HELP & RESOURCES section located in the top-right corner of any screen. In the next section, we'll discuss the newest feature of the WFA solution: Headlines.

13.4   Headlines

The Headlines feature of the WFA solution is aimed at bringing attention to noteworthy findings in your data by presenting them in a common business language (similar to headlines in a newspaper). This innovative feature epitomizes the intuitive aspect of the SuccessFactors HCM suite. With the Headlines tile on the SuccessFactors HOME page, workforce insights can be delivered to HR and business managers, providing insight into the performance of their workforce. While traditional workforce analytics applications require managers to comb through hundreds of data points, Headlines continually mines your data according to the parameters that you define, finds hot spots and pain points that are relevant to subscribers, and pushes alerts to them.

The following sections will delve deeper into this game-changing feature of WFA.

13.4.1 Using Headlines

While traditional analytics solutions serve data, charts, and metrics, Headlines serves true "insights" by interpreting metrics and delivering conclusions in a common business language. Essentially, Headlines is a mobile device–ready SuccessFactors solution that pulls insights from workforce analytic data automatically and pushes them out to managers who need them.

These insights are communicated in simple human language and offer actionable next steps for any critical issue. Users or administrators can decide which metrics to track by subscribing to alerts that are flagged when a metric goes out of bounds. Metrics can be compared to targets, a prior period, or overall company values.

An example of a Headline alert sent to a manager might be, "Your team is losing high-potential employees. Sixty-six exited this month, which is double last month's count," or, "Only 60% of your team has completed training." End users can easily click (or tap, if using a mobile device) to get the details behind the finding to better understand the issue without having to "slice-and-dice."

In addition to giving end users true insight and guided data interpretation in a compelling way, Headlines also provides options for taking action to mitigate the identified risk. At the bottom of a Headlines page, there is a section populated with targeted strategies for how to address the issue at hand, pulled from an embedded strategy bank that encompasses more than 30 years of HR strategies based on client experiences.

The first time you use Headlines, you see a blank page until you add subscriptions. To add a subscription, click the MANAGE SUBSCRIPTIONS link, and a new MY SUBSCRIBED INSIGHTS page refreshes. If you click the blue PLUS button, an ADD CONTENT window pops up, where you can choose from the shared insights that have been defined by your administrator. Users can also deactivate insights in the same window. After you add one or more subscriptions, you see the topmost subscription appear in the HEADLINES tile on your SuccessFactors HOME page. To enable the Headlines tile, go to the ADMIN TOOLS section and click the MANAGE HOME PAGE (under SYSTEM PROPERTIES in the old Admin Tools or COMPANY SETTINGS in OneAdmin). From here, move the Headlines tile to the DEFAULT (always shown on HOME page) or AVAILABLE (available via the TILE BROWSER) tab.

Figure 13.25 shows the HEADLINES tile on the SuccessFactors HOME page and clearly demonstrates how easily HR and managers can quickly learn the details of concerning workforce issues.

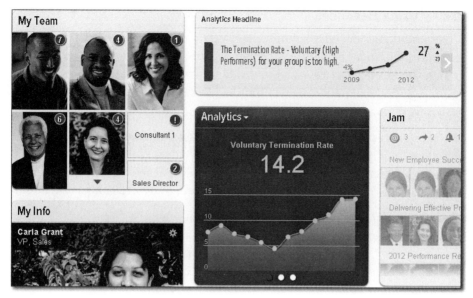

Figure 13.25 Headlines Home Page Tile

13.4.2 Headlines Mobile Integration

The Headlines feature integrates via a mobile tile through the People Insights enhancement in the SuccessFactors HCM Mobile application. There are a few important points to note:

▸ In provisioning for your instance, you need to turn on the People Insights feature.

▸ You also need to load the hybrid YOUCALC tiles into your instance (ADMIN • YOUCALC DASHBOARD MANAGER). These tiles must be uploaded as type Hybrid. After they are uploaded to your instance, you can add them in the People Insight iPad app.

One of the most exciting new features of the Mobile Headlines product is that you can write notes to a colleague on the iPad and send them directly to the other person, as shown in Figure 13.26.

The Headlines feature of the SuccessFactors WFA solution is revolutionizing the way organizations leverage workforce data to make decisions. People managers need more advice, not more data, and Headlines makes this possible by turning complex data into instant, actionable insights.

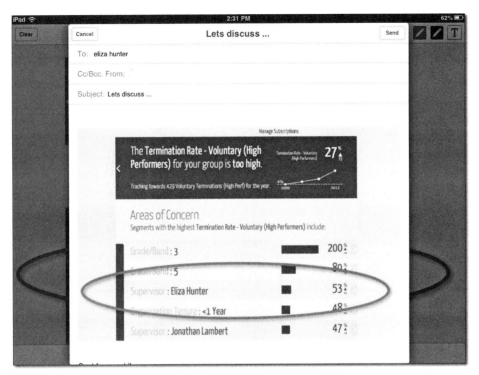

Figure 13.26 Emailing Headlines from an iPad

13.5 Summary

In conclusion, you should now have a thorough understanding of the SuccessFactors WFA solution and how this innovative technology, combined with best practices, helps organizations achieve quantifiable business results. By providing clients with a standardized metrics catalog across the various HR domains and business functions, coupled with powerful and intuitive data analysis tools such as Query Workspace or Analytics Workspace, organizations can begin to uncover the insights in their data that translate into cost savings or increases in revenue. The metric methodology we covered in the beginning of this chapter aids organizations in adhering to the standard definitions and tried-and-true formulas, which in turn allows organizations to communicate metrics in a common language across the business. Further, the Benchmarking program allows clients to make comparisons to external data and is a key differentiator from competitors in the analytics solution marketplace. The Report Designer capability brings all of these data elements together by allowing users to easily create scorecards, dashboards, and standard reports across the business in a scalable and repeatable manner.

Lastly, the Headlines functionality is taking the WFA solution to the next level by acting as an "automated data analyst" that interprets your data, provides guidance on which strategic actions should be considered, and minimizes the time spent discussing data quality while maximizing the time spent on obtaining desirable results. This enhancement has not only made the WFA process more scalable and repeatable, but also reduces the amount of time analysts spend combing through the data, allowing them to perform more value-added activities. The SuccessFactors WFA solution continues to make fact-based decision making a part of HR's day-to-day business operations, which is the ultimate goal of WFA.

In the next chapter, we'll cover the five-step SuccessFactors methodology for Strategic Workforce Planning (SWFP). In conjunction with the theory behind WFP, we'll provide an in-depth review of the SuccessFactors WFP technology from both a Strategic Workforce Planning and Operational Planning standpoint.

Organizations often overlook the necessity of strategically planning their human capital to meet the needs of the business in the future, and the result is often expensive interventions to fill talent gaps. SuccessFactors Workforce Planning provides the tools to ensure that organizational strategy can be executed with the right skills, in the right place, at the right time, and at the right cost.

14 Workforce Planning

Strategic Workforce Planning (SWFP) is a process-based business planning activity that often gets overlooked, despite its clear importance in enabling execution of business strategy with the proper staffing of underlying talent management initiatives, now and into the future. Although SWFP has been steadily practiced for more than 30 years in other regions of the world, such as Asia-Pacific and Europe, it's still an emerging discipline in North America. Even when utilized as a regular step in the strategic planning process, SWFP often results in plans for the near term, rather than looking at whether the organization has the right talent infrastructure in place to meet future demand. Without modeling capabilities, organizations rely primarily on "gut feelings" to make long-term strategic decisions, and more often than not, the resulting plan isn't an accurate representation of the future landscape and doesn't leverage the wealth of historical workforce data that resides in the organization's HCM system.

SuccessFactors Workforce Planning (WFP) provides a platform and proven process to aid organizations in proactively planning for the types of business challenges associated with critical talent shortages and surpluses. In effect, the solution facilitates the process of matching workforce supply with workforce demand to determine where talent gaps exist and provides the ability to forecast and model changes to the workforce across the business. The tool also highlights risks, capability and skill gaps, cost modeling, and best-practice strategies to successfully execute strategy and plan action for the long term.

While SWFP is primarily focused on the next three, five, and ten years, it's still crucial for organizations to operationalize Year 1 and Year 2 of the workforce plan. Consequently, the SuccessFactors WFP solution includes an embedded Operational Planning tool to supplement the SWFP process.

The Workforce Planning application is an extension of the SuccessFactors Workforce Analytics (WFA) module and is fed underlying data from that WFA engine for planning purposes. In addition, the WFA module plays a key role in the ongoing monitoring and reporting of critical areas of the business, which is the final step in the SWFP process. In this chapter, we'll cover the basic methodology and theory behind SWFP, as well as the key functionality within the SuccessFactors WFP application for both Strategic and Operational Workforce Planning. This includes an in-depth review of the key activities in SWFP, such as demand and supply forecasting and gap analysis (see Section 14.3), risk identification and action planning (see Section 14.4), and what-if financial modeling (see Section 14.5).

14.1 Defining Strategic Workforce Planning

Let's begin by defining SWFP as it is mirrored in the SuccessFactors WFP tool. Essentially, SWFP entails creating a process that works for your organization to make sure that you have the right people in the right place with the right skills at the right time, and all for the right price. In theory, if you're doing all of these things properly, you can execute your business strategy successfully and proactively mitigate risks along the way.

People tend to have different ideas about SWFP and define it differently in their individual organizations (e.g., some organizations consider staffing, budgeting, and headcount planning to be SWFP). However, at its core, the process helps companies understand what is going to happen to workforce supply and demand across a three- to five-year timeframe (typically) and how that will impact the organization's strategic plan. On a related note, it's important to understand what SWFP is *not*: it's not short-term resource planning to fill open headcount, and it's not succession planning for named resources.

In general, organizations tend to be better at considering the right place and time when planning for future demand, but they place less emphasis on the right skills and the right price. With SWFP, you start to ask questions such as the following:

▶ Do we know what skills we'll need in the future?

▶ Do we have sufficient quantities?

- If so, where are they located in the organization (e.g., which business units or job roles)?
- If not, can we build or borrow them, or do we need to buy them from the external labor market?
- Can we buy them, or is there a shortage of that particular skill in the external labor market?

When you're thinking about price, there are many paths that lead to having the right people with the right skills in the right place at the right time. However, the challenge is figuring out which mix is most cost effective. In other words, can you answer what your traditional approach costs versus what the alternatives would cost—in both the short term and the long term?

To answer questions like these, organizations need a proven process to guide strategic decision making. Essentially, SWFP focuses on making decisions that will have the most impact, which means making a decision about what you will and will not do. The end goal of SWFP is to move away from firefighting mode to being more proactive about planning for the workforce.

To summarize, the aim of SWFP is to reduce business strategy execution risks associated with workforce capacity, capability, and flexibility. SWFP is an ongoing process to identify the workforce needs for the future that allows organizations to identify the gap between demand and supply for talent, both in terms of capacity and capabilities. Possibly the most important outcome of the SWFP process is that it provides a view of the degree of business risk the organization is facing—or in other words, the magnitude of the gaps. Lastly, it's a plan to inform business decision making and assign action and accountability. SWFP is the process of answering the "how" with scenario planning, creating demand and supply forecasts to assess the gap(s), forecasting the critical skills and capabilities needed in future roles, and financial modeling to help drive action. In this chapter, we'll cover each of these steps in greater detail.

14.2   The Five Steps of SuccessFactors Workforce Planning

SuccessFactors WFA provides the foundation for the data used in SuccessFactors WFP and supplies the following core data elements:

- ▸ Headcount

- ▸ External hires

- ▸ Terminations

- ▸ Retirements

- ▸ Movements (e.g., promotions and transfers)

In addition, the WFP tool utilizes the same organizational structures and analysis options available on the WFA site to allow users to create meaningful forecasts for critical areas of the organization or critical job roles. Clients can access the WFP application by clicking the PLANNING tab within the ANALYTICS pane on any page within the WFA application, as shown at the top left of Figure 14.1.

Figure 14.1 Accessing the SuccessFactirs WFP Application

Because the SuccessFactors WFP application is part of the acquired Infohrm technology (explained in Chapter 14), the product mirrors the Infohrm five-step SWFP methodology:

1. Strategic analysis

2. Forecasting

3. Risk analysis

4. Strategy, impact, and cost modeling

5. Actions and accountability

The five-step process flow can be seen on the HOME screen of the WFP application, as shown in Figure 14.2. Note that, in the past few years, SuccessFactors has updated the methodology to include a "pre-step" that is known as the Workforce Planning Foundations and shown at the base of the staircase. While this isn't an actual step in the process, it was added to act as a blueprint to ensure that clients have the critical data elements (e.g., job family framework) and support mechanisms in place before kicking off the SWFP process.

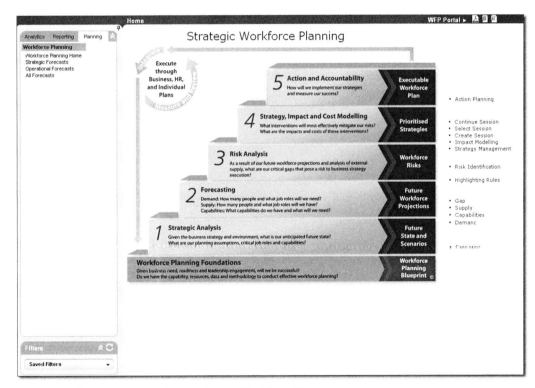

Figure 14.2 The Home Screen of SuccessFactors Workforce Planning

The WFP tool acts as a wizard, taking users through each of the steps to consolidate the qualitative and quantitative data in one forecast for a complete yet simplified analysis. Because SWFP is very much a qualitative process, much of the information is collected in workshop- or interview-style settings and then input into the tool. In addition, the HELP button located at the top of every screen is populated with valuable information about tips and tricks for navigating the tool and populating the various tabs throughout the WFP process.

Let's walk through each of the phases, beginning with how to create a forecast in WFP.

14.2.1 Forecast List

The first entry point in the WFP tool is the *forecast list*, which can be accessed on the PLANNING tab in the ANALYTICS pane on your WFA HOME page (refer to Figure 14.1). Within the PLANNING tab, there are a few options:

▸ WORKFORCE PLANNING HOME
▸ STRATEGIC FORECASTS
▸ OPERATIONAL FORECASTS
▸ ALL FORECASTS

For the purposes of this example, we'll look at how to access an existing strategic forecast or build a new one from scratch. When you click the STRATEGIC FORECASTS link, a new page refreshes that shows all previously built strategic forecasts, as shown in the center of Figure 14.3.

From here, you can edit or copy an existing forecast by clicking the EDIT dropdown, or you can build a new forecast from scratch by clicking the NEW dropdown. The forecast details for the selected forecast are shown on the right-hand side of the screen, in the SUMMARY window. Directly below the SUMMARY window is another box called EXPLORE FORECAST, which contains quick links to the various phases of the five-step methodology (see Figure 14.3). Also, each forecast within the list is color coded, with green denoting a completely built forecast, yellow indicating that the forecast is in the process of being built, and gray indicating incomplete forecasts.

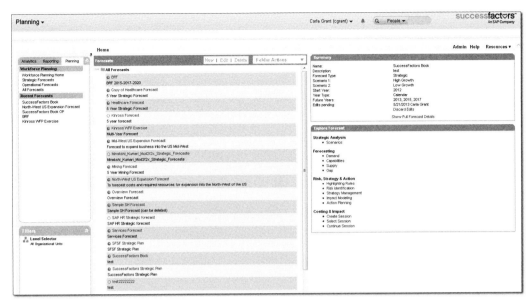

Figure 14.3 Strategic Forecast List

Users can build as many forecasts as they like, but keep in mind that all users can see all forecasts. The WFP tool does give administrators the ability to determine what level of access users of the system will have—either full access for building forecasts (power users) or a more limited WFP role that allows users only to modify the demand or supply numbers of existing forecasts.

In the next section, we'll walk through the steps of building a new strategic forecast.

14.2.2 Creating a Strategic Forecast

Within the WFP solution, strategic plans are called *forecasts* and fall into three types of forecasts:

▸ Strategic forecast (two or more years into the future)

▸ Operational forecast (six months to 48 months into the future)

▸ Amalgamate strategic forecast (combine separate strategic forecasts into one)

After a forecast type is selected, a new window opens with six main tabs, which are outlined in the chevron process flow at the top of the screen, as shown in Figure 14.4. These six steps to build a strategic forecast include defining all data elements that will be analyzed, as well as the future scenarios that we'll plan against:

1. FORECAST BASICS

2. SET SCENARIOS

3. SET DIMENSIONS

4. SET RETIREMENTS

5. SET STRUCTURE

6. BUILD

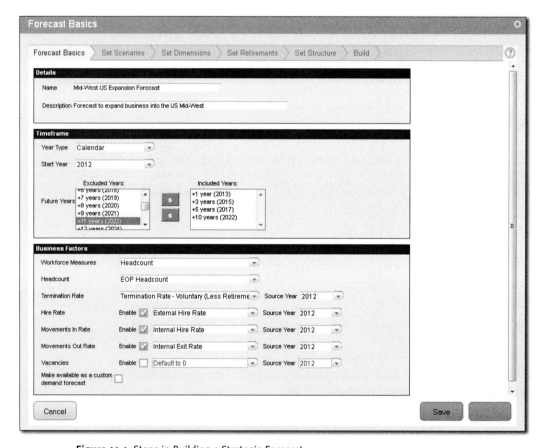

Figure 14.4 Steps in Building a Strategic Forecast

Let's walk through an example of how to build a strategic forecast for a company expanding its retail operations.

Forecast Basics

Again, the first step of creating a strategic forecast is to provide the basic information for the forecast, which you can do by clicking the NEW button and selecting NEW STRATEGIC FORECAST. Doing so causes a new window to appear with the title FORECAST BASICS, and you're prompted to enter the details and factors of your forecast. Essentially, the information in the following sections and fields is the backbone of your workforce plan (refer to Figure 14.4):

▶ DETAILS
Name and description of your forecast

▶ TIMEFRAME
Year type (calendar or fiscal), start year, and future years you'll be forecasting against

▶ BUSINESS FACTORS
Headcount or full-time equivalent (FTE), termination rate, hire rate, movements-in rate, movements-out rate, and vacancies

Starting with the DETAILS section, you're prompted to enter the name and description for the forecast. Additionally, you have the option of switching between fiscal and calendar years in the YEAR TYPE dropdown. Please note that you must have fiscal years configured as a dimension in the WFA application for this to appear as an option in the YEAR TYPE dropdown.

The next window is the TIMEFRAME, where you must define the number of years your forecast will include. For the START YEAR field, clients typically select the default option, which shows the current year (in this case, 2012). As an example, for FUTURE YEARS, you select the values +1 YEAR (2013), +3 YEARS (2015), and +5 YEARS (2017), which means you want to identify any significant risks/gaps in your forecast for next year, within three years, and, finally, in five years' time. If you double-click the year, it moves to the INCLUDED YEARS window.

The next section that must be populated is the BUSINESS FACTORS, where you choose which underlying measures the tool will leverage from the WFA application. This information is used mainly to populate the SUPPLY tab with predictions on headcount, terminations, hires, movements, and vacancies based on historical data. For instance, users can choose to forecast against end-of-period (EOP) headcount or FTE, depending on how headcount is reported in their organization. This section of the WFP tool must be configured to show the measures that you want to make available for users to choose from.

Additionally, different termination measures can be configured to choose from in the TERMINATION RATE dropdown (refer to Figure 14.4). Typically, forecasts leverage the voluntary termination rate (minus retirements) measure as the standard. The reason this is the most common slice of termination rate for SWFP purposes is that retirements are broken out, which allows users to define the retirement logic in the SET RETIREMENTS tab (covered later in this section).

Another custom termination measure that is commonly used in SWFP is a three-year rolling voluntary termination rate average. This type of measure allows users to take an average over a set number of years, eliminating the possibility of skewing the forecasted terminations due to an unusually high year of turnover.

The additional measures that can be enabled for the forecast are movements in, movements out, external hires, and vacancies. The external hire rate is generally included; however, best practice states that movement data (e.g., promotions and transfers) should be incorporated in the forecast only if there is a clearly defined career path program for the specific job roles you're planning against. The reasoning here is that, in this phase, you're defining the available talent supply that you expect to have over the forecast period (here, five years). Therefore, you include movement data only if you can predict how many employees in a specific job role will be moving through the career path program by the end of the forecast period, meaning that they are available talent to source for filling identified gaps. Lastly, the VACANCIES field can be enabled only if a client has configured the WFA tool to include vacancy rates.

For all data elements after the termination rate, users have the option to leverage the underlying WFA data for that specific measure (e.g., external hire rate) or *default to zero*. The premise behind defaulting to zero is called *zero-based forecasting* and essentially allows you to start with a clean slate for forecasting supply. This is a commonly used method because, in theory, organizations can't count on supply from external hiring (or movements) that has not yet happened, and by defaulting to zero, the tool doesn't forecast out predicted hires based on historical patterns. Instead, a user can choose to manually override the zero that is input by the tool, which makes sense for roles that don't have a shortage in the external labor market.

The final piece to consider when filling out the BUSINESS FACTORS section of the forecast is the source year for each data element. Next to each measure, there is a dropdown list called SOURCE YEAR, which shows all the previous years of historical data that are captured in the WFA application. Using the external hire rate as an example, if you select 2011 as the source year, the tool leverages the 2011 external hire rate as a baseline to predict the number of hires for the next five years. However, if 2011 was an unusual year in terms of hires, you might decide to use 2008 as a baseline instead because it was a more "normal" year to represent the organization's hiring patterns.

After you've entered these details, the screen should look like Figure 14.5.

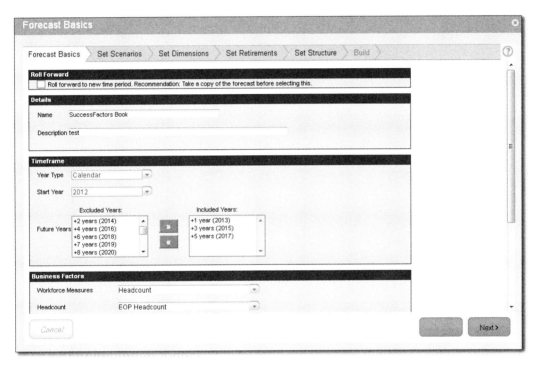

Figure 14.5 Completed Forecast Basics

After you fill out the necessary information, click the SAVE button, and then click the NEXT button to advance to the next tab (SET SCENARIOS).

Set Scenarios

Defining plausible future states, known as scenarios, is a key step in the SWFP process, and it typically takes place in a workshop setting with key business leaders and workforce planners. At this stage of the process, the key stakeholder group comes together to discuss the strategy of their areas of the business in relation to the overall company strategy for the forecast period. The objective is to identify a set of unknowns that could potentially affect demand for the critical talent necessary to execute strategy. Simply stated, scenarios are an articulation of what you predict will significantly impact the business during the forecast period.

We develop robust scenarios for the following reasons:

▶ To understand the drivers of demand to estimate the future demand for labor

▶ To help identify critical job roles

▶ To get risks/issues out in the open, including workforce capacity and capability

▶ To understand the organizational strategy in conjunction with the drivers of change, with a focus on the talent impacts

During scenario planning, the focus is mainly on external business factors that are outside of the organization's control (e.g., regulations, politics, socioeconomic factors, etc.). In addition, because the goal is to limit the number of scenarios to a maximum of three, scenarios should be plausible, rather than possible. Often, organizations start the SWFP process with a "steady-state" scenario, meaning the demand doesn't change throughout the forecast period. Essentially, the purpose of the steady-state scenario is to show the members of the organization where they will be at the end of the forecast period if they do nothing, which can be a very powerful message. The final step of scenario planning is to obtain sign-off on the scenarios that will be included for forecast purposes.

Because setting scenarios is entirely text-based, the WFP tool allows users to enter qualitative descriptions of the scenarios. This plays a key role in helping your demand forecasters understand the business goals for the next few years, so the level of granularity is important here. The more detail you can give in each scenario, the easier the job of the demand forecaster is when they are determining how many people with what skills they are going to need to be successful in the future.

As an example, let's create a common set of two scenarios, one for high growth and a second for low growth. As shown in Figure 14.6, the SET SCENARIOS tab has SCENARIO 1 entered as the default.

If you click SCENARIO 1, a new window opens where you can enter the details and comments that are critical to capture from the scenario planning session. In this window, you can rename the scenario and give a short optional description, so let's change the name to "High Growth." You can add any information that will be helpful to consider during the demand forecasting process into the accompanying text box. Lastly, you can add assumptions common to all scenarios, which are defined as factors that are likely to happen regardless of either scenario's playing out.

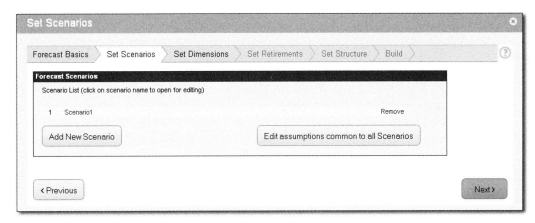

Figure 14.6 The Set Scenarios Step of Creating a Strategic Forecast

After the High Growth scenario is defined, click the SAVE button, and repeat the process for Scenario 2 by clicking the ADD SCENARIO button. When all scenarios are entered, click NEXT to advance to the SET DIMENSIONS tab. After your forecast is built, all scenarios can be accessed on the STRATEGIC ANALYSIS tab in the tool.

Set Dimensions

The third step of building a forecast is to set *dimensions*. In this step, you can add multiple *dimensions*, which is how you define the critical population that you'll be forecasting against. This is where you determine what those critical jobs roles are and how you're going to analyze them. The most commonly used dimensions for SWFP are job family, grade, and critical job role. Essentially, you're segmenting the critical population that you've previously identified as at risk over the forecast period. Typically, this is referred to as the Critical Role Identification process and is completed during the initial planning workshops.

For this example, let's say that you're planning for job roles in specific job families, and you want to analyze those that have been marked as critical. When you click the ADD DIMENSION button, a list of available dimensions that have been configured for the WFP tool populates in a dropdown list, and you add JOB FAMILY. The dimension populates with the various nodes that have been defined. Users can select or deselect specific nodes to be included in the forecast by highlighting them or choose to include all nodes by checking the CLICK ON A NODE'S NAME TO SELECT IT AND ALL OF ITS DESCENDANTS ONE LEVEL BELOW checkbox in the NODE selection window. In this specific example, select all nodes within the JOB FAMILY dimension.

You still need to add a second dimension for CRITICAL ROLES, which you can do by clicking the ADD DIMENSION button. In this example, you want to include only employees marked YES (critical), and not employees that are marked NO (not critical) or UNALLOCATED employees, so highlight only the YES node, as shown in Figure 14.7.

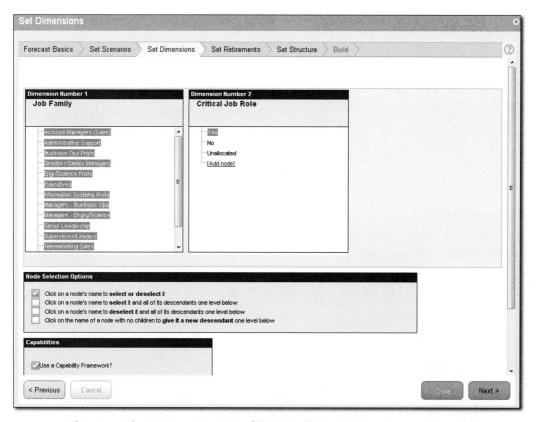

Figure 14.7 The Set Dimensions Step of Creating a Strategic Forecast

All dimensions have an [ADD NODE] link at the bottom of the node list. This is for users to create a placeholder for anticipated future nodes that don't exist yet. For example, under JOB FAMILY, you may not have an existing job family today for a job that you know will be critical in the future, but you can create a place to capture that in your forecast here in the SET DIMENSIONS tab. Because there are no employees in the JOB FAMILY today, there is no underlying data associated with the new node.

Finally, the order of the dimensions is important because this is how they appear on your demand spreadsheet. Simply click the red left or right arrows to move certain dimensions up or down in the order list. To delete a dimension, click the red REMOVE X.

One final tip in the SET DIMENSIONS tab is that if you scroll to the bottom of the window, you see the option to choose whether to leverage a *capability framework*. By checking the USE A CAPABILITY FRAMEWORK? checkbox, you have the ability to forecast by capabilities (also known as skills, competencies, etc.), as well as build a rating scale to rate the current and future skill levels of employees in critical job roles. If you build your forecast without selecting this checkbox, you'll be unable to enter capability demands in the forecasting section of the tool.

The WFP tool does come with an embedded capability framework, which can be selected as the default in the SELECT A FRAMEWORK dropdown. However, most clients opt to enter an organization-specific capability framework into the tool instead. To create a new capability framework, select the CREATE A NEW FRAMEWORK option in the SELECT A FRAMEWORK dropdown.

Next, you're prompted to choose an importance scale, which can be either a five- or ten-point scale. Typically, the five-point scale will suffice, although both options are available. The rating scale also includes both a five- and ten-point option. For both, select the FIVE-POINT SCALES. We'll cover how to enter a custom capability framework and assign values to the rating scales in Section 14.3.1. Click SAVE and then NEXT to move to the next step, which is to set the retirement profile.

Set Retirements

The set retirements step allows you to define the *retirement profile(s)* that can be applied to your critical job roles in the SET RETIREMENTS tab. The default retirement profile is set to NOT SET, and you can define it by selecting the EDIT DEFAULT RETIREMENT PROFILE button in the DEFAULT RETIREMENT PROFILE section. There are two options for defining the retirement profile: FIXED RETIREMENT AGE or MATHEMATI-CAL APPROXIMATION.

The FIXED RETIREMENT AGE option allows a fixed value to be defined for the retirement age. For example, if you know based on historical data that employees in Job Role X typically retire by age 68, you can set this age as the cutoff.

The second option, MATHEMATICAL APPROXIMATION, shows the curved line progression of retirements by defining the start and end age of the retirement wave. Users can either show this in a STRAIGHT LINE or EXPONENTIAL CURVE, with EXPONENTIAL CURVE being the typical selection. From here, you can select the START AGE from the dropdown menu and define the END AGE, as well. The last option is to enable the USE CUTOFF AGE checkbox, which says that all employees will retire by age X. As you change your retirement model criteria, the chart at the bottom of the window updates with a graphical representation of your selection showing the rate at which you can expect employees to retire.

For this example, we chose to enable the MATHEMATICAL APPROXIMATION model with the EXPONENTIAL CURVE, with a START AGE of 65 and an END AGE of 75, as shown in Figure 14.8.

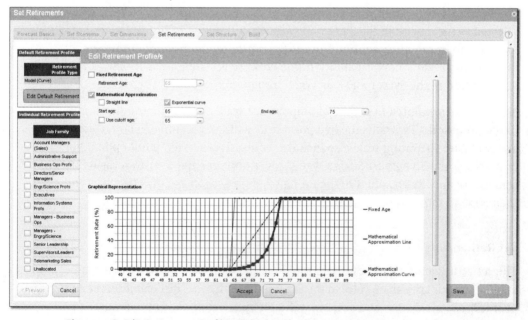

Figure 14.8 Edit Retirement Profile/s Screen in the Set Retirements Step

In addition to defining the general retirement model, you can set individual retirement profiles for specific job roles in your forecast, which overrides the default retirement model for only the job roles that you assign, as shown in Figure 14.9. This becomes very useful when you're forecasting for a job such as an airplane pilot, wherein there are regulations specifying the specific age when pilots must retire. You can set individual retirement profiles at the job family level by checking the box next to the job family and clicking EDIT SELECTED RETIREMENT PROFILE/S at the bottom of the window.

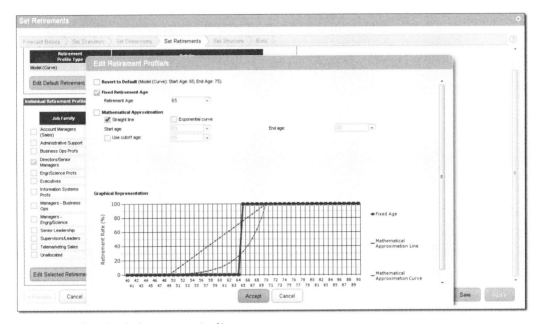

Figure 14.9 Edit Individual Retirement Profiles

As an example, let's create an individual retirement profile for the directors/ senior manager job family. One reason this might be necessary is that your company has a contractual retirement age of 65, and therefore, you don't want to include any employees who meet this criteria in your supply forecast.

In the INDIVIDUAL RETIREMENT PROFILES section, select the checkbox for the DIRECTORS/SENIOR MANAGERS JOB FAMILY, and select the EDIT SELECTED RETIREMENT PROFILE/S button. Enter the EDIT RETIREMENT PROFILE/S screen, and change the FIXED RETIREMENT AGE value to 65. Note that this is the same screen that you used to set the default retirement profile. After clicking ACCEPT to confirm the change, you can see the new retirement model for the DIRECTORS/SENIOR MANAGER JOB FAMILY shown in Figure 14.10.

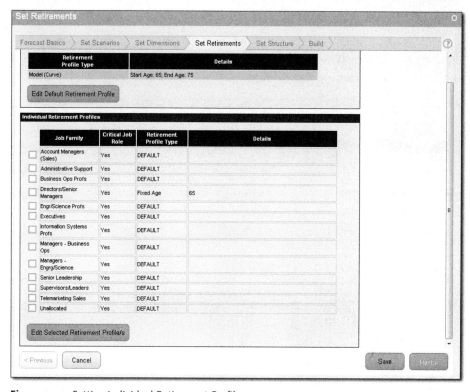

Figure 14.10 Setting Individual Retirement Profile

Click SAVE and then click NEXT, and the tool moves to the next tab: SET STRUCTURE.

Set Structure

In the SET STRUCTURE tab, you can define the organizational structure for your forecast. As defined in Chapter 14, clients can have multiple organizational hierarchies, such as cost center structures, supervisor rollups, or location structures. Depending on how the organization reports workforce data, users can choose to apply the structure that most closely represents how the business views the organization.

When you click the STRUCTURE dropdown arrow, all available structures are displayed, but only one can be selected. The most common hierarchy is the organizational unit structure; select it by clicking the name.

As an example, let's say you are expanding your retail operation into the Midwest region of the United States. First, click the plus (+) button to expand the top node of the organizational structure called ALL ORGANIZATIONAL UNITS. From here, expand the RETAIL level, and select RETAIL and all departments located one level below, which are denoted by red icons to the left of each node, as shown in Figure 14.11. Also, all existing hierarchies show a link node called ADD LEVEL, which is used to create a node for a business unit, cost center, location, and so on that doesn't exist today but that you predict will exist in the future.

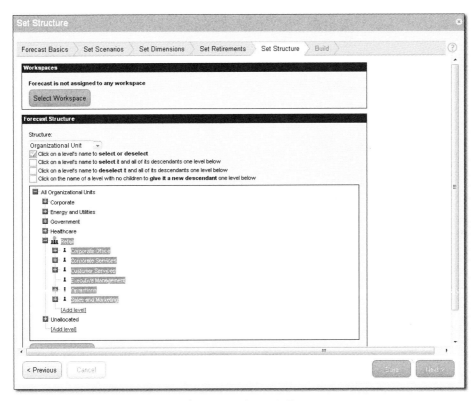

Figure 14.11 The Set Structure Step of Creating a Strategic Forecast

At the bottom of the SET STRUCTURE tab, you'll see the SUMMATION LEVEL EDITING ENABLED checkbox. By clicking this checkbox, users can edit the total level (top level) of the forecast. While all forecast data entered at the business unit or depart-ment level automatically rolls up to the top-level node selected, sometimes it's necessary to edit at the total level, as well. It's important to take this step at this stage of the process because it can't be enabled after the forecast is built. Check the box, click SAVE, and then click NEXT to advance to the final tab.

Build Forecast

The final step of building the forecast is to verify your forecast selections and cre-ate the forecast using the BUILD FORECAST button. Figure 14.12 shows the final overview prior to the creation of the forecast. Until the build is complete, your forecast has a yellow dot next to it in the STRATEGIC FORECASTS list. After the fore-cast build is complete, you receive an email notification, and the dot turns green in the STRATEGIC FORECASTS list.

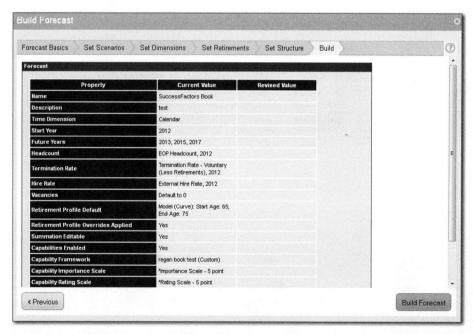

Figure 14.12 The Build Step of Creating a Strategic Forecast

After the forecast is created, you're taken back to the STRATEGIC FORECASTS screen. If you try to edit the forecast after you've clicked BUILD, you see a red note at the top of each tab that reads, "This forecast already has data attached to it. Changes will not take effect until after a rebuild."

On the right-hand side of the Forecast List screen, you can see an overall summary of what you've selected, as shown in Figure 14.13. To summarize, you're looking at two different scenarios (high growth vs. low growth), and you're starting in the 2012 calendar year and forecasting out for 2013, 2015, and 2017. Finally, you're analyzing job family by critical roles for the retail business unit and incorporating the 2012 voluntary termination rate (minus retirements).

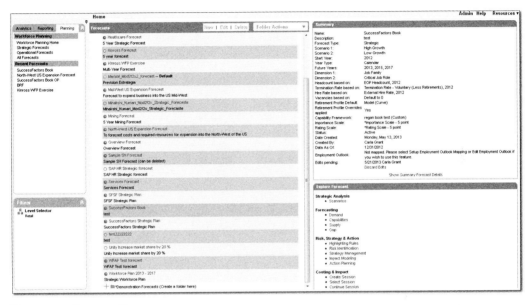

Figure 14.13 Summary View

Now that the forecast has been built, we'll cover the forecasting step in the SWFP process.

14.3 Forecasting

Forecasting is the process of evaluating scenarios to identify any gaps between your existing talent pool and the optimal organizational mix of people and skills that will be needed in the future. In SWFP, forecasting is generally broken down into two separate steps: *demand forecasting* (includes both capability and capacity forecasting) and *supply forecasting*.

14.3.1 Demand Forecasting

Forecasting demand is the process of determining the number of people you'll need in each of the critical job roles that have been identified under each scenario. Critical job roles are defined as those that do the following:

- Conduct the core business of the organization
- May become part of the core business under either scenario
- Have had a high number of vacancies in the past 12 months
- Have been historically difficult to fill
- Require a long training time to develop the skills for the role
- Have the largest number of staff

From a demand standpoint, directors/managers who have expert knowledge of the business are asked to forecast how many people they will need in each critical job role over the next one, three, and five years to meet the demand of each scenario (high growth vs. low growth).

In addition, many organizations forecast demand in terms of not only the number of people needed, but also the specific capabilities that will be necessary to execute the organizational strategy. In *capability forecasting*, you're looking to differentiate between skills needed today and those that will be needed in the future.

Typically, the process of determining demand is done in a demand workshop setting or through a series of demand interviews. Lastly, the demand forecasting should be zero-based to estimate demand as if you're starting from scratch. However, it's helpful to understand the current headcount of each critical job role to give forecasters a frame of reference in terms of the amount of growth or downsizing that needs to occur.

After you've collected your demand numbers by critical job role, you can enter the forecast into the WFP tool. To navigate to the FORECASTING screen, select the DEMAND link under the FORECASTING heading in the EXPLORE FORECAST section (refer to Figure 14.13).

When you enter the DEMAND screen, you first see a graphical representation of your demand forecast. Because we haven't yet input any demand numbers, the tool automatically assumes a steady-state forecast. This means simply that the demand for each job family over the five-year forecast period remains the same as the starting headcount in 2012 (the beginning year of our forecast). Figure 14.14 shows the steady-state demand forecast for the RETAIL business unit.

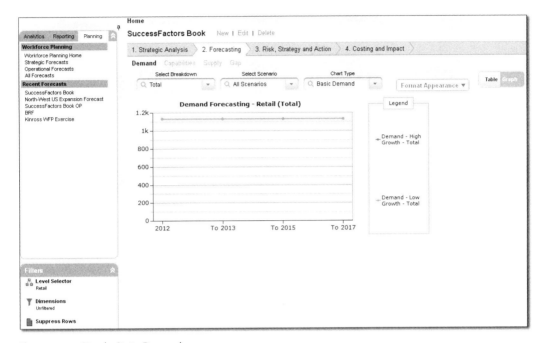

Figure 14.14 Steady-State Demand

When you click the TABLE/GRAPH toggle button, the demand forecast is also shown as a table. In the table view, you can modify the demand numbers for each critical job family, scenario, and year of the forecast. The demand page view can be customized to show the data elements or cuts that are of specific interest (e.g., only one scenario, only the first two years, etc.). Similarly, if you want to focus on only one department at a time, you can do so by clicking the LEVEL SELECTOR in the FILTER pane and selecting a specific node.

Let's say you want to forecast demand for CUSTOMER SERVICES and select this node only. Figure 14.15 shows the new demand forecast for each critical job family within only the CUSTOMER SERVICES department. Users can export this demand forecast to Excel by clicking the EXCEL icon in the top-left corner of the spreadsheet (also shown in Figure 14.15). By providing this customized view to Customer Services managers, they can more easily forecast demand for their critical job families (as opposed to seeing the entire Retail business unit). After the head-count demand is finalized by managers for the Customer Services department, you can upload the revised demand forecast into the WFP tool by clicking the Upload (Import from Excel) link, eliminating much of the manual data entry.

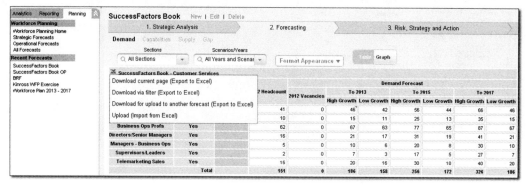

Figure 14.15 Export Demand for Customer Services Department

If a demand forecaster's preference is to modify the demand numbers directly in the WFP tool, you can simply click a cell and manually override the existing entry in a new window called Edit Values, as shown in Figure 14.16.

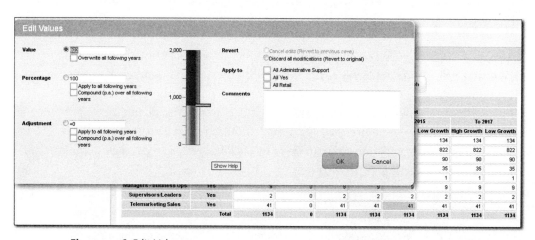

Figure 14.16 Edit Values

Forecasters repeat the process for each critical job family, under each scenario, for each year until the forecast is complete. Often, it's helpful to enter comments in the Edit Values window so that others can quickly understand a forecaster's logic for the demand estimates. This becomes especially useful when you revisit demand forecasts a year or so after the SWFP process is completed and modify or update the demand numbers.

For the Customer Services department example, let's say you want to add +5 headcount and compound this number year over year for each critical job family in the high-growth scenario. For the low-growth scenario, you add +1 headcount compounded over the forecast years. Note that this is for example's sake only, and in an actual demand forecast, the numbers would not necessarily follow a straight linear increase. To make these changes, click the 2013 High Growth cell, check the Adjustment option, change the value to +5, and then check the Compound over all following years option. Repeat the same process for the low-growth scenario, only adding +1 to the value.

After you've accepted all changes, the edited cells display a red font, and you must click Save to move to the next step. If a forecaster enters a comment while editing a value, that cell has a red icon in the top-right corner, which denotes that there is a comment attached. After the demand forecast is saved, the comment icon turns green, and all cell fonts revert back to black, as shown in Figure 14.17.

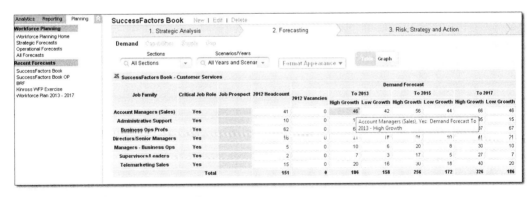

Figure 14.17 Edited Customer Services Forecast

If you toggle back to the Graph view of the demand forecast, you can visualize how the different demand forecasts vary for each scenario. Figure 14.18 shows the graphical representation of the demand forecasts for Customer Services.

Figure 14.18 Customer Services Demand Graphs

Now that the demand forecast is entered for Customer Services, we can move to the next link in the FORECASTING tab called CAPABILITIES. This tab is available only if you've enabled the capability framework when building your forecast.

14.3.2 Capabilities

When you click the CAPABILITY link, a new screen refreshes that shows each critical job family with no capabilities attached, as shown in Figure 14.19.

The first step is to click the empty cell called [NO CAPABILITIES SPECIFIED] and assign the capabilities for each critical job role that will be important over the forecast period. A new window called EDIT CAPABILITIES opens; if you've entered a capability framework, it is displayed here for you to select. To enter a capability framework, click the EDIT dropdown at the top of the page, and select EDIT CAPABILITIES. A new window opens that allows you to add a two-level framework, as well as customize the importance and rating scales. If your organization does not have an organization-specific capability framework, capabilities can be added on the fly in the CAPABILITY tab. Let's walk through an example of how to add a communication capability to the directors/senior manager's job family.

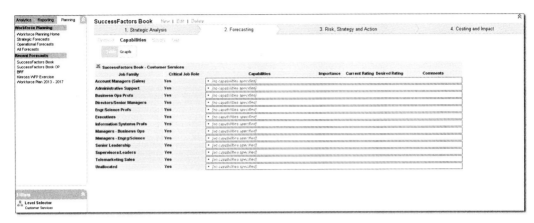

Figure 14.19 Customer Services Capabilities

First, click the empty [NO CAPABILITIES SPECIFIED] row corresponding to the DIRECTORS/SENIOR MANAGERS JOB FAMILY, which causes a new window to appear that doesn't have any capabilities listed to assign. Click OPEN CAPABILITY EDITOR, and click ADD to enter the COMMUNICATION capability (see Figure 14.20). Click OK, and then click SAVE; the editing window closes, and you are taken back to the main CAPABILITY tab.

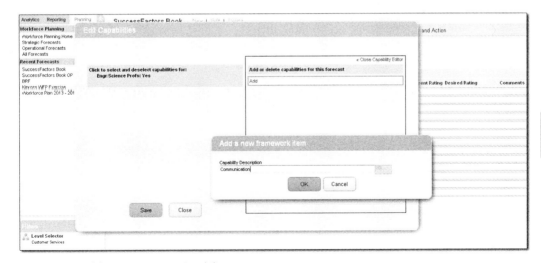

Figure 14.20 Add Communication Capability

Now, when you click [NO CAPABILITIES SPECIFIED] for the DIRECTORS/SENIOR MANAGERS JOB FAMILY, COMMUNICATION is an available capability to choose, and it turns green with a checkmark, signifying that it has been successfully applied.

The next step is to assign an importance rating to the COMMUNICATION capability for DIRECTORS/SENIOR MANAGERS by clicking the empty cell in the IMPORTANCE column. Because you've built the forecast with a five-point rating scale, you can assign a value ranging from 1—NOT AT ALL IMPORTANT to 5—EXTREMELY IMPORTANT to the COMMUNICATION capability, which denotes how critical the capability will be at the end of the forecast period. For directors/senior managers, communication is a very important capability, so assign the highest value (5—EXTREMELY IMPORTANT).

You're also prompted to enter ratings of the capability in this window, which is intended to show the gap between the directors'/senior managers' current communication capability level and the desired communication level by the end of the forecast period (e.g., 2017). For directors/senior managers, enter the CURRENT RATING at 4—ABOVE AVERAGE. However, you want them to be at the highest possible level by 2017, so select 5—EXCELLENT as the DESIRED RATING. You can also enter comments about the importance and ratings you've assigned.

Figure 14.21 shows the completed capabilities table for the DIRECTORS/SENIOR MANAGERS JOB FAMILY. Multiple capabilities can be added to each job family and, similar to other tabs in the WFP tool, the capability spreadsheet can be exported to Excel. Users can also toggle between a table and graph view.

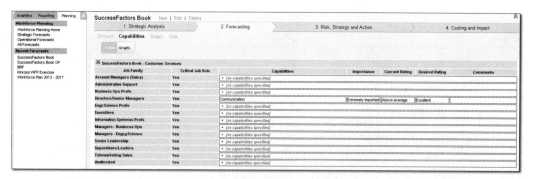

Figure 14.21 Completed Capability Row

Now that we've walked through how to forecast capabilities, let's discuss supply forecasting, which you can access by clicking the SUPPLY link.

14.3.3 Supply Forecasting

Supply forecasting is where you leverage the measures taken from the underlying analytics engine, meaning that the tool is applying historical rates to forecast estimates for terminations, hires, movements, and vacancies (depending on what you enabled while building the forecast). Similar to the DEMAND tab, when you click SUPPLY, the first screen shows a graphical representation of supply for each critical job family over the forecast period. By clicking the TABLE/GRAPH toggle button, you can view the supply figures in a table, which is the preferred format for forecasting supply.

In the table view, we're starting with the 2012 headcount for each critical job family, and the tool is using the 2012 voluntary termination rate (minus retirements) as a baseline for supply into 2013, 2015, and 2017. This measure truly is a baseline, meaning that you can edit the historical supply estimates to more accurately model out expected future patterns. Exactly as you did in DEMAND, you can click any one of the cells in the supply table to modify the value.

To the right of the current headcount, terminations, retirements, and external hires are incorporated to give a more granular understanding of what the forecast will look like from a supply perspective across the next five years, as shown in Figure 14.22.

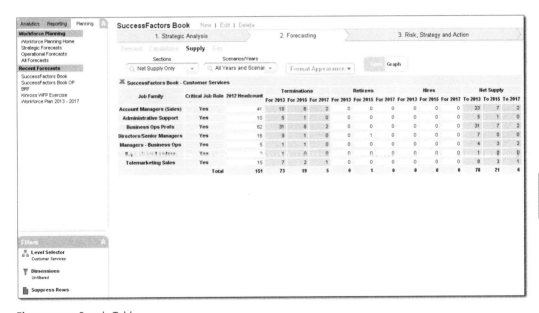

Figure 14.22 Supply Table

As with demand, you can view the supply forecast in a graph, and there are a few different charting options. One particularly useful view is the NET SUPPLY EXCLUDING INFLOWS view, which essentially shows you where you'll be at the end of the forecast period if you do nothing differently. In other words, the supply curve is only showing outflows (terminations and retirements), without factoring in any new hires (internal or external) to backfill positions. Figure 14.23 depicts the net supply excluding inflows for Customer Services; by 2017, there will be nearly no one left in the internal talent pool.

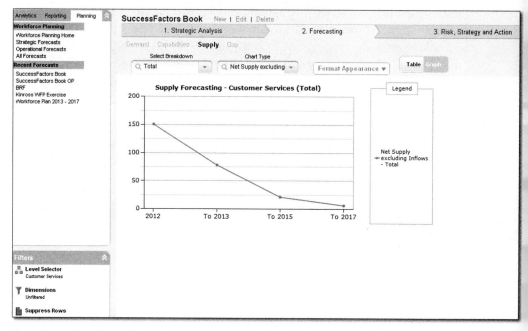

Figure 14.23 Supply Graph

Now that the necessary changes have been made to the supply forecast, let's move to the final forecasting step: analyzing the gap.

14.3.4 Gap Analysis

Gap analysis is a simple calculation of demand minus supply, and it helps you identify the key workforce risks for both capacity (numbers) and capabilities. In the GAP tab, you're pairing together supply and demand and breaking it down by scenario. Once this is calculated, you can see the overall net supply, as well as the magnitude of the gap per scenario, as either a shortage or a surplus.

Similarly to all tabs within the Forecasting section of the tool, you access the Gap tab by clicking the Gap link. This shows a graphical view on the initial screen. By toggling to the Table view, you can see a more granular view of both demand and supply in one table, and you can customize the columns shown in the table by clicking the Sections dropdown. The last column in the table shows the Gap (Shortage/Surplus), and all negative deltas (shortage) are shown in red font, while all positive deltas (surplus) are shown in green. Figure 14.24 shows the Gap table for the Customer Services department, which identifies shortages across all critical job families, regardless of scenario.

Job Family	Critical Job Role	2012 Establishment Headcount	Demand						Net Supply				Gap (Shortage - / Surplus +)					
			To 2013		To 2015		To 2017		2012 Headcount	To 2013	To 2015	To 2017	To 2013		To 2015		To 2017	
			High Growth	Low Growth	High Growth	Low Growth	High Growth	Low Growth					High Growth	Low Growth	High Growth	Low Growth	High Growth	Low Growth
Account Managers (Sales)	Yes	41	46	42	56	44	66	46	41	23	7	2	-23	-19	-49	-37	-64	-44
Administrative Support	Yes	10	15	11	25	13	35	15	10	5	1	0	-10	-6	-24	-12	-35	-15
Business Ops Profs	Yes	62	67	63	77	65	87	67	62	31	7	2	-36	-32	-70	-58	-85	-65
Director/Senior Managers	Yes	16	21	17	31	19	41	21	16	7	0	0	-14	-10	-31	-19	-41	-21
Managers - Business Ops	Yes	5	10	6	20	8	30	10	5	4	3	2	-6	-2	-17	-5	-28	-8
Supervisors/Leaders	Yes	2	7	3	17	5	27	7	2	1	0	0	-6	-2	-17	-5	-27	-7
Telemarketing Sales	Yes	15	20	16	30	18	40	20	15	8	3	1	-12	-8	-27	-15	-39	-19
Total		151	186	158	256	172	326	188	151	78	21	6	-108	-80	-235	-151	-320	-180

Figure 14.24 Gap Table

As with demand and supply, the gap can be shown in a variety of graphs. After receiving sign-off on both the demand and supply forecasts for each department within the Retail business unit, it's time for the *Risk, Strategy, and Action* phase (also known as the Act Module), which you can access by selecting the Risk, Strategy, and Action tab.

14.4 The Act Module

At its core, SWFP is a risk mitigation exercise, with the end goal of identifying the highest-priority risks an organization is facing in the future and creating action plans to put in motion today to minimize the impact of risks in the future. After you've identified the gaps, you need to analyze where the largest shortages and surpluses are occurring and what might be causing them. Typically, there are three main drivers of gaps:

- Growth
- Resignations
- Retirements

By looking at the various data elements on the gap spreadsheet, such as terminations or retirements, you can identify which of these three drivers are causing the gaps. Next, you must prioritize the gaps in terms of significance and impact. Are there large shortages in critical job roles that you know are historically difficult to attract and retain? Or, are the largest gaps in roles you know are easily sourced in the external labor market? You'll also want to consider how the gaps differ by scenario and what impact changes in capabilities have on gaps. Ultimately, you're trying to determine the risks that are most likely to occur and have the largest impact on your ability to execute your strategy.

In the Risk, Strategy and Action phase, workforce planners can model the impact of different strategies to mitigate the identified risks. When you first access the Act Module, a screen prompt appears, asking whether you want to use the Act default template or start with an empty slate. To leverage the SuccessFactors strategy bank and other best-practice defaults, you must click YES.

14.4.1 Highlighting Rules

The first screen is HIGHLIGHTING RULES, which leverages the data highlighting tool embedded within Analytics Workspace in the WFA application (see Chapter 13). The first step is to define the rules that you want the tool to search for in the data. A few common rules are listed here as defaults (e.g., high turnover, significant gaps, and large numbers of forecasted retirements).

Next to the list of rules is a summary window that shows the criteria of the selected rule. To view the criteria of each rule, simply click the rule description until that row turns green, and the summary window refreshes with the selected rule's details. You can add multiple rules by clicking NEW RULE or edit the parameters of the default rules by clicking EDIT. You must click SAVE after editing a rule to go back to the HIGHLIGHTING RULES screen. For the RETAIL business unit example, let's leverage the three existing default rules, which are shown in Figure 14.25.

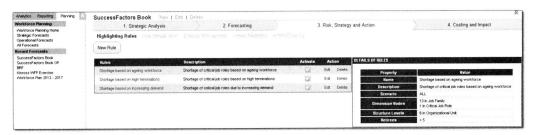

Figure 14.25 Highlighting Rules

14.4.2 Risk Identification

The next link within the Act Module is RISK IDENTIFICATION, which also comes pre-populated with common risks associated with the rules that you defined in the HIGHLIGHTING RULES section. The risks are listed at the top of the screen, with the selected risk highlighted in green and a table below showing where in the forecast (by business unit, department, or job family) each specific risk is an issue (denoted by a green cell). You can also add new risks by clicking the NEW RISK button. Essentially, in this step, the tool has listed specific risks that map to the rules you've previously defined.

For example, you might have a shortage of critical job roles due to high projected termination rates, as shown in Figure 14.26. If you scroll down, you can easily see where in the forecast this particular risk is an issue because it's highlighted in green.

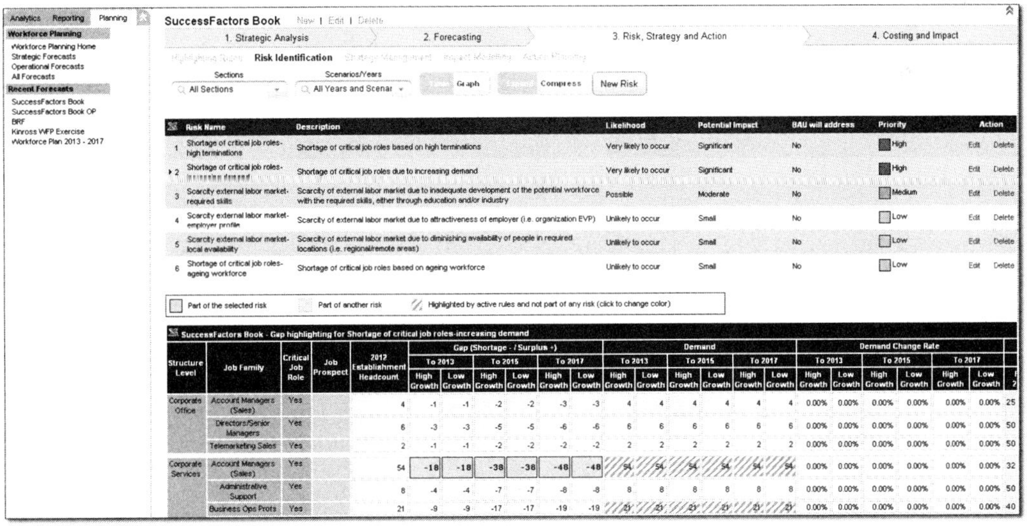

Figure 14.26 Risk Identification

Data highlighting is an easy method of sifting through all of the data in your forecast to quickly highlight the areas with the greatest risks. In this case, you can see that account managers in the Corporate Services department are at risk for a shortage due to increasing demand, as well as high termination rates.

In Figure 14.26, you can also see that each risk is color coded in the Priority column. However, the priority level always defaults to low (gray color). To change the priority level based on your organization's circumstances, select the risk you want to modify (the row turns green), and then click Edit. A new window appears that shows the description of the risk and requires a rating on the likelihood that the risk will happen, the potential impact, and whether business as usual will address the risk. Depending on the risk level assigned, either a red, yellow, or gray color is assigned to the risk. A few quick tips are that risks are listed in order of priority (red to gray) and any cell in the table can be manually overridden and coded according to the specifications a user defines.

The last feature of the Risk Identification section that we'll cover is the graphical view of the risk matrix. When you toggle from Table to Graph view, the risks are shown in a three-by-three matrix utilizing the same color coding assigned in the Table view to visually highlight the highest-priority risks. High-priority risks, again, are defined as the most likely to occur and have the greatest impact, as shown in Figure 14.27.

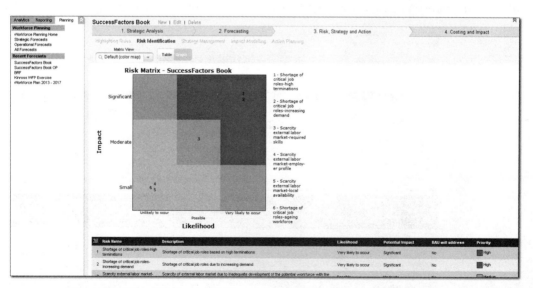

Figure 14.27 Risk Matrix

14.4.3 Strategy Management

Now that you've defined the highest-priority risks and where they are occurring in the forecast, you can begin to determine which strategies will be most impactful in terms of mitigating the identified risks. SWFP focuses on making decisions that will have the most impact, which means you'll make decisions about what you will and will not do to address workforce risks related to the following:

▶ Critical job roles

▶ Significant capability gaps

▶ Significant staff surplus/deficit

▶ Significant turnover in key roles

▶ Workforce trends, such as an aging workforce

When you click the STRATEGY MANAGEMENT link, a new screen refreshes with your risk list, as well as suggested tactics for the selected risk (highlighted in green). Tactics are pulled directly from the SuccessFactors strategy bank, which is embedded in the tool and contains more than 30 years of best-practice strategies. You can view the full strategy bank by clicking the ADD OR REMOVE TACTICS button; a new window opens, where specific tactics can be checked or unchecked, depending on whether you want to include them.

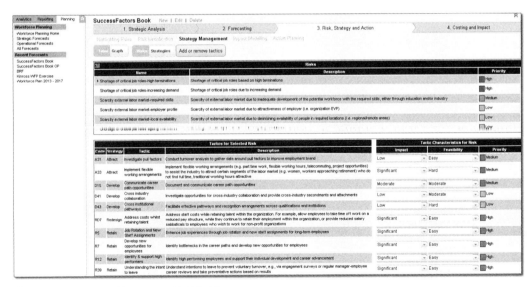

Figure 14.28 Strategy Management Table View

To the right of each tactic is the TACTIC CHARACTERISTICS FOR RISK window, which allows users to rate each tactic on both impact and feasibility. Similarly to Risk Identification, the color associated with each tactic changes based on how the tactic is rated. You can toggle between the RISK and STRATEGY views, depending on the format you prefer. Figure 14.28 shows the STRATEGY MANAGEMENT screen.

After you've assigned and rated tactics for each identified risk, you can toggle to the GRAPH view to see a three-by-three matrix of the strategies that will be most feasible to implement and have the greatest impact. The GRAPH view also includes a legend defining the tactics, as shown in Figure 14.29.

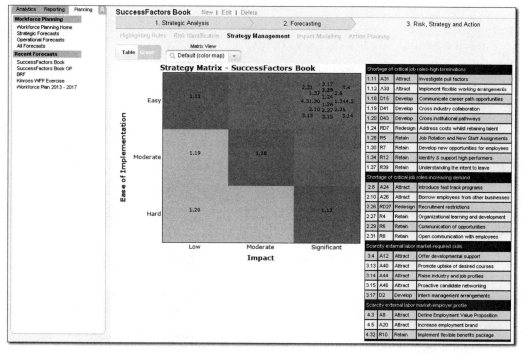

Figure 14.29 Strategy Management Graph View

In the next section, we'll cover how to model the impact of strategies to mitigate the risks already identified in the forecast.

14.4.4 Impact Modeling

Impact modeling can be a powerful tool for identifying which strategies are going to be the most impactful and cost-effective to implement. Typically, clients create different models by strategy type and can then compare the models side by side to determine which strategy should move forward to the action planning phase.

For example, let's say you've identified a high-priority risk due to high turnover in critical roles. The two strategic options you have to mitigate this risk can be grouped into buy versus build scenarios, meaning you either need to buy talent from the external market or invest in programs to internally develop additional talent. While the specific tactics may vary under each sourcing strategy, impact modeling can help you understand whether the benefits of one strategy significantly outweigh the other.

To access the IMPACT MODELING section of the Act Module, click the IMPACT MODELING link. A blank screen refreshes, alerting you that you haven't yet assigned any risks to the model, and therefore, it's blank. To assign risks, click the VIEW/EDIT MODEL DETAILS link in the FILTERS pane, which generates a list of risks. If you click the checkbox next to each risk, the tool lists the tactics that can be applied, and you can check the ones you want to include in the model.

For the first model, let's select tactics that apply to a buy sourcing strategy (e.g., RAISE INDUSTRY AND JOB PROFILES, PROACTIVE CANDIDATE NETWORKING, etc.) and then click SAVE. Figure 14.30 shows the complete list of selections.

Now, the page displays a table view of where the selected risks and gaps are occurring within the forecast. If you click the MODEL dropdown, you can then click ADD to save this model, and title it, "Buy Sourcing Strategy".

Next, you repeat this process by clicking ADD in the MODEL dropdown menu and naming it, "Build Sourcing Strategy". The tool asks whether you want to copy the selected risks and tactics from the current model or start with a clean slate. Because you're changing your strategies, choose to start with a clean slate, and repeat the process of assigning risks/tactics by clicking VIEW/EDIT MODEL DETAILS and changing your selections to strategies designed at internal capability building. Now, when you click the MODEL dropdown, you can see both models displayed in the list and compare them side by side after making edits to each model.

Similarly to demand and supply forecasting, the IMPACT MODELING section allows users to change the numbers in the forecast depending on a specific strategy's expected outcomes. For example, in the buy sourcing strategy, we've chosen to focus recruitment on critical roles, so we expect to see hiring rates for critical roles change significantly, ultimately affecting the gap.

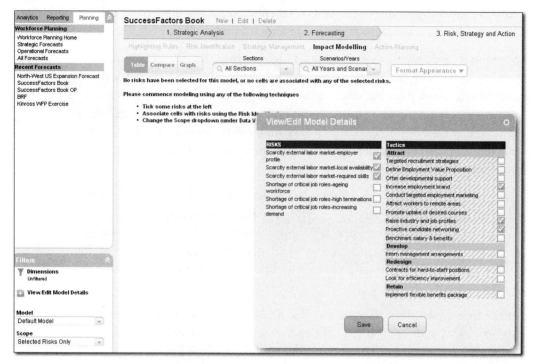

Figure 14.30 Impact Model: Buy Strategy

Let's model this scenario as an example. The first step is to switch back to the buy model, which you can do by selecting BUY SOURCING STRATEGY in the MODEL drop-down in the FILTERS pane. Again, the table view refreshes with the CUSTOMER SERVICES account managers because this is the department you identified with the largest risks/gaps. The default hiring rate is 0%, but let's change it to 3% year over year by clicking the 2013 cell. Doing so prompts a new window to open, similar to the EDIT VALUES window you saw in the FORECASTING section. In this window, you can change the hiring rate to 3% in the value window (change 0 to 3), and check the OVERWRITE ALL FOLLOWING YEARS box.

Before you can exit this window, you must assign this change to a specific tactic in the ASSOCIATE EDITS WITH dropdown menu. For example, associate the hiring increase with the PROACTIVE CANDIDATE NETWORKING tactic, and click OK. Now your hiring rates are displayed in a red font as 3% for the next five years of the forecast, as shown in Figure 14.31.

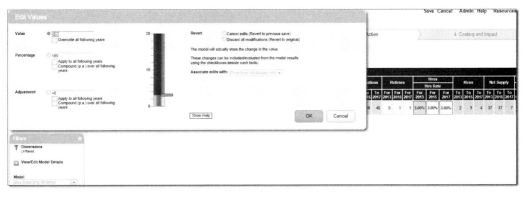

Figure 14.31 Impact Model Change Hiring Rate

The gap is automatically modified as a result of the hiring rate increase; in this example, it has decreased across all years for both scenarios. Before you can move on, you must click SAVE at the top of the screen to confirm the edits, and the cell font reverts back to black. Each edited cell also has a blue border around it, signifying that the cell has been edited.

After the page refreshes, toggle to the GRAPH view to see a graphical representation of your before-and-after results for the buy sourcing strategy, as shown in Figure 14.32.

Figure 14.32 Before-and-After Comparison

After you repeat a similar process for the build sourcing strategy, the final step of impact modeling is to do a side-by-side comparison of both strategies. When you click the COMPARE toggle, a table view refreshes, displaying both models in one view, as shown in Figure 14.33.

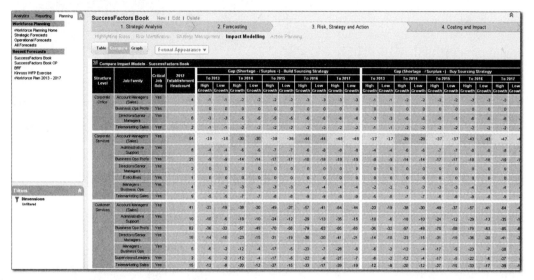

Figure 14.33 Compare Models

Now that you've modeled a few different strategies to reach a decision on which tactics should be implemented, you can build an action plan and assign activities to individuals in the final section of the Act Module.

14.4.5 Action Planning

The final portion of the Act Module is where users can assign responsibility to either individuals or teams to ensure that the selected initiatives are completed in a timely fashion. In effect, this is a great tool to drive accountability and ultimately brings workforce planning from an "exercise" to an "executable strategy." In addition, based on the strategy, you can start to frame the workforce planning discussion in terms of the business. In many ways, this is the beginning of the SWFP process, not the end.

The *action plan* should include an outline of how the strategy will be executed, targets for achievement, the required resources, and timelines and key milestones. Figure 14.34 shows the ACTION PLANNING screen in the WFP tool.

There are several different buttons at the top of the ACTION PLANNING screen. If you click TACTIC PRIORITY SETUP, a new window opens that allows users to modify the strategies included from the strategy bank, the tactic priority rating scale, the tactic feasibility rating scale, the associated color coding, and where the tactic falls on a three-by-three tactic matrix. For example, you might identify a tactic that has a high feasibility of being implemented and will have a significant impact if prioritized. Alternatively, you might identify a tactic that has a low feasibility of being implemented and will have a low impact, so it would not be a priority.

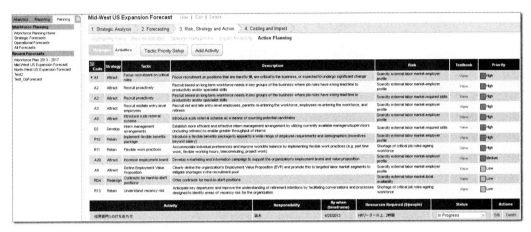

Figure 14.34 Action Planning Screen

For each tactic, activities must be added using the ADD ACTIVITY button. A new window opens called ACTIVITY EDITOR, where you enter the name of the person who will be held accountable, the timeline for implementation, and any additional resources needed. Figure 14.35 shows an example of an activity assignment.

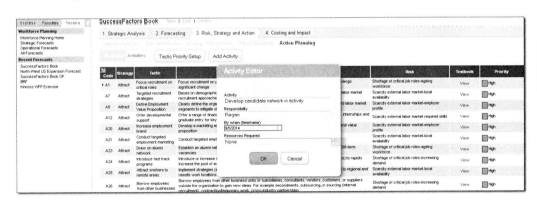

Figure 14.35 Activity Editor

After activities have been assigned, you can toggle between the Strategies/Activities tab to see different views. Until an activity has been added, the activity view is unavailable. While the action planning step is the final phase of the SWFP process, some organizations opt to integrate financial data for modeling purposes before determining which strategies to implement. In the next section, we'll cover the Costing and Impact tool, which is also known as the What-If Financial Modeling tool.

14.5 What-If Financial Modeling

The final tab of the WFP tool is Costing and Impact (also known as What-If Financial Modeling). This section provides context around the financial ramifications of the decisions that you're making today, helps to optimize the composition of the workforce from a financial perspective, and allows organizations to prove that WFP is a necessary business process and not just an HR exercise.

Financial modeling quantifies the financial impact of implementing interventions that address risks to move the business to the desired future state. Organizations that have the Financial Metrics Pack implemented in the WFA application can also configure the financial metrics to flow through to the What-If tool. Essentially, you're connecting the workforce plan and identified future gaps with historic financial and compensation data to model financial variables related to workforce costs, both now and in the future. However, even without the Financial Metrics Pack, users can manually enter the critical financial data elements for modeling purposes.

When you first click into the What-If tool, you're provided with an overall financial dashboard that outlines your company's financial profile (assuming the Financial Metrics Pack is configured) and includes things such as overall total cost of workforce, total operating revenue, and profit per FTE. There is also a chart displaying the cost to fill the gap broken down by the two scenarios across the forecast period. From a financial perspective, all figures take into account measures such as salary growth, composition of the workforce, different costs of training, recruitment, and cost of turnover. The ability to model the numbers to generate different outcomes is what makes the tool truly "What-If?"

The FINANCIAL DASHBOARD in Figure 14.36 provides a number of visualizations from a financial perspective. There are also other dashboards that can be viewed, including the following:

▸ COMPARISON VIEW

▸ GAP ANALYSIS DASHBOARD

▸ MARKET COMPARISONS AND PRODUCTIVITY

▸ EFFICIENCY ANALYSIS

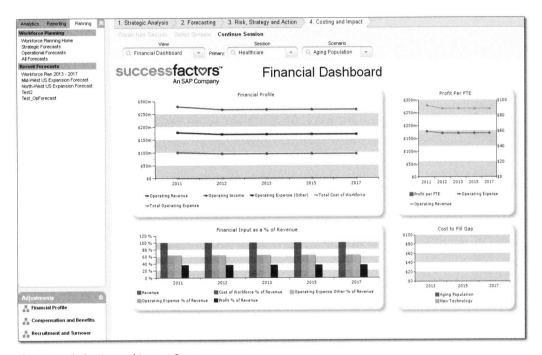

Figure 14.36 Costing and Impact Screen

Let's walk through an example of how to set up a What-If Financial Modeling session for the Retail business unit. The first step is to select the CREATE NEW SESSION link at the top of the screen. A new window opens that prompts you to enter the session details and select the forecast from the existing forecast list. After selecting the RETAIL business unit forecast, you must choose a dimension and model. For this example, choose to analyze by JOB FAMILY in the BUY SOURCING STRATEGY model, as shown in Figure 14.37. To exit this window, click SAVE.

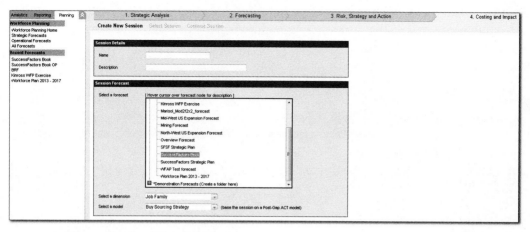

Figure 14.37 New What-If Session

A new FINANCIAL DASHBOARD refreshes based on the data from the Retail Business Unit Forecast. From here, you can begin to model various changes to your workforce to understand the financial implications of these actions by clicking the three tabs in the ADJUSTMENTS pane (FINANCIAL PROFILE, COMPENSATION AND BENEFITS, and RECRUITMENT AND TURNOVER).

Click COMPENSATION AND BENEFITS first; this causes a new window to open, showing the job families by AVERAGE ANNUAL SALARY, SALARY GROWTH (%), and BENEFITS (%), as shown in Figure 14.38.

Let's say that your account managers across the next 5 years are expecting 10% annual salary growth, so you can click the 5% and change it to 10% in each year. After the change is accepted, the Revised Chart on the right-hand side of the screen (see Figure 14.38) updates to show the financial impact of this salary increase on factors such as operating revenue or total cost of workforce. The Original Chart stays the same, allowing you to compare the before and after effect of this compensation strategy. This ability to make changes dynamically within the tool and then see how the changes affect the overall organization from a financial perspective is a very powerful functionality.

In addition to modeling compensation strategies, you can start to model different workforce mixes (e.g., temporary vs. permanent vs. contractors) or bonus structures to see the impact on your financial profile. You can do the same type of modeling for recruitment and turnover and start to factor in things such as cost to fill, turnover costs, and training expenses. Last, the FINANCIAL PROFILE tab allows you to model different growth scenarios to determine how increases to operating revenue or expenses will affect your overall financial profile.

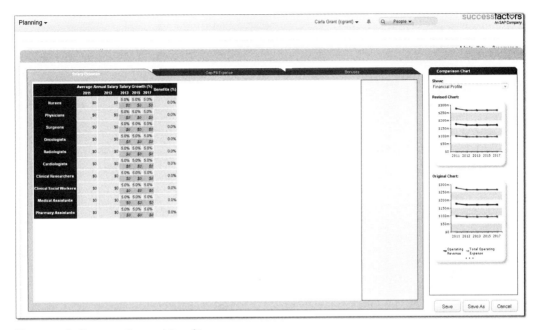

Figure 14.38 Compensation and Benefits

Now that we've covered how the What-If Financial Modeling tool bridges the gap between HR and financial planning, we'll touch on the Operational Planning tool embedded within the SuccessFactors WFP application.

14.6 Operational Workforce Planning Forecasts

Operational Workforce Planning (referred to as Operational Planning) is often known as Headcount Planning, Strategic Staffing, or Budget Planning and can be either a standalone process or a method for operationalizing Year 1 and Year 2 of a strategic workforce plan.

The aim of Operational Planning is to enable each business unit to continue its daily functions by having the right people available to do the work. The process is such that managers forecast how many people they will need to proceed with their day-to-day operations over the next 1-5 years. If they don't perform this forecasting as accurately as possible, managers are less likely to secure the appropriate budget allocation to have the required resources and/or may not have the right people to effectively execute on their near-term goals. Figure 14.39 shows a few key differences between Operational Planning and SWFP.

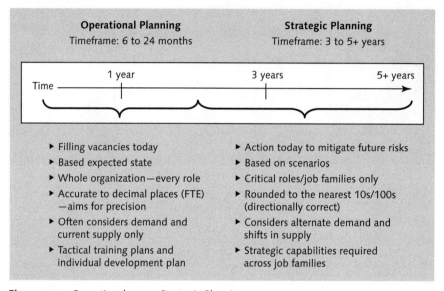

Figure 14.39 Operational versus Strategic Planning

To meet clients' short-term planning needs, the WFP application includes an Operational Planning tool, which you can access on the WFP HOME screen by selecting NEW FORECAST and then NEW OPERATIONAL FORECAST.

For an operational forecast, three sets of parameters must be defined:

▸ DETAILS
NAME and DESCRIPTION fields

▸ TIMEFRAME
START YEAR and NUMBER OF MONTHS (up to 48) fields

▸ BUSINESS FACTORS
WORKFORCE MEASURES, HEADCOUNT, TERMINATION RATE, MOVEMENTS IN RATE, MOVEMENTS OUT RATE, MISCELLANEOUS INFLOWS, MISCELLANEOUS OUTFLOWS, and RECRUITMENT SCHEDULE

Figure 14.40 shows the Forecast Basics screen for an operational forecast.

Figure 14.40 The Forecast Basics Screen for an Operational Forecast

Building an operational planning forecast is very similar to the process for building a strategic forecast in that users must define the source data year for enabled data elements when building a forecast. The key difference in Operational Planning is that the source data is by month instead of year (e.g., May 2013 voluntary terminations are sourced from the May 2012 historical voluntary terminations data). The rest of the forecast building screen follows the same process as building a strategic forecast (e.g., set dimensions, set structure, and build).

Using the same selections as the strategic forecast (e.g., job family and critical roles for the Retail business unit), you click Build and are taken back to the WFP forecast list. A tip here is to click the Operational Forecasts link in the Planning window on the left-hand side of the screen to display only Operational Planning forecasts. After selecting the forecast, you see in the Explore Forecast window that there is only one option to click: Operational Planning. Click this link, and a screen refreshes with the month-by-month forecast for the next six months, as shown in Figure 14.41.

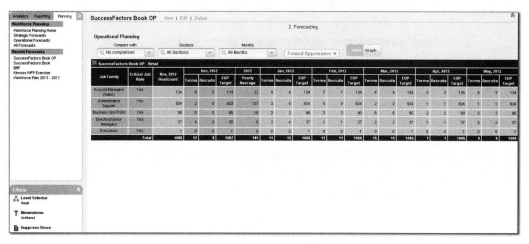

Figure 14.41 Retail Business Unit Operational Plan

In this screen, you can begin to edit the forecasted headcount by job family for the next six months. Note that cells can't be edited at the total retail business unit level, meaning you must click the Level Selector and drill into a department to make edits. Select Customer Services for this example.

In this example, December 2012 has already occurred, so the cells can no longer be edited and are highlighted in green. However, you can edit all remaining months in the forecast by clicking the cell and adjusting the number. The numbers populating the future months are based on the source month and year that you defined while building the forecast.

If you toggle to the Graph view, you're given a quick visualization of where hiring activity increased in previous years, as shown in Figure 14.42.

In this view, you can easily see that January and March are predicted to be your busiest hiring months, based on historical data. In theory, if you expect termination patterns to remain consistent, then you can be more proactive in your hiring by starting the recruiting process before you find your organization in firefighting mode.

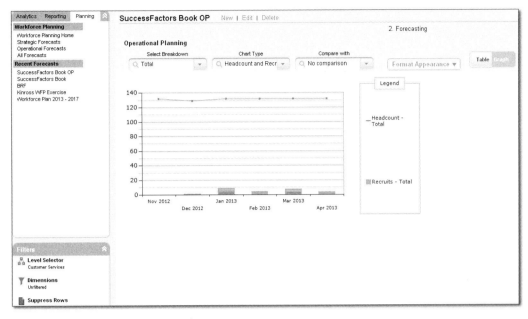

Figure 14.42 Retail Business Unit Graph View

14.7 Summary

Now that we've covered the main features and functionality of the SuccessFactors Workforce Planning solution, you have a thorough understanding of how organizations use this innovative solution to create strategic plans to ensure that you have the right people in the right place at the right time for the right cost. The SuccessFactors WFP methodology has very much evolved while working with hundreds of clients and learning what has helped most organizations do SWFP well. Clearly, SWFP is a qualitative process; even with sophisticated tools and technology, the quality of the workforce plan is going to depend on the key conversations with the business, as well as the vision and strategy of the organization.

In addition, SWFP is a continuous process that does not stop with the action plan. For the process to be sustainable, it must feed other strategic planning processes undertaken by the business, such as Financial Planning, Operational Planning, and Strategic Planning. Furthermore, prior plans must serve as the basis for future ones, testing old assumptions, and monitoring progress. In effect, this year's plan serves as the starting point for next year's plan. Throughout the year, an ongoing

587

process for monitoring and reviewing the key elements of your plan is critical and includes regular reviews of the scenarios, changes to company strategy, unexpected internal events, and operational workforce metrics through WFP dashboards and KPI reports.

In the next chapter, we'll cover SuccessFactors HCM mobile, which assists with bringing new employees into the organization.

SuccessFactors' HCM Suite mobile app is focused on putting the most critical talent management functions in the hands of users when they need them. It takes the virtual teaming concept to the next level by enabling users any time and from anywhere.

15   SuccessFactors HCM Mobile

SuccessFactors has taken the ease of its HCM suite of applications and delivered the most critical processes to the mobile device through its mobile app. This enables employees and managers to stay connected and keep the development process moving forward both at the desk and away from it. The mobile app supports users finding each other through the Org Chart and directory, collaborating via SAP Jam, approving critical recruiting forms and providing candidate feedback, keeping track of pending items from Employee Central, keeping up with Performance Manager To-Do items, and enabling managers to touch base with their employees from anywhere.

Many enhancements have been added to the mobile app over the last year that improve usability, look and feel in the app itself, and administrative functions, as well as expand mobile learning options, including offline learning. Users can also now manage their Time Off via the mobile app, and Onboarding features enable even the newest employees to stay connected from day one.

SuccessFactors HCM Mobile empowers employees and managers to make talent management an everyday event, not just a once a year occurrence. It also enables managers and HR business partners to stay on top of critical employee changes away from their desks. This chapter will review the features currently available to users via the mobile app.

Several mobile features that are currently available encompass finding and staying connected to your team and other employees and enabling collaboration among teams on-the-go:

- Employee Profile, Org Chart, and Directory

- SAP Jam

- Learning

- Mobile Touchbase

- Who's in the Meeting

- Mobile Onboarding

- Mobile Time Off

Other features allow managers to stay current with critical processes, such as creating performance reviews and approving recruiting actions like requisitions and offers:

- Recruiting

- Employee Central

- Performance To-Dos

We'll now take a brief look at some of these features and tools.

15.1   Employee Profile, Org Chart, and Directory

SuccessFactors Mobile has made the Employee Profile view in the mobile app much more synced with the web version. Enhanced APIs pull data directly from the profile and makes it available in the mobile Profile view. The user interface is also much more in line with the web version. Org Chart and Mobile Directory features, which are shown in Figure 15.1, allow employees to see how their company is connected and organized and find the people they need quickly. Users can now search by data elements such as location, department, and position. The Mobile Org Chart gives a visual representation of how people within the organization are connected.

The Mobile Directory offers contact details such as phone numbers, email addresses, and instant message details. From the Mobile Directory, employees can reach out directly to contact their colleagues and create new contacts directly on the mobile device.

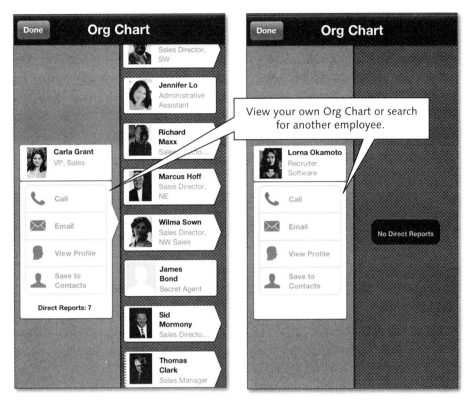

Figure 15.1 Mobile Org Chart and Mobile Directory

15.2 SAP Jam on SuccessFactors HCM Mobile

Continuous collaboration—the theme of SAP Jam mobile—enables employees to stay connected to and involved with projects and groups right from their mobile devices. Employees can set up their notification preferences so that they receive emails immediately as posts are made to the SAP Jam wall or as direct messages. Posts can be made directly to the SAP Jam wall from the mobile device, or users can reply from their email to reply to wall posts and post other comments.

Active conversations in the feeds encourage engagement and keep employees up to date with dialogue as it occurs and highlights items that have not yet been viewed. The SAP Jam mobile app gives employees access to any group they are a member of and provides tools to move projects forward, right from their smartphone or iPad.

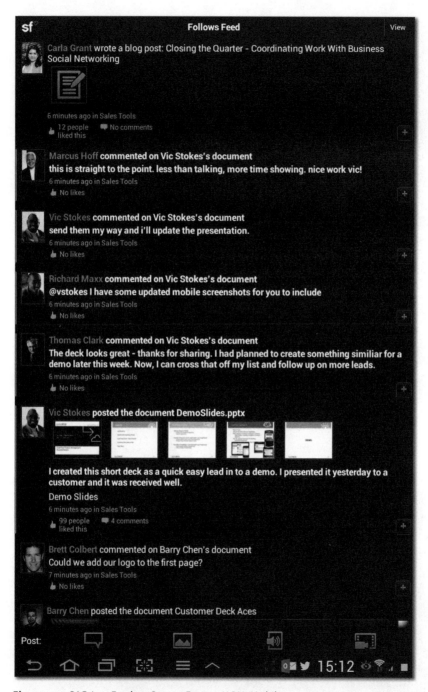

Figure 15.2 SAP Jam Feed on SuccessFactors HCM Mobile

SAP Jam content search puts even more information in the hands of employees when they need it. Allowing users the ability to search for content such as videos, wikis, documents, people, and conversations via the mobile app reduces the aggravation of having to search through a news feed to find what employees are looking for. Staying connected to the conversation is made easier with feed updates coming right to the mobile device, or even to users' email, so response is almost immediate. In Figure 15.2, users can view their feed and keep up to date on the latest posts, reply to comments and questions, posts blogs, and view documents. Users can now also contribute to Ideas Forums in Jam right from the mobile app.

15.3 Mobile Learning

Mobile Learning frees users to pursue learning on-the-go. From the Mobile Learning app, managers can approve courses for their team members, and employees and managers can receive notifications of assignments and upcoming due dates. The Learning To-Do list now looks more like the web view with grouped and/or sorted items on the Learning Plan and the item graphics that can accompany all items in the catalog. All employees can access content to learn anywhere, anytime, which can help them get the training they need, when they need it. This can be especially helpful with a dispersed workforce or those in the field that don't have the time or opportunity to participate in formal learning in the office or classroom.

Real-time social learning keeps content current because it's constantly being updated. Employees can upload videos and images of white boards and samples, or demonstrate complex procedures right from their mobile device to keep the learning process going, despite being on the road or in an airport. By making comments from their mobile device, adding tips and tricks to formal training, employees can participate in learning without being tied to a classroom.

Late in 2013, SuccessFactors introduced offline mobile learning for iPad users. This allows users to download content items to the app, where it is encrypted and stored. They can launch the item at a later time, complete it, and upload completion results the next time the app is connected and synced. This is especially helpful for employees who spend a lot of time traveling or away from the office. Further enhancements in 2014 have included support for AICC content, including the AICC Wrapper, and support for various file types such as .xls, .doc, and .pdf, among others.

15.4 Recruiting

In today's environment, recruiting is a 24/7 process. Candidates view open positions, apply for jobs, and monitor their progression through the process at any time of day or night. Likewise, recruiters often deal with hiring managers and approvers who are traveling or based in different time zones all over the globe. The Recruiting features of the mobile app keep the most crucial elements of the recruiting process accessible across the globe at any time.

Requisitions can be approved via the mobile app. The app supports iterative route map steps. Configuration on the requisition identifies those fields that should appear on the mobile app. With Interview Central access on the mobile device, SuccessFactors enables the fastest interview feedback possible. Interviewers can provide candidate ratings by competency, an overall rating, and comments along the way. The side-by-side feature of Interview Central lets interviewers rate candidates against each other in an easy interface. In Figure 15.3, requisition approval and interview feedback are easily performed on the mobile device, keeping the recruiting process moving forward.

Figure 15.3 Mobile Recruiting

After a candidate is selected for hire, approving the official offer becomes a time-sensitive task. Mobile offer approvals again put the right information in the hands of the right people to provide recruiters, hiring managers, and candidates with the fastest, smoothest hiring process possible.

15.5 Employee Central To-Dos

Just as recruiting is a time-sensitive business process that requires input from multiple people to keep the process moving forward, many HR processes require up-to-the-minute attention. Each Employee Central workflow configuration might require multiple parties' involvement before an employment or compensation action gets approved. The Employee Central To-Do list puts change requests at the fingertips of each approver to keep the personnel action process moving, as shown in Figure 15.4. Approvers can stay informed of pending actions through feeds on items requiring their attention and make the best personnel decisions possible while still on-the-go.

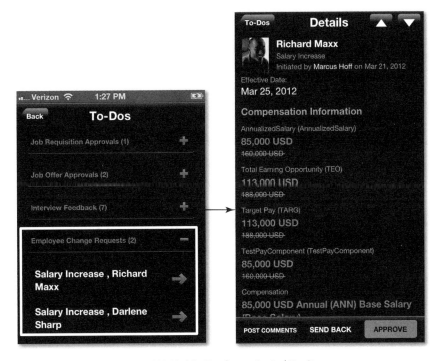

Figure 15.4 SuccessFactors HCM Mobile Employee Central To-Dos

As of the b1408 release in August 2014, the following Employee Central workflows are supported on the mobile app for iPhone and iPad:

- Job Relationship
- New Hire
- Termination
- Employment Change
- Compensation Change (recurring and non-recurring)
- Personal Info Change
- National ID Change
- Address Change
- Time Off
- Leave of Absence

15.6 Performance Manager To-Dos

With the Performance Manager To-Do list, managers have the capability to complete employee performance reviews by electronically signing them from the SuccessFactors HCM mobile app. They can view overall ratings, add comments to the review, and approve or reject it from their devices. Likewise, employees with mobile app access can sign and confirm their performance reviews from their devices. With push notifications, proactive users can receive email notifications and respond to email without needing to access the mobile app To-Do list.

15.7 Mobile Touchbase

One of the most exciting features of the SuccessFactors HCM mobile app is Touchbase, as shown in Figure 15.5. This innovative tool allows managers to stay in touch with their teams at the touch of a button, regardless of distance or time zone. Touchbase enables team collaboration from the device by facilitating the following:

- Setting up meetings with team members and sending recorded messages to them
- Keeping informed of employee goal progress

▸ Scheduling one-on-one meetings with direct reports

▸ Sending email agendas for meetings

The multimedia feature of Touchbase enables note-taking and adding photos and videos. Any items created via Touchbase are available to view as comments within Performance Manager and the performance review. Touchbase has been revamped for iPad users so that the UI matches the rest of the iPad app, helping to reinforce the mobile platform as a unified app for all modules with the Success-Factors HCM suite. Additionally, Touchbase icons have been added to all profiles for easy communication.

Figure 15.5 Mobile Touchbase

15.8   Who's In the Meeting

A newer feature of the mobile app is Who's In the Meeting, a feature that provides an integrated view of your calendar from within the app. Get quick information about attendees for any meeting, capture action items and decisions from the meeting, and quickly email them to all attendees after the meeting.

15.9 Mobile Onboarding

For customers using the SuccessFactors Onboarding module, there is a mobile feature for new hires called the Mobile First Day Experience. This provides them a countdown to their first day on the job and answers the "who," "what," and "where" questions that accompany a new job. The interactive manager and buddy "mobile quickcard" answers the "who" on day one by connecting new hires with their new manager and their "buddy." Meeting timelines and agendas and a link to the Mobile Profile help answer the "what" and alleviate many questions from the new hire on how they will spend their first days of employment. Finally, the "where" is answered via information on office location(s) that comes with a mobile map app integration.

15.10 Mobile Time Off

Now, users can manage their Time Off requests and check balances right from their mobile devices. With the Mobile Time Off features, users can view their balances, submit time-off requests, and view public holiday calendars. They can also view their team absences to ensure that they are not requesting time off during a time period with low team coverage. The monthly calendar navigation increases the usability of this feature and makes it easier for users to move through the calendar. Also, there is now Before You Go for future-dated Time Off requests available in the mobile app. Now, users can set up the things they want to remember to do before they leave as soon as the request is submitted.

15.11 Data, Security, and Administration

SuccessFactors HCM Mobile enables team management and collaboration on the go within a secure environment. Administrators control who has access to the mobile app, and, with the user authentication, it can be accessed only from an active user account. Further, access to each component of the mobile app is permissioned in OneAdmin by system administrators, as demonstrated in Figure 15.6. For example, a company can permission all employees to the Mobile Org Chart and Directory, and only managers to the Performance Manager To-Dos. Permissions for mobile now match permissions for the web version of SuccessFactors HCM suite, and administrators have a consolidated view of all mobile permissions. These increased permissions mean the mobile app is now more of a platform for data that is already available to users via a browser.

Figure 15.6 SuccessFactors HCM Mobile Permissions

An extra layer of security is provided by PIN activation. Data accessed via the mobile app remains secure because all data can be erased from the device if it's lost or stolen via a computer. Activation is now easier and can be completed from directly within the mobile app itself. Administrators now have the option to send an email to each user with a link that can be used to activate the device. Activation is still possible from the OPTIONS menu, using the activation code provided by the app and setting a PIN, as represented by Figure 15.7.

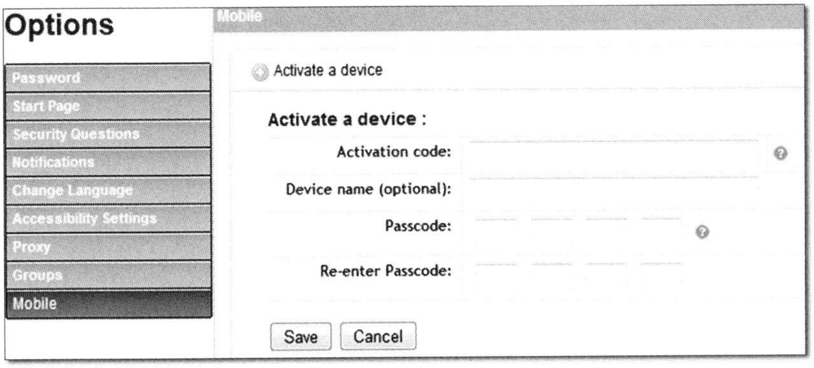

Options

Mobile

Password
Start Page
Security Questions
Notifications
Change Language
Accessibility Settings
Proxy
Groups
Mobile

Activate a device

Activate a device :

Activation code:

Device name (optional):

Passcode:

Re-enter Passcode:

Save   Cancel

Figure 15.7 Mobile PIN Activation

Administrators now have more control in managing mobile features in OneAdmin. They can manage mobile-specific settings, such as activating theming and on-device support for users. They can also manage module-specific features, such as enabling the various components of mobile, as illustrated in Figure 15.8.

The Profile Switcher feature now enables multiple users to log in and out from the app without activating and deactivating the application. Now a single user can access multiple SuccessFactors HCM instances from the same device and the same app. This is great for users who are involved in testing because they can now log in and out of the test instance and production instances from the same mobile device.

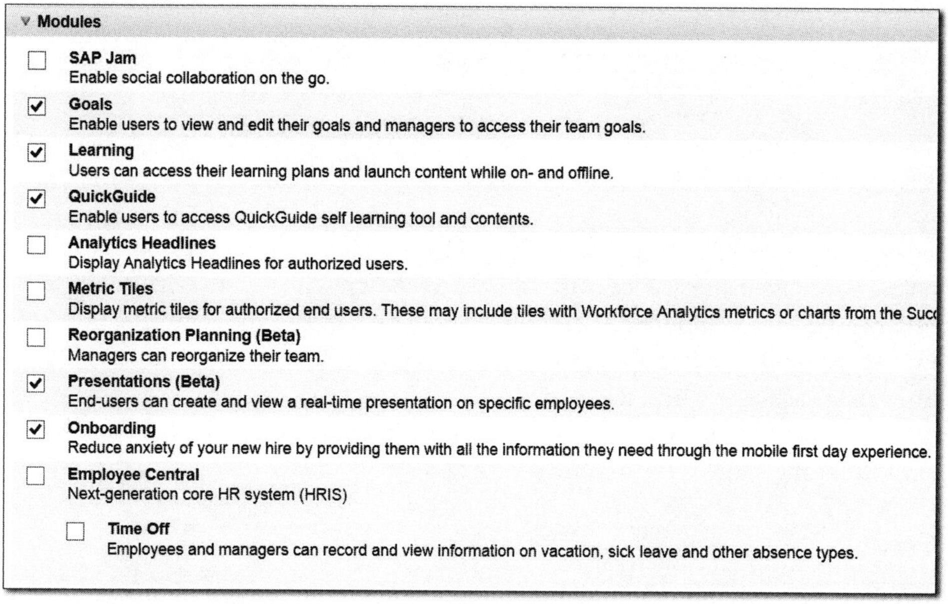

Figure 15.8 Enabling Mobile Modules in OneAdmin

15.12 Summary

With the collaborative features of SuccessFactors HCM mobile, users are empowered to stay connected to their teams and actively participate in critical business processes, regardless of where they may be working on any given day. It delivers the tools they need to find and communicate with each other, stay current with learning needs and activities, and participate in collaborative teams or projects managed via SAP Jam. Managers can keep critical performance-related processes and tasks moving right from their mobile devices by signing performance reviews, monitoring goal progress, scheduling Touchbases with their teams, and approving critical recruiting forms to ensure that the best talent is evaluated for their open positions.

In the next chapter, we'll look at SAP Jam, the social collaboration and knowledge-sharing solution designed to improve cross-functional cooperation and support for achieving team, project, and strategic goals and initiatives.

SAP Jam is an innovative, professional, social collaboration and networking solution that supports cross-functional collaboration, ensuring that organizations leverage their skills, knowledge, and experience to enhance productivity. It brings together people, data, content, and processes to deliver business results in a secure, social foundation.

16   SAP Jam

Social networking is a relatively recent phenomenon that has created new methods for individuals to connect and interact. These networks have become powerful ways of sharing information, opinions, and different types of content. With the increased ability to gain attention and traction, there has been an increase in the level of content creation and sharing. Now, SuccessFactors and SAP have created a solution to leverage this type of social networking, content creation, and sharing in a professional collaboration environment.

SAP Jam is a cross-functional social collaboration and networking solution designed to increase productivity and knowledge sharing in a professional environment. SAP Jam brings together the strengths of SuccessFactors Jam and SAP StreamWork to provide a new social experience for SAP customers.

Social collaboration enables sharing knowledge to create empowerment, engage employees, and enhance expertise. It increases overall organizational competency levels, facilitates faster decision making, and onboards individuals into an organization more quickly. It also provides a platform for teams to discuss common topics, find answers to problems within their everyday work, and work toward achieving shared goals. SAP Jam also offers the possibility to collaborate with individuals who are based outside of the company, such as partners or customers.

To enable social collaboration, SAP Jam supports business processes in all of SAP's cloud business pillars, as well as on-premise systems and processes. It uses common social networking features that can be seen in popular social networking platforms such as Twitter, Facebook, and Google Plus. In this chapter, we'll focus on SAP Jam for the people pillar, although we'll briefly cover the benefits it offers across different business areas, as well.

16.1   Using SAP Jam

SAP Jam supports a number of different business scenarios inside and outside of the HCM domain. It covers four main capabilities:

▶ **Enterprise social networking**
Groups, feeds, discussions, content creation and sharing, bookmarks, and so on

▶ **External collaboration**
Collaboration with customers, partners, suppliers, and so on

▶ **Structured collaboration**
Brainstorming, problem-solving, and decision-making with business tools (ranking, pro/con tables, etc.)

▶ **Business processes**
People, customers, money, and supplier processes

The following list gives a set of examples of the business processes and scenarios that SAP Jam supports:

▶ Employee

- Informal learning

- Onboarding

- Recruiting

- Collaborative goals and performance management

- Expert finding

- Career growth through mentoring

▶ Customers and sales

- Opportunity management

- Campaign management

- Partner and vendor management

- Suppliers and partners
  - Supplier collaboration
  - Sales and operations planning

Note that these are not exhaustive lists of use cases—SAP Jam supports many more possibilities. Through the *work patterns* concept (which we'll cover later in this chapter), various scenarios are provided to match the ways in which organizations do business. The flexibility of the SAP Jam solution means that creative organizations may find numerous ways to leverage the functionality for specific internal and external activities. The core to SAP Jam is the *groups* functionality; using groups to target specific audiences enables targeted sharing and collaboration.

Now we'll look at some of these use cases to understand how SAP Jam can support social collaboration.

16.1.1 Work Patterns

Work patterns are pre-built collaborative processes that combine content, expertise, and best practices with real-time business data and applications. Work patterns enable collaboration within existing business processes and applications that employees already use. This enables them to introduce efficiency and speed into common activities, as well as remove silos and add collaborative working to their everyday work.

SAP applies these to SAP Jam with a variety of pre-built scenarios. Group templates with combined integration to external systems are one of the main areas where SAP Jam provides value-adding work patterns, but there are many other examples. Sales is a key area where work patterns can add real value because of the collaborative nature of sales and the need to access data from a number of different systems in the course of a sales cycle.

Work patterns really give an advantage by leveraging functionality into a scenario that relates to a particular type of work. For example, a group becomes a deal room, and a feed becomes the real-time deal status board.

16.1.2 Sales

Sales organizations can leverage the collaboration aspect of SAP Jam to share critical information to help close team deals, build pro/con tables for sales tactics, ask questions, and request documentation. For teams working with similar products/ services or customers, it can be beneficial to collaborate over the handling of accounts or share new information that colleagues can use to position or sell additional products or services. At-risk accounts can be discussed and remedy tasks can be set up to track actions. Marketing colleagues can be invited to groups so that sales and marketing can collaborate on campaign strategy and execution. External vendors can be invited to collaborate on the sales cycle of their products.

16.1.3 Informal and Social Learning

SAP Jam can be used for informal learning or to support learning activities in the SuccessFactors Learning module. By leveraging the groups functionality, groups can be created to share learning materials in the following ways:

▶ Members can share additional documents to help other members increase their learning.

▶ Wikis and blogs enable users to add new learning information and post their thoughts on what they have learned.

▶ The agenda and task functionalities allow members a way to complete a structured learning program.

▶ Videos enable learners to create inline annotations to support the video content from a learning perspective.

▶ The questions functionality enables members to ask questions, for either the course instructor or their fellow group members.

16.1.4 Social Onboarding

The process of onboarding new employees can be significantly streamlined in SAP Jam. The availability of a private external group provides new employees with access to an onboarding group before even commencing their employment.

Using the first-time welcome announcement can introduce employees to the purpose of the group, what information and resources they can find in the group, which people to follow, what related groups to join, and what activities they need to perform. Recommendations can help new employees understand what content is important and which contributors are worth following. By familiarizing themselves with new colleagues, the new employees can begin to orient and integrate themselves into their new company.

16.1.5 SuccessFactors HCM Mobile

SAP Jam is also available via SuccessFactors HCM mobile, as we covered in Chapter 15. Now that we've evaluated the ways SAP Jam can be used, let's look at the features within the application.

16.2 Features and Social Networking Capabilities

SAP Jam streamlines business processes by making them social. It offers a number of social networking features that Twitter and Facebook users are familiar with. The Enterprise Social Networking functionality forms the backbone of the process-driven business scenarios that bring business value through social collaboration.

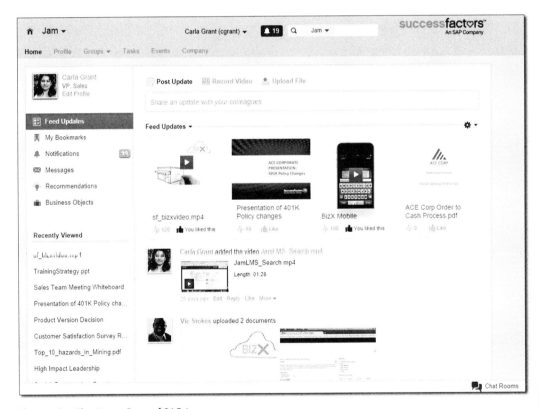

Figure 16.1 The Home Page of SAP Jam

For example, when entering the SAP Jam solution, users are taken to the Home page with their feed, which shows content from all of the groups of which they are a member (see Figure 16.1).

The core functionality and features available in SAP Jam include the following:

- Profile
- Feeds and comments
- Bookmarks and notifications
- Groups
- Content authorship and distribution

Now let's run through these features.

16.2.1 Profile

SAP Jam gives users the opportunity to create a *profile* about themselves, with some data already populated from SAP ERP HCM. This is accessed by clicking Profile at the top of the page. When entering their profiles, users are presented with their overview, which displays their basic profile data, such as name and position, and their updates. They can also post updates, record videos, and upload files here, as well as add a variety of other types of content. Additionally, they can check the individuals they follow and the individuals that follow them. Figure 16.2 shows the Profile overview of Carla Grant.

The left menu bar gives users access to the following content and details:

- Overview
- Achievements
- Blog Posts
- Documents
- Groups
- Links
- Photos
- Polls
- Social Graph

▶ TASKS

▶ VIDEOS

▶ WIKI PAGES

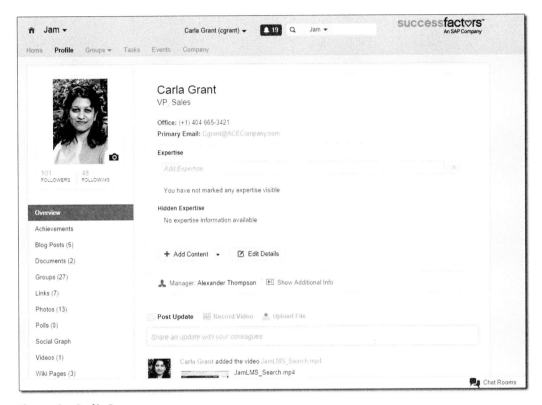

Figure 16.2 Profile Page

By selecting COMPANY at the top of the page, users can access the COMPANY profile page, which contains all of the public feeds from the company, as well as options to see the same content for the entire company in the user's PROFILE page. In addition, the following content and features can be accessed for the company:

▶ ALUMNI
Displays all company alumni

▶ CHAT ROOMS
Provides a platform for employees to discuss topics

- COMPANY WIKI PAGE
  Acts as a company intranet

- DASHBOARD
  Shows the most-followed and most active individuals in the company, as well as how much of the preset (50 GB) storage has been used

- DIRECTORY
  Provides search functionality for company employees

- EMPLOYEE OF THE MONTH
  Allows employees to vote for the employee of the month

- LOCATIONS
  Displays the company locations

- TAGS
  Allows tagged content to be searched by tags

- TOP CONVERSATIONS
  Shows the conversations with the most comments

16.2.2 Feeds, Comments, and Notifications

Every user, group, and company page has a *feed*. The feed shows actions such as updates (with comments and likes), upload of documents, and replies to questions. Each action in the feed can be commented on, liked, or bookmarked. Administrators also have the ability to delete actions.

At the top of the screen, the number of notifications of new actions or content is displayed. Selecting this displays the most recent notifications.

Figure 16.3 shows the COMPANY NEWS FEED. Here, you can also see the notifications icon at the top of the screen.

Embeddable widgets for Feed and Recommendations are available to embed into the web UIs of external applications, so SAP Jam feed functionality can be extended beyond SAP Jam itself, across the enterprise, and beyond.

Figure 16.3 Company News Feed Page

16.2.3 Groups

With SAP Jam, users can create, manage, and join internal and external groups. Groups can be created for a variety of topics and purposes and allow individuals to participate in discussions and share and consume content. This forms the backbone of collective collaboration and creates a permanent history of conversations and documents that can be reused in future business scenarios, such as employee onboarding or sales cycles.

Users can access the groups they are members of by selecting GROUPS at the top of the page and selecting either the group from the list or selecting the menu option VIEW ALL GROUPS. All groups are displayed, and users can view or leave any groups. When they select a group, users are taken directly to that group. Depending on the group settings, they are taken to either the ABOUT page or the FEED page. Figure 16.4 shows the SALES LEADS group, as an example.

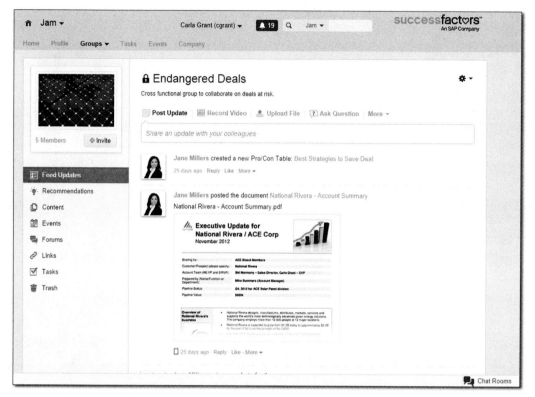

Figure 16.4 The Endangered Leads Group

The group OVERVIEW page provides a dynamic page that not only displays information about the group, but also provides embeddable widgets to allow group administrators to filter the information displayed about people, discussions, documents, decision-making tools, and planning tools within the group. A page designer exists so that an OVERVIEW page can be created easily and customized with widgets for text; video; images; and other group features like feeds, forums, and content listings. Users can easily add columns and rows to the initial layout, drag cells to resize them, and drag and drop widgets.

Within groups, there is a lot of the same functionality available in other feeds and profiles, such as posting updates and uploading documents. For example, in groups, users can share links, ask a question, add an idea, start a discussion in the forum, record a video, and add tasks. Members can also get recommendations of the most popular content in the group, as well as stop following a group, change the regularity of their email notifications, invite members (depending on group settings), and leave the group. Within the CONTENT page of a group, members can also create blogs, wiki pages, polls, pro/con tables, and rankings. Administrators can also download CSV reports of various metrics about activity, consumption, and contributions.

Users can create groups by selecting GROUPS at the top of the page and selecting the menu option CREATE A GROUP. In the pop-up window the group creator can select a template or define the name, description, and select the group permissions (PUBLIC, PRIVATE, or EXTERNAL; see Figure 16.5). The group creator can setup the home page, navigation, and access rights for the group easily after creating the group. The ADMIN page allows the group creator to modify the name, description, and group type as well as define the invite policy, Terms of Use (discussed later in the section), any announcements, the photo, sub-pages that are available, and the participation level.

In the PARTICIPATION tab, the creator can set the allowed participation level for members, the upload policy (all members or just administrators), and whether a moderation policy should apply (the moderation policy applies to documents, photos, videos, wikis, and blogs). The allowed participation has three different levels:

▶ (READ ONLY)
Members can view and download only content and discussions; polls and tasks are disabled.

▶ LIMITED
Members edit, post updates, comment, like, and view content.

▶ FULL
All members have full read and write access.

Private groups require an invitation to be sent out by a group administrator before a user can access the group. Bulk invites can be sent out to multiple users.

Administrators have the ability to turn off Questions, Ideas, and Discussions forums within Forums. Administrators can even go further and turn off Forum sections within groups, in addition to turning off Content sections within groups.

Terms of Use for groups can be created by group administrators. A user must accept the terms before they can gain access to group content or receive notifications from the group. The Terms of Use are also enforced on both the iPhone and iPad apps. An Acceptance log records each user's acceptance of the Terms of Use—including different versions of the Terms of Use—for audit purposes.

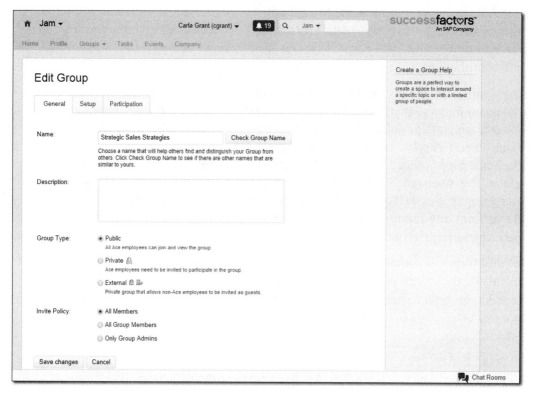

Figure 16.5 Create a Group Page

Auto Groups

Groups with auto-membership—called *auto groups*—can be created by administrators in *Jam Admin* (see Section 16.3 for more details on Jam Admin). Auto groups are created using almost the same process as standard groups, except that membership can be set to be automatic. Membership is defined by selecting one or more attributes, such as country, department, division, or location.

Group Templates

A number of group templates are provided in the system. They feature a professionally designed overview page, placeholder content, and group structure. Templates include Help & Support, Mentoring & Coaching, Knowledge Sharing, Learning Room, Topic-Based Collaboration, Team Collaboration, Planning and

Implementation, Order to Cash, and Quote Management. Administrators can also create their own group templates.

The Order to Cash group template is an example of a group template influenced by the Work Pattern concept. The Order to Cash group template provides administrators the ability to create SAP Jam groups around Orders and their related Invoices from SAP ECC to support account teams. The Quote Management group template is another example.

As part of the integration to SAP Customer Relationship Management (CRM) v7 and SAP Cloud for Customer, a number of prebuilt templates are provided. These templates enable CRM-specific groups to be created that pull SAP CRM or SAP Cloud for customer data into them, specifically data focused around Accounts, Opportunities, and Service Request Resolution.

Subgroups

In order to better organize large and/or complex groups, subgroups can be created. Subgroups can help segregate topics, activities, work streams, and/or individuals from the core group for better management and more organized collaboration. Child groups are linked to the parent group, so permissions and membership are inherited by the subgroup from the parent group. Likewise, if membership to the parent group is rescinded or cancelled, the membership of the subgroup follows. Tasks and Events in a subgroup are available in the parent group for those members who are also a member of the subgroup.

Microsoft SharePoint Integration

Content from Document Libraries and folders in Microsoft SharePoint 2010 or 2013 can be displayed in a read-only capacity within groups. Microsoft SharePoint documents can be previewed, commented on, and copied into groups to be edited.

Additionally, SAP Jam content from internal public groups can be searched in Microsoft SharePoint.

Alfresco One Integration

Like with Microsoft SharePoint integration, documents from Alfresco One can be displayed in a read-only capacity within groups, to be previewed and commented on. However, documents cannot be copied into groups to be edited like with Microsoft SharePoint integration.

16.2.4 Content Creation and Sharing

SAP Jam allows various types of content to be created, uploaded, edited, and shared, including photos, videos, documents (such as Word or PowerPoint documents), and blogs. Creating content is simple and intuitive, and uploading content is as easy as opening a file in any application. For example, creating blog posts features a rich text editor (see Figure 16.6), while videos can be recorded using a screen capture of a webcam.

Any content posted on a feed, in a wiki, or in a blog can be previewed. This preview screen—called a *lightbox*— displays a preview of the content and allows comments and tasks to be added to content.

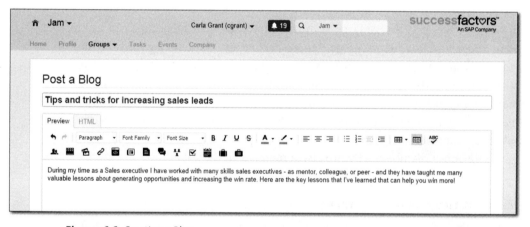

Figure 16.6 Creating a Blog

16.2.5 Tasks

Tasks enable users to create and track activities that have a finite timeframe in which to be completed. Tasks are accessed from the top menu by selecting the TASKS hyperlink. Here, a user can add, edit, view details of, and delete tasks. Tasks can be sorted by due date, priority, group, and status. Figure 16.7 shows the TASKS page with a task being created. Tasks can be created easily by typing in the name of the task to the ADD A NEW TASK box.

Tasks can be attached to any content object, and multiple task assignees are supported. Tasks can be placed onto Overview pages, wikis, and blogs.

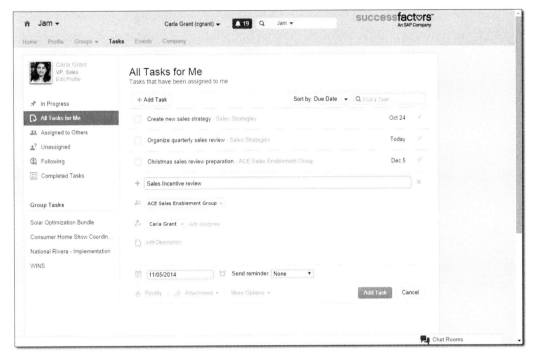

Figure 16.7 Creating a Task in the Tasks screen

16.2.6 Events

Events represent—as the name suggests—events that are planned to occur. They are used to represent events and invite other users to attend them. Users can accept, decline, or indicate tentative attendance. A calendar exists in both groups and for users so that events that they are part of can be displayed together by month, week, or day. Agendas and Tasks can be added to Events and, thus, extend the collaboration use cases. Events can also be placed onto Overview pages, wikis, and blogs.

16.2.7 Gamification

SAP Jam can leverage external gamification platforms to provide a full range of gamification features, such as badges, challenges, missions, and leader boards. These can then be viewed on an individual's Profile page under ACHIEVEMENTS.

16.3   SAP Jam Administration

SAP Jam has an excellent set of administration features in the Jam Admin function. Jam Admin is accessed in the user menu by selecting JAM ADMIN. Here, an administrator can configure a number of options, including the following (see Figure 16.8):

- AUTO GROUPS
  Create groups with automatic membership

- BRANDING
  Configure branding features for SAP Jam such as the name, logo, and colors of the instance

- COMPLIANCE
  Monitor flagged content, define keywords, and view history

- CONTENT ADMINISTRATION
  Enable or disable administration of all content across the SAP Jam instance, set abuse flagging level, and audit users

- FEATURES
  Enable or disable many of the features in SAP Jam, such as file sharing, wikis, videos, gamification, and so on

- REPORTS
  Download CSV reports of various metrics about activity, consumption, and contributions

- SECURITY
  Enable or disable RSS, shared session service, or content creation via email, and set session length, IP restrictions, and valid domains for users

- USERS
  Manage users—including assignment of administrator rights—and review usage

- OAUTH CLIENTS
  Configure OAuth clients

- SAML TRUSTED IDPS
  View and register SAML trusted identity providers

- EXTRANET MANAGEMENT
  Manage external access and users for external groups

A number of the pages include a right HELP sidebar that provides help, tips, and definitions for the administration options.

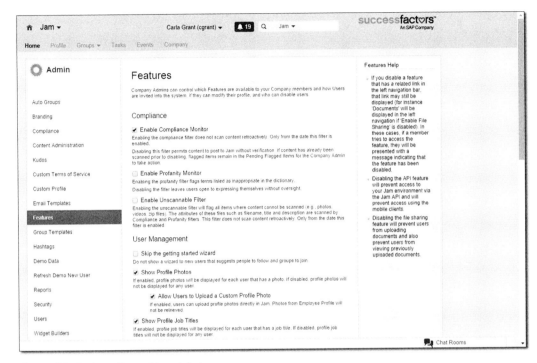

Figure 16.8 Features Page of Jam Admin

16.4 Integration

Various functionality-specific integration points have been mentioned throughout this chapter, but it is important to look at more general and application-wide integration.

SAP Jam is integrated within the SuccessFactors HCM suite and can be accessed from the dropdown menu in the same way that other solutions, such as SuccessFactors Recruiting Execution and Succession & Development, can be accessed, as well as being integrated into SuccessFactors HCM Mobile. It is also integrated with solutions such as Learning so that social learning discussions and activities can take place. SAP Jam leverages employee data such as name, email address, and organizational data (e.g., job code, department, location, etc.).

SAP Jam integrates with SAP ERP HCM for this employee and organizational data, and authentication with Single Sign-On (SSO) is also possible. It also natively integrates with the rest of the SAP Business Suite, SAP CRM on-premise, SAP Cloud apps, and third-party applications. For more information on integration, refer to Chapter 3.

Additional integration exists between SAP Jam and Microsoft Outlook in the form of an add-in for Microsoft Outlook. It enables users to post the following types of content to SAP Jam from Microsoft Outlook:

- Status updates to profile wall or group feeds
- Post emails as blogs and wikis to groups
- Post emails as forum posts to groups as Ideas, Questions, or general Discussions

16.5 Summary

SAP Jam is a powerful tool for increasing collaboration and knowledge sharing within organizations. In this chapter, you've seen the business processes that SAP Jam supports and functionality that the solution provides.

By using SAP Jam, organizations can reduce onboarding time and costs, increase sales, enhance learning opportunities, and produce a more knowledgeable and efficient workforce. Leveraging groups and discussions can be a foundation for targeting focused productivity and giving individuals easy access to tools that can make their everyday work easier and more enjoyable.

In the final chapter we'll go through a number of different channels, events, and organizations that can provide you with further information to help you become even more knowledgeable on SuccessFactors.

In light of the continuous innovation in SuccessFactors software, constant development of strategy, and changes within the market, it's important to ensure that you stay abreast of all the latest information available. A number of resources and channels are available to do this.

17 Further Resources

Due to the nature of cloud software and the evolution of enterprise software, many changes are occurring to the SuccessFactors HCM suite, SAP's strategy, and the overall market. We recommend that you stay as up-to-date and well-informed as possible because the pace of change is quick.

Due to the differing nature of SuccessFactors as a product suite and the lack of access to information, there can sometimes be a difference in understanding of the SuccessFactors HCM suite compared to SAP ERP HCM, so it's more important than ever for customers to do their homework and look at a number of sources to get the most accurate and relevant information.

This chapter will recommend reliable channels of information for your ongoing research.

17.1 SuccessFactors

SuccessFactors does a great job of providing news and new release information on its website (*www.successfactors.com*) and via its Twitter account (*@successfactors*). Customers can also find new release information, detailed product information, training materials, videos, support information, event details, thought leadership topics, and discussion forums at the SuccessFactors Community website (*http://community.successfactors.com*), as shown in Figure 17.1.

SuccessFactors partners can access a wealth of resources via the SuccessFactors Partner Portal (*https://partners.successfactors.com*). Partners can access a variety of information on products, training, implementation, sales, and marketing.

In addition, SAP's sales and pre-sales executives can provide up-to-date information on the company's products, as well as information on subscription prices, implementations, and partner recommendations. Customers can get in contact with their regional SuccessFactors representatives via their SAP account executives.

Figure 17.1 The SuccessFactors Community Website

17.2   SAP

SAP continues to improve the release and distribution of information to customers and partners. We recommend several outlets of information that are maintained by SAP.

SAP's sales and pre-sales executives, as well as Production Management and Solution Management, are a source of the latest information on products, integration, and roadmaps. Although information from this channel can have a strong marketing feel, it's nevertheless a good starting point to understand the capabilities of the SuccessFactors HCM suite and the integration content and technology that SAP is releasing.

The SAP website hosts high-level information on both SAP products and SAP's range of Rapid Deployment Solutions (RDS) packages for integration. The information is extremely high level but can be useful to distinguish SAP's various offerings.

17.2.1 SAP Help Portal

The SAP Help Portal (*http://help.sap.com*) is a useful resource for getting detailed and technical information on SAP's products. Although light on SuccessFactors HCM suite information, the website does host information on the iFlows released for the hybrid scenario and includes documentation on SSO. The most recent content (*http://help.sap.com/erp_sfi_addon30*) covers all Talent Hybrid content, as shown in Figure 17.2.

17.2.2 SAP Service Marketplace

The SAP Service Marketplace (*http://service.sap.com*) contains solution documentation and SAP notes for the integration add-on that have been released for the hybrid model. There are four areas of interest to customers regarding SuccessFactors.

SAP & SuccessFactors Integration Add-on Administration Guides

The SAP & SuccessFactors Integration Add on Administration Guides can be found on SAP Service Marketplace, as shown in Figure 17.3. Access requires an S-username and password. To access the Administration Guides, visit *http://service.sap.com/support*, and log in using your S-username and password. On the top menu bar, select RELEASE & UPGRADE INFO; in the bar below, select INSTALLATION & UPGRADE GUIDES.

In the navigation pane to the left side of the screen, follow the path INSTALLATION & UPGRADE GUIDES • SAP BUSINESS SUITE APPLICATIONS • SAP ERP ADD-ONS • INTEGRATION ADD-ON FOR SAP ERP HCM AND SUCCESSFACTORS BIZX.

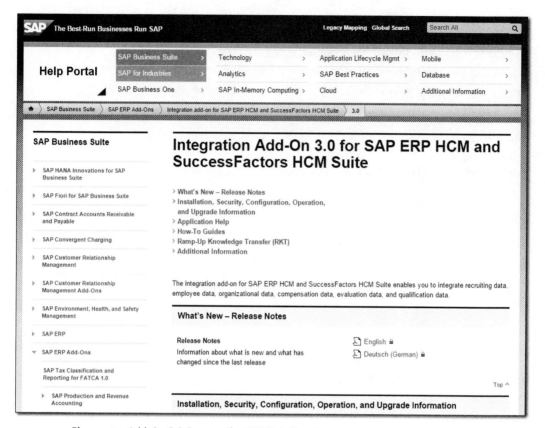

Figure 17.2 Add-On 2.0 Page on the SAP Help Portal

SAP & SuccessFactors Integration Add-on Release Notes

You can find the SAP & SuccessFactors Integration Add-on Release Notes on SAP Service Marketplace by visiting *http://service.sap.com/support* and logging in using your S-username and password. On the top menu bar, select RELEASE & UPGRADE INFO; in the bar below, select RELEASE NOTES. In the navigation pane to the left side of the screen, follow the path RELEASE NOTES—WHAT'S NEW • SAP SOLUTIONS • SAP ERP ADD-ONS • INTEGRATION ADD-ON FOR SAP ERP HCM AND SUCCESSFACTORS BIZX.

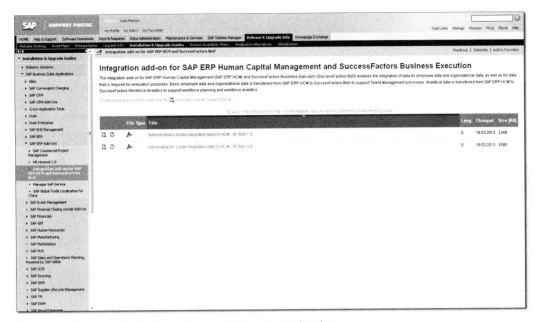

Figure 17.3 iFlow Administration Guides on SAP Service Marketplace

Hybrid Scenarios

SAP has launched a website called Hybrid Scenarios. This gives high-level information on the different hybrid integration scenarios for both Full Cloud HCM and Talent Hybrids deployment models. This is available via the URL *https://service.sap.com/public/hybrid* using your S-username. You can also access it by navigating from the front page of SAP Service Marketplace via the navigation path Products • Hybrid Scenarios.

Media Library

The *Media Library* contains a variety of documents relating to SuccessFactors and the SAP & SuccessFactors Integration Add-on. To access the Media Library, visit *http://service.sap.com/erp-hcm*, log in using your S-username and password, and, in the navigation pane to the left side of the screen, follow the path SAP ERP • SAP ERP Human Capital Management • Media Library—SuccessFactors Integration.

Product Handbooks

SAP publishes handbooks for many of the SuccessFactors HCM suite applications on Service Marketplace. Handbooks can be accessed via *http://service.sap.com/sfsf*. Although the Employee Central handbooks can be accessed there, they can also be accessed directly via *http://service.sap.com/ec-ondemand*. To navigate directly, select RELEASE & UPGRADE INFO on the top menu bar. In the bar below, select INSTALLATION & UPGRADE GUIDES. In the navigation pane to the left side of the screen, follow the path INSTALLATION & UPGRADE GUIDES • CLOUD SOLUTIONS FROM SAP • SUCCESSFACTORS. Select the folder for the relevant application.

SAP Notes

SAP regularly releases SAP Notes for corrections to the SAP & SuccessFactors Integration Add-on and other integrations, as well as information notes. These can be found on the SAP Service Marketplace in the same location as all other SAP Notes. To access these notes, visit *http://service.sap.com/support*, select SAP SUPPORT PORTAL, and log in using your S-username and password.

On the top menu bar, select HELP & SUPPORT, and, in the bar below, select SEARCH FOR SAP NOTES & KBAS. In the main panel, enter a component code (see below) in the APPLICATION AREA text box, and click SEARCH to display all of the SAP notes for the selected component. Components include the following:

- PA-SFI-TM for Talent Hybrid integration
- PA-SFI-EC for Employee Central integration
- LOD-EC-INT-EE for ERP to Employee Central integration
- LOD-EC-INT-ORG for Employee Central to ERP Organizational Integration
- LOD-EC-GCP-ANA for Employee Central Reporting and Analytics
- LOD-EC-GCP-PY for Employee Central Payroll & Integration
- LOD-EC-GCP-PY-GLO for Employee Central Payroll & Integration—Globalization

17.2.3 SAP PartnerEdge

The SAP PartnerEdge website (*http://partneredge.sap.com*) is the primary resource for SAP Partners and provides resources for sales, training, solution brochures, and general information. To access the SAP PartnerEdge page for SuccessFactors, as shown in Figure 17.4, visit *http://partneredge.sap.com/cloud*, log in with your

S-username and password, and select LEARN MORE under the SUCCESSFACTORS BIZX heading.

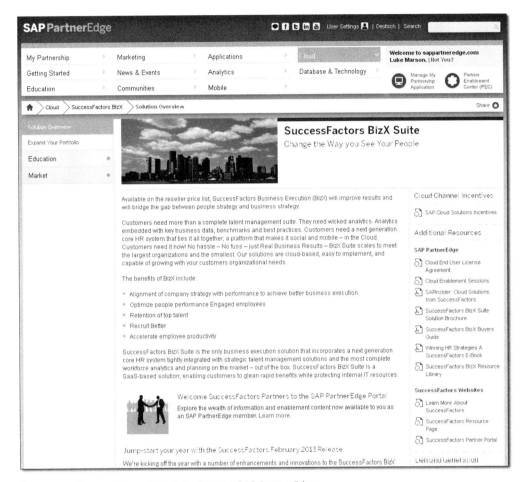

Figure 17.4 SuccessFactors BizX Suite Page on SAP PartnerEdge

17.2.4 SAP Community Network

The SAP Community Network (SCN) is the official user community of SAP and has more than two million members. The SCN contains a wide range of spaces covering different SAP areas and disciplines with content largely focused around blogs and forum discussions. Within both the SAP ERP HCM space (*http://scn.sap.com/community/erp/hcm/*), as shown in Figure 17.5, and the SAP Social Software space (*http://scn.sap.com/community/socialsoftware*), there is a growing collection of blogs and documents covering SuccessFactors and SAP Jam. Two popular collections are the *SuccessFactors—Useful Resources and Documents* document (*http://scn.sap.com/docs/DOC-41539*) and the *SAP Jam—Useful Resources and Documents* document (*http://scn.sap.com/docs/DOC-50789*).

Figure 17.5 The SAP ERP HCM Space on SCN

17.2.5 SAP Jam

SAP and SuccessFactors leverage SAP Jam for social collaboration and knowledge sharing and host a number of groups for partners. As a partner, you automatically get access to SAP Jam, and a number of SuccessFactors product-specific groups are automatically available, along with the SUCCESSFACTORS PARTNER NEWSFLASH group (see Figure 17.6). For consultants who have completed application training, an application-specific group may be available. The following groups are available to some or all partners:

▸ SuccessFactors Partner Newsflash

▸ SAP Jam Partner Enablement

▸ SuccessFactors Quarterly Releases for Partners

▸ Partner Up!

▸ SAP SuccessFactors Integration For Partners

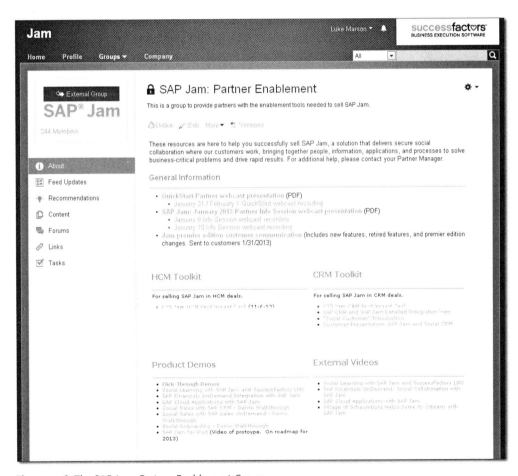

Figure 17.6 The SAP Jam: Partner Enablement Group

17.3 Social Media

Social media plays a large role in disseminating information, and a number of high-profile contributors and influencers are involved in this activity. You can use several different social media platforms to source the latest information.

17.3.1 LinkedIn

LinkedIn hosts a number of groups focused on SuccessFactors. The most prominent of these groups is the 11,000-member *SAP and SuccessFactors* group (*http://www.linkedin.com/groups?gid=4278743*). This group is updated with content multiple times daily and is where most of the experts and industry influencers are present.

17.3.2 Google Plus

Google Plus is still a heavily underutilized platform with a lot of great features, and this is reflected in the level of engagement on Google Plus pages versus LinkedIn groups. The *SAP and SuccessFactors* LinkedIn group has a presence here (*https://plus.google.com/communities/113841560495002390957*), while Success-Factors EMEA (*https://plus.google.com/106910022434033585064*) also has a page.

17.3.3 Twitter

Twitter is a special networking site geared around providing tweets (messages up to 140 characters) to followers. Individuals can be followed, or with the help of a Twitter client or app, hashtags (keywords beginning with a # that categorize tweets) can also be followed. We recommend that you follow a few accounts (beginning with @) or hashtags (beginning with #):

▶ *@SuccessFactors*

▶ *#SuccessFactors*

▶ *@SAPHCM*

Additionally, other individuals can be found by searching or following these hashtags. The authors of this book are also found on Twitter.

During conferences, you can follow hashtags to hear the latest information as it is announced. For example, attendees at the SAPPHIRE show used the hashtag #SAPPHIRENOW. Similarly, the #ASUG hashtag can be used for the ASUG annual conference. #SConnect is the hashtag of the annual SuccessConnect conference.

17.3.4 YouTube

SuccessFactors maintains a channel on the video-hosting platform YouTube at *www.youtube.com/user/SuccessFactorsInc*. Additionally, SuccessFactors also has a playlist for videos about its SuccessFactors Community website that can be accessed by selecting the PLAYLISTS tab in its channel.

17.4 Publications

There are a number of professional publications for SAP, including SAP ERP HCM, that regularly publish articles and reports on SuccessFactors, including the following:

▶ SAPexperts (*http://sapexperts.wispubs.com/HR*)

▶ SAP Insider (*http://sapinsider.wispubs.com/Channels/HR*)

▶ SearchSAP (*http://searchsap.techtarget.com/resources/SAP-HR-management*)

17.5 Conferences

The regular SAP conferences serve as another great source of information. Informal networking provides an opportunity for customers to talk to other customers or have off-the-record conversations with experts, consultants, and SAP executives. The following are some of the popular conferences:

▶ SuccessConnect

▶ SAP Insider HR conference (known as HR2014, HR2015 etc.)

▶ SAPPHIRE NOW and the ASUG annual conference

▶ Mastering SAP

▶ ASUG chapter meetings

17.6   SAP User Groups

SAP User Groups are country-based organizations that are comprised of companies using SAP and SAP partners, such as consulting partners or software developers. They provide a valuable channel of information to members and provide SAP an opportunity to work with SAP users to improve its software and services.

There are a number of these groups globally, including the following:

- ▸ Americas' SAP Users' Group (ASUG)
- ▸ German SAP User Group (DSAG)
- ▸ UK & Ireland SAP User Group (UKISUG)
- ▸ SAP Australian User Group (SAUG)

These groups often hold events or provide information to members about SAP ERP HCM topics that include SuccessFactors. ASUG also hosts its annual conference in conjunction with SAPPHIRE and has a strong influence within SAP.

17.7   SuccessFactors Value Innovation Program

SuccessFactors runs a customer program called the Value Innovation Program (VIP). As part of the VIP, SuccessFactors run a number of complimentary "Customer Success" engagements for existing customers, often hosted by a customer. These occur around the world at different times and usually involve customers from a particular region or geography. They can be useful for customers to share experiences and insights with fellow customers, network, share tips and ideas, learn better ways to use SuccessFactors, provide input into future innovations, and their customer engagement executive or account executive.

Customers can access the VIP program on the SuccessFactors Community website or reach out to their sales executive. Platinum Support customers can reach out to their Customer Support representative.

The Authors

Amy Grubb is a founder and principal at Cloud Consulting Partners, Inc., an SAP/SuccessFactors reseller and consulting partner and full-service HCM consultancy focused on implementing cloud solutions. She has consulted in the HCM space for more than 15 years, spending 8 years in Deloitte's Human Capital Management practice.

Amy has implemented the SuccessFactors suite since 2007 and implemented SAP HCM on-premise solutions for many years. She holds three SuccessFactors consultant certifications in Align & Perform, Talent Sourcing, and Talent Management. She currently teaches Mastery Courses for SAP Education including Recruiting Management Mastery, Succession Mastery and Performance, and Goal Management Mastery. Amy has implemented numerous modules within SuccessFactors, including Performance and Goal Management, Succession Planning, CDP, Recruiting, Compensation, and Learning for clients globally. Her experience with LMS dates to 2000, and she has implemented every market-leading LMS, including Plateau. She is an expert in Learning business processes and best practices and led the development of LearningPrint for Saba™ while at Deloitte.

Luke Marson is a C-level leader, architect, and principal consultant for SuccessFactors HCM solutions and is a Certified Professional in Employee Central. In addition to being an author, writer, speaker, and go-to individual on HCM and SuccessFactors topics, he is also a member of SAP's SAP Mentor program and an ASUG volunteer.

In his current role, Luke delivers strategy, advisory, roadmap, and consulting services to customers and also provides strategic guidance and expertise to support various internal and industry initiatives. His implementation and strategic experience covers SAP ERP HCM, SuccessFactors, Talent Management, and Visualization Solutions by Nakisa (VSN). He has delivered more than 40 projects in multiple countries across North and Central America, Europe, the Middle East, and Asia to organizations of various sizes and types in different industries and sectors, including oil and gas, defense, retail, manufacturing, the public sector, telecommunications, and media.

He is an active Twitter user (@*lukemarson*); a regular writer and blogger on SuccessFactors, HCM in general, cloud, and various thought leadership topics; and an active contributor to the SAP Community Network (SCN). He has also contributed to numerous articles, reports, and podcasts for *SAPinsider* magazine, SAPexperts, SearchSAP, and other publications. He has spoken at numerous events internationally and in various webinars and podcasts.

Jyoti Sharma co-wrote the first edition. Jyoti has expertise in strategy development, business process analysis, process re-engineering and global HR transformation.

In her current role as Vice President, Consulting and Services for the Cloud HCM LoB at HRIZONS, she has been instrumental in setting up and leading the LoB with innovative approaches to assist customers undergoing cloud migration and business transformation initiatives. Jyoti has more than nine years of information technology and SAP experience implementing core SAP ERP HCM modules and partnering with customers across industries to formulate and execute cloud migration and business transformation strategies.

Jyoti is widely regarded as an expert in Employee Central, is an active contributor to the SAP Community Network (SCN), and has presented at ASUG events. She is an SAPexperts author and an international speaker who has presented on the subject in the USA and Europe.

Atif Siddiqui has contributed to both editions of this book. He is an experienced ERP professional specializing in cloud solutions. His areas of expertise are Compensation Management, e-Recruiting, and Performance Management for both on-premise and cloud systems; as someone who also specializes in IT governance, compliance, and regulation, he has also led successful global ERP initiatives in the human resources and finance areas. He became an active member of the SuccessFactors community in Canada, particularly in the Compensation area. Atif also holds several professional qualifications and certifications in SAP ERP HCM, SAP HANA, cloud security, project management, information systems auditing, and risk and information systems control.

Index

T

U

V

W

■ Integrate SuccessFactors with SAP ERP, SAP ERP HCM, and third-party applications

■ Explore SuccessFactors deployment models and best practices

■ Get step-by-step instructions for using rapid-deployment solutions

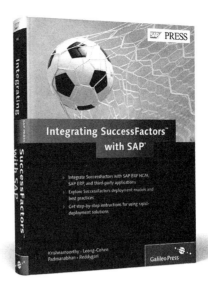

Venki Krishnamoorthy, Donna Leong-Cohen, Prashanth Padmanabhan, Chinni Reddygari

Integrating SuccessFactors with SAP

Whether you're making the jump to SuccessFactors all at once or in parts, explore your deployment options and how to integrate this cloud-based functionality into your HR landscape. Learn to apply prepackaged or planned integration scenarios and walk through case studies that model the use of templates and APIs. With SuccessFactors, the question isn't what to aim for--it's how to get there.

approx. 500 pp., 69,95 Euro / US$ 69.95
ISBN 978-1-4932-1185-2, April 2015

www.sap-press.com

■ Learn how to work with the SAP ERP HCM architecture and data models

■ Program for custom enhancements, reports, performance, and more

■ Understand what SuccessFactors, SAP HANA, SAP Fiori, and HR Renewal mean for you

Dirk Liepold, Steve Ritter

SAP ERP HCM: Technical Principles and Programming

Your SAP ERP HCM system needs more than just a pretty face—get the information you need to work with your backend system! This book will help you to master the technical aspects of SAP ERP HCM, starting with the basics of its architecture, and moving to more advanced concepts like authorizations and performance programming. With the help of screenshots and detailed instructions, you'll acquire new skills in no time flat. In addition, get the latest updates for SAP HANA, SAP Fiori, and HR Renewal.

approx. 863 pp., 2. edition, 79,95 Euro / US$ 79.95
ISBN 978-1-4932-1170-8, Dec 2014

www.sap-press.com

- ESS and MSS: what it is, how it has evolved over the years, and how it fits into an HR Service Delivery model

- Learn how to implement an effective self-services approach

- Explore the latest core HR enhancements like HR Renewal and SAP Fiori

Kris Bland, Jeremy Masters, Justin Morgalis, Brandon Toombs

Self-Services with SAP ERP HCM

ESS, MSS, and HR Renewal

Wrap your mind around the HCM Self-Services picture with this guide to on-premise self-service offerings. Understand the benefits, functionality, and business processes enabled by new technology like the HR Renewal Add-on for HCM and SAP Fiori, and integrate them into your self-services strategy. Take advantage of HCM solutions that extend your reach and keep you adaptable to the HR environment.

approx. 400 pp., 69,95 Euro / US$ 69.95
ISBN 978-1-59229-984-3, Jan 2015

www.sap-press.com

Galileo Press